Fresh From the Word

the Bible for a change

FRESH from the WORD

the Bible for a change

Foreword by Revd Leslie Griffiths

Edited by Nathan Eddy

International Bible Reading Association

MONARCH
BOOKS

Published by
Lion Hudson Limited
Wilkinson House, Jordan Hill Business Park,
Banbury Road, Oxford OX2 8DR, England
www.lionhudson.com
and by the International Bible Reading Association
5–6 Imperial Court, 12 Sovereign Road, Birmingham, B30 3FH
Tel: 0121 458 3313; Fax: 0121 285 1816
www.ibraglobal.org
Charity number 1086990

ISBN 978 0 85721 883 4
e-ISBN 978 0 85721 919 0
ISSN 2050-6791

First edition 2018

A catalogue record for this book is available from the British Library

Printed and bound in the UK, July 2018, LH26

Fresh From the Word aims to build understanding and respect for
different Christian perspectives through the provision of a range of
biblical interpretations. Views expressed by contributors should not,
therefore, be taken to reflect the views or policies of the Editor or the
International Bible Reading Association.

The International Bible Reading Association's scheme of readings is listed
monthly on the IBRA website at www.ibraglobal.org and the full scheme
for 2019 may be downloaded in English, Spanish and French.

Contents

Foreword

From the very beginning of my life as a committed Christian, not far off my 20th birthday, I knew I had to do something to undergird the faith I had so recently embraced. I needed some kind of spiritual infrastructure. I knew that an important element of this would be a better grasp of the Bible. In day school and Sunday school I had learned some of its stories and some of the psalms. But now I was launching out into the deep and I felt the need to equip myself for the journey. I determined to read the Bible from cover to cover. That would give me the ballast I needed at such a time.

Well, I got there. In the end. And with relief. I was a student of literature, so I was used to reading books; even complicated books. But this was different. For a start there wasn't a readily perceptible 'plot'; a narrative line to get me turning those pages. And then there was the perpetual mixing up of different types of literature – poetry, history, legal documents, prophecy – with great abandon. It was almost too much. I knew I needed help.

And that's what led me to two precious resources: the Daily Study commentaries of William Barclay and the daily study notes of IBRA. It's such a pleasure to have this opportunity to pay my tribute to the way those two streams built up my faith, deepened my knowledge of the Bible, and eventually gave me the courage to turn to longer and more systematic kinds of scholarship.

I learned the important truth – stated so simply at one point in the letter to the Hebrews – that it's important to enjoy easily digestible food before ordering heavier dishes. I shall be eternally grateful to IBRA for supplying my needs at that turning point in my life.

These notes are written with due regard for the best scholarship, and I have never hesitated to recommend them to the congregations I have served down the years. And I commend them to you now, dear reader. May they build your inner life and equip you to face the increasingly bewildering world we live in. May they be a lamp unto your feet.

Revd Leslie Griffiths

How to use *Fresh From the Word*

How do you approach the idea of regular Bible reading? It may help to see daily Bible reading as spiritual exploration. Here is a suggestion of a pattern to follow that may help you develop the discipline but free up your mind and heart to respond.

- Before you read, take a few moments – the time it takes to say the Lord's Prayer – to imagine God looking at you with love. Feel yourself enfolded in that gaze. Come to scripture with your feet firmly planted.

- Read the passage slowly before you turn to the notes. Be curious. The Bible was written over a period of nearly 1,000 years, over 2,000 years ago. There is always something to learn. Read and reread.

- If you have access to a study Bible, pay attention to any echoes of the passage you are reading in other parts of the biblical book. A word might be used in different ways by different biblical authors. Where in the story of the book are you reading? What will happen next?

- 'Read' yourself as you read the story. Be attentive to your reactions – even trivial ones. What is drawing you into the story? What is repelling you? Observe yourself 'sidelong' as you read as if you were watching a wild animal in the forest; be still, observant and expectant.

- What in the scripture or in the notes is drawing you forward in hope? What is closing you down? Notice where the Spirit of Life is present, and where negative spirits are, too. Follow where life is leading. God always leads into life, even if the way feels risky.

- Lift up the world and aspects of your life to God. What would you like to share with God? What is God seeking to share with you?

- Thank God for being present and offer your energy in the day ahead, or in the day coming after a night's rest.

Introduction from the Editor

Waiting, stillness, seeking, finding ...

In a world that never stops, these simple words invite us to take a step outside the rush. What might we find when we pause to reflect? The desert was a place of danger in the Bible, but it was also a place of reassessment and renewal, where the Israelites were formed as a people, where prophets sought God, and where Jesus found space before beginning his mission.

Going beyond the wilderness, Moses discovered the presence of the Holy One himself, waiting in a fiery bush. This year, IBRA invites you to journey, listen, seek and find as we consider the modern desert in the midst of our busy lives and communities.

We can find that space of the desert – the space of solace and challenge – in the Bible itself. Morning or evening, on a train or on the sofa, reading the Bible can open spaces of comfort and hope even in the midst of difficulty. Our mission has always been to encourage faithful people to read the Bible daily, right from the day we first published a reading list of Bible passages more than 130 years ago and encouraged people to form reading groups. We still offer that invitation today. What might come of your time in the desert with the Bible this year? How might it change your life, and the life of your community?

Other themes this year include the power of the word, music in the Bible, and fruits of the Spirit. We consider women in the Bible, with a twist. We look at gossip – freshly relevant in our social media age – and familiar sayings in the Bible. We take the Bible with us to the movies, and to the beach. We also have continuous readings through the books of Luke, Philippians, Psalms, Daniel, Deuteronomy, and Romans 1–8. We even mark the 500th anniversary of Magellan's circumnavigation of the globe with a theme entitled 'An interconnected world'.

As we do every year, we have reached out to creative writers around the world to bring their gifts to this book. This year we feature writing from Samoa, Australia, New Zealand, Argentina, Brazil, Nigeria, and the Caribbean, as well as Wales, Scotland, England, Northern Ireland, and many other places.

Find your space outside the rush this year. Come to the modern desert with these writers. And may God's Spirit inspire and energise your reading of the Bible there, opening up your life in fresh and surprising ways.

Yours in Christ,

Nathan

Acknowledgements and abbreviations

The use of the letters a or b in a text reference, such as Luke 9:37–43a, indicates that the day's text starts or finishes midway through a verse, usually at a break such as the end of a sentence. Not all Bible versions will indicate such divisions. We are grateful to the copyright holders for permission to use scriptural quotations from the following Bible versions:

NIVUK Scripture quotations marked NIVUK taken from the Holy Bible, New International Version Anglicised. Copyright © 1979, 1984, 2011 Biblica, formerly International Bible Society. Used by permission of Hodder & Stoughton Ltd, an Hachette UK company. All rights reserved. "NIV" is a registered trademark of Biblica. UK trademark number 1448790.

NRSVA Scripture quotations marked NRSVA taken from the New Revised Standard Version Bible: Anglicised Edition, copyright © 1989, 1995 the Division of Christian Education of the National Council of the Churches of Christ in the United States of America. Used by permission. All rights reserved.

KJV Scripture quotations marked KJV taken from The Authorized (King James) Version. Rights in the Authorized Version are vested in the Crown. Reproduced by permission of the Crown's patentee, Cambridge University Press.

NIRV Scripture quotations marked NIRV taken from the New International Reader's Version Bible: Copyright © 1995, 1996, 1998, 2014 by Biblica, Inc.®. Used by permission. All rights reserved worldwide.

THE MESSAGE
Scripture quotations taken from *The Message*. Copyright © by Eugene H. Peterson 1993, 1994, 1995, 1996, 2000, 2001, 2002. Used by permission of NavPress Publishing Group.

p. 85 Lyrics from "Lean on Me" by Kirk Franklin © 1998 Kerrion Publishing/ Bride Building Music/Lilly Mack Music, Capitol CMG Paragon (capitolcomg.com UK&EIRE Song Solutions www.songsolutions.org). All rights reserved. Used by permission.

p. 126 Extract from "I Am Your Mother (Earth Prayer)". Words: Shirley Erena Murray. © 1996 Hope Publishing Company, Carol Stream, IL 60188. All rights reserved. Used by permission.

The power of the Word

Notes by **Carla A. Grosch-Miller**

 Carla is a practical theologian and educator working in the areas of congregational trauma and sexual-spiritual integration, and a poet. She lives with her husband in Northumberland, England, and travels around the UK to lecture and speak. She is the author of *Psalms Redux: Poems and Prayers* (Canterbury Press, 2014) and articles in the *Journal of Adult Theological Education* and *Theology & Sexuality*. An avid swimmer, she recently fell in love with hillwalking. Carla has used the NIVUK for these notes.

Tuesday 1 January
In the beginning

Read John 1:1–14

In the beginning was the Word, and the Word was with God, and the Word was God.

(verse 1)

You would not be reading these words (and I would not be writing them) if we had not been given or stumbled upon a Bible at some point in our lives. Whether it was the Bible or a Bible-shaped life, something got our attention ... and we began. We began to open ourselves to let God shape us into the person God created us to be. In this way Word becomes flesh.

Beginnings are big deals. Without them we would not get anywhere! The Chinese philosopher Lao-Tzu observed that a journey of a thousand miles begins with a single step.

Today is the first day of a new year, a day for new beginnings. On 1 January 2012, on an airplane en route to California, I began anew a recommitment to daily prayer and Bible reading. The unusual setting for day one helped me to learn that I could read and pray anywhere, anytime, anyhow. The journey begun that day led me to discover in myself and in God things that surprised and delighted me, as the Divine melted, moulded and made me anew. What journey is God nudging you to begin or to begin again?

† Word of Life, my beginning is in you. Step into this new year with me, that I may discover who you created me to be.

Wednesday 2 January
The Word calls us

Read Jeremiah 1:1–12

'Before I formed you in the womb I knew you, before you were born I set you apart ...'

(verse 5a–b)

The Word of God comes to Jeremiah and he wrestles it. He wrestles his capability; he knows his limitations. Jeremiah's resistance, some say, is a true sign of a calling. When the Word comes to us, like Jeremiah we tend to marshal all the reasons why we are not the ones to do it. The list can be long: too young, too old, undereducated, overeducated, too ordinary, too much an outsider. Our humility (our fear?) in the moment is stunning. But God sees our potential as well as our limitations. The attributes that we think may disqualify us are sometimes the very qualities that God needs to speak a new word into the world.

The testimony of the Bible is clear: God chooses to work *with and through* human beings, all sorts of human beings. Desmond Tutu quotes Augustine of Hippo as saying, 'We, without God, cannot; God, without us, will not.'[1]

The real difficulty is discerning if what has come to us *is* a word from God. The voice in our heads sounds distinctly like our own, even if the idea is not one we could have come up with ourselves. After a few years in ministry I decided that when I received an uninvited, possibly divine nudge I would just do it and see what happened. Twenty-five years on I can testify that the vast majority of those nudges bore fruit; they were exactly the right thing to do.

The best news: once we hear and respond, God follows through.

† Living God, whose Word is meant to bear fruit, sharpen my listening and make bold my response so that I may participate in your outflow of love and justice into the world.

For further thought

Frederick Buechner says that our call is where our deep joy and the world's deep need meet.[2] What does your joy lead you to offer?

---

1   United Methodist News Service, 'Tutu stresses justice, mercy, humility in remarks to students' (https://across.co.nz/TutuSpeaks2Students.htm).

2   Buechner, F. (1993), *Wishful Thinking: A Seeker's ABC* (New York, NY: HarperCollins).

Thursday 3 January
The Word calls us Home

Read Deuteronomy 30:1–16

… the word is very near you; it is in your mouth and in your heart so you may obey it.

(verse 14)

The word the Deuteronomist speaks of is one that lingers in the mind and is harboured in the heart. Sometimes it is like a catchy tune that appears when you least expect or want it; other times it is the word you have been thirsting for, arising like a stream in the wilderness. It can chide or it can comfort, but its purpose is always the same – to point us in the right direction, the direction of Home.

It is a marvel to me that what we read or sing makes its home so deeply within us, with little effort on our part. The grand design is wonderful. Our immersion in the Word creates pathways in the brain that get tickled when most needed. It is the origin of our conscience, the soundtrack that keeps us on track.

A wise rabbi said that when we study the Word, it is written on our heart so that when our heart breaks, the words will fall in.[3] The Deuteronomist, speaking to people in exile, called the people to remembrance and obedience, reminding them (and us) that the Word is life. We choose life when we heed the holy words that bubble up when we are in trouble.

† Holy God, write your Word on our hearts in bold print and hold us in our heartbreak as we turn towards Home.

For further thought

What are you reading? Is it worthy of a place in your mind and heart? Will it lead you Home?

---

3   Recounted in LaMott, A. (2005), *Plan B* (New York, NY: Riverhead Books).

Friday 4 January
The Word is a treasure

Read Psalm 119:11–25

I have hidden [treasured] your word in my heart that I might not sin against you.

(verse 11)

Psalm 119 is an artfully crafted love song to the Law (the Torah). The longest psalm in the book, it is written in acrostic form in Hebrew – meant to teach the surpassing value of living a Torah-oriented life. Our modern concept of 'law' does not hold a candle to the Hebrew understanding of Torah, which sought to participate in God's life in the divinely well-ordered world. To us the word *law* connotes regulation and restriction. To the ancient Hebrews the Torah provided the structure that enabled love and freedom in community. To sin against God by neglecting or failing to obey the Torah would be to cut oneself off from the very source of life.

Here we stumble on one of the paradoxes of the life of faith: that structure enables freedom. We need structure when we are children so that we may know the security of the love that keeps us safe and teaches us how to interact in the world. And we need structure as adults. Chaos is not conducive to community building or to being a human.

In the contemporary West freedom is often equated with being able to do whatever one wants, when one wants, including and especially accumulating financial treasure. The ancient Hebrews knew that true freedom comes from a life lived in communion with God and with others. A pearl of great price, this teaching is revealed in the treasure that is Torah. Living a God-oriented life opens the way to the joy and love that bring us fullness of life.

† Gracious God, I thank you with all my being for the gift of Torah. Lead me in your ways to life abundant.

For further thought

How do the structures of your day, week, month and life free you to love God and others as yourself?

Saturday 5 January
The Word transforms

Read John 17:13–21

'I have given them your word ...'

(verse 14)

In his Farewell Discourse Jesus prays for all who will follow. He knows that what he has left us with may put us on a collision course with the powers that be. Our encounters with the Word change us, altering our framework for making sense of the world and our lives, our most basic assumptions and our most deeply held values. The Word transforms us, bit by bit, over and over again, as we dwell in it.

And this transformation may cause us to be at odds with the way things are usually done ... in the world and sometimes even in the church. Look where it got Jesus.

I often look at my 'non-Christian' neighbours and wonder how, really, is my life different from theirs? They keep their lawns tidy, give to charity, take care of their families, are helpful in a pinch and contribute to the community. Most of the time I see very little difference, other than how I spend my Sunday mornings and what I do for a living. In one sense this troubles me: shouldn't my life look different? In another sense it reassures me: God is at work in the world regardless of labels or perceptions. But most of all it humbles me. And it calls me to ask whether there is yet more transformation to come in my life by the grace of God.

The Word is our inheritance – not an object to put in a display case, but a living force that never stops making us anew.

† Living God, thank you for not being done with me yet. I open my heart and my mind to receive what you have for me.

For further thought

It has been said that our lives may be the only Bible that some people read. What good news does your life share with the world?

Readings in Luke (1) – 1 Births and beginnings

Notes by **Catherine Williams**

Catherine is an Anglican priest working for the Archbishops' Council in the Church of England. She facilitates the processes by which new clergy are selected to train for ordained ministry. Catherine lives in Tewkesbury and works in London. She is married to Paul, also a priest, and they have two adult children. Catherine is also an experienced Spiritual Director. She enjoys singing, theatre, cinema, and reading and writing poetry. Catherine has used the NRSVA for these notes.

Sunday 6 January
Tale as old as time

Read Luke 1:1–17

I too decided, after investigating everything carefully from the very first, to write an orderly account for you, most excellent Theophilus, so that you may know the truth concerning the things about which you have been instructed.

(verses 3–4)

Today many churches celebrate the Feast of the Epiphany, marking the coming of the Magi to the infant Jesus, indicating that God's salvation is for all nations. In our readings this week we are beginning an exploration of Luke's Gospel, where that message of salvation for all has been carefully compiled so that those who come after the first witnesses to Christ may have a thorough, accurate and 'orderly account' with which to engage.

Luke begins his Gospel by taking us to a particular time and place, and a specific person, Zechariah, indicating that the cosmic good news he wants us to explore is rooted in a real place and involves ordinary people. The Holy Spirit plays a major part in these opening chapters – empowering local people to step up and undertake risky and surprising roles in God's salvation plan. We witness as another world breaks into everyday life through angels and miracles. Prophecy, which has been silent for hundreds of years, bubbles forth. While the central character of the Gospel is always Jesus, today we enter the story before his birth in order to set the scene for his arrival.

† Lord God, prepare my heart to explore with Luke. Open my eyes and mind to new ideas this week as I engage with this Gospel.

Monday 7 January
Struck dumb!

Read Luke 1:18–25

Zechariah said to the angel, 'How will I know that this is so? For I am an old man, and my wife is getting on in years.'

(verse 18)

What a day for the priest Zechariah! His once-in-a-lifetime opportunity to enter the sanctuary of the Lord and offer incense has changed his life forever. He's encountered the angel Gabriel and heard incredible news: after years of waiting, praying and longing he and Elizabeth are going to have a child. The gift of a son would be sufficient to fill them with deep joy and gratitude, but this child is chosen by God; he will be filled with the Holy Spirit from his conception and will be the one to prepare the people to receive the Messiah. It's overwhelming, and no wonder that Zechariah questions Gabriel and asks for certainty – a sign to help him believe. The sign is given and poor Zechariah is struck dumb. He won't speak again until he brings his newly born son for circumcision and names him John.

While the story that Luke is unfolding has cosmic ramifications, he is also able to show how God's extraordinary plan for the salvation of the world is worked out through ordinary people going about their everyday lives. Even holy and righteous folk have doubts and struggle to believe that God can work through improbable or impossible ways. We can appreciate that Zechariah and Elizabeth – who had borne the stigma of childlessness – would have been astounded to find themselves following so closely in the footsteps of their ancestors Abraham and Sarah, those great heroes of the faith. In fulfilling his purposes God calls ordinary people like you and me to surprise, adventure and fulfilment. Are you ready?

† Lord, help me to be open to your surprising call. May I recognise and trust your power to transform and save, even in very difficult circumstances.

For further thought

Spend some time today in silence and pray for those who are unable to speak or communicate with others.

Tuesday 8 January
Nothing is impossible

Read Luke 1:26–38

'The Holy Spirit will come upon you, and the power of the Most High will overshadow you; therefore the child to be born will be holy; he will be called Son of God.'

(verse 35)

God chooses where God chooses – irrespective of age, gender or location. Gabriel undertakes another visit – to a young woman in Nazareth. This time the news is not just improbable, it seems impossible. A virgin has been chosen to bear a child who will be the Messiah – the Son of God. Unlike Zechariah, Mary, with the benefit of youth and inexperience, doesn't doubt the angel – though she does request some technical clarification. She's informed that the Holy Spirit will enable her to be and do more than could ever be possible on her own. This soon-to-be-teenage-mum accepts with appealing freshness and lack of cynicism that God can work miracles. Humility and obedience focus her response: 'Here am I … let it be with me according to your word.'

We don't know why God chose Mary and Luke doesn't say. But her willingness to embrace God's astonishing call and receive his unmerited grace can educate and inspire us as we seek to grow in faith. Often God's call is surprising and beyond our unaided ability: it requires some growing into. With the gift of the Holy Spirit to guide, empower and equip we can serve God in ways we never would have imagined possible. But it's also important to remember that Mary doesn't 'go it alone'. The Spirit empowers her, and she also fulfils her calling with the help of her supportive partner Joseph, Elizabeth her confidante, and later the disciples and followers of her son. We all need the community of faith around us as we seek to serve and follow Christ.

† Lord, help me to trust in your surprising call. Like Mary may I be humble, obedient and willing to embrace the adventures you have in store for me and those I walk alongside.

For further thought

What can we learn from teenagers and young adults? What are the particular gifts they bring to our communities?

Wednesday 9 January
Jumping for joy

Read Luke 1:39–56

'As soon as I heard the sound of your greeting, the child in my womb leaped for joy. And blessed is she who believed that there would be a fulfilment of what was spoken to her by the Lord.'

(verses 44–45)

Have you ever been so excited that you have literally 'jumped for joy': the adrenalin pumping through your body making you feel more alive than ever before? There are times in our lives when we are so excited, or amazed, deeply thankful or filled to the brim with delight that we can't contain ourselves and our joy overflows, affecting all of those around. This is the situation in which Mary, Elizabeth and John find themselves as the astonishing news that Gabriel has brought becomes reality.

Mary carrying the Messiah runs to Elizabeth, who on meeting her cousin proclaims a prophetic blessing. John, in Elizabeth's womb, quickens and leaps for joy. Mary opens her mouth in praise and her song – the Magnificat – pours forth. The Holy Spirit is active in all three as this meeting with the unborn Jesus occurs. Stitching together verses learned by heart from the scriptures and drawing heavily on the song of Hannah from 1 Samuel 2, Mary sings of the God who turns worlds upside down: keeping his promise to rescue, save and restore. This song, which is sung, said and prayed by Christians every day, is a shout of triumph and a display of firm trust in the God who will not let his people go and whose love is everlasting. We can imagine Mary, Elizabeth and John – old, young and not yet born – all celebrating with wild excitement and dancing for joy. Luke is indicating that wherever Jesus is acknowledged lives will be transformed. May we never forget the wild excitement of those who first met Jesus.

† Lord Jesus, like Mary, Elizabeth and John, may the Holy Spirit make my heart jump for joy whenever I take time to meet with you.

For further thought

As you carry Jesus to and for others, pray that the Holy Spirit will release joy both in you and in all those you meet.

Thursday 10 January
Names matter!

Read Luke 1:57–66

He [Zechariah] asked for a writing tablet and wrote: 'His name is John.' And all of them were amazed.

(verse 63)

Do you know the meaning of your name? Has it shaped your life in any way? Names are incredibly important, and parents take time and care to choose a name for their child. When I'm baptising children I spend time finding out the meaning of the names that have been chosen, and tie those meanings in with the promises of God given in baptism. I hope and trust that the Holy Spirit will bring to fruition a strong faith in Jesus and the latent potential indicated by the child's name.

Zechariah and Elizabeth's baby has been hoped and longed for down the years. When they bring him to be circumcised everyone expects him to be named after his father, as would be common practice. However, Gabriel told Zechariah in the temple that this baby is to be called John – meaning 'God is Gracious'. Elizabeth holds fast to the plan and Zechariah's confirmation of the name loosens his tongue so that for the first time in nine months he is able openly to praise God. His faithfulness to God brings liberation. The onlookers at the celebration wonder about this baby – there is obviously something very special about him, and this creates fear. God is breaking into ordinary lives in extraordinary ways, causing ripples and change which not all find comfortable. John will live up to his name and God will indeed be gracious to his people through this new prophet, but much will be demanded of him and the people as the paths to God are restored and made straight.

† Thank you Lord that you know me and call me by my name. Help me to become fully the person you are calling me to be.

For further thought

Make an artistic representation of your name. As you spend time creating it, give thanks for the people who named you and ponder the ways that your name shapes you.

Friday 11 January
A new prophet

Read Luke 1:67–80

'You will go before the Lord to prepare his ways.'

(verse 76)

When I held each of my newborn children and met them for the first time, I can remember being filled with awe and wonder at these tiny bundles of humanity placed into my care. My body had nurtured each for nine months and knew them intimately but this was still a first meeting. These new infants were brimming over with potential and I was filled with hopes and dreams for them and for us as a family, but I had no idea who they would become. Both have surprised me with the paths they have taken and one of them in particular has astonished everyone.

The crowd wonders about the baby John, but Zechariah knows that this child will be 'the Prophet of the Most High' – Gabriel told him, and now filled with the Holy Spirit this new father speaks his own prophecy, pouring out both the agony and hope of his people. All that he has desired down the years is coming to fulfilment. The child he holds will prepare the way for the return of the Messiah, by calling people to repent of their sins and turn back to the Lord. Political and religious freedom is on the horizon – God is faithful despite humanity's lack of faith and trust. Zechariah and Elizabeth's son 'strong in spirit' will be deeply challenging for them to parent – and his journey to fulfil his vocation will ultimately cost him his life. Retreating to the wilderness to embrace solitude is a time-honoured discipline to enable spiritual preparation and here sets the scene for John's role as the forerunner.

† Lord, thank you for John the Baptist who prepared the way for Jesus the Messiah. Enable me to be a signpost to Jesus for those around me.

For further thought

Need to discern a way forward or prepare spiritually for what lies ahead? Consider slowing down and taking a retreat in a quiet place.

Saturday 12 January
Our manifesto

Read Luke 4:14–30

'The Spirit of the Lord is upon me, because he has anointed me to bring good news to the poor.'

(verse 18)

Today we leap forward in Luke's Gospel and meet with Jesus ministering in Galilee, returning to his home town and visiting the synagogue. There he astounds everyone as he claims that he is the fulfilment of the prophecy written in Isaiah 61. This local lad identifies himself with the Lord's anointed who will come to liberate those imprisoned in a variety of contexts. The amazement of the locals turns to rage as Jesus identifies himself also with Elijah and Elisha and suggests that God's salvation is open to all. Those who believed themselves to have a secure inheritance are deeply threatened by God's grace and generosity attested to by one who is not just the carpenter's son but the Son of God too. Though they are called to be the light to the nations, they would prefer to keep the light to themselves – going so far as to try to hurl Jesus off a cliff, fuelled by the fear that their privilege is being eroded.

The passage that Jesus quotes from Isaiah is a good checklist for Christians. Our mission is to follow in Christ's footsteps, bringing freedom to those in adversity and proclaiming the good news that in God's economy there are no 'outsiders': in Jesus the kingdom is open to all. In our readings this week we have seen how the Holy Spirit dwelling in ordinary people empowers them to do extraordinary things for God. May the Holy Spirit gifted to each of us at our baptism enable us to hear and respond to God's surprising call on our lives too.

† Holy Spirit – thank you for being in my life. Empower me to follow and serve Christ. Fill me with courage and joy as I explore God's surprising call.

For further thought

How is your church fulfilling Christ's manifesto in Luke 4:18–19? What is your part in that? Whom might you encourage to join you in serving?

Readings in Luke (1) – 2 Spreading the word

Notes by **Alistair Milne**

Ali is an accountant for Christian charity Tearfund, which works with local churches and other organisations to help communities around the world escape the worst effects of poverty and disaster. He lives in London and studies Theology, Ministry and Mission at St Mellitus College. Ali has an interest in apologetics, which led him to take a course at the Oxford Centre for Christian Apologetics. He also enjoys spreadsheets! Ali has used the NRSVA for these notes.

Sunday 13 January
News spreads!

Read Luke 4:31–44

As the sun was setting, all those who had any who were sick with various kinds of diseases brought them to him; and he laid his hands on each of them and cured them. Demons also came out of many, shouting, 'You are the Son of God!'

(verses 40–41)

In Luke 4, we discover that the world, which was thought to be under Roman rule (Luke 2:1; 3:1), is ruled by Satan. God's intention for the world is being revealed: to save it and release it from the powers that are set up in opposition to God. There is a battle at hand and as the sun sets, marking the end of the Sabbath, more and more casualties are brought to Jesus. This week we are also invited to be with Jesus – and to see where and how he is still at work around us.

Sometimes the word 'atonement' is used to describe what happened on the cross. Somehow God is unifying the heavens and the Earth, making them 'at-one' (atonement). In Leviticus, on the day of atonement sacrifices are made, and the trumpet is sounded throughout the land (25:9). Here in Luke 4, the trumpets are starting to sound. Jesus is acting on his statement of intent, bringing about what the Jubilee envisaged: releasing captives, setting the oppressed free, defeating the powers that are opposing God's rule, and proclaiming the good news of the kingdom of God (verse 43). His campaign will climax at the cross, where the enemy is finally defeated, and the trumpets are sounded throughout the land on the day of atonement. The battle is won.

† Dear God, thank you for defeating sin and death, freeing us to follow your calling. Help us to walk in your paradoxical, cross-shaped victory.

Monday 14 January
The fishermen

> **Read Luke 5:1–11**
>
> *But when Simon Peter saw it, he fell down at Jesus' knees, saying, 'Go away from me, Lord, for I am a sinful man!' For he and all who were with him were amazed at the catch of fish that they had taken.*
>
> (verses 8–9)

Fish everywhere! The fishermen, whose day-to-day lives were dependent upon their connection with creation, catch a taste of Jesus' divinity. There's no reason to think that at this point they know him to be God incarnate, but seeing his right relationship with creation and command over it, they at least recognise him to be someone special. Instead of trying to control this power in Jesus (as did the crowds who wanted to prevent him from leaving in Luke 4:42), or dismissing it as something ungodly (like the scribes and the Pharisees in Luke 6:6–10), Simon Peter recognises how he himself has turned away from the God who is at work in Jesus. He realises that on his own terms he is not fit to be in God's presence. This humbleness is what Jesus values. Not how nice they are, how much they know or how many fish they've caught (fortunately!). Simon Peter and the others recognise the inadequacy of all that they had previously put their identity in. They are ready to leave behind everything that had been of value, to find their identity in relation to Jesus, the community being built around him, and his mission to bring good news to the poor and set the captives free.

Tearfund's vision is one where the local church in unstable and economically deprived areas is mobilised and empowered to bring transformation to the communities around them. The stories I have heard from our beneficiaries during staff prayers have inspired my work: tales of hopeless lives being empowered to be cultural drivers in areas lacking opportunity and vision. Jubilee!

† Dear God, I praise you for your love for those suffering under worldly social and political structures. Thank you for seeking out these people and for bringing restoration and justice.

For further thought

In what way can you seek to bring justice to those who are shackled by social and political structures?

Tuesday 15 January
The leper

Read Luke 5:12–16

... there was a man covered with leprosy. When he saw Jesus, he bowed with his face to the ground and begged him, 'Lord, if you choose, you can make me clean.' Then Jesus stretched out his hand, touched him, and said, 'I do choose. Be made clean.'

(verses 12–13)

Jesus' mission is gathering momentum. He has been recognised as the Holy One of God by the demons and his actions are providing an understanding of what the title means. Holiness is an important term in the narrative of Israel. To be holy is to be unique. God, as the only one who can create a universe, is unique. But this uniqueness is also very powerful, like an author who is unique in relation to the characters in her story, bringing them to life.

In Ancient Israel, many of the things stopping them being in God's presence were related to death: disease or touching dead bodies, for example. Being the source of life, things related to death are contrary to God. Normally, unclean things contaminated those around them so that they also become unclean. But here, we see the God who is life (John 1:4) undoing this. God becomes present in the world and his cleanness contaminates anything that is unclean (verse 13), pointing to the day when the world will be filled with the Holy God's contaminating, living presence (Isaiah 11:9).

Not only does God's cleanness overcome contamination, God in Jesus desires to be in that place of social isolation and stigma, and to bring life there. Some of the most important work that Tearfund have done over the years has been working with victims of leprosy as well as HIV/AIDS. These diseases carry a social stigma that isolates those suffering from them. We support those who, with Jesus, work to bring life to places of despair.

† Thank you, God, for stepping into our world and bringing life. Please help me wait expectantly for the revealing of your kingdom.

For further thought

Where do you see Jesus' mission taking shape around you today?

Wednesday 16 January
The paralytic

Read Luke 5:17–26

He said to the one who was paralysed – 'I say to you, stand up and take your bed and go to your home.' Immediately he stood up before them, took what he had been lying on, and went to his home, glorifying God.

(verses 24b–25)

Both of Mark's and Matthew's accounts of this episode set the scene by telling us that Jesus had returned home. Throughout chapters 4 and 5, Luke uses each episode to build his characterisation of Jesus' mission: a mission that involves the God of the universe coming home and being present in his creation. In this section, Jesus continues his mission to bring about the vision of Jubilee: liberating the paralysed man from the bondage of sin, healing creation and, in the same command, sending him home. Off he goes, liberated to return home to be who he was made to be, glorifying God. Luke tells us that the Pharisees and teachers of the law represent not only every Jewish village, but the city of Jerusalem as well (verse 17). Their lack of faith is contrasted to the faith of the friends of the paralysed man, telling us that, at this point in the narrative, at the heart of God's home, the city of Jerusalem, where the Prince of Peace will reign on David's throne (Isaiah 9:6–7), God's mission is being opposed.

Last year, 2018, was Tearfund's 50th anniversary, their year of Jubilee. Tearfund and its partners used the opportunity to reflect on the work God has been doing through them. I personally am constantly amazed and challenged by the generosity of our supporters and the interest that they show in our work. They are the unseen foundations of Tearfund's Jubilee work. It seems to me, when we give of our resources – time, practical or financial – we become more of who we were made to be.

† Dear God, thank you for who I am in you. Please continue your transforming and liberating work in my life, and show me how I can be an envisioning light to others.

For further thought

Check out Tearfund's Learning website for videos, pictures, blogs, the *Footsteps* magazine and stories of what Jubilee in practice can look like: learn.tearfund.org.

Thursday 17 January
The tax collector

Read Luke 5:27–39

Then Levi gave a great banquet for him in his house; and there was a large crowd of tax collectors and others sitting at the table with them. The Pharisees and their scribes were complaining to his disciples, saying, 'Why do you eat and drink with tax collectors and sinners?'

(verses 29–30)

Today we continue to see the outworking of Jesus' Jubilee vision as he brings good news to the poor. Being poor in Middle Eastern culture is about being poor in social status, not necessarily in terms of wealth. By using the term 'sinners', the Pharisees are labelling those with Jesus as outsiders with no status. Moreover, in the Greco-Roman world, tax collecting had a social stigma. Therefore, Levi is an outsider to the Jews and was looked on with disdain in the Greco-Roman world. He is poor in social status and in need of an identity. But there's good news for Levi, Jesus has come to the poor! Levi follows Jesus, using his wealth selflessly, and it becomes a part of God's mission, hosting a banquet where many tax collectors, poor in social status, can come to hear the good news. Throughout the Middle East, shared meals symbolise shared lives – intimacy, kinship and a shared identity – and in following Jesus, Levi has found his true identity.

In many cultures today, woman and girls are faced with violence and a lack of human rights simply because they were born as women. Tearfund work with partners around the world to change this social stigma and bring good news to those who have been marginalised. Like Jesus sitting at banquets with those whom society has rejected, our partners prepare feasts in Jesus' name for all to share in. I see it as God's banquet continuing through us; and tax collectors (and accountants) are welcome.

† Dear God, thank you that you gave up your status as God of the universe, facing rejection on the cross, to give us the hope of restored identity for those treated as outsiders by the world.

For further thought

What groups have been marginalised by our cultures? How can we challenge how people are labelled through our use of language and our actions?

Friday 18 January
The apostles

Read Luke 6:1–16

One sabbath while Jesus was going through the grainfields, his disciples plucked some heads of grain, rubbed them in their hands, and ate them. But some of the Pharisees said, 'Why are you doing what is not lawful on the sabbath?'

(verses 1–2)

The Sabbath theme runs throughout the Old Testament and is a way of summarising Israel's identity and hope. The Sabbath is a day set aside to remember that God is the Creator God (Exodus 20:8–11) and the God who liberates from slavery (Deuteronomy 5:12–15). Israel's hope was that God will one day restore creation and liberate it from its bondage to sin and forces of evil, and the Sabbath day helped them remember this hope they had. Throughout this week Jesus has been embodying these themes. He's shown authority over creation through his healings and his calling of the fishermen, and he's liberated those held captive to evil powers or oppressed by social and political structures. But the Pharisees have only taken the Sabbath at its face value. They have missed its meaning and how Jesus is fulfilling this.

Tearfund's approach of working through local churches is a core strength. Imagine being part of a church community where people are struggling to survive, and becoming empowered through resources, knowledge and social education, to become a community of hope, transforming lives. In unstable countries, this may be providing shelter, medicine, food and water, for those whose houses have been burned down or who are fleeing war. In more stable countries, it may be teaching simple farming techniques. One beneficiary, Polly, said, 'After I learned about these techniques I was filled with joy because I could see things were going to change. Now people look at me and my family differently – I support others and I'm useful to the community.'

† Dear God, I praise you for your power. The whole of the universe is your creation. Please empower me to actively pray for and seek out those whose lives need compassionate love.

For further thought

How can you find rest in the knowledge that God creates and liberates? How does this affect what we value, and impact who we are?

Saturday 19 January
Blessings and woes

> **Read Luke 6:17–26**
>
> *He came down with them and stood on a level place, with a great crowd of his disciples and a great multitude of people from all Judea, Jerusalem, and the coast of Tyre and Sidon. They had come to hear him and to be healed of their diseases.*
>
> (verses 17–18a)

This setting to the 'Blessings and Woes' is full of symbolism. Just as Moses went up the mountain to meet with God, Jesus goes up the mountain to be with the Father in prayer. He then descends the mountain, choosing the 12 disciples, echoing God's choosing the 12 tribes of Israel, and proclaims a new way of life, a new way of valuing the world, through the Blessings and Woes, repeating Moses' proclamation of the Ten Commandments. Jesus is revealing the way that God sees, and wants us to see, the world, each other and ourselves. Those who are unacceptable in the socially defined world in which they live, are embraced and restored in the new world. But those who measure their worth by social definitions are building false hope.

Human trafficking is a major problem today. Some of the factors which play a part in its persistence are: poverty, weak family and community support systems, poor law enforcement, government and societal corruption, and fatalistic worldviews which make people believe they have no power to change their lives. A lot of this stems from a cultural worldview or belief system which influences who or what we value, and the decisions that are made based on these values. Learning to throw off our cultural lens and to see the world through God's eyes is a significant part of the Christian journey. It is one that I am still trying to learn by trying to understand the story of God, the world and humanity in the Bible, learning from those who have journeyed before me, and prayer.

† Dear God, thank you for restoring vision and cleaning the muddied way in which we see the world, and value ourselves and each other. Please create in me more of your vision.

For further thought

Reflect on the world-defining actions of Jesus we have read this week. What does it look like and feel like to live in a world with these values?

Readings in Luke (1) – 3 Are you the one?

Notes by **Michiko Ete-Lima**

Michiko serves alongside her husband, Peletisala Lima, at the Congregational Christian Church Samoa in Fairfield, Australia. She is passionate about working with women of the parish, as well as the young people, and watching them grow spiritually in God's Word and ways. She loves visiting different eateries and then burning off the calories at the local gym. She enjoys her quiet times and learning more about Jesus Christ daily. Michiko has used the NRSVA for these notes.

Sunday 20 January
Sawdust and planks

Read Luke 6:27–42

'Why do you see the speck in your neighbour's eye, but do not notice the log in your own eye?'

(verse 41)

Mediation is the process of trying to reach a solution that is acceptable to both parties involved. At the beginning of mediation, both parties are firmly holding onto views that they feel are the correct ones and believe any solutions should satisfy their concerns. Throughout mediation, the parties are then made to consider the other parties' situation and place themselves in each other's shoes. It is remarkable how, suddenly, views start changing and walls start breaking down. Their stance is from a different place and they start realising that there is some validity to what the other party is proposing.

In essence, it is through this process that they start taking out the 'plank' from their eyes and start seeing that what is in their neighbour's eye is only a 'speck'.

At times we find ourselves in situations where we feel that only our views are correct and the truth. It is only when we are forced to see things from another's point of view that we start to see things a lot clearer and without a 'blurred' vision. When we learn to see from the other's perspective we have a clearer and untainted view. This then leads to the building of firm Christian relationships.

† Lord, help us to take the plank out of our eyes, so that we can see your greatness in one another.

Monday 21 January
Good foundations

Read Luke 6:43–49

'I will show you what someone is like who comes to me, hears my words, and acts on them. That one is like a man building a house, who dug deeply and laid the foundation on rock; when a flood arose, the river burst against that house but could not shake it, because it had been well built.'

(verses 47–48)

There is a well-known Samoan proverb: *'e fafaga tama a manu i fuga o laau ma i'a, ae fafaga le tama a le tagata i upu ma tala.'* Translated it means that animals feed their offspring with plants and fish whereas people feed their children on words and stories. It is a saying that conveys the importance of constantly feeding our young people with words or instructions that will serve as a great foundation for them. These words are so important that they take precedence over food.

It is the hope of the elders that these words will be engraved in the young people's hearts and minds, allowing them to be equipped with powerful tools that will prove beneficial in their later years.

The most stable of foundations is that founded on Christ Jesus. When we are assured of this foundation there is hope in the knowledge that, whatever we may encounter, we will not waver or be led astray.

We all have an awesome responsibility to create a firm and stable foundation for all our young people. It is the hope that with such a firm foundation, no matter what problems they may encounter in later years, the foundation will be solid enough that they do not falter. When their foundation is firm, then they will grow up to be good citizens of our villages, countries and churches.

† Lord, provide us with the wisdom to build a firm foundation that is based solely on you, Jesus Christ.

For further thought

Give thought to the kind of stable foundation you would like to build for your life in your Bible reading this year.

Tuesday 22 January
Just say the word

Read Luke 7:1–17

'Therefore I did not presume to come to you. But only speak the word, and let my servant be healed.'

(verse 7)

In reading the story of the centurion, I cannot help but admire his faith in the words spoken by Jesus. The centurion is confident that Jesus will heal his servant by simply saying so. The centurion identifies himself with Jesus and knows that in his line of work, he also makes a command to his soldiers and they will listen. It then begs the question, had the centurion not experienced such a trust in his soldiers, would he have been so trusting in Jesus' word? Perhaps not, but this story is indicative of the fact that our trust really lies in the actions of others. For the centurion then, his experience of faithful workers, coupled with his faith in Jesus, means that his faith is strong.

The story of the woman and her dead son is different. Her situation differs in that she does not address Jesus personally, but rather her tears and great sadness are evident to all around her and especially Jesus. Her tears are then turned into joy by Jesus bringing her son back to life. Obviously, it was not her personal plea to Jesus but rather her heart that caused Jesus to speak words of life back to her dead son.

These stories relay the message that Jesus hears our hearts' yearning and pleas at all times. Whether we utter them or not, Jesus hears and it is through this hearing that Jesus will speak the word of life into our hearts.

† Lord, in faith we pray that you will answer the desires of our hearts, and speak words of life in all areas of our lives.

For further thought

What cries for healing do you hear around you today?

Wednesday 23 January
'Are you the one?'

Read Luke 7:18–35

'Are you the one who is to come, or are we to wait for another?'

(verse 19)

Our family has now been working at Congregational Christian Church Samoa in Fairfield, Australia for over a year. One of my joys is writing plays for our Sunday school for special occasions, like Christmas. I also enjoy telling stories each Sunday and at times I get actors to act our various roles.

I have learned throughout our time at our parish to recognise various young people who would be ideal for certain parts of a play. If I know a person who can easily and quickly learn the role in the Samoan language then they would be given that role. If it is a musical, I would choose the person with a good voice and who is musically talented to fill the role. I find myself asking, are they the one? Is he or she the one for this particular role?

John the Baptist also needed to be sure that Jesus was the person who would fit the role that he was told to prepare for. Jesus responds to the question by relaying his deeds and miracles and in so doing, it was an assurance to John that Jesus is indeed the one.

We have all been given roles to play in our Christian walks. The question is whether or not we have been acting out these roles in the ways that we should. We need to regularly ask ourselves, are we the one? And if so are we acting accordingly?

† We pray for your guidance Lord to help us realise that you have chosen us and that we must act according to your will and ways. Amen.

For further thought

What unlikely person around you might be 'the one' for some particular task?

Thursday 24 January
A fragrant offering

Read Luke 7:36–39

And a woman in the city, who was a sinner, having learned that he was eating in the Pharisee's house, brought an alabaster jar of ointment.

(verse 37)

In our first year as students at Malua Theological College we had a ylang ylang (*moso'oi*) tree that grew outside our house. This tree produced flowers which gave the most beautiful aroma that wafted into our house. It also made walking by our home a most pleasant task. At times, when I was returning from an arduous day, I would be uplifted just from the scent and in the awareness that I was nearing home. The flowers' scent would trigger the sensation of much-welcomed relaxation after a hard day's work.

This ylang ylang flower was always highly sought after when it was time to make garlands for special events at the college. Their sweet aroma would permeate the venue and produce a scent that was most welcoming and inviting. It never ceases to amaze me how much a pleasant smell can represent a positive and happy sensation.

The ointment that the woman had in the alabaster jar most certainly produced a scent that was pleasant. When it was used to anoint the feet of Jesus, the aroma would have filled the house. With its pleasant smell there would have been a most inviting sensation that filled the room. The aroma that was most fragrant, however, would have been the heart of the woman: her willingness to give all that she had and her eagerness to be accepted into the family of Jesus.

As Christians, we all strive to produce that pleasant aroma. This aroma will only be authentic, however, if our hearts are at one with the heart of Jesus.

† Lord, we pray for courage to be that sweet aroma in your presence. Amen.

For further thought

Do you think your Bible reading this year can be a source of beauty and sweetness in your day, like the ylang ylang flower?

Friday 25 January
Sowing seeds

Read Luke 8:1–15

'Now the parable is this: The seed is the word of God.'

(verse 11)

It is routine in our parish that after every Sunday service, our church secretary would make a speech that greets the preacher of the day and to welcome all the church members and visitors. Often in the church secretary's speech, he would identify the encouraging sermon and go on to say words like, 'May the word of God be like seeds that fall upon good soil and may the listeners' spiritual lives continue to flourish.' These words give recognition to the fact that the preacher has attempted to sow seeds in the heart of the congregation. The desire is that these seeds would flourish and be evident in the lives of the hearers.

The task of sowing seeds is somewhat cumbersome at times. We are at times burnt out with the weekly services, running Sunday school programmes, youth groups, choir, mothers' fellowship, fathers' fellowship and various other bodies of the church. However, when we recognise that we should be totally reliant on God's spirit, then we are at peace.

There is true satisfaction when the growth of the seeds becomes evident. As any keen gardener knows, the magic moment comes when seeds bear fruit. When this is seen in the lives of the parishioner, there really is a great sense of joy. As it is written in 3 John 4:3, I could have no greater joy than to hear that my children are following the truth.

† Lord, give us boldness to sow your word and give us strength to grow in your Spirit.

For further thought

What do you hope might take root in your community? How might you sow that seed yourself?

Saturday 26 January
Where is your faith?

Read Luke 8:16–25

He said to them, 'Where is your faith?'

(verse 25)

In 1990, our family set out for a Christmas holiday from New Zealand to Samoa. That very year, a storm ravaged the islands of Samoa and a lot of damage was done.

I remember that as a young child, we were at my mother's family home in Apia, and the storm raged on outside. We saw corrugated iron roofs flying around and yet I remember a sense of peace. The extended family all sat in the sitting room area and had brought cyclone lamps and really made the most of enjoying each other's company. I am guessing that it was due to my great sense of dependency on my parents and knowing that in their presence, everything was fine.

I saw this time as one of true bonding with the extended family, as we not only heard stories from our elders, we were also allowed to play card games at all odd hours.

The greatest lesson for me during this time is that even when we possess a childlike faith, we are able to come through the storms we may experience in our lives. It also highlighted the fact that we must learn to see these times of trial as moments that God has blessed us with to bond with families, friends and neighbours.

When Jesus' disciples recognised the power that Jesus had, they must have gained some form of quiet confidence and faith. So too must we also gain that faith when we become aware of Jesus' greatness and power.

† Lord, help us to see your power and greatness and let not our faith waver in times of adversity. Blessed be your name Lord Jesus Christ, Amen!

For further thought

As you begin a year reading the Bible, where is your faith? Share honestly with God.

The Bible at the movies – 1 Epic beginnings

Notes by **Liz Clutterbuck**

 Liz is a priest in the Church of England, combining parish ministry with work as a researcher and writer. Her particular focus is on fresh expressions of church and measuring its impact. Liz is part of Matryoshka Haus, a missional community that eats together every week and works to build community in London. She is passionate about social media, film, baking and travel – and loves combining as many these as possible! Liz has used the NRSVA for these notes.

Sunday 27 January
God's care

Read Psalm 140:1–13

I say to the Lord, 'You are my God; give ear, O Lord, to the voice of my supplications.' ... I know that the Lord maintains the cause of the needy, and executes justice for the poor.

(verses 6, 12)

The violent imagery of Psalm 140 is worthy of a summer blockbuster movie! The traps and snares set; the burning coals; and the enemies thrown into pits – I imagine it would take some masterful CGI to depict it all!

Against this violent imagery is a recurrent theme: that God cares. The God of the psalmist hears their prayers, and their cries for help and mercy. In a world where violence seeks to take control, the God of the psalmist advocates mercy and justice for the poor and needy.

This week begins a two-week series on 'the Bible at the movies'. In twenty-first-century society, it is in film where life becomes exaggerated as it is played out upon the screen in front of us. Over the years, there have been many attempts at portraying the stories of the Bible in film, but biblical themes and imagery have also been played out in 'secular' storytelling – because they are the themes of God's world.

As we explore a series of themes through scripture and film, one thing needs to be understood above all else: God cares.

† Lord, listen to our cries for justice and mercy in a world so stricken with violence.

History of IBRA

The International Bible Reading Association (IBRA) was founded by the Sunday School Union (SSU) committee under Charles Waters in 1882, a bank manager in King's Cross. A devout young man and Sunday school teacher, Waters had arrived in London in 1859 to further his career, and there encountered the inspirational teaching of Charles Spurgeon. He threw himself, heart and soul, into working with Spurgeon and the SSU who wrote to all members in Britain and overseas inviting them to join the newly formed IBRA, circulating lists of daily Bible readings supported by brief commentary notes.

The response was amazing. By 1910 the readership had exceeded a million people and was touching the lives of soldiers fighting wars, sailors on long voyages to Australia, colliers in the coal mines of Wales, schools in Canada, Jamaica and Belfast and prisoners in Chicago. People all over the world, alone and in groups, felt comforted and encouraged by the idea of joining other Christians throughout the world in reading the same Bible passages. And they still do!

We often receive endorsements from people whose lives are transformed through IBRA. Below are extracts from two letters; one from 2015 and the other from 1907. Can you tell which was written when?

> *I can truly say the Daily Bible reading is a great help and blessing to me. It seems to bring me daily nearer Christ and higher up in the sunshine of God's love.*
> **A. Roberts, Buryas Bridge**

> *People are really excited … In a country where the daily income is low, some are unable to buy [a] printed guide of daily Bible readings. They are expressing a deepest gratitude for free available IBRA material.*
> **Baptist Community of the Congo River, Democratic Republic of the Congo**

Today, over 135 years later, this rich history lives on, touching the lives of hundreds of thousands of people across the world. God is the same yesterday, today and forever – therefore our original mission continues today and will do into the future!

Monday 28 January
Evolution of a man

> **Read Genesis 2:4b–9**
>
> *… then the Lord God formed man from the dust of the ground, and breathed into his nostrils the breath of life; and the man became a living being.*
>
> (verse 7)

The 2014 film *Boyhood* chronicles the life of Mason, a child we first meet aged 6 and revisit at intervals to the age of 18 and his arrival at university. Unusually, it was filmed over 12 years, meaning that we watch the actors growing up as their characters age, too. It is a profoundly moving and thought-provoking film, which I am still pondering years after having first seen it.

One of the themes of *Boyhood* is how our lives are shaped by events over which we have no control. Mason's parents are divorced, and we watch as his father's chaotic life and his mother's choices of partner send his life spinning in different directions. By the end of the film, as he is setting out on his adult life, we the viewers are aware of how these experiences have moulded him.

The breath of life that God breathed into humanity at creation fills each one of us. But our lives then take different directions, dependent upon where we are born, our family's circumstances and numerous other factors. We know the path that God's first human creations were to take – the evolution of their journey and that of their descendants. But we don't know how our own lives (and those of the humans to whom we give life) will evolve.

I don't know what happened to Mason after the film ended, but it's something I often think about. I don't know where God may take my life either, but I am grateful that as God breathed life into me, so God carries me forward.

† God of creation, we thank you for the breath of life that began our time on Earth. Lead us and guide us as we try to follow the path you have laid out for us.

For further thought

Watch *Boyhood*. Who are the people in your life that the stories bring to your mind? Pray for them.

Tuesday 29 January
The fight for equality

Read Genesis 2:18–24

Then the Lord God said, 'It is not good that the man should be alone; I will make him a helper as his partner.'

(verse 18)

The account of God's creation of women has repeatedly been used throughout history as justification for inequality between the genders. Calling her man's 'helper' set the tone of women's role in society over centuries – but gradually equality is now being achieved.

Many important moments in feminist history have been depicted in film, but one of my favourites is 2010's *Made in Dagenham*. It dramatises the 1968 strike at the Ford car plant in Dagenham, east London, where female workers protested against sexual discrimination that took the form of women being paid less than their male counterparts. It is regarded as a turning point in British equalities legislation, as it contributed to the passing of the Equal Pay Act in 1970.

The women's role at the plant was to sew together the car seat covers. When they went out on strike, production of Ford cars across the UK had to cease because they could not be finished. A job that management had thought insignificant and worthy of less pay turned out to be crucial!

Those of us who fight for gender justice often need inspiration from those who have gone before us. The events of *Made in Dagenham*, now 50 years ago, are a stark contrast to the inequality still present in the church.

Women are an equal part of God's creation, and when they are relegated to the role of 'helper' our world is imbalanced. Instead, we should remember that we are 'one flesh' and united in our call to steward God's world.

† Creator God, we thank you for all who have sought equality in our world. Let your Spirit continue to encourage equality between the genders in our world today.

For further thought

Where is there inequality in the news this week? Pray for these situations.

Wednesday 30 January
The curse of temptation

Read Genesis 3:1–13

But the serpent said to the woman, 'You will not die; for God knows that when you eat of it your eyes will be opened, and you will be like God, knowing good and evil.'

(verses 4–5)

The 'crafty' snake and its encouragement to the woman to eat from the tree of the knowledge of good and evil is the very first instance of temptation in humanity's long struggle with it. In modern-day society, so many things are labelled 'temptation' – from a decadent chocolate cake, to the purchase of an unnecessary (but seemingly so necessary) new gadget. But by far the biggest temptation that our culture gives us is sex. Not in the sense that sex is sinful, but that in certain scenarios it hurts us and those with whom we are in relationship.

Numerous films depict this struggle and the fallout that occurs when temptation is given in to. However, what are often more meaningful are stories in which temptation – in spite of everything – is resisted. The 1945 British film *Brief Encounter* does just this, against the backdrop of a humble train station tea room.

It is an agonising watch, as we see Laura and Alec fall in love with each other over the course of their Thursday rendezvous at the station, and witness Laura's emotional turmoil over the attachment she is forming in spite of her husband and children at home. In some ways it is a film in which nothing really happens – tea is drunk and conversations had – and at the end of the film, both realise that there is no future for their relationship. It is beautiful yet heart-wrenching.

We all face temptations of different kinds. But in each struggle, God is with us and can lead us to the right decision.

† Creator God, lead us not into temptation, but deliver us from evil. For yours is the power, the kingdom and the glory, now and forever.

For further thought

Think over those lines from the Lord's Prayer. What are the temptations in your life?

Thursday 31 January
Frozen in exile

Read Genesis 4:1–16

'Today you have driven me away from the soil, and I shall be hidden from your face; I shall be a fugitive and a wanderer on the earth, and anyone who meets me may kill me.'

(verse 14)

Cain's self-imposed banishment is just one example of exile that we find in scripture. In yesterday's passage, Adam and Eve hid themselves in the presence of God once their eyes had been opened to their sin. Exile is a common reaction to acting in a way that displeases God.

One of the most popular Disney films of all time, *Frozen* (2013) broke the mould of the traditional 'princess movies'. Instead of a 'true love's kiss' from a prince saving a princess close to death, it was her sister's love that saved her.

Frozen is a tale of exile: the exile of a sister fleeing into the mountains when her curse of turning all she touches into ice is discovered, and the exile of another sister, motivated by love, following her at all costs.

Although Elsa is hidden from the community she has hurt, she is never separated from the love of her sister Anna. Ultimately, the love between the sisters saves both of them from danger. Similarly, Cain flees from God's eyes, but God continues to protect him. Exile is physical, not emotional, and you cannot hide from the love of others.

When our lives take an unexpected turn or when we believe that we have failed those whom we love and God, exiling ourselves may seem the best way out. But the truth is that love continues to search us out and surround us. We cannot ever truly hide our faces from the one who created us.

† All-seeing God, we thank you that you do not turn your face from us when we turn from you. Surround us and protect us with your love today and always.

For further thought

Is there anyone in your life from whom you are exiling yourself? Bring the situation before God in prayer.

Friday 1 February
Denying the betrayers

Read Matthew 26:20–29

'The Son of Man goes as it is written of him, but woe to that one by whom the Son of Man is betrayed! It would have been better for that one not to have been born.'

(verse 24)

The disciples' disbelief at Jesus' declaration that one of their number would betray their Messiah is understandable. They had journeyed together for some time, witnessing miracles and receiving hours of teaching – why would one of them turn against Jesus?

Judas' betrayal is a bitter moment in Jesus' last days. Turning him over to the authorities results in the ultimate act of violence towards our Messiah.

It can be argued that every act of violence carried out in the name of Jesus is an act of betrayal akin to Judas'. Time and again in history we have seen wars emerge from religious fervour and violence justified as being 'for Christ' – from the crusades to the more recent phenomenon of white supremacy and neo-Nazi movements.

American History X (1998) delves deep into the dark world of American white supremacy – a theme that still resonates deeply two decades on. The story follows two brothers as they become entangled with a neo-Nazi group called the 'Disciples of Christ'. Having distanced himself from the group, the older brother then fights to get his younger sibling out of its clutches.

The film depicts horrific violence conducted under the guise of Christianity – but it is not a Christianity that true disciples of Christ can condone. It is a betrayal of the love that Jesus bestows upon each of his followers.

† Loving Jesus, give us the strength to stand against violence justified in your name. Help us to spread your light in our world and may it overcome the darkness.

For further thought

Research some examples of violence seemingly done in Jesus' name and seek to educate others in what true discipleship is.

Saturday 2 February
Christ who breaks down walls

Read Ephesians 2:14–22

For he is our peace; in his flesh he has made both groups into one and has broken down the dividing wall, that is, the hostility between us.

(verse 14)

The history of humanity is littered with brutal attempts to keep different races separate from each other out of a belief that one was superior to another, but it feels as though these have been particularly prevalent over the last century. The extermination of the Jews in the Holocaust; the genocide of Muslims in Srebrenica; and the Rwandan genocide are just a few examples of the horrific ways in which societies have turned upon each other in living memory.

Apartheid in South Africa is another example of a belief in racial supremacy, enshrined in law for 43 years. The release of Nelson Mandela in 1991 from 27 years of imprisonment marked the beginning of negotiations between the white government and black majority population, a process that was painful and violent. South Africa's first free elections took place in 1994 and marked a new era for the nation.

In 2013, Mandela's autobiography was turned into the film *Mandela: Long Walk to Freedom* and was released in the same month that the globally revered politician and freedom fighter died. It is difficult for a 140-minute movie to do justice to the story of decades of discrimination, political upheaval and imprisonment, but it brings home the brutality of the regime as well as the struggle to unite two groups into one nation.

History and current events demonstrate our tendency to form factions, while the New Testament tells us again and again that in Christ all are one. If only we could remember that Christ has indeed broken down the dividing wall and made all groups into one.

† God the three-in-one, unite humanity and break down those walls that seek to separate us from one another. We pray especially for those places in the world where division begets violence today.

For further thought

Where is there division in your own society? What could you or your church do to help break down walls?

The Bible at the movies –
2 Pass the popcorn

Notes by **Dave Brock**

Dave is a massive film and Bible geek, and came to faith 12 years ago. He is a graduate of Moorlands Theological College, a worship leader, and runs a film and theology club called The One Door Cinema Club in Swanage, Dorset. His favourite films include, in no particular order: *Star Wars: Return of The Jedi*, *The Matrix*, *Scott Pilgrim vs. the World*, *A Bronx Tale*, *The Shawshank Redemption*, *Man of Steel*, *Iron Man*, *Risen* and *Back to the Future*. Dave has used the NIVUK for these notes.

Sunday 3 February
God is everywhere?

Read Acts 17:22–28

For as I walked around and looked carefully at your objects of worship, I even found an altar with this inscription: to an unknown god. So you are ignorant of the very thing you worship – and this is what I am going to proclaim to you.

(verse 23)

One day I was watching *Iron Man* for about the fifth time and God said, 'This is just the story of Paul retold!' Surprised, I rushed off to grab my Bible and a study of Acts, and *Iron Man* revealed startling parallels between the story of Paul and Tony Stark, the maverick entrepreneur who builds the famous metal suit which enables him to fly. Like Paul, Stark is a flawed human being who nevertheless does the right thing. Like Paul, a Damascus-like experience changes his life forever.

I did my research and found the biblical heritage of nearly all my favourite film superheroes. Nearly all my favourite films were just the greatest stories ever retold. Paul today would be preaching the unknown God not from inscriptions on stone idols but from Hollywood idols. I hope this week the God you know will inspire you and speak through our films in ways you have never considered!

Like Paul and his audience in Athens, your friends and neighbours and you will have different beliefs, but the same culture in common. This week, look at film through the lens of scripture, and introduce your friends to the unknown God!

† Lord, show me the films that declare you and your word so I may point to the master author with the one true story. Amen.

Monday 4 February
The all-seeing God

Read Psalm 139:12–17

even the darkness will not be dark to you; the night will shine like the day, for darkness is as light to you.

(verse 12)

A boy worried before bedtime asks his father, 'Does God see everything I do?' The dad, sensing his fears, replies, 'God loves you so much he can't take his eyes off you.' As the psalmist knows, nothing can separate us from the love of God, or indeed his gaze. Jesus is the light shining in the darkness, the darkness that sometimes hides us from God.

But people naturally want to hide in the dark. The 2015 science fiction film *Tomorrowland: A World Beyond* shows people in another dimension able to see into our lives and world and also, like God, into our future. They build a machine that sees us and also has a way of influencing, even warning, humankind. The film shows humanity rejecting this warning and not repenting but embracing the dark path to destruction.

The film is about a simple choice. As one character puts it, there are two wolves: one of darkness and despair and one of light and hope, and they are always fighting. Which one survives? Whichever one you feed.

God does indeed know our innermost being and God sees everything, from the time he knitted us together in our mother's womb to the day we rise in glory with him, or not. Do we live our lives aware of God's hope, sharing with others the knowledge that God loves you so much he can't take his eyes of light off you? Alternatively, do we embrace the dark future the world says we have coming? There are two wolves; which one do you feed?

† Lord, you are the light that the darkness cannot put out. Thank you that you came to save me from darkness and despair. Amen.

For further thought

Do you ever really think about what God sees in our lives? If we believe this, how do we then live life?

Tuesday 5 February
The Word of God

Read Isaiah 40:1–8

A voice of one calling: 'In the wilderness prepare the way for the Lord; make straight in the desert a highway for our God. Every valley shall be raised up, every mountain and hill made low; the rough ground shall become level, the rugged places a plain.'

(verses 3–4)

The Book of Eli is a rare film. It features a Christian actor playing a positive, tough Christian hero set in a dystopian post-apocalyptic future. However, *The Book of Eli* is not a Christian film and presents a horrible vision of a world without order, without hope, seemingly without God. It is a total contrast to the vision of the future presented by yesterday's film.

But there is a voice in the post-apocalyptic wilderness preceding the giving of the Word of God, just as John the Baptist preceded Jesus, the Word made flesh. Eli is a walking miracle. Although blind, Eli is the one chosen to protect a copy of the Bible and carry it across the wasteland. Fending off bandits and a bitter rival for the book, Eli prevails. God removes every obstacle and overcomes all odds, working through Eli to protect his word. God shows the same perseverance in the Isaiah reading today.

The word of God dwells in Eli. Eli is not a stranger to hardship and suffering but the word is in him and Eli meditates on it day and night, walking in faith with the Lord. The voice of one crying out, indeed.

† Lord, please birth in me a fresh love of your word and take me deeper. Help me to hear you speaking through your word. Amen.

For further thought

God's word the Bible is 70 per cent narrative. Why do you think God chooses to communicate his truths through one connected collection of stories?

Wednesday 6 February
Overcoming evil

Read Psalm 37:1–11

A little while, and the wicked will be no more; though you look for them, they will not be found.
But the meek will inherit the land [earth] and enjoy peace and prosperity.

(verses 10–11)

The geek shall inherit the Earth! Well, not *geek*, but this geek came out of the cinema loving the new addition to the canon of Star Wars, *Rogue One: A Star Wars Story*, and I cannot wait to watch it again. It's not just theologians who talk about canon and tradition – and it's not just the psalms that tell stories of unlikely people overcoming wickedness and bringing about peace.

Rogue One tells a story of meek rebels brutally suppressed by the wicked Empire. The story resonated with my experience walking around Jerusalem, the birthplace of a group of men and women who were waging a new type of peaceful rebellion while being hunted down by the Roman Empire and its allies.

As with the rebels in *Rogue One*, this small group known as the Church of Jesus Christ had an important message, the key to freedom for everyone, even those in the Roman Empire. This message, if it got out, would change everything. Like the rebels in *Rogue One*, there was a message that the Galactic Empire would have the power to destroy entire planets and bring the galaxy to submission. The rebels would sacrifice their lives to see the message of hope, the key to defeating this Death Star, and broadcast it to save the galaxy.

The Church did exactly the same and still does to this day, with Christians giving their lives to proclaim a message of love that will set this whole planet free. God still calls the meek and humble as his revolutionaries; God empowers them to overthrow hostile forces; and God still promises that this unlikely group will inherit his blessing.

† Lord, give me the strength and courage to overcome, with my fellow Church rebels of love, social or physical persecution, in Jesus' mighty name. Amen.

For further thought

Despite the persecution against the Church, in just over 2,000 years it overcame, with my fellow Church rebels all over the planet!

Thursday 7 February
Blessed are the peacemakers

Read Matthew 5:1–16

'Blessed are the peacemakers, for they will be called children of God. Blessed are those who are persecuted because of righteousness, for theirs is the kingdom of heaven. Blessed are you when people insult you, persecute you and falsely say all kinds of evil against you because of me.'

(verses 9–11)

Every now and again an amazing film will briefly appear in a cinema and, before you can tell your friends, be gone just as quickly. Its real life begins the moment it is released for viewing at home. These films are often a simple story that seems to resonate within your spirit, usually a true story told well.

The war movie *Hacksaw Ridge* (2016) is one of those films. It is the true story of Desmond T. Doss, a pacifist in the Second World War. He was blessed: persecuted but blessed, reviled but blessed, with all kinds of evil falsely said against him. Branded a coward by his peers – but so very blessed. Although he probably didn't *feel* blessed at the time.

But this peacemaker did bless others, even those who said all this false evil about him. The film tells the story of him becoming a medic, refusing to fire a weapon due to his pacifist beliefs and his faith. People with his convictions often became conscientious objectors, but Doss did something different. He rescued 75 wounded men during the Battle of Okinawa, praying each time, asking God for 'just one more'. He became the first man in American history to receive the Medal of Honor without firing a shot.

As peacemakers, our weapons and warfare are not like those of the world. We fight with the power of prayer against principalities and powers in the heavenly realms, as men and women under the authority of Christ who has all authority. We are on a rescue mission to pull wounded and broken people from the very jaws of eternal death, bringing them to eternal life in the kingdom of heaven and sending them to do the same.

† Heavenly Father, Abba, help me to be a peacemaker and bring glory to your name. Please give me one more. Show me whom you want, whom you have been calling. In Jesus' name, Amen.

For further thought

How often do we ask Jesus whom you should pray for, rescue, lay hands on, bless or befriend?

Friday 8 February
God's good work

Read Nehemiah 2:12–20

I also told them about the gracious hand of my God on me and what the king had said to me. They replied, 'Let us start rebuilding.' So they began this good work.

(verse 18)

The Lego Movie features a hapless hero, Emmet, blissfully unaware of his reality and calling. Falling in with a group of master builders who aim to overthrow the rule of the villain Lord Business, Emmet discovers he, too, has powers to build with Lego without instructions. He, too, is a master builder. Nehemiah, by contrast, would prove to be the original master builder. At the time of Nehemiah, tasked with rebuilding ruined Jerusalem in the fifth century BC, everything was *not* (as Emmet would describe) 'awesome'! Israel's capital, Jerusalem, was a shadow of its former glory days.

At the zenith of Jerusalem's history, Solomon had built walls and palaces, and the temple where God himself would reside! God in the temple would become the centre of everything: the city, the walls, the nation and the region.

Now all lay in ruins and disrepair. God had put a desire into Nehemiah for a good work that needed doing – to rebuild. Like Emmet, who had seen a vision of his Creator's hand, Nehemiah knew God had given him a job to do and Nehemiah raised up his master builders, normal men and women, to restore Jerusalem. There was unity, a purpose and instructions!

Like any Lego construction, the Creator gave Nehemiah instructions, resources and fellow builders. The enemy was not far away, wanting to stop the good work: people rallying crowds against the project. But if God dreams it, who can stop it?

† Lord, what good work or vision of yours do you want to put in me and stir up in my spirit, or what do you want me to join in with? Please show me. Amen.

For further thought

The calling, purpose and good work God has called you to will affect others, as with Emmet and Nehemiah. Let the resistance to these God-given plans drive you forward.

Saturday 9 February
Father and son

Read Proverbs 19:18–23

Discipline your children, for in that there is hope; do not be a willing party to their death. A hot-tempered person must pay the penalty; rescue them, and you will have to do it again.

(verses 18–19)

The theme of a father chastening his son is key to the Marvel comic book film *Thor*. In the Marvel heavenly realms the father, Odin, is betrayed by his adopted son Loki, a liar and deceiver (as in Proverbs 19:22), which forces a multidimensional war. The father sends his true son, Thor, to Earth: a mighty and powerful warrior considered a god by some, stripped of his powers at the start of his mission but later gathering a small band of followers.

There are many similarities here with the gospel story. For some viewers, these father–son relationships may mirror their view of God, the obedient son Jesus, the betrayer Lucifer, and ourselves as adopted children. Hebrews 12:6 tells us that God only chastens the son that he loves, and this film does tell us something about the good father's parenting style.

But this film is a twisted version of the gospel story, in that Thor's powers are stripped because of his own shortcomings. Thor is a 'man of great wrath' who needs to be chastened by his father for his own benefit, to develop his character.

By contrast, Jesus willingly humbled himself from the beginning, laying aside his power. Jesus came to Earth as the sinless God/man on a rescue mission, taking on humanity's sin and overcoming it.

But in both cases, it is humble self-sacrifice that enables the son to defeat the powerful enemy, to save humanity and to be restored to full power and status as son of the father.

† Father, help me, your child, to know that when you do correct me it's because you love me as your son/daughter. Increase the fruit of the Holy Spirit in my life. Amen.

For further thought

In what ways is Jesus like a comic book hero? In what ways is he very different?

The Bible at the movies – 2 Pass the popcorn

Philippians – 1 Paul's longing

Notes by **Kat Brealey**

After studying theology at university, Kat went on to spend a formative year working with Coventry Cathedral's reconciliation ministry team. More recently, her work has focused on interfaith engagement, and she is particularly interested in understanding the way religion can contribute to peace. Kat enjoys cycling, sings in a gospel choir and is part of her local Anglican church. Kat has used the NRSVA for these notes.

Sunday 10 February
Work in progress

Read Philippians 1:1–12

I am confident of this, that the one who began a good work among you will bring it to completion by the day of Jesus Christ.

(verse 6)

The letter to the Philippians was written from prison, where Paul had to rely on the generosity of others to survive. His gratitude suggests the 'good work' was probably a financial gift which the Philippians had sent. Paul interprets this act of generosity as evidence that God has brought about a shift in their perspective and priorities. The broader implications of this for God's work in our lives are encouraging. When it feels difficult to find the energy to continue growing more like Christ, this verse urges us to cling to God's faithfulness and maintain an openness to God's transformative power. The Greek words used for 'begin' and 'complete' are technical terms relating to religious sacrifice, reminding us that God's work in our lives is a sacred and sometimes mysterious act.

As we will see throughout this week, Paul encounters challenges. Yet he never loses hope, because his eyes are fixed on Jesus. He draws deep encouragement from his fellowship, or partnership, with the Philippians – knowing that though separated by distance and circumstance, they are united in God's service. We too need people who celebrate what God is doing in our lives, and spur us on to seek its completion.

† Eternal God, we rejoice in your transforming love. Continue to mould and shape us, that by your grace we may better reflect your glory.

Monday 11 February
Surprise, surprise?

Read Philippians 1:13–18

What does it matter? Just this, that Christ is proclaimed in every way, whether out of false motives or true; and in that I rejoice.

(verse 18)

It might seem like things are going wrong for Paul – a travelling evangelist, he now cannot travel. But in fact he celebrates, because his predicament means that people are talking about Jesus – even if some of them are just trying to make trouble. Paul was guarded by a member of an elite Roman unit at all times, and possibly even chained to them. Presumably he didn't miss an opportunity to talk about Jesus – and if different guards took it in turns to watch him, then during his imprisonment he had the chance to share the good news with many of the most important people of the time. Not all of them would have believed him – but even if they mentioned it to others to dismiss it as madness, the message spread. Thus being in prison was not the end of Paul's ministry but a new phase. Acts 23–24 tell us that high-ranking governors got wind of him, sending for him to come and share his message. Furthermore, the local church was emboldened by Paul's experiences and preached more passionately than ever.

Paul was not surprised by all this. After all, his faith was one in which the horror of the crucifixion resulted in the ultimate good, and so he was open to the idea that things don't always turn out as expected! Indeed the Bible is full of stories which demonstrate that our God is perpetually turning things on their head. Does this unnerve us, or do we embrace it?

† Surprising God, we celebrate that your ways are not our ways. Sustain our trust when we face challenges, and open our hearts to seek and know your ever-present love.

For further thought

Where, when, and in whom will you encounter the unexpected God today?

Tuesday 12 February
A change is gonna come

Read Philippians 1:19–26

… for I know that through your prayers and the help of the Spirit of Jesus Christ this will turn out for my deliverance.

(verse 19)

Paul's assertion that 'this will turn out for my deliverance' is a phrase also found in Job 13:16, where Job tells his friends that he will not renounce his belief that God is good, despite the horrendous things he has experienced. Paul draws on the story of Job to understand his own trials, seeing it as a source of confidence that the situation he finds himself in will have a positive resolution, as Job's eventually did. By deliverance, he isn't referring to salvation after death – although the following verses indicate that he is assured of this – but rather his release from prison instead of execution.

How can Paul be so sure? There are two reasons. Firstly, he asked people to pray for him and believes in prayer bringing about changes in history. Secondly, he believes in the power of the Spirit being on his side. We may well find Paul's assuredness challenging. What can we honestly say we know, in the midst of global change and uncertainty? Yet it is a helpful reminder that as Christians we are not called simply to trust in the existence of something better after death, but to work and pray for a better world.

The US civil rights movement is a good example – the title of Sam Cooke's famous song 'A Change is Gonna Come' embodies the sentiment of those who committed their lives to pursuing racial justice, believing that they would see progress. It took time, it was costly, and there is still more to be done – but they were right.

† Sovereign God, situations in our world and in our lives exhaust and overwhelm us. Grant us fresh hope to envision change, and the courage to pursue it.

For further thought

Big changes are made up of lots of small ones! Take one action today to make a difference to a situation you're concerned about.

Wednesday 13 February
Dare to be different

Read Philippians 1:27–30

Only, live your life in a manner worthy of the gospel of Christ, so that, whether I come and see you or am absent and hear about you, I will know that you are standing firm in one spirit, striving side by side with one mind for the faith of the gospel.

(verse 27)

The Greek verb Paul uses for the phrase 'live your life' is related to the word *polis*, meaning city – so although we might be inclined to read this verse as an instruction relating to our personal life, this was not Paul's intention. Rather he is addressing the Philippian community as a whole. He is particularly concerned with how their life together is carried out in the public eye. What message does the way they conduct themselves communicate to those around them who are looking on?

We could ask the same question of our churches and Christian communities today. This term *polis* also draws an analogy with the fact that Philippi was a Roman colony, situated in Macedonia. Those who lived there were Roman citizens, but far from Rome. As such their culture would have contrasted in various ways with the way of life of those around them. This situation is not dissimilar to the spiritual reality; the Philippians are citizens of the kingdom of God and called to live accordingly, despite (and in fact because of) their present location among those who do not share this citizenship. Following Christ has implications not just for their beliefs but also for the attitudes, behaviour and priorities which stem from these.

Paul's words remind us that maintaining our distinctive identity as followers of Christ is at the heart of our calling. Today, as our Christian communities continue to differ from others that surround them, how can we ensure this is in positive ways which point people towards the gospel?

† Generous God, give us wisdom to discern ways our shared life can be a sign of your abundant grace to those around us.

For further thought

Business guru Stephen Covey suggested, 'The main thing is to keep the main thing the main thing.' What practical steps could help keep Jesus your 'main thing'?[4]

---

4   Covey, S. (1989), *The 7 Habits of Highly Effective People* (New York, NY: Free Press).

Thursday 14 February
Considering our culture

Read Philippians 2:1–11

Let the same mind be in you that was in Christ Jesus.

(verse 5)

There is so much which can be said about this rich passage that we will restrict ourselves to focusing on 12 words today!

Yesterday we considered the Philippians' status as a Roman colony and the fact that this had a distinct culture. While this was a useful analogy to help them understand their role as Christians in relation to those around them, in fact the culture itself was something of an impediment. Philippian culture placed great importance on strength and self-reliance. Their status as a Roman colony brought with it financial and political benefits, and so it was something they took great pride in. Yet Paul points out that such concerns are at odds with who they are as Christians, and as such should be traded in for an attitude of humility and self-sacrifice, following the example of Jesus.

What does this mean for us? Well, another way of defining culture is simply 'the way we do things round here'. We are all part of various cultures – whether related to where we live, the social circles we move in, our hobbies and interests or our family. These inform the way we are as individuals and as a Christian community – often without us even realising! Particularly when it comes to the Church, we need to stop and consider if 'the way we do things round here' is in line with the mind of Christ Jesus – or whether his attitudes as related in this passage might suggest some alterations are needed.

† Loving God, reveal to us the aspects of our culture which do not reflect the mind of Christ, and help us to root ourselves in you, our Creator and Sustainer.

For further thought

What five words would you use to describe the culture of your church or Christian community? Would people from other social, ethnic, age or interest groups fit within this?

Friday 15 February
Stepping up, stepping out

Read Philippians 2:12–18

… work out your own salvation with fear and trembling; for it is God who is at work in you, enabling you both to will and to work for his good pleasure.

(verses 12b–13)

As we approach the end of our week looking at the first half of Philippians, this verse provides an opportunity to reflect on our personal journey of faith. You may have been introduced to Christian faith at Sunday school, discovered it as an adult – or both! Either way, Paul offers a reminder that each of us must take responsibility for the ongoing task of working out what our faith means on a day-to-day basis. He isn't suggesting that we somehow bring about our own salvation, but rather that part of being a Christian is to unpack more fully over time what salvation means for us, as we mature in our faith. As the Philippians cannot rely on Paul to do this for them, now that he is far from them, so we cannot leave this to our own leaders and teachers. Instead let's commit to doing it ourselves – trusting that God will energise, equip and sustain us along the way.

Why is this associated with fear and trembling? The language evokes Exodus 19, where God revealed himself at the giving of the Torah, or the Law. Mount Sinai trembled – and so did the people! Taking our faith into our own hands and figuring out what it means for us can be a scary experience. It requires navigating difficult questions which arise as we encounter life's challenges, and questioning things we've previously taken for granted. Yet as we commit to engaging deeply with our faith, God is revealed and we find that we are on holy ground.

† Gracious God, equip us for the task of working out our own salvation – that this lifelong adventure of faith may be a source of deep joy.

For further thought

Are there ways you could invest in your spiritual growth – perhaps going on a retreat, reading a helpful book or joining a Bible study group?

Saturday 16 February
What are friends for?

> ### **Read Philippians 2:19–30**
>
> *Still, I think it necessary to send to you Epaphroditus – my brother and co-worker and fellow soldier, your messenger and minister to my need.*
>
> (verse 25)

The theological theme of partnership in the gospel which runs throughout Philippians is illustrated practically in this verse. Epaphroditus was a member of the Philippian Church who had served as the messenger to deliver their gift to Paul in prison. Somewhere on the journey he became seriously ill, but now has recovered and so Paul is able to send him back along with this letter.

Paul often names individuals in his letters who were particularly important to him. Sometimes we can piece together their stories, like here, but in other places the limited information means that we tend to overlook them. This can lead to the inaccurate impression that Paul operated in isolation or that his relationship with God meant he had no need for human relationships. In reality, his missionary work actually meant that relationships were more important to him – their shared faith making them like a family – rather than less. The continuation of his ministry was dependent on the support and assistance of friends whether named or unnamed in the Bible, and the way he describes Epaphroditus here indicates the deep affection he felt for them.

Similarly, we need friends to journey alongside us, sharing our joys and sorrows and helping us in practical ways. We have seen this week that Paul viewed Christianity primarily in corporate terms, and this was backed up by his own experience. How can we nurture these faithful friendships in our own lives and communities?

† Living God, we thank you for the gift of friends who support and encourage us, asking that we too may grow in our ability to be a faithful friend to others.

For further thought

How intentional are you about nurturing your Christian friendships? Are there people in your community who could use a friend?

Philippians – 2 Rejoice always

Notes by the **Very Reverend Bruce Jenneker**

Bruce is Rector of All Saints' Anglican Church, Durbanville, in Cape Town, and Senior Priest of the Diocese of Saldanha Bay. After 26 years in the USA he served at St George's Cathedral, Cape Town. He chaired the Standing Commission on Liturgy and Music of The Episcopal Church, serves on the Liturgical Committee of the Anglican Church of Southern Africa and is convenor of the Prayer Book Revision Project. Bruce has used the NRSVA for these notes.

Sunday 17 February
Surpassing value

Read Philippians 3:1–11

I regard everything as loss because of the surpassing value of knowing Christ Jesus my Lord. For his sake I have suffered the loss of all things, and I regard them as rubbish, in order that I may gain Christ and be found in him.

(verses 8–9)

In this poignantly pastoral letter, Paul now addresses the challenge of opposition from outside the church and division from within. But first he insists that the Philippian Christians be joyful. A joyful spirit will engage abuse and attack and not be overwhelmed by them. The joy that comes from knowing Christ and sharing the hope of glory is a powerful antidote to legalistic confrontation. 'Rejoicing in the Lord' is an essential and recurring theme of this letter. To be found by Christ is joy, to live in Christ is joy, to receive and trust the salvation Christ offers is joy, sublime and complete.

Employing a ringing alliteration in Greek, Paul exhorts his readers to beware of dogs, evil workers and mutilators. They are 'dogs' because like dogs (as seen at that time by Jews) these people are unclean since they disregard the spirit of the law; they are evil workers because they emphasise the 'works' of the law; they are 'mutilators' because they circumcise the flesh and not the heart.

Paul considers every other achievement or commitment as 'rubbish' – 'dung' in some translations. He wants nothing whatsoever to stand in the way of his knowing Christ and the power of Christ's resurrection.

† When the gospel calls me to witness bravely to Christ's all-embracing love, fill me, O God, with joy that triumphs over narrow legalism.

Monday 18 February
Knowing and being known

Read Philippians 3:12–16

Beloved, I do not consider that I have made it my own; but this one thing I do: forgetting what lies behind and straining forward to what lies ahead, I press on towards the goal for the prize of the heavenly call of God in Christ Jesus.

(verses 13–14)

The joy of knowing Christ and complete participation in Christ's resurrection is always a work in progress: it is never complete. Surrendering to the encompassing and liberating love that Christ offers is a lifetime commitment. Paul offers the example of his own abandonment of all that came before, his exertion in the present as he intentionally pursues this goal, and the living hope of the glorious prize that summons him to the end of the race. Paul frequently uses imagery from sport and athletics. Here it is a marathon runner he calls to mind: the past steps and effort don't matter, the present exertion demands no less than everything, and the goal beckons: the prize of the crowning glory of life in and with Christ.

The effort involved is not 'hard work' demanded to earn salvation; no, it is the passionate and active commitment required to render ourselves open to the gift Christ offers. The offer Christ makes is whole and complete, direct and immediate. On the other hand, our readiness to receive the offer requires an abandonment of our instinct for self-preservation; the openness to embrace it demands a vulnerability acknowledging that we cannot save ourselves. Perhaps hardest of all is the necessity to affirm that we are broken, fallen down and hopeless – and in urgent need of redemption.

The gospel that Paul proclaims here is that it is Christ who saves, it is Christ who invites us to claim that salvation and it is Christ who, by grace, empowers us to open ourselves, wholly and entire, to receive the gift Christ offers.

† Recreate me, Lord Jesus Christ. Transform my need to save myself into an embrace of your love. Take me as I am and remake me in the fullness of your grace.

For further thought
Life demands that we 'make it', be successful, get to the top – and all of that, supposedly without help from anyone. Reflect today on the dangers of being arrogantly self-sufficient.

Tuesday 19 February
The heresy of apathy

Read Philippians 3:17–4:1

But our citizenship is in heaven, and it is from there that we are expecting a Saviour, the Lord Jesus Christ. He will transform the body of our humiliation so that it may be conformed to the body of his glory.

(verses 20–21)

Paul distinguishes between those who live according to his example and those who are 'enemies of the cross of Christ' (verse 18). Paul was probably referring to several groups: among them, those who insisted that the fledging church remain a Jewish sect following the Laws of Moses, those who interpreted the gospel in ways that diminished the reality of the crucifixion, those who believed that the end of time was at hand and so lived licentiously.

Paul had discovered the power of the cross. He lived in the redeeming power of the self-sacrificing love of Jesus Christ: 'the message about the cross is foolishness to those who are perishing, but to us who are being saved it is the power of God' (1 Corinthians 1:18). For Paul, the cross is nothing less than the charter, compass and portal to the citizenship to which we are called and graced. The cross stands for grace unbounded, infinite forgiveness and absolute love. This is the universe in which Paul lives and into which he invites the Philippians.

In the international turmoil between the First and Second World Wars, when many Christians were drawn to an escapist and distracting view of Christianity, H. Richard Niebuhr (using the language of his time) wrote challengingly about the heresy of proclaiming that 'a God without wrath brought men without sin into a Kingdom without judgment through the ministrations of a Christ without a Cross'.[5] His words echo Paul's and address us powerfully in our time.

† Fix my gaze on your cross, Lord Jesus. Let me see, in your wounds and agony, love reaching out to find me, embrace and save me, filling me with the joy and freedom of abundant life.

For further thought

Reflect on what your daily life would be like if you were able to live moment by moment in the depth of Christ's self-sacrificing love, knowing that you are precious, beloved and saved.

5   Niebuhr, R.H. (1988) *The Kingdom of God in America* (Middletown, CT: Wesleyan University Press).

Wednesday 20 February
Sharing one mind

Read Philippians 4:2–3

I urge Euodia and I urge Syntyche to be of the same mind in the Lord.

(verse 2)

As Paul urges his readers to 'stand firm' (verse 1) in the redemptive power of Christ's loving self-sacrifice, he writes very tenderly to his brothers and sisters whom he loves and whom he longs for, describing them as his 'joy and crown' (verse 1). In the context of this pastoral intimacy, he appeals to them to come to the aid of these two women who have 'struggled together' for the sake of the gospel and now are at odds (verse 3). Here again Paul deliberately used the word 'struggle', from the language of the sports arena, denoting extreme exertion and total dedication.

Rather than focus on the details of the quarrel, Paul lists the women among his co-workers 'whose names are in the book of life' (verse 3) and proceeds to exhort the community to live the life to which they have been called and graced: rejoicing in the Lord, gentleness in all things, turning away from anxiety, confident prayerfulness and living in 'the peace of God, which surpasses all understanding' (verses 4–7).

Do not be distracted by your quarrels and differences, Paul is counselling his readers. Rather, recognise your co-workers for the heralds of the gospel that they are. Rise above the distractions of factiousness and self-serving to find your identity and peace in the joy of the Lord.

Personality and temperament often confuse the issues for us too, causing us to be distracted from the goals we share by the opinions and attitudes we don't. 'All things work together for good for those who love God, who are called according to God's purpose,' Paul wrote in Romans 8:28.

† Keep me alert, Lord Jesus Christ, to the ministry I share with you in my sisters and brothers. Fill me with joy in the work I share with them for the sake of your cross.

For further thought

What behaviours of others have the power to unsettle you and alienate you from them? What can you change in your responses to enable you to live more fully into the freedom of abundant life?

Thursday 21 February
The Lord is near

Read Philippians 4:4–7

Do not worry about anything, but in everything by prayer and supplication with thanksgiving let your requests be made known to God. And the peace of God, which surpasses all understanding, will guard your hearts and your minds in Christ Jesus.

(verses 6–7)

Having exhorted the Philippians to deal with interpersonal conflict by entering fully into the life to which they have been called and graced, Paul affirms two essential aspects of Christ's gospel: to live in the joy of the Lord and to turn away from worry, anxiety and stress. These are two consistent themes of the gospel Christ proclaimed: that there is no need to be afraid of anything whatsoever, and that therefore anxiety and stress do not have any hold over us. The lavish gift of salvation that Christ offers frees us, always and forever, from whatever seeks to threaten, diminish or destroy us. This freedom is joy, overflowing, pressed-down and running over. Those who live in Christ receive this freedom and inherit this joy.

Perhaps Paul meant that the end time was at hand when he wrote that the 'Lord is near'. But for us who live in this in-between time, the nearness of the Lord is the intimacy that John the Baptist proclaimed in his message of repentance: 'Repent, for the kingdom has come near.' The new reign of Christ, the abundant life Christ inaugurates, is within our hands' reach. We do not have to wait for the moment of the end of all time to know the nearness of the Lord; that embrace is Christ's offer to us here and now.

Our time and our context make us worriers. Our heightened stress levels result from our striving to save ourselves rather than trust the extravagant grace of God in which, as the mystic Julian of Norwich (1342–c. 1426) wrote, 'all will be well, and all manner of thing will be well'.

† Deliver me, O Jesus, from the pride that insists that I control all that happens to and around me. Turn my eyes upon you alone, to find in you my confidence and my joy.

For further thought

Reflect on the words of Jesus today: 'Peace I leave with you; my peace I give to you. I do not give to you as the world gives. Do not let your hearts be troubled, and do not let them be afraid' (John 14:27).

Friday 22 February
The truth of wherever

Read Philippians 4:8–13

Finally, beloved, whatever is true, whatever is honourable, whatever is just, whatever is pure, whatever is pleasing, whatever is commendable, if there is any excellence and if there is anything worthy of praise, think about these things.

(verse 8)

Paul has been at pains to exhort his readers to live in 'the harvest of righteousness that comes through Jesus Christ for the glory and praise of God' (1:11). In this summation, he urges his readers to right living by encouraging them to right thinking, calling them to consider a list of virtues that appears nowhere else in the New Testament, although most of them are referred to singly. As a collection of virtues they would have been familiar to Paul's Greek readers since they are characteristic 'goods' of Greek moral philosophy.

In this connection it is challenging to ponder whether Paul is inviting Christians to recognise true goodness round about them and to honour it wherever they find it. Is there an echo here of Jesus' teaching that 'whoever is not against you is for you?' (Luke 9:50).

There are times when we are called to live the unique distinctiveness of life in Christ. According to Paul in this letter, that is life characterised by intimacy with Jesus Christ, convinced of the power of Christ's resurrection, full of gentleness and abounding in joy. On the other hand, we are also called to recognise and acknowledge the power and grace of God in goodness that is present everywhere, emerges where we least expect it and erupts without our aid: 'the earth is full of the steadfast love of the Lord' (Psalm 33:5).

God is at work everywhere and all the time, not just in the Church and certainly not just with us Christians. 'The earth is the Lord's and all that is in it' (Psalm 24:1).

† Keep me rooted in the power of your love, O Christ, and filled with the joy of your embrace. Then open my eyes to recognise with joy your hand at work in the world.

For further thought

Joy is a gift, but also a commitment and a discipline. Life often ambushes joyfulness and we surrender to its power to paralyse us into cynicism and hopelessness. How can you sustain joyfulness?

Saturday 23 February
A fragrant offering

Read Philippians 4:19–23

And my God will fully satisfy every need of yours according to his riches in glory in Christ Jesus. To our God and Father be glory for ever and ever. Amen.

(verses 19–20)

It is clear from this letter that the Philippians had provided generous financial support for Paul. Now he affirms that support for the mission and ministry of the gospel and provision for the welfare of its ministers are 'a fragrant offering' and 'an acceptable sacrifice' (verse 18) because the offering of the sacrifice itself is accompanied by the offering of the heart as well. It is not just 'stuff' that is sacrificed but with it the heart too is offered in love.

In this conclusion to his letter (verses 10–23), Paul declares the contentment in which he lives and which comes from his faith. He has lived with abundance as well as with scarcity. He has learned the secret of living always in the joy of the Lord, because he can do 'all things' through Christ who strengthens him (verse 13). It is this confidence that Paul desires for the Philippians. The God Paul knows and loves, and whom the Philippians desire to know and serve, will satisfy fully their every need: not just some needs, but every need; not just partially met, but fully satisfied.

In relation to 'God's riches in glory in Christ Jesus', our needs, however enormous they might seem, are very small requirements indeed. God's riches are predicated on God's glory. In the English translation of Paul's letters, 'glory' appears 56 times. The God Paul knows, loves and serves acts in all things 'to make known the riches of God's glory for the objects of mercy, which God has prepared beforehand for glory' (Romans 9:23). This is what God offers; this is the joy of the Lord.

† You, O Christ, are my strength and stay. Make me ready to trust you in all things, on the good days and the bad, when the road is smooth or when it is rough.

For further thought

How can you serve the needs of the mission and ministry of the gospel? What can you support with your time and talents? How can you speak, serve or act for Christ?

Psalms of Ascent – 1 Let us go up

Notes by **Carla A. Grosch-Miller**

For Carla's biography, see p. 1. Carla has used the NRSVA for these notes.

Sunday 24 February
Prayer from the heart

Read Psalm 120

In my distress I cry to the Lord, that he may answer me.

(verse 1)

From ancient times Jewish men and women have made annual pilgrimages to the temple in Jerusalem during the Feasts of Passover, Weeks and Tabernacles. As Jerusalem is a city on a hill, they would walk uphill to get there and, after a ritual bath, climb the steps leading onto the Temple Mount. The Psalms of Ascent are thought to be those recited on the road as well as on the steps.

These psalms cover a range of situations and emotions, enabling the pilgrims to voice the prayers of their hearts. Over the centuries Christians too have found these psalms to open the gate of honest prayer.

Psalm 120 is spoken by a war-weary alien. We can imagine these words on the tongues of fleeing refugees. We are reminded how difficult it is to speak a word of peace when we are surrounded by the winds of war. Rage and righteous indignation trump thoughtful reflection; fear fuels cycles of violence. As it was then, so it is now.

A number of the Psalms of Ascent express a longing for peace and security, a longing as old as our species. May God prosper the praying of these psalms on the Earth.

† Merciful God, in a world of seemingly intractable conflict, lead us into peace. Be in our longing and our living, our words and our actions.

Monday 25 February
Healing balm

Read Psalm 121

I lift up my eyes to the hills – from where will my help come?

(verse 1)

Before ever we knew the name God, we sought God in high places. Mountaintops, hills and plateaus have been worship sites from time immemorial. In our tradition, the Great I AM is revealed to Moses on Mount Horeb/Sinai, first in the burning bush and later with the Ten Commandments. Peter, James and John witnessed the transfiguration of Jesus on a mountaintop. Is it any wonder that the psalmist looks to the hills?

The first time I experienced a mountaintop in all its glory and wonder – clouds billowing up from below, birds coasting on thermals – was when I took the train up Snowdon in Wales. The experience of standing on the edge, enthralled with all I could see, made me turn to my husband to say, 'We have to climb this mountain tomorrow.' I wanted to earn whatever mystery was enfolding before me and to experience the journey.

Since then I have developed a love affair with hillwalking. When my brother was killed, I longed for the hills. Driving from the Lake District to the Isle of Skye, I drank them in. Nothing else satisfied my wounded soul. They were healing balm, witnessing to eternity and to the power of unseen forces.

Silently the hills testify to the steadfast and solid love of the One who called them, and us, into being. Wordlessly we are consoled and reassured. Our small lives, with their great pains and hardships, are put into perspective. Beauty binds our hearts.

† Maker of Mountains, I stand in awe and wonder at the mystery of your healing, strengthening love. May I never forget to lift my eyes to the hills.

For further thought

If there are no mountains or hills nearby, search online for mountain images and choose one that speaks to you. Spend some time with it.

Tuesday 26 February
Pray for peace in Jerusalem

Read Psalm 122

For the sake of my relatives and friends I will say, 'Peace be within you.'

(verse 8)

Some say that Jerusalem is the navel of the universe. The night I first arrived, my friend Leah, who was living there for her first year of rabbinical training, took me to pray at the Western Wall. Exhausted from the long flight and with knees shaking, I leant my forehead and hand against the cold stone. I felt myself to be standing in the vortex of the world – a terrible beauty engulfed me as I sensed the power and mystery of the Holy. I have never been the same. In Jewish tradition, the name of God is never uttered; even the writing of the name is forbidden so 'G-d' is used. I get this. We bandy about the name too readily, as if we really know what we are talking about. We don't.

It is no surprise to me that Jerusalem, whose name means 'City of Peace', knows so little peace. Located at the crossroads of two continents (Africa and Eurasia), it was passed between occupying superpowers for centuries. As the birthplace of the three monotheistic traditions called the People of the Book, Jews, Christians and Muslims lay claim to its holy sites. The city pulses with humankind's deepest longings and fears. The Holy, in all its beauty and all its terror, is held in trembling hands.

To pray for the peace of Jerusalem is to pray for the peace of the world. If people in the Middle East can learn to live with difference and reconcile conflicting claims, humanity will have found a way to rise above some of the violence that marks our presence on Earth.

† God holy and unknowable, limit not your love to the measure of my understanding, but make clear the way of peace in my life and our world.

For further thought

Buddhist monk Thich Nhat Hanh in his 1987 book *Being Peace* observes that one person being peace makes a difference. What practices enable you to be peace?

Wednesday 27 February
Have mercy

Read Psalm 123

Have mercy upon us, O Lord, have mercy upon us, for we have had more than enough of contempt.

(verse 3)

We need mercy as much as a garden needs sunshine. We make a lot of mistakes, don't or can't always anticipate the consequences of our actions, and sometimes choose to do things that are unavoidably hurtful. While I've never been keen on the concept of original sin, I recognise the inherent fallibility and frailty of humankind. Let one who is without sin cast the first stone.

Becoming aware of one's need for mercy goes hand in hand with becoming a person who is self-aware, self-accepting and accepting of others. No one is perfect; we are all works in progress. Knowing that I need mercy helps me to extend it to others. Ian MacLaren (1850–1907) said it well: 'Be pitiful [often quoted as kind], for everyone you meet is fighting a hard battle.'[6]

The psalmist seeks a particular mercy: one of favour shown in the face of the contempt and scorn of the rich, the proud and the self-satisfied. Contempt chokes off compassion; scorn suffocates sympathy. Those attitudes are particularly sin-laden, as they denigrate the dignity of others made in the image of God. The psalmist recognises that the true source of our dignity is God, in whose image we are made and whose mercy is from everlasting to everlasting. By the grace of God, we need not be ashamed and we need not be afraid. We can stand tall, leaning towards the light and growing in the light of grace.

† God merciful and just, let your light illumine the shadows we are tempted to hide in and enable us to accept and extend mercy.

For further thought

Is there someone you find it difficult to forgive? Might it be time? When you are ready, simply hold that person before God in light.

---

6   MacLaren, I. (1898) 'Be Pitiful', *The British Weekly*, 76.

Thursday 28 February
God is for us

Read Psalm 124

If it had not been the Lord who was on our side …

(verses 1a, 2a)

God is for us. Can any statement be more powerful? Or more dangerous? In today's psalm of victory, we hear a grateful song of deliverance from the snares of an enemy. I have no doubt that some causes are more holy and in line with the divine will for humanity than others, but I am always nervous about claims that God is on a particular side in a conflict.

God is for us. Yes, indeed. I believe human and planetary flourishing are at the heart of God's desire for the creation. All revelation is geared towards that end. Yet in our self-interested myopia, we readily claim that what we ourselves want is what God wants. That may not always be the case.

Still there are times when we prevail by the power and presence of God, and we might not recognise it until after the fact. There was a time when I was so defeated by a series of bereavements and human failings (my own and others) that I could hardly hold my head up. Even attending church was painful; God and I were not exactly on speaking terms. But looking back, there were a series of invitations and occurrences that, while honouring my freedom and my pain, nudged me back towards fullness of life. God is for us, and never stops sending emissaries to bring us back to ourselves and to the life God has for us. Thanks be to God.

† God wise and wonderful, give me a discerning mind that I may know the path you have for me. Let not my ignorance or self-interest blind me to your will.

For further thought

Search online for Mark Twain's short story 'The War Prayer' to get a sense of what we are really praying for when we pray for 'our side'.

Remembering joy

Read Psalm 126

May those who sow in tears reap with shouts of joy.

(verse 5)

Remembrance is a powerful tool. Speaking to a people beset by devastation and sorrow, the psalmist calls to mind a time when God acted powerfully to restore their fortunes.

Psalm 126 is traditionally said on the Sabbath day in Jewish worship as well as on high holidays. Its weekly recitation keeps both history and hope before people's eyes. When all is well, the laughter of the first paragraph enlivens gratitude. When times are hard, the prayer of the second paragraph is an earnest plea.

I remember a particularly difficult political time in my home country of the United States when one of the Weavers, a folk quartet that survived being blacklisted in the 1950s for political speech, said: 'This too will pass. I know. I've had kidney stones.'[7] It turns out laughter is allied both to celebrating the joy of fulfilment and to marshalling persistence in the face of adversity.

Week by week Christians gather in worship with both history and hope before our eyes. We call to mind the good things God has done for us, not least in sending us the Word made flesh that we might know how to inhabit our own skin with grace and purpose. We celebrate the joy that comes with belonging to the ragtag, beleaguered but beloved family of God and we draw deeply from the well of salvation to meet the challenges of the day. Thanks be to God for never letting us forget.

† When my memory of your love begins to fade, Good God, set before me both history and hope so that I may be renewed by remembering.

For further thought
Choose a lovely notebook and each day write down some good thing you may want to remember when times get hard.

---

7   *The Weavers: Wasn't That a Time!* (1982), J. Brown, [film], (California: United Artists Classics).

Saturday 2 March
True security

Read Psalm 127

Happy is the man who has his quiver full of sons.

(verse 5a)

From where does our security come? What is security anyway? The word derives from the Latin *securus* meaning 'free from care, quiet, easy' or 'free from danger, safe'.

In the millennium before the Common Era, when the psalms were first sung, security looked like an expanding tribe of kinsmen capable of wielding sword and shield. Hence the desire for a 'man's' (or woman's) quiver full of sons or daughters. In the twenty-first-century West, individuals tend to think of accumulated wealth as our greatest security while nations that are able stockpile nuclear weapons to make themselves feel secure.

It is worth asking: where do these obsessions really get us as a human family? What would the world look and feel like if more of the time, energy and material that go into creating bulging portfolios, holiday homes and weapons of mass destruction were spent instead on the things that make for peace and the flourishing of the human family on this planet – education, health care, sustainable development and agriculture, reversing global warming, and the arts?

It is beyond my pay grade to know what the right answer is regarding nuclear deterrence but it is not rocket science to see that our efforts at creating our own personal and national security may be undermining that security by fuelling inequality and creating dangerous possibilities.

The psalmist reminds us that our true security is in aligning our desires and our work with God's. We are cast back on the Great Commandment to love God and neighbour as self. What does the Love Commandment say about excessive personal wealth and the weaponising of the world?

† God true and trustworthy, enable me to let go of my hold on the things that falsely promise security so that I may grasp the true security of living within your love.

For further thought

Fear is the driver of our worst behaviours. What are you afraid of, and how are you managing that fear?

Psalms of Ascent – 2 Calm and quiet

Notes by **Carla A. Grosch-Miller**

For Carla's biography, see p. 1. Carla has used the NRSVA for these notes.

Sunday 3 March
Rest and resonance

Read Psalm 131

But I have calmed and quieted my soul, like a weaned child with its mother.

(verse 2a)

Imagine yourself as an infant, belly full, sleeping on your mother's chest. Feel the deep relaxation, the complete absence of fear or want. Is there any more powerful image of the soul at rest, secure in love?

What most fascinates me about this passage is the agency of the writer: *I* have calmed and quieted my soul. Not *God* has calmed and quieted my soul. We can rest secure and trust in the love of God, but we have to make the choice to do that. The writer's soul is compared to a weaned child – one who no longer feeds directly from her mother's body, one no longer dependent in the same way.

This language recognises our maturity as well as our need for resting secure in the arms of a loving parent. The infant is picked up and cuddled, but we need to walk over and sit on our mother's lap. It is up to us to make the choices that enable us to rest secure in God's love.

Every human being needs moments of complete rest. We need it for our bodies and our souls. Unrelenting stress and anxiety will diminish our health and our capacity to be the person God created us to be. We also need resonance – the feeling of being known and loved, heard and cared for … as a child being held by a parent can feel. This is a gift we can receive from God and that we can give to one another. God bless our resting and our being a restful and resonant place for others. We are beloved, held in the warm embrace and loving gaze of God.

† Holy One, our only Home, call me back to your loving arms often, and enable my arms to embrace those who need your love.

Monday 4 March
The dwelling place of God

Read Psalm 132

'I will not give sleep to my eyes or slumber to my eyelids, until I find a place for the Lord, a dwelling-place for the Mighty One of Jacob.'

(verses 4–5)

It is the penultimate day of our ascent with the psalms, our final approach to the temple. The psalmist's eyes turn towards the magnificent edifice. Built by David's son Solomon, it was a wonder to behold. For all its beauty, its real significance was that it was the physical manifestation of God's presence and God's promise to keep a son of David on the throne so long as the king was faithful.

Millennia have passed. Being made of stone, wood and precious materials, the first temple is long gone, as is the second, both destroyed by occupying forces. Since the seventh century AD, the Temple Mount has been home to the Muslim shrines the Dome of the Rock and the al-Aqsa Mosque. We are led to contemplate impermanence and change. Even stone structures are vulnerable.

How remarkable, then, that in the Christian tradition we understand God's dwelling place to be in that most vulnerable of creations – the human body. The incarnation seems insane. But perhaps there is method in this madness ... perhaps God's dwelling place has always been where the divine meets the human *in the flesh*. Human beings full of the Spirit create monumental edifices, compose sacred music, write life-giving stories and serve their fellow humans with humility and kindness. In a vulnerable, impermanent world, perhaps the living God can only come to be known and loved through faithful flesh.

The last verses of the psalm detail the real physical manifestation that comes from God's dwelling with us: abundance shared with all and joy. May it be so among us.

† Make me a dwelling place for your Spirit, so that joined with others we may grow into your holy temple and be a blessing to our world.

For further thought

Read Solomon's dedication of the temple in 1 Kings 8 and Paul's understanding that Jesus and his people are God's temple in Ephesians 2:19–21.

Tuesday 5 March
The blessing of unity

Read Psalms 133–134

How very good and pleasant it is when kindred live together in unity!

(Psalm 133:1)

We have reached the summit. Our Psalms of Ascent have brought us to the holy place, and what do we find here but the fulfilment of our deepest longing for peace in our families and in our world. For the psalmist, God is the focus of unity, its source and its sustenance. It is God who draws people and the nations to the temple (Isaiah 2:3).

Psalm 133 exudes gladness and fulfilment of the divine purpose. So life-giving is unity that it is like the dew on sacred Mount Hermon, the natural provision of life-giving moisture to the parched wilderness. Oil running down the beard of Aaron calls to mind the dedication of temple priests.

The blessing of unity is life forevermore. The curse of disunity is the devastation and trauma our world knows all too well. For in our day, rather than being a focus of unity, ideas about God are too often at the centre of disunities. Extremist Christians, Jews and Muslims seek to impose their beliefs on others, sometimes using violence to seek their ends.

What is clear is that unity cannot be forced. People cannot be shamed, shoved or shunted into the commonwealth of God. Only love opens that gate, love and life shared together for the good of all.

We end our consideration of the Psalms of Ascent as we began it, with a heartfelt prayer for the peace and security of all who inhabit this planet, so that we may live out our diversity in a unity of respect and love.

† Gracious God, I bless you for the vision of the human family at peace in unity. I pledge myself to your purpose: use me in whatever way you can.

For further thought

Watch on YouTube the TED Talk by former Chief Rabbi Lord Jonathan Sacks (author of *The Dignity of Difference*) on facing the future without fear, together.

Life in the (modern) desert –
1 The way to the desert:
Luke 3–4

Notes by **Kate Hughes**

Kate worked for the Church in Southern Africa for 14 years. Since returning to the UK she has edited books on theology, gardening, dog training, climate change, sociology and gender studies. She lives in Coventry with Ruby, her Cavalier King Charles Spaniel, is involved in her local community and preaches regularly at her local Anglican church. Kate has used the NRSVA for these notes.

Wednesday 6 March (Ash Wednesday)
A voice in the wilderness

Read Luke 3:1–14

'The voice of one crying out in the wilderness: "Prepare the way of the Lord."'

(part of verse 4)

We start our Lent theme with Jesus. Before he began his public ministry he went out into the wilderness, the rocky scrubland around the River Jordan that could not be cultivated. Jesus went into the desert firstly to be baptised by John and then to grapple with his own temptations. The coming of God to his people was first proclaimed in the wilderness on the way out of Egypt, and Jesus died in a desert of pain and loneliness on the cross. Christians have followed Jesus into physical and spiritual deserts ever since.

In the desert there is nowhere to escape to, no distractions, nothing to stop you being confronted by God and by yourself. We may not leave our everyday life for a physical desert, but there is no shortage of desert experiences in modern life: the spiritual wasteland where God seems absent, the patience needed to wait for his word in a culture that demands instant answers, the aloneness experienced in a crowded city. But being in the wilderness can also be a preparation for the coming of the Lord. How God and we can use our desert experiences is our Lent theme.

† Lord, lead us through the desert this Lent so that we may come to our Promised Land at Easter.

Thursday 7 March
'You are my Son'

Read Luke 3:15–22

Now when all the people were baptised, and when Jesus also had been baptised and was praying, the heaven was opened.

(verse 21)

The wilderness, the arid desert of scrub and sheep around the Jordan, was the right place for Jesus to emerge from the obscurity of his life as a village carpenter in Nazareth and come into the public eye. It was from the desert that the people of Israel had crossed over the Jordan into the Promised Land, and Isaiah prophesied that it would be from the desert that the glory of the Lord would be revealed (Isaiah 40:5).

But, as so often with Jesus, things didn't happen quite as expected. To the onlookers he was simply one person in a crowd of people coming from the surrounding towns and villages to be baptised by John. Unlike Matthew's account (Matthew 3:14–15), Luke doesn't record that John even recognised his cousin Jesus, let alone acknowledged him as the one he was expecting. It is not clear whether the dove and the voice from heaven (verse 22) were seen and heard by anyone else except Jesus, who then later shared the experience with his disciples. So the first event of the public ministry of Jesus takes place in the desert, alone in a crowd, having his unique nature affirmed by the Spirit of his heavenly Father.

In the scrubland, in the place of desolation far from a town, Jesus heard words of confirmation and hope for his coming ministry. What words from God do you seek this Lent, as you enter the desert? What do you desire for the next stage of your life, which you can seek in this period of searching, waiting and hoping?

† As your family, Lord, may we too know ourselves affirmed and beloved.

For further thought

How was Jesus 'alone in a crowd'? Do you have experience of being 'alone in a crowd'?

Friday 8 March
Truly God and truly human

Read Luke 3:23–38

... son of Enos, son of Seth, son of Adam, son of God.

(verse 38)

It took some time for the first followers of Jesus to realise that he was more than just a charismatic human teacher. The early Christian communities also had to explore the implications of saying that Jesus was in some way God as well as a man. Could God really translate himself into a form that could communicate with human beings, live like one of them, suffer like one of them, die like one of them? What did this say about God loving the world so much that he was prepared to do it? What did this say about human beings, that God needed to rescue them personally from the mess they had got themselves into?

In today's reading, Luke provides Jesus with a family tree, containing the names of many of the notable men of the Bible. Unlike Matthew, in his family tree for Jesus (Matthew 1:2–16), Luke doesn't include any women in his list, but he takes it further back, beyond Abraham. In doing so, he states clearly, in only six words, what the first disciples and their early converts had discovered about Jesus: he was son of Adam and son of God.

The word Adam means humankind. So here Luke is saying that Jesus is the son, the image of humankind – truly a man, and also the son, the image, of God – truly God. Luke's readers need to bear this in mind when they read the rest of the Gospel – it is the story not only of a great man, but of God in action. Salvation has indeed started out from the wilderness.

† Jesus, help me this Lent to enter more deeply into the mystery that you are both truly man and truly God.

For further thought

What does the fact that Jesus was both 'son of Adam' and 'son of God' say about both humanity and God?

Saturday 9 March
In the desert

Read Luke 4:1–13

Jesus, full of the Holy Spirit, returned from the Jordan and was led by the Spirit in the wilderness.

(verse 1)

Apart from the incident in the Jerusalem temple when he was 12 years old (Luke 2:41–51), Jesus seems to have had an ordinary childhood growing up in Nazareth. In time, he became the village carpenter. A lot of questions are left unanswered: when did he begin to realise that he was more than just the eldest child of Mary and Joseph? What did he think he was called to do? God had affirmed Jesus as his son after his baptism, but what should happen now? So the Spirit of God prompted him what to do next: take some time out away from other people to think and pray and wait for God's guidance. The Spirit led Jesus into the wilderness.

Because Jesus successfully resisted temptation during his time in the desert, we can assume that the Spirit stayed with him, although the only other being mentioned in Luke's account is the devil, the tempter, the accuser. What tempts Jesus is to take shortcuts – to stampede people into following him through miracles and secular power, and to be so doubtful of God's authority that it needs to be constantly tested. But this is not how God works, and it is not how Jesus will work.

When we go through desert times of temptation and doubting God's power to sustain us, God's Spirit is still there with us. Indeed, he may have led us there, as he led Jesus, because working through temptation and doubt with him enables us to come out of the desert stronger and more faithful.

† Lord, may your Spirit lead me through my desert times, so that I may come out of them stronger and more faithful.

For further thought

What tempts you in your Christian life and ministry? How do you deal with it?

Life in the (modern) desert – 2 Waiting

Notes by **Kate Hughes**

For Kate's biography, see p. 66. Kate has used the NRSVA for these notes.

Sunday 10 March
Waiting for God's moment

Read Psalm 27:1–14

Wait for the Lord; be strong, and let your heart take courage; wait for the Lord!

(verse 14)

After our first few days with Jesus in the desert, most of the readings for this theme are from the Old Testament, because for the Ancient Israelites the desert was a very special place, where God had led them to a new land and formed them into a nation. It was also a place where they had trudged for a very long time and done some pretty stupid things, so a place of failure and learning too. Often the Israelites rebelled against Moses and their long journey; they looked nostalgically back to Egypt, they tried to worship an idol – the golden calf, they grumbled and complained. But whether they liked it or not, they had no alternative but to wait, to get to the end of their journey in the Promised Land. Most of us are not very good at waiting; when we are in a desert of difficulty, suffering, seeming abandonment, we want to take some action.

When I lived in South Africa in the 1980s, a group of mainly black theologians produced a booklet called *The Kairos Document: A Challenge to the Church*, looking at the social and political situation in the country from a biblical and theological perspective, as God's time for change. The Greek word *kairos* means 'the right time', 'the moment of truth'. That is what the psalmist is telling his readers to wait for: God's moment, the moment when he will act, intervene, direct, lead, rescue. It takes strength and courage to wait in what may be an intolerable situation. Wait! Wait for God's *kairos*. It will surely come.

† Lord, teach me to wait for you, for your time, your *kairos*.

For further thought

In your own life, the life of your country, the affairs of the world, what are you waiting for, what is God's time to act?

Monday 11 March
Pulled from the pit

Read Psalm 40:1–8

I waited patiently for the Lord; he inclined to me and heard my cry. He drew me up from the desolate pit ... and set my feet upon a rock.

(verse 1, part of verse 2)

Yesterday the psalmist urged us to 'wait for the Lord'. Today he tells us what will happen if we wait patiently. Patience is something that we can only learn by doing. It includes elements of trust and expectation. You don't wait patiently unless you believe that there is something at the end that will be worth waiting for. If there doesn't seem to be anything worthwhile to wait for, if you believe that the present bad situation will never end, then you give up on patience and give way to resignation or despair.

But patient waiting believes that even when there is no tangible evidence of it, things are working themselves out. There will be an ending, and that ending will be brought about by God, whose Spirit is actually beside you in the darkness, listening to your crying and helping you to wait patiently. Eventually, when the time is right, God will act. He will bring you out of the wilderness, pulling you out of the pit of desolation and putting you down on firm ground. In the Old Testament God is often referred to as a rock, so when you emerge from your desert experience, your faith in him, your relationship with him, will be even stronger, more rocklike, because you will be based on God the rock.

† Help me, Lord, to grow in patience this Lent, to be willing to wait for you.

For further thought

How patient are you? What will help you to become better at waiting?

Tuesday 12 March
Woven in prayer

Read Lamentations 3:25–33

The Lord is good to those who wait for him, to the soul that seeks him.
It is good that one should wait quietly for the salvation of the Lord.

(verses 25–26)

We don't like being in the desert. We twist and turn and fight against it. We panic and are terrified by our situation. We feel that we might die before we get rescued. But this only wastes our energy and makes us less able to live in the situation. In the desert, we need to conserve our strength to deal with a barren and unknown territory. But we also need to believe that we are on a journey, not just wandering aimlessly without a guide. We need to seek God in the desert, trust that he is guiding us even if we cannot see or feel him. The writer of Lamentations wrote the words of today's reading in the midst of the destruction of Jerusalem by the Babylonians.

The Desert Fathers, Christian hermits and monks in the deserts of Egypt in the fourth and fifth centuries, had plenty of experience of temptation, doubt and suffering. And what the experienced monks said repeatedly to the newcomers when they started to doubt their calling was, 'Stay in your cell, and your cell will teach you everything.' Go back to your simple hut of mud brick, do your work of weaving rush baskets, carry on praying. In other words, 'Wait quietly for the salvation of the Lord' (verse 26). Stop twisting and turning, trying to escape, doubting that God knows what he is doing, imagining that you would do better somewhere else. Wait for God to lead you where he wants you to go, seek him and his will, and the Lord will be good to you.

† Lord, it is so easy to grumble, to tell you what you ought to do. Teach me to wait quietly.

For further thought

What do you think the Desert Fathers meant when they said, 'Stay in your cell, and your cell will teach you everything'? Were they right?

Wednesday 13 March
Waiting and hoping

Read Psalm 130:1–8

I wait for the Lord, my soul waits, and in his word I hope.

(verse 5)

We can only survive our time in the desert if we have hope. The writer of this psalm speaks 'out of the depths' (verse 1), but he has hope – he looks for the Lord to rescue him, with more concentration than the nightwatchman or the soldier on sentry duty who wearily longs for morning to come so that they can be released from their duty (verse 6).

St Paul wrote that 'hope that is seen is not hope. For who hopes for what is seen? But if we hope for what we do not see, we wait for it with patience' (Romans 8:24–25). Our readings this week and this Lent are concerned with the great Christian virtues: faith, trust, patience, hope. Waiting for what is to come. Trusting that it will come, because God has said that it will. And for Christians, though not for the psalmist, 'word' has a double meaning. It is not only what God says, it is also his definitive saying that translates him into a form that can be understood and trusted and hoped in by human beings – the person we call the Word of God. 'In him every one of God's promises is a "Yes"' (2 Corinthians 1:20) and so we, too, can have hope.

It is harder to have this hope in the desert than it is in the Promised Land. Yet precisely when times are hard and resources are scarce we are asked to hope. Can we embrace this challenge? Can we live in trust, even in the desert?

† My hope is in your word, Lord – both in your promises and in Jesus the Word of God.

For further thought

What is hope? How would you describe it? As a Christian, what do you hope for?

Thursday 14 March
Keeping watch

Read Habakkuk 2:1–4

I will stand at my watchpost, and station myself on the rampart ... If it seems to tarry, wait for it; it will surely come, it will not delay.

(verses 1a, 3b)

In yesterday's reading the psalmist compared himself to a watchman waiting for the dawn, and felt that his longing hope that God would deliver him exceeded even their wish to end their time of duty. In today's reading, the prophet Habakkuk sees himself as the watchman. He is a sentry, standing on the ramparts of the city, staring into the distance, waiting and longing for deliverance for himself and his city. The Lord says to him that the end time will surely come, the time when God will deliver his people and deal with their enemies (verse 3).

Our time in the desert of the spirit can seem endless. St John of the Cross called it the dark night of the soul. Everything we have ever discovered about God seems to disappear. We cannot pray. Anything we try to say seems to lack authenticity. All we can do is hang on for grim death in a seemingly unending darkness. And wait, saying over and over again that somehow God is still here in the night ('the darkness is not dark to you; the night is as bright as the day, for darkness is as light to you', Psalm 139:12), that he is to be trusted though everything, seems to contradict this ('though he slay me, yet shall I trust in him', Job 13:15 KJV; other translations have 'yet shall I hope in him'). 'Wait for it; it will surely come, it will not delay.'

† Lord, my soul waits for you; I believe you are with me always, even in the desert and the darkness.

For further thought

Another translation of Psalm 139:12 is 'the darkness and light to you are both the same'. What does this say about the faithfulness of God?

Friday 15 March
God's faith

> **Read Psalm 69:1–15**
>
> *My eyes grow dim with waiting for my God.*
>
> (verse 3b)

We may be in a desert of apparent abandonment by God, of loneliness, of temptation, of frustration at being unable to act or help in a situation, of sheer exhaustion. And it can seem endless. The psalmist speaks not of a dry desert but of drowning in mud or deep waters, struggling to survive. The struggle seems so long to him that his eyes seem to be tired out, or growing dim with age. But whether we think of ourselves as in a dry desert or a raging torrent, we can still only wait it out, wait for God to show himself and bring us out into fertile land, light or dry ground – however we see it.

Often our spiritual struggles in the desert are invisible to other people; they may have no idea what we are going through. At other times, however, outward circumstances will make it clear to others that the going is proving tough for us. Then, how we handle it can help or hinder their own faith. This does not mean that we always have to present a serene, untroubled face to the world, or always be cheerful. But neither should we be constantly complaining, as if God doesn't know what he is doing. I hang on to St Paul's words in his first letter to the Christians in Corinth: 'God is faithful, and he will not let you be tested beyond your strength, but with the testing he will also provide the way out so that you may be able to endure it' (1 Corinthians 10:13).

† Lord, I may feel that I cannot go on, but I know that you will not let me be tested beyond my strength.

For further thought

Have you experienced a desert of the spirit? If so, how do you think you handled it?

Saturday 16 March
Spirit journey

Read Isaiah 30:15–18

In returning and rest you shall be saved; in quietness and in trust shall be your strength ... the Lord waits to be gracious to you.

(parts of verses 15, 18)

Deserts can perhaps be divided into two kinds – the bleak and the hectic. The bleak desert is one of abandonment and darkness. There is no one in sight – least of all God. There are no paths to follow. No landmarks. No guides. All you can do is be still and wait – as today's writer says, keep trying to return and reconnect with God; rest quietly in the darkness; trust that you are not just standing still in a wilderness, but actually on a journey through it in the company of God's Spirit.

The hectic desert is one of rejection. 'I hate this empty space! I want to be out of it, I want to be doing things, people need my help! Temptation is driving me mad! I can't go on!' But God also is one who waits. One of my friends, John, has a daughter called Lucy. When she was small, Lucy was a very determined child and if she was getting upset over something, John would suggest that she had a tantrum. And Lucy would lie on the floor for a few minutes, shouting and screaming, waving her arms, kicking her heels – then she would stand up, shake herself and go to her father, who would hug her and say, 'Now let's quietly sort out your problem.' God waits patiently for us to stop kicking and screaming, or in Israel's case get defeated in the war they insisted on, so that he can get a word in edgeways. When we can wait quietly in the desert, the Lord will graciously wait with us.

† Forgive me, Lord, when I make so much noise that I cannot hear what you are waiting to say.

For further thought

What is God waiting for in your time in the desert? What is God hoping for in your life this season of Lent?

Life in the (modern) desert – 3 Stillness

Notes by **Peter Langerman**

 Peter pastors a Presbyterian Church in Durbanville, Cape Town, and is Moderator-Designate of the General Assembly of the Uniting Presbyterian Church in Southern Africa. He and wife Sally have four daughters. Peter is passionate about the dynamic rule and reign of God. He believes God invites all to be part of his transformative mission through love, and that the most potent and powerful agent for the transformation of local communities is the local church. Peter has used the NIVUK for these notes.

Sunday 17 March
A time for everything

Read Ecclesiastes 3:1–8

There is a time for everything, and a season for every activity under the heavens … a time to be silent and a time to speak …

(verses 1, 7b)

Recently my wife Sally and I, together with our good friends Wayne and Jenny, walked the Camino Frances, an ancient pilgrimage route. We covered 800 kilometres in 33 days from St Jean in the south of France to Santiago in northern Spain. One thing I learned from this journey is that what these verses say is true. There is, indeed, a time for everything. A time to walk and a time to rest. A time to speak and a time to be silent. When walking this ancient pilgrimage, there is time to speak and a time to be silent. Much of the Camino is spent in silence, even though you are surrounded by people right through the day. Eight to ten hours a day spent on the road means that for large parts of the day you are alone with your thoughts and able to talk to God and to hear God speak to you. Although not everybody has the privilege to walk the Camino, we can all take the time to be silent and listen to what God might be wanting to say to us. Today, as you listen, what might God be saying to you, in the stillness and silence?

† As I take time to listen, what is it that God might be saying to me today? What is God calling me to pay attention to in my relationship with God or others?

Monday 18 March
Selective hearing

Read Ezekiel 3:22–27

I will make your tongue stick to the roof of your mouth so that you will be silent and unable to rebuke them, for they are a rebellious people. But when I speak to you, I will open your mouth and you shall say to them, 'This is what the Sovereign Lord says.'

(verses 26–27a)

Ezekiel had to learn to be silent to hear what God had to say. Not only was he required to be silent, but he was also bound so that he could not move until he had heard what God wanted him to hear. Only then could he be trusted to speak out in God's name. Thankfully for us, such drastic action is not usually required, but the principle remains the same. Stephen Covey spoke about the need to 'seek first to understand'[8]. Listening is not a passive exercise. We must learn to listen actively, to listen well if we are to communicate effectively. For us on the Camino, learning to be silent took discipline and patience, especially when meeting new people. We often overwhelm people with information about ourselves and don't make space for them to tell us about who they are and where they are. In addition, our tendency is sometimes to hear without listening or to hear selectively or to hear to be able to make a counter-argument. In the same way, we must learn to be quiet and to listen if we are to be able to hear what God is saying to us and if we are then to speak in God's name to others.

To listen to God we need to practise being silent with God and to listen actively to what God might be saying. What do you hear in the desert places around you today?

† As you meet people today, ask God to help you to listen actively and to make sure that every person with whom you have contact knows that you care about them enough to listen well.

For further thought

What can you do today to be a better and more attentive listener to the people to whom you are the closest: to your spouse or partner, children or work colleagues?

---

8   Covey, S. (1989), *The 7 Habits of Highly Effective People* (New York, NY: Free Press).

Tuesday 19 March
Be still and know

Read Psalm 46:1–11

He says, 'Be still, and know that I am God; I will be exalted among the nations, I will be exalted in the earth.' The Lord Almighty is with us; the God of Jacob is our fortress.

(verses 10–11)

The imagery of this psalm at the beginning is turbulent and violent. It is as though Table Mountain, that stands guard over the city of Cape Town, were to be tossed into the midst of Table Bay harbour. Life can do that to us sometimes. Unexpected tragedy, the loss of a loved one, the diagnosis of a serious and life-threatening disease, retrenchment, divorce or death can all leave us feeling rocked and disorientated.

Then the tone of the psalm changes. Amid turbulence and upheaval there are calmness and peace that defy explanation. Many people have experienced just this. Amid profound disturbance, they are the ones who know a peace and a stillness that defy logic. There are the emotions that accompany the experience of disorientation: anger, fear, anxiety, sadness and despair. But, for people of faith, there is the pervasive sense of the presence of God and the assurance that these are not the final words on the matter: death is followed by resurrection and new life. Such is the nature of Christian hope: the assurance that just as Jesus was raised to new life, so those who have faith in Jesus will be raised to new life in him.

Where is the turbulence in your time in the desert today? Where are the calmness and peace? Psalm 46 challenges us to find God in both.

† Today, as you face surprising challenges for which you were neither warned nor prepared, ask God to help you to have faith in God's infinite love and unending compassion.

For further thought

How can I help somebody today who might be experiencing great turmoil in their lives to also experience the love and compassion of God?

Wednesday 20 March
Refuge and refugee

Read Psalm 62:1–8

Truly he is my rock and my salvation; he is my fortress, I will not be shaken. My salvation and my honour depend on God; he is my mighty rock, my refuge. Trust in him at all times, you people; pour out your hearts to him, for God is our refuge.

(verses 6–8)

The psalms don't give us a rulebook for a faith-filled life, but a snapshot of what a faith-filled life looks like. The psalms are not a play book, but a photo album in which we are allowed to see what it looks like to live this way. And what a photo album it is. It contains neither carefully posed nor meticulously Photoshopped images of people living perfect lives, but gritty and very real representations of real life.

In Psalm 62, the psalmist is grappling with something we have all experienced at points in our lives. Enemies who are trying to destroy the psalmist, trying to topple him – where will the psalmist find help? Should he defend himself, should he fight back? He decides to do a rather strange thing. He decides to find a place of stillness and silence and there to draw strength from God. This is a very difficult thing to do since we have been taught that it is a dog-eat-dog world and you must fight for yourself. The psalms suggest that if we allow ourselves to find rest in God when we are being threatened, then God will fight for us. This doesn't mean that we should not take further action – report a crime to the authorities for instance – but it does mean that we can choose to fight ourselves or to let God deal with the matter.

† When you are in a conflict situation, ask God to help you not to fight yourself, but to allow God to fight for you.

For further thought

What can you do today to stand up for a friend, colleague or family member who is being unfairly attacked or targeted by someone else?

Thursday 21 March
The place of quiet trust

Read Psalm 39:1–9

I said, 'I will watch my ways and keep my tongue from sin; I will put a muzzle on my mouth while in the presence of the wicked.' … I was silent; I would not open my mouth, for you are the one who has done this.

(verses 1, 9)

Yesterday we saw the psalmist choosing to allow God to fight for him rather than to fight for himself. In this psalm today, we see something even more profound and more difficult to understand. The psalmist finds himself assailed, not by some outside enemy, but by the enemy within. It is the fleeting nature of his own life; his own transgressions; the frantic nature of the society in which he lives where all people are just looking after themselves and trying to get ahead that disturb him. What do we do when the enemy is not outside us, but inside us? Which of us does not know that feeling? We try and try to do better, to be better, but no matter how hard we try, we just seem to dig ourselves into a deeper hole.

The psalmist decides to take radical action: to stop digging. He realises that the awareness of his own sin is a gift from God and rather than defend himself, he should simply be quiet and put his trust in God. In such a situation, silence is not easy. We want to explain, to justify, to point out that we are the exception to the rule and that we deserve special treatment. The psalmist decides to do none of this, but rather to trust in God's mercy.

† Today take time to confess your sin: those things of which you are deeply conscious and ashamed, but also those things that you don't even notice any more.

For further thought

In what ways can you allow your failures and weaknesses to reveal things that you never knew about yourself so that you can become a stronger, more resilient person?

Friday 22 March
On sleeping well

Read Psalm 4:1–8

Tremble and do not sin; when you are on your beds, search your hearts and be silent … In peace I will lie down and sleep, for you alone, Lord, make me dwell in safety.

(verses 4, 8)

Do you sleep well or do you toss and turn at night while sleep remains elusive? Although there are many causes for insomnia, usually when I battle to sleep it is because there are things on my mind that just won't settle down. Sometimes they are incidents from the day gone past that I keep reliving or there is anxiety about something up ahead.

In Psalm 4, the psalmist decides against counting sheep or drinking warm milk to help him sleep. He decides that he will call upon the Lord and that, having called upon God for help, he will be able to sleep peacefully. The psalmist is disturbed by those who serve false gods and refuse to give honour to the only true God. He searches his own heart to see whether he has not been guilty of doing the same thing. In a world where the wicked seem to prosper while the faithful struggle, the psalmist decides that true prosperity is seeing the face of God. It is this reality that finally brings him peace and allows him to lie down to sleep in peace.

Perhaps there are issues that keep you awake at night. Regrets from the past or anxiety about the future. Perhaps you are worried about how you are going to care for yourself or your family. If so, then this psalm is for you. Read it today, again and again, and through its words let God begin to bring its safety and peace into your life.

† Bring your regrets, your fears and anxieties to God. Search your own heart and if you need to confess something, then do so and thank God for his forgiveness.

For further thought

If you are having trouble sleeping because of anxiety, would you consider speaking to a friend or a medical professional and getting some help? Too little sleep can seriously impact our health and ability to function.

Desert whisper

Read 1 Kings 19:11–13

And after the fire came a gentle whisper. When Elijah heard it, he pulled his cloak over his face and went out and stood at the mouth of the cave. Then a voice said to him, 'What are you doing here, Elijah?'

(verses 12b–13)

This incident in the life of Elijah is difficult for us to understand. Elijah had just experienced a great miracle on Mount Carmel where God had proved his superiority over Baal. Elijah had gone up against, and triumphed over, 450 prophets of Baal. Then the seven-year drought for which Elijah had prayed was broken, again, as Elijah prayed. He should have been on a high. Yet when Jezebel, with whom Elijah had several run-ins over the years, threatens to kill him, he runs away in sheer terror. He heads deep into the wilderness and runs so hard that he faints from exhaustion and fear. While we cannot be absolutely sure, it seems possible that Elijah was suffering from burnout and exhaustion. Although his ministry has been a success, it has taken its toll on the prophet physically, emotionally and spiritually. And God does not judge Elijah. God sustains Elijah on his journey and then meets him on the mountain, not in earthquake, fire or tempest, but in the still, small, thin voice. And the question God asks? 'What are you doing here?' Ever ended up in that place? Somewhere where you wondered how you got there?

Be aware that God might want to meet you in that very place. As successful as you may be, we all need to take time apart. Take time, be silent, embrace stillness and be open to listening.

† Instead of praying in words today, why not take time to be silent for 5–10 minutes and ask God if there is anything he would like to say to you?

For further thought

Consider inserting time into your regular schedule to be quiet and still. Even if it is only a few minutes a day at the beginning, you can always make it longer as you go.

Life in the (modern) desert – 4 Seeking

Notes by **Aileen Quinn**

Aileen is a copywriter, playwright and lay member of the Church of England who lives in South Manchester with her son, Isaac. Her blog, 'The (mal)Contented Mother: Motherhood, Mental Health, Miscellany' takes an honest look at parenting culture and mental illness. Aileen has had several short plays performed in Manchester and continues to write as much as possible from her box room/office. Aileen has used the NRSVA for these notes.

Sunday 24 March
What is it to seek God?

Read 1 Chronicles 28:9

'If you seek him, he will be found by you.'

(part of verse 9)

In today's reading, King David is essentially handing over the mantle of leadership to his son, Solomon. In this speech, I think, he's being a tad melodramatic. I say this because the idea of David telling anyone that if they forsake God 'he will abandon you forever' seems a bit rich. This is, after all, the guy who had a loyal soldier killed so that he could steal his wife (2 Samuel 11). David knows, really, that one can repent, return to God and change one's heart repeatedly; God is always there to be sought.

That's what Lent is about isn't it? Reflecting, repenting and returning to God. It is a time when we set aside more of ourselves and our lives for God. This week we will reflect on what it means to 'seek' God, how that might look and how we might do it in a humble, human way. I'm not sure I have any answers to these 'whats and hows', but I have some questions for us to ponder as we move ever closer to Holy Week.

† Steadfast God, strengthen us as we reflect on how we may seek you out, that we may find you, right where we are.

Monday 25 March
The consequences of seeking

Read Proverbs 2:1–11

Then you will understand righteousness and justice and equity, every good path.

(verse 9)

A few years back I discovered a gospel album called *The Nu Nation Project*. Recorded in 1998, it was groundbreaking for bringing hip-hop, funk and R 'n' B motifs into worship music.

Every track on the album is a gem, but I often skipped track three: 'Lean on Me'. It wasn't the famous Bill Withers song, but carried a similar sentiment: 'Here's my shoulder, you can lean on me.' The lyrics of the verses were about homelessness and disease and offering a hand to people who were suffering. I confess, I wasn't that into it; I preferred the praise music and found this track almost out of place on the album. Then, one day, the lyrics in the song's bridge caught my attention: 'Tell me how can I, how can I love Jesus, when I've never seen his face? Yet I see you dying and I turn and walk away.'

I felt utterly stupid. This song wasn't out of place on the album, it was essential. Seeking out God means very little if it doesn't translate into a compassion for our fellow humans.

The extract I've chosen from today's text reminds me of this same sentiment. Though seeking God may feel utterly personal, the consequences of finding God – God's wisdom in this context – have just as much of an impact on the wider world as they do on the individual. Righteousness, justice, equity; this is the wisdom that God invites us to seek out 'like silver'.

† Gracious God, though we seek you for ourselves, let the experience of finding you be transformative not only to our inner worlds but to the world around us.

For further thought

If you found God, where would you take him? Where in your outward life could you invite righteousness, justice and equity today?

March

Life in the (modern) desert – 4 Seeking

85

Tuesday 26 March
All of your heart

Read Jeremiah 29:11–14

When you search for me you will find me; if you seek me with all your heart.

(verse 13)

My four-year-old, Isaac, has a mind like a sponge. He soaks up information from kids' TV shows and remembers everything I say (much to my occasional dismay). One day recently I asked him if he knew what the heart did. 'It pumps blood around the body and gives you love,' he replied confidently. Indeed, from further conversations it seems that he thinks these two functions are interconnected.

We hear a lot about 'all of your heart' in the Bible, and I often struggle with the imagery. I'm not sure what it means to incline my whole heart to the divine, especially when I know that God very much requires me to love others, too.

Perhaps, though, I am not starting from the right place. I think Isaac's understanding might be more in keeping with scripture than the lovey-dovey, 'romantic comedy' vision I have of the heart and its metaphorical functions.

In Hebrew, and throughout scripture, the 'heart' is more than an organ of romance – it is the very centre of one's being: physical, emotional, moral and spiritual. This definition is helpful to me when trying to understand what it means to seek God with all my heart. Rather than being consumed only by thoughts of him, he asks to be put at our centre – that we seek him from the very core of who we are. If we do this, then concern and compassion for others are natural by-products. It's still a tall order, but put like this it is one that feels more real and reachable.

† Loving God, we invite you into our hearts and ask you to sit at the centre of all we are and all we do.

For further thought

What's in your heart? Draw a picture of it and fill it up with all of the stuff that concerns you at your centre.

Wednesday 27 March
In the still of the night

Read Isaiah 26:7–12

My soul yearns for you in the night, my spirit within me earnestly seeks you.

(verse 9a)

Ever since I was a child I have had trouble settling at bedtime. At first, perhaps, it was wilful, but I can't remember a time when I've had a string of head-hits-the-pillow evenings. Taking an hour to get to sleep is a regular occurrence and taking much longer than that is all too familiar to me, as is the peculiar, simultaneous feeling of exhaustion and restlessness. Bouts of serious insomnia almost always occur during times of stress, and sometimes they can be indications of unacknowledged issues within me, too.

The verse I've selected today speaks to me about more than sleeplessness, though. When times are hard we can often power on through, keep moving and avoid reflection at all costs. It saves us from pain. But in the still of night there's suddenly no escape. The thoughts and feelings we have been running from suddenly descend and we wish to escape.

I don't mind admitting that, sometimes, one of the things I'm avoiding is God. We all do it, perhaps because we feel unworthy or we don't want to face some truth about an unhealthy behaviour, or because we are experiencing that resistance to the Spirit that some would describe as 'the devil'.

Whatever it is, when we are in the dark, alone and quiet, that is when we feel a yearning and when, despite ourselves, our spirit stirs and inclines itself heavenward. If we are to seek God, we must stop running, for a moment at least.

† Patient God, there is a place within us that is always seeking you, Lord. Let our restlessness turn to calm so that we can hear that still, small voice.

For further thought

If you can today, find a time to retreat from the busyness of doing and take a moment to sit in the quiet.

Thursday 28 March
On seeking and understanding ...

Read Isaiah 55:6–13

For my thoughts are not your thoughts, nor are your ways my ways, says the Lord. For as the heavens are higher than the earth, so are my ways higher than your ways and my thoughts than your thoughts.

(verses 8–9)

As a teenager, I sang in a choir at the local Anglican church. I went there primarily to sing, I hadn't been a churchgoer before I joined the choir and wouldn't have called myself a Christian. There was something about the liturgy, though, that never left me. In my twenties, I flitted about from church to church, trying, I suppose, to find something that 'fit' me. Eventually, though, I felt myself called back to the Church of England and the rhythm of those ancient words that are, by and large, the same week to week. These words have little bearing on the personality of the preacher, or the politics of the congregation; instead they offer an unchanging structure within which to meet God. It's not so much the words themselves that are important, but the space their familiarity creates not to think about 'doing' worship and instead to ease into the rhythm of it.

I think I took to the comfort of liturgy so much because at some time it struck me (somewhat ironically as I'm writing for this book right now) that human language will never adequately capture God. Although it's important and affirming to try to understand and debate the 'ways' of the Almighty, that understanding is, finally, unachievable. If we could pin God down intellectually, what would that say about God?

So how do we go about seeking something we will never fully understand? Honestly, I'm not sure. But perhaps it begins with a kind of surrender and the humility that comes from us letting God be God. Transcendent; surpassing; intangible; and yet, mysteriously, here.

† Unknowable God, the deepest mystery of all is that you are completely present and utterly transcendent. Help us surrender our intellectual grasping, in the hope that your inexpressible presence will draw nearer.

For further thought

Is there an aspect or teaching of God that you think you fully understand? Spend some time today considering the idea that you might be wrong ...

Friday 29 March
Crying out

Read Psalm 77:1–15

I cry aloud to God, aloud to God, that he may hear me.

(verse 1)

We've all done it, haven't we? In a moment of despair or desperation, we've literally cried out to God. We often do this in times of crisis, regardless of whether we've prayed or worshipped at all recently. Even atheists do sometimes, just in case.

In less dramatic circumstances, many of us pray aloud, even when we're alone. That's a funny thing, isn't it? As if God has ears and needs to tune in, or if we don't recite with a list from our mouths then God will have no idea of our concerns, needs or wishes. I don't say this to mock praying aloud to God; there's certainly some power in it. I think of Job, of the writers of Lamentations, of Jesus in the garden and on the cross. Of course, I've done it too: pleaded aloud with a deity I believe to be all-knowing, all-loving.

I wonder if these cries are for God at all; maybe they are for ourselves. We are the ones with ears, the ones whose attention needs focusing, the ones, perhaps, who need to make promises and keep them.

When we cry out to God we tap into an incredibly raw, vulnerable part of ourselves that we rarely acknowledge. This part is one that seeks more earnestly, is more willing to accept our flawed humanity, and so is a powerful tool for 'finding' God and letting him in.

† Today, say your own prayer, let the words of desperation, vulnerability and hope pour out of you. Listen to yourself as you say them, and then listen a little longer.

For further thought

When was the last time you cried aloud to God? Who are some models of this kind of prayer in the Bible?

Saturday 30 March
Hide and seek

Read Colossians 3:1–11

So if you have been raised with Christ, seek the things that are above, where Christ is, seated at the right hand of God. Set your minds on things that are above, not on things that are on earth, for you have died, and your life is hidden with Christ in God.

(verses 1–3)

Do you ever want to hide from your life? As someone who has suffered several bouts of severe depression and anxiety, it's a feeling I'm all too familiar with. Nothing is quite as seductive to a weary, broken mind as a darkened room and a cosy duvet.

Of course, you don't have to be ill to want to hide; life is perpetually overwhelming. For me that's because I have a small child and a mortgage and a job and wish to remain a creative, engaged, social creature. Life is work, and so is church for many people. Those who are actively involved in the life of their congregation can feel more drained than nourished on a Sunday. If we're not careful, we begin to associate God with that feeling and want to hide from him, too.

That's why, though there are many challenges to Paul's call to 'seek the things that are above', I take great comfort from the idea that we are 'hidden with Christ in God'. Even when I feel like I'm utterly rubbish at 'doing life' and want to disappear into myself, Jesus is there too, waiting for me. I can retreat under the blanket of Christ, who is 'all in all'.

Sometimes, the very idea of seeking God is, in itself, exhausting. Ironically, we become overwhelmed by the task that could ease our burdens the most. And, though God requires work from us, God himself is not work. God is present in our hiding places. He will meet us when we seek him, wherever we are; even under the duvet.

† Loving God, when we wish to retreat from the world, may we find in you a hiding place where we can rest and be nourished, and may you send us out again clothed in your love.

For further thought

Can you take time to retreat from the stresses of your life today? Allow yourself to hide awhile and invite Jesus to watch with you.

Life in the (modern) desert – 5 Finding

Notes by **John Birch**

Based in South Wales, John is a Methodist preacher who writes prayers, worship resources and Bible studies for his website faithandworship.com. Some of the prayers have been adapted for use within choral and contemporary worship settings. John has four published books including *The Act of Prayer*. In his spare time plays guitar, sings, tends his allotment patch and walks the beautiful Welsh coastline. John has used the NIVUK for these notes.

Sunday 31 March
Finding hope

> **Read Habakkuk 3:17–19a**
> *Yet I will rejoice in the Lord, I will be joyful in God my Saviour.*
>
> (verse 18)

How can Lent be a time of discovery in the wilderness?

Several of our readings this week are written to be sung, and our passage from the prophet Habbakuk tells us it's for the 'Director of Music'. That makes sense of our theme as so many songs of our time have been about 'finding' something – be it love, justice or hope in times of trouble. Occasionally, I watch films of folk singers of the 1920s onward featuring men and women sat outside dusty old shacks with their family, banjo in hand, singing about the times in which they were living. Even though their words reflect the inequalities and struggles they are enduring, there's often a thread of hope running through, that this is a temporary situation, and they look (often to God) for better times to come.

Expressing how we feel is important. Within the poetry and songs of those who have experienced desolation first-hand we can often find words of comfort and hope in someone who understands where I am, who expresses my thoughts better than I ever could. Habakkuk's song was possibly written with Babylonian invasion in mind, and his hope that God would bring deliverance. What is our song? Where will we find hope this season?

† Thank you, Lord, for those who write songs that inspire us. May their words lighten our hearts in life's darker days. Amen.

Monday 1 April
Finding blessing

Read Hosea 14:1–9

People will dwell again in his shade; they will flourish like the corn, they will blossom like the vine – Israel's fame will be like the wine of Lebanon.

(verse 7)

Hosea is writing to a disobedient people, and like many Old Testament prophets he offers a choice between judgement and blessing. But Hosea is also a poet. This is no hastily scribbled note; every word has been carefully considered, and with them he paints pictures even we today can appreciate.

Having been told to turn their lives around, the people assumed the sacrificial offering of a young oxen was a necessary demonstration of repentance. But no, God wants them to put living words, not dead animals, on the altar. Their repentance comes with the offering of 'the fruit of our lips', words which could also mean 'we offer our lips as sacrifices of calves'. Doesn't that put our own prayers of repentance into context, if they too can be offered sacrificially!

The blessing that the people receive might not be instant. Hosea talks of cedar trees sending down roots from which young shoots will grow, and that takes time. But the wise among you, he says, will realise that walking with God is far better than stumbling along without him.

I have days where I feel that I've let God down and need to seek his blessing once more. I am sure we all do. We may also find ourselves turning to repentance, and perhaps, as we do so, we could also humbly bring those words as a sacrifice and place them upon the altar as our offering to God. If we are able to do so, what restoration will we find?

† Merciful God, accept the sacrificial offering of our prayer, and renew and refresh our hearts that we might better serve you in this world. Amen.

For further thought

Is there a general reluctance to say 'sorry' these days, particularly in the media spotlight, and why might that be?

Tuesday 2 April
Finding answers

April

Read Matthew 7:7–11

'Ask and it will be given to you; seek and you will find; knock and the door will be opened to you. For everyone who asks receives; the one who seeks finds; and to the one who knocks, the door will be opened.'

(verses 7–8)

Two of our young grandchildren have a thirst for knowledge. One has devoured books on science and history since he first began to read. Now at senior school he's the first to answer questions from his teachers. The other, aged two, discovered the planets, learning not only their names and positions relative to the sun but the names of all their tiny moons as well, and there are lots! They both learn because they have questions that need answers.

We think of these verses in Matthew as referring to prayer – that invitation to ask and knock because God has an open-door policy and will not refuse our requests. The tense of the language means we must 'go on asking or knocking'; we must be persistent.

In my own life there are things I want to ask God about that aren't necessarily normal prayer requests. I want to know more about the origins of the universe, how it works, my place in it, how I can best care for it. I want to know how my gifts and abilities fit into this bigger picture. I too have a thirst 'to know', and I can ask God to reveal these things to me – through the Bible, through other books or in many other ways – just as my grandchildren pester their parents for answers in their own insatiable thirst for knowledge.

'Keep on asking, seek and you will find!'

† Thank you, gracious Father, for the wisdom contained within scripture's words that inspires, guides and brings us hope and joy. Amen.

For further thought

Do you have conversations with God about things other than the more familiar prayer requests?

Life in the (modern) desert – 5 Finding

Finding our way

> **Read Psalm 107:1–9**
>
> *Then they cried out to the Lord in their trouble, and he delivered them from their distress. He led them by a straight way to a city where they could settle.*
>
> (verses 6–7)

This is one of the psalms I used to sing as a boy in a church choir. Chanting meant that I had to read the verses more slowly than I would normally, held back by the speed of the organist, and the words were able to speak to me.

The psalm was composed for one of Israel's annual religious festivals, and the writer praises God for his unfailing love, because he hears the prayers of those who are struggling and reaches out to help them. It talks of desert wastelands that the people had travelled through, dangerous places, and how they had cried out to God for help.

Getting lost or finding yourself in unfamiliar places is a fear for many who are travelling. I'm not good at navigation, and if driving I rely on the satellite navigation app on my phone. If I didn't have my hands on the wheel then I'd be holding the hand of the lady on the phone app giving me instructions. I like her, because if there is an accident ahead she sees the bigger picture and will offer me an alternative route to my destination – and generally I find that I can trust her advice.

God sees the bigger picture in our lives, both joys *and* dangers, and if we are struggling and cry out for help, God is our guide and will lovingly, and reliably, lead us towards our destination as he did the people of Israel.

† Thank you, merciful Lord, that you are never far away, and if we call to you in distress you will hear and respond, bringing us to a safer place.

For further thought

Remember those who are fleeing persecution and seeking refuge in another land.

Finding refreshment

Read Isaiah 41:17–20

'The poor and needy search for water, but there is none; their tongues are parched with thirst.
But I the Lord will answer them.'

(part of verse 17)

There are times in every believer's life when they feel – like the nation of Israel – exiled, trapped far from where they want to be, and even abandoned by God. When this passage from Isaiah was written, and possibly sung, the people were exiled in Babylon and desperately thirsty to see God's blessing once again.

If we forget to drink enough water when the sun is hot, our bodies soon start complaining. I know that from experience. It passes from the familiar dry mouth to tiredness, headache, confusion and eventually pain. But I've also had times when I've ignored my spiritual life, particularly when things seemed, at least on the outside, to be sunny. And that, too, can lead to a dry, tired and confused state of mind.

At times like this it can seem that God has walked away from us. But in my experience that is never the case. It's more likely that we have inadvertently wandered off and temporarily lost sight of God. That's when, like the people in our reading, we need to call out and discover that God was not far away, and just waiting to hear our voice. And the blessing will come, water will flow through our desert, and it will turn green and flourish as this beautiful song promises, so that we and others will know that this is the work of God's own hand.

† Be close to all who feel that their faith has simply become a desert, dry and barren. Be close to them, Lord, and grant them refreshment and blessing.

For further thought

Remember to pray for those who are currently in real situations of exile, as refugees in foreign lands.

Finding nourishment

> **Read Mark 8:1–10**
>
> *He told the crowd to sit down on the ground. When he had taken the seven loaves and given thanks, he broke them and gave them to his disciples to distribute to the people, and they did so.*
>
> (verse 6)

We went to a couple of Christian festivals this year, which involved camping among crowds of people. There were discussions over what kind of long-life foods we could take so we didn't have to rely on expensive food vendors. It also meant that at times we could share some of the things we'd brought. They were good times, the teaching and worship uplifting. We planned well, ate well and there was little waste.

Not quite the same for that large crowd following Jesus around for three days, with nothing but a handful of food they'd grabbed before they set off, and now mostly eaten. No time to plan, just the feeling that here was something that they needed to be a part of, one of those 'once in a lifetime' moments when they'd be able to say to their grandchildren, 'I was there.' I know people who think that way about being at Billy Graham rallies in the 1950s or 1960s.

In our reading, we see the compassion shown by Jesus to the crowd, and a willingness of those present to share the little they had, which resulted in all being fed. But there's more here, because after Jesus blessed the food he gave it to his disciples to share out. Jesus needs you and me to not only offer the little we have, but also be his hands, share his blessing, and help nourish the spirit and souls of those in our own crowd, wherever that might be. Perhaps finding what we are seeking means discovering that we are strong enough to feed others, even as we have been fed.

† May life be full of 'I was there' moments, Lord, as we follow you day by day!

For further thought

Remember the many aid organisations daily sharing bread and water with those who have travelled far, maybe fleeing persecution for their faith.

Saturday 6 April
Finding fulfilment

Read John 12:24–26

'Very truly I tell you, unless a grain of wheat falls to the ground and dies, it remains only a single seed. But if it dies, it produces many seeds.'

(verse 24)

Around 160 years after the death of Christ, the Christian writer Tertullian wrote his most famous work, *Apologeticus*, in which he states, 'the blood of the martyrs is the seed of the Church'. The history of the world is populated with Christian martyrs, giving up their lives rather than giving up their faith. Now, I maybe suffered a few snide comments in school, and have had to answer the occasional 'Why?' about my own faith, but that's about it, if I'm honest. And yet I often read about the suffering of Christians in other parts of the world and wonder if my faith would be strong enough to survive under similar circumstances.

Jesus isn't saying, of course, that we will all have to make this ultimate sacrifice for our faith. But some things do have to die if we as Christians are to produce fruit. When Jesus told his disciples to leave everything and follow him, he was asking them to put aside human pride and selfishness and the natural desire for security that so many people hang onto – to let those seeds fall to the ground, die and be buried. Then their lives could become free to be used by God and produce seed that would become fruitful. The fact that I am free to write this says much about the fruitfulness of the lives of those first disciples. That is Jesus' challenge to us all, as together we follow on our journey of faith and service. This Lent, can we find the strength to let die what needs to die?

† Thank you for your faithful servants throughout the centuries, who have sowed the seeds of faith that now bring fruit into my life.

For further thought

Think of those who shared their faith with you, and be thankful for the seed they sowed within your heart.

April

Life in the (modern) desert – 5 Finding

97

Readings in Luke (2) – 1 The stone rejected

Notes by **Delroy Hall**

Delroy is a bishop in the Church of God of Prophecy, UK, and sits on the Bible Doctrine and Polity Committee of the church in Cleveland, Tennessee, USA. He is an academic with more than 25 years' experience as a trained counsellor. Delroy keeps himself fit and hopes to compete in an Iron Man. In 2017, he was appointed as the Sports Chaplain for Sheffield United Football Club. He is married to Paulette and the proud father of twin young women. Delroy has used the NIVUK for these notes.

Sunday 7 April
The stone rejected

Read Luke 20:1–19

'... I will send my son, whom I love; perhaps they will respect him.'

(verse 13)

The story of the vineyard owner sending various workers to receive a harvest is a tragic one. The workers were treated badly and sent away. He sends his son hoping for a different response, but alas, no.

There will be times as Christians we will be rejected by those whom we will interact with. I recall a time when I worked for a large telecommunications company and all the engineers on my group had been promoted. My boss asked me why I was not making a claim for promotion. I responded by saying, 'You are the one who determines whether I should be promoted or not.' He replied that I should do like the others have done. 'What is that,' I said, 'stab my colleagues in the back? No way, I will never do that.'

However, later I was summoned to see the head of the department who told me, 'Delroy, I hear you have some traditional values.' I replied, 'Yes, I do.' I was promoted to another group on a job which no one wanted to do, but which I loved.

Even in the face of rejection, we must hold fast to our values. In this way, we too might be built into cornerstones (verse 17) in our communities and places of work.

† Father and master builder of my life, help me to endure the hard times that may come my way. Prepare me in being an important rock in your kingdom and in the life of your creation.

Monday 8 April
Give to God what is God's

Read Luke 20:20–26

He said to them, 'Then give back to Caesar what is Caesar's, and to God what is God's.'

(verse 25)

What really belongs to us? I was raised in the home of Caribbean parents who emphasised that we should always give liberally to God. How many times did these opponents of Jesus try to catch Jesus out? Each time they failed, miserably.

I remember an incident years ago when carpet-fitters came to our church to install new carpets. My father was a joiner and he was very particular when it came to houses, construction and maintenance. The carpet-fitters did a shoddy job and my father was livid. They eventually did the job correctly and they were paid. My father came home still angry and expressing very clearly that it was God's house which needed proper attention, but more so because it was 'God's money, not ours'.

I think this little episode carries much to consider. We are God's, and as people who claim that we follow God we ought to give all of ourselves to him. Not only do we give back to God, but we must give of our best to God. In the story before us the citizens of Rome could not, and dare not, short-change Caesar. Neither are we to short-change God in all our doing. Now for the Christian what does that mean? All our doing means in all our interactions on the Earth, not only in church.

† Lord, you have blessed me more than I realise. Let me not short-change you, ever, but let me give to you and give of my best in all that I have and do.

For further thought

What material possession is most important to you? Will you give it to God liberally?

The questioners questioned

April

Readings in Luke (2) – 1 The stone rejected

Read Luke 20:27–47

'Beware of the teachers of the law. They like to walk around in flowing robes and love to be greeted with respect in the market-places and have the most important seats in the synagogues and the places of honour at banquets. They devour widows' houses and for a show make lengthy prayers ...'

(verses 46–47a)

A Christianity based on appearances seems to have been around for a long time. The spirit of the scribes is not a new thing, either. The scribes had important work to do as copyists and teachers of the word, but look at what they loved: all the external stuff, public showing, rubbing shoulders with the right people, sitting in the best seats and being seen with the biggest plates at parties. They preyed on the most vulnerable and loved to show how spiritual they were with long public prayers. I know plenty of scribes in today's church. Maybe you know a few, too.

As a teacher, I have learned over the years that when some people ask questions they often know the answer already, or sometimes they are trying to catch you out. There is an uncomfortable attitude that accompanies the question.

Jesus dealt with his questioners effectively. Is there something that we can learn from Jesus' style of teaching and ministry with those who are simply being difficult? Jesus' strategy of turning questions back onto the questioners is effective. I recall one of our church bishops who told us that his theological lecturer was an atheist for many years until he met a Christian who caused him to reconsider what he believed. You can do the same, too, by becoming skilful in knowing what other people think and challenging them, in discussion, to consider their own beliefs.

† Saviour and friend, help me not to get drawn into a skin-deep and showy Christianity. If I am to boast, let it be because of who you are and what you have done for me.

For further thought

The Bible teaches us to give an intelligent response of the hope within us. Let us equip ourselves by learning how to question the questioners.

Wednesday 10 April
Standing firm

Read Luke 21:1–19

'And so you will bear testimony to me. But make up your mind not to worry beforehand how you will defend yourselves. For I will give you words and wisdom that none of your adversaries will be able to resist or contradict.'

(verses 13–15)

How is it possible to act in the way that Jesus was describing to his disciples? It is a challenge for many of us. We worship God with relative ease. Our lives are not under threat, and if we go to church we do not even consider whether or not we will return home to eat our fine Sunday feast. Yet in some parts of the world people do not have such security.

One of the things that enables us to become strong in faith and being able to stand is practising the Christian disciplines. One of these, in fact, is a discipline you might have begun to practise this year: daily Bible reading.

Regular Bible reading is not important merely so that we can remember scripture and repeat it at a given moment. It is important to enable us to speak a penetrating word at the right moment when it is most needed. This comes about by spending time with God and the Bible. If we practise this kind of meditation, we will be able to speak a significant word of truth in those special moments when something outside our normal sphere of understanding is required.

My wife has often reminded me that God's work is not about me. 'All you need to be is the pipe that God can flow through,' she says. We can all be vessels of God if we give time to scripture and let it 'settle in our hearts', as Jesus said.

† Loving God, let me be willing and give the unrushed time to deepen my walk with you so I can live, be fruitful and stand firm, especially during times of desperation and crisis.

For further thought

As human beings we are prone to lethargy, but we must learn the principles of being proactive and disciplined in developing our walk with God.

Readings in Luke (2) – 1 The stone rejected

Thursday 11 April
Be watchful

Read Luke 21:20–38

'Be careful, or your hearts will be weighed down with carousing, drunkenness and the anxieties of life, and that day will close on you suddenly like a trap. For it will come on all those who live on the face of the whole earth.'

(verses 34–35)

Our scripture today is, frankly, terrifying. Many believers are uncomfortable talking about end times and especially the prospect that the world could end in our own lifetimes. We dread it. Yet Luke is clear that we must not avoid thinking about it. There is clear instruction to readers: they must wake up to what is happening in the world as this is no time for believers to bury their heads in the sands. We have been warned and encouraged to take note of what is happening, not to be caught off guard. We must be watchful.

When was the last time you were caught off guard? Being caught off guard can happen to anyone. It has happened to me on more than one occasion and when it does, for a few moments there is a feeling of confusion, madness and chaos. It can really leave you feeling all messed up and scared.

On reflection, many painful experiences could have been avoided. I recall in my early days as a pastor there was so much conflict which I could have avoided had I listened more, asked a few more questions of the right people and not rushed into things with youthful eagerness. I should have taken the time and been more watchful, and I would have, had I not been so busy.

Being watchful must be intentional and focused. It cannot be rushed and is a learned discipline.

† My heavenly Father who never rushes, help me resist over-busyness so I can take the time to be watchful of what is happening in your world and be ready for your coming.

For further thought

Today's scripture might be scary, but looking into areas of discomfort and wanting to learn is where we often make significant growth. Try it.

Friday 12 April
The die is cast

Read Luke 22:1–6

And Judas went to the chief priests and the officers of the temple guard and discussed with them how he might betray Jesus. They were delighted and agreed to give him money. He consented, and watched for an opportunity to hand Jesus over to them when no crowd was present.

(verses 4–6)

If the previous reading was scary, this one is sad. Judas, who has been loved, cared for and taught by Jesus for three years, decides to betray him. How could he do that to such a meek and humble human being?

Of course, we are talking about Jesus and most of us know the story well. But let us consider one aspect of the story. I wonder where you, the reader, find yourself in this short story. Do you identify with the priests, the scribes or perhaps even with Judas? Judas is our key character today. Judas goes behind Jesus' back and sets him up. Have you ever done that, out of anger or hurt? Maybe you know someone who has – a work colleague or a family member. Maybe you identify with Jesus, the innocent one. You have gone out of your way to help someone only to discover they have betrayed you. You have done much for them and this is how they repay you. Now, that hurts.

I recall an Anglican vicar talking about a grand event that was taking place at his church. On the day of the event, the organist did not show up. The vicar was devastated. Years later, the organist apologised to the vicar and admitted that, because of an argument between them, the organist wanted to hurt and humiliate the vicar in one of the cruellest ways possible.

Betrayal and cruelty are realities in our world. Yet even this most familiar of stories has an extraordinary outcome. As one convicted criminal found out, even in dire circumstances Jesus will open doors of forgiveness (Luke 23:43).

† Father of all forgiveness, help us to forgive others when they have hurt us and help us not to have the characteristic of Judas, betraying those who have treated us with love and kindness.

For further thought

What were Judas' options that he didn't consider?

Saturday 13 April
Bread and wine

Read Luke 22:7–23

After taking the cup, he gave thanks and said, 'Take this and divide it among you. For I tell you I will not drink again from the fruit of the vine until the kingdom of God comes.' And he took bread, gave thanks and broke it, and gave it to them, saying, 'This is my body given for you; do this in remembrance of me.'

(verses 17–19)

Bread and wine, Holy Communion, the Lord's Supper, the Eucharist: all words for this mystic and mysterious meal. A meal that had violent origins in the salvation history of Israel, and now Jesus embraced in his body the symbolism of the Passover lamb and the other elements used in the Exodus. This new meal was now instituted by Jesus to bring liberation, healing and salvation to millions. This new meal was not only for the apostles sat there on the floor, but for millions of people who would become believers in the time of Jesus and times to come.

This was a meal Jesus eagerly desired to eat with his disciples. It is a meal he intended believers throughout the world to join in with him to remember his suffering, crucifixion, burial and resurrection and also to signify real hope for a fallen humanity.

As Jesus showed in his own actions, the real story of sharing bread and wine in Jesus' name begins after the meal ends. After eating together, we are called to engage with the world and bring life to all. In other words, like Jesus, we are to demonstrate incarnational ministry in our lives.

The breaking of a body, the shedding of blood are violent in action. Yet if ever there was a time to recognise the attempt Jesus made to nullify violence, that time is now. We are called to nullify violence any way we can in this frequently violent world.

† Lord, you took the dehumanising effects of violence into the being of your body so that we might have life. Partaking of the bread and wine means we bring life into a dark, broken world.

For further thought

Here is a challenge for believers. How is it possible to live the bread and wine existence in the twenty-first century?

Readings in Luke (2) –
2 Who is the greatest?

Notes by **Edel McClean**

 Edel is a Roman Catholic laywoman currently employed as a learning and development officer with the Methodist Church in Great Britain. She is a spiritual director, supervisor, facilitator and coach. Edel grew up in Northern Ireland and now lives in Bury, UK. She is passionate about Ignatian discernment and about integrating a lived awareness of God into all that we do as individuals and in groups. Edel has used the NRSVA for these notes.

Sunday 14 April
One who serves

Read Luke 22:24–38

'… I am among you as one who serves.'

(part of verse 27)

At the beginning of Holy Week it's useful to think about expectations. Those with Jesus as that fateful week unfolded held very different views of what might happen and why. The religious leaders had such clearly defined expectations that they were clear that Jesus was a distraction from the coming of God, not the main event. Many of those who'd surrounded Jesus and followed him for years had hopes that finally Jesus would become the Messiah of their dreams. The week would not unfold as any of them imagined.

So, if we're tempted to expect Jesus to come this week in solemn remembering, soaring music or beautiful church services, we too maybe need to widen our gaze. Jesus is among us as one who serves. He may catch our attention and cause us to catch our breath, in the quietest of ways and most unexpected of places. It may be wise to create a space in ourselves to allow this week to unfold in a way beyond what we can imagine, to allow Jesus to show us who he really is, beyond all our imaginings and expectations.

† Jesus, friend and brother, help me to be open to the surprise of encountering you as you really are.

Monday 15 April
An expedient kiss

Read Luke 22:39–53

Judas … approached Jesus to kiss him; but Jesus said to him, 'Judas, is it with a kiss that you are betraying the Son of Man?'

(verses 47b–48)

Have you ever done something unsavoury because you thought it served the greater good? Maybe we tolerate someone's bad behaviour because of the good they can do with their skills or money. Maybe we allow someone to be bullied in a meeting because we agree with the bully's position if not their methods. One of my own struggles is that I fly to visit my father on a regular basis. The command to honour my father doesn't give me the right to contribute to global warming. It is beguilingly easy to defend bad choices with good intentions.

Did Judas believe that what he was doing was wrong? Or did he think he was doing something difficult and unsavoury in order to get Jesus to stand up and be accounted for? Did he think he was urging on the kingdom? He may have assumed that the end result would be good (and ultimately the end was good, if not in the way Judas imagined) but the covert plotting, the accepting of personal gain, neither of these point towards a pure heart.

Before we condemn Judas, we need to be honest about the shades of grey of our own consciences. Sometimes we innocently make bad decisions with the best of intentions. Sometimes our motives and intentions are tangled and unclear. But none of us can claim an entirely pure heart. What we can do is desire to be pure of heart, ask God's help, and commit ourselves to seeking to make right decisions with right intentions.

† Jesus, friend and brother, help me to be honest with you and with myself about the choices I make and to seek to be true to you in everything that I do.

For further thought

What might beguile you to defend bad choices with good intentions? How might God be inviting you to make better choices?

Tuesday 16 April
God believes in us

Read Luke 22:54–71

The Lord turned and looked at Peter. Then Peter remembered the word of the Lord, how he had said to him, 'Before the cock crows today, you will deny me three times.' And he went out and wept bitterly.

(verses 61–62)

If you remember back to Sunday, Jesus told Peter, 'but I have prayed for you that your own faith may not fail; and you, when once you have turned back, strengthen your brothers' (Luke 22:32). Peter had been quick to bat that assurance away, confident that Jesus needn't concern himself on that front.

I suspect that Peter remembered that conversation as he went outside to weep, feeling the hot flush of the shame, realising that promises he'd so confidently, publicly made lay shattered on the courtyard floor.

Peter learned humility. It must have helped that Jesus had stated his faith in him and given him a job to do, even in full expectation of him stumbling. Jesus had given Peter work to do among the disciples. Whatever his heartbreak, he had brothers to strengthen and so, no matter how disheartened he might have felt, he did not have the luxury of wallowing in his guilt.

It's an example of one of the great truths of our faith. Even when we struggle to believe in ourselves, and struggle to believe in God, God continues to believe in us. Even with our brokenness, our bluster, our tendency to deny our need for Jesus, our tendency to deny Jesus himself, we're still needed for kingdom building. Jesus never gives up on us. We may cry bitterly, repent our sin, but Jesus keeps holding us in his steady gaze, believing in us and seeing the very best of us.

† Jesus, friend and brother, forgive me when I am not as good a friend to you as I aspire to be. Help me to find myself again in your unwavering belief in me.

For further thought

Have you ever asked Jesus what he sees in you? What difference might it make if you believed in God's belief in you?

Wednesday 17 April
'He stirs up the people'

Read Luke 23:1–12

They were insistent and said, 'He stirs up the people by teaching throughout all Judea, from Galilee where he began even to this place.'

(verse 5)

They say the best deceptions always include a germ of truth. The chief priests, though manipulating the story to their own ends, put their finger on the nub of the problem: the unquestionable truth that Jesus is in the habit of stirring up the people.

For those of us who are fairly mature in our Christian life, even more for those of us who are somehow 'professional' Christians, the life and words of Jesus and even the tragic events of this week are in danger of becoming smooth, well-worn, familiar.

Yet Jesus is a man who stirs things up. This is what Jesus does, it's who he is. In the presence of this man something in us is disturbed. Yes, his friendship often brings us peace, offers reassurance and a solidity on which we build our lives, but his friendship also challenges us, pushes us to become people who join him on his mission.

When were you last truly stirred up by Jesus? When did you last find yourself moved at a visceral level? If you've lost that, perhaps this week is a chance to encounter again this challenging, loving, unpredictable, generous, revolutionary teacher. Perhaps this week, as you walk with him through his passion and death you can open yourself to be stirred again by whatever it was that first drew you to him. Stay by his side, pay attention and notice how being alongside him changes you.

† Jesus, friend and brother, stir my soul this week. Help me to pay attention to you and how you live through this week, so that I am transformed by what I see.

For further thought

How can you help the Church to help people to be stirred up by Jesus?

Thursday 18 April (Maundy Thursday)
Who will speak for the innocent?

Read Luke 23:13–25

So Pilate gave his verdict that their demand should be granted. He released the man they asked for, the one who had been put in prison for insurrection and murder, and he handed Jesus over as they wished.

(verses 24–25)

Those who stand by are also part of the story. Listening to people who've experienced bullying, they often say that it wasn't the bully who caused the greatest hurt but the friends and colleagues who kept silent in the face of the injustice.

Recently, in the UK, two men were acquitted of criminal damage after breaking into a manufacturer of war jets with the intention of irreversibly damaging a plane bound for a war zone. Their defence was that they believed that the jet's intended owners would use it in war crimes against civilians. Believing this, and having exhausted all other avenues, they argued that to do nothing would have been to be complicit in the slaughter of innocents – to hand those innocent civilians over to the mercy of another power with the intention of slaughtering them.

I'm challenged by the actions of those two men, and by the actions of people across the world who every day refuse to play Pilate, handing the innocent over to be harmed in the name of political expediency. One way to read Jesus' passion is to notice how person after person fails to speak up for Jesus. When I choose not to stand with the innocent against tyrants, I join forces with Pilate. When I choose to side with the innocent on a local or on a world stage, I choose to stand with Jesus.

† Jesus, friend and brother, encourage today all who seek to stand with the innocent in the face of injustice and oppression. Give me the courage to add my voice to theirs, in your name.

For further thought
Who do I know who stands with the innocent in the face of injustice? How can I support them and their work?

Friday 19 April (Good Friday)
Remember me

Read Luke 23:26–46

Then he said, 'Jesus, remember me when you come into your kingdom.' He replied, 'Truly I tell you, today you will be with me in Paradise.'

(verses 42–43)

I've long struggled with the enthusiasm I sometimes encounter in Christian circles to attempt to recapture the gruesome reality of the crucifixion, second by bloody second. It is not that I don't recognise the tremendous significance of this day, the life-changing and world-changing truth that the Son of God was put to death by those he sought only to love.

But Jesus is my friend – someone about whom I care deeply, someone who has made more of a difference to my life than anyone else, someone whose love is the most steadfast that I have ever encountered. This man is dear to me and so I cannot bear to remember on an annual basis the grim details of how he was tortured, how he was harassed, how he was broken.

For me it's more helpful to remember those who stood by Jesus and stayed with him though they could do nothing more than continue to witness the truth of who he was, whatever filth the world threw at him. That is the staggering insight of the criminal hanging by Jesus' side, who somehow, in the midst of everything that is happening to him and around him, finds a space for hope. Who sees, even marred by the dirt, blood and brutality, the shining truth of Jesus that nothing can blot out.

† Jesus, friend and brother, I want to stay by your side today. Help me to recognise the truth of your presence even when the world seems bleak.

For further thought

When in your life have things seemed particularly bleak? How have you seen the light of God shining through in those times?

Saturday 20 April (Holy Saturday)
A day of remembering

> **Read Luke 23:47–55**
>
> *This man went to Pilate and asked for the body of Jesus. Then he took it down, wrapped it in a linen cloth, and laid it in a rock-hewn tomb where no one had ever been laid. It was the day of Preparation, and the sabbath was beginning.*
>
> (verses 52–54)

Holy Saturday is a day of emptiness. If you've had a loved one die, you'll have lived through those painful days between the death and the funeral, the early, disorientating shock of bereavement.

In Irish Catholic tradition it is still normal for the deceased to be buried on the third day after the death. The time between the death and the burial is marked by the wake. Friends and family flood the home of the deceased, surrounding the bereaved with love, food and memories of their loved one. The life is remembered, grieved and celebrated. It is a deeply intimate and personal process to remember the particularities of a person, the lived experience of knowing them and loving them.

Jesus' friends were forced into quietude by the Sabbath. And in the quietude they turned to their God, to the rituals of their tradition and to each other. They turned over in their hearts their memories of Jesus, the highlights and lowlights of their relationship with him, the particular things that they cherished about him.

I think this is at the heart of Holy Saturday – a holy waiting and remembering, an intimate and personal recollection of who this particular man has been in your particular life. We remember not just a figure on the world stage, but a friend. What do you cherish about this man, how has knowing him changed you, what do you need to hold onto in your memory?

† Jesus, friend and brother, in the quiet of this day, help me to remember with gratitude all that I cherish in our friendship.

For further thought

If, on Holy Saturday, you had to write a eulogy for Jesus, what would you want to say?

Readings in Luke (2) – 3 Easter in Luke and John

Notes by **Alex Cameron**

Alex is passionate about community transformation. She studied International Politics and Conflict in Belfast before returning to London to help found the Christian International Peace Service (CHIPS) project. She has done interfaith work for West London Synagogue, church planting for the Diocese of London and taught in Trenchtown, Jamaica. She blogs at: ascameron93. wixsite.com/alexsadventures. Alex has used the NIVUK for these notes.

Sunday 21 April (Easter Sunday)
Hope bursting through!

Read Luke 24:1–12

'He is not here; he has risen!'

(verse 6a)

The sound of a mother losing her child never leaves you.

Grief is not like in the movies. That heart-wrenching cry can come days … weeks … months … later. Instead it's an eerie normalcy. The pouring of tea … rustle of tissues … lighting of a cigarette …

Before the grief can really be processed, there are practical arrangements that need to be made. A body must be identified … family should be told … a funeral needs to be planned …

It's at this junction that our reading joins these women, as they go to perform the final burial rituals. But something is deeply wrong; the body isn't there! Instead two men appear next to them and utter the words that redefine all our futures – 'He is not here; he has risen!' Jesus is alive!

Over this week, Easter week, we will explore how even in the darkest moments hope can still shine through. Today is the greatest celebration of the Church throughout the world. Death is beaten. Jesus is alive!

So no matter whether you're meeting the day full of joy or struggling to see through the darkness …

HAPPY EASTER!

† Lord, thank you for your sacrifice; your ultimate display of love! We pray for your Church around the world as they meet today to celebrate your victory.

Monday 22 April
God's plans are like an onion ...

Read John 20:10–23

Mary Magdalene went to the disciples with the news: 'I have seen the Lord!' And she told them that he had said these things to her. ... When the disciples were together ... Jesus came and stood among them.

(part of verses 18–19)

When I finished university I had no intention of returning to London; I wanted to change the world, not come back home! But God had other plans. As I was looking for opportunities overseas I discovered a small charity called the Christian International Peace Service (CHIPS). CHIPS does long-term, grassroots peacebuilding in communities across the world. I fell in love with their philosophy for Christian peacemaking and hoped they would send me. They did; the only problem was it was to London! CHIPS was invited to start a missional community on Angell Town Estate in Brixton and I became a founding member.

God's plans are like an onion ... they are often revealed in layers.

John tells the intricate story of Jesus slowly revealing himself to the disciples. Mary Magdalene doesn't even recognise Jesus to begin with, then he sends her to warn the other disciples before he appears in their midst. Jesus doesn't spontaneously arrive; instead he peels back the layers one by one.

Finally Jesus reveals to the disciples his message of forgiveness. Each successive generation of Israel has peeled back a layer of the story to this climax.

Why does God do this? Because he doesn't just arrive for the climax at the end. He is with us throughout the journey!

A year before I finished university (before I'd even heard of CHIPS) I was walking round Brixton. I turned to my mum and said, 'You know, if I ever move back to London, I'm moving back here.' Little did I know God was already peeling back a layer ...

† Thank you for being the God of yesterday, today and tomorrow. We are sorry for our frustration when we cannot see your plan. Help us to rest in the knowledge that you have yet to peel back the layers.

For further thought

Take five minutes to ponder how you got to where you are – making a timeline might be helpful. Bring before God your hopes of where you want to end up.

Tuesday 23 April
Peace in the midst of conflict

Read John 20:24–31

Though the doors were locked, Jesus came and stood among them and said, 'Peace be with you!'

(verse 26b)

What a powerful opening line! 'Peace be with you!' I spend a lot of time talking about peace. As part of CHIPS we were invited to live in Brixton because of the violence between young people, and those inviting us expect us to somehow bring peace. But the godly peace we talk about is not what they are expecting.

Jesus walks into the room and announces that peace is with them. He has not changed the hearts of the authorities who still want to persecute the disciples, he has not overthrown the Roman Empire that still holds power in the Holy Land, he has not even unlocked the door; yet peace is with them because he is with them.

A heavenly peace is not the absence of conflict, it is the presence of God.

It is this peace we try to demonstrate in Brixton. We do not always try to stop all the different conflicts that are present on our estates, because conflict can be creative, character-building and progressive. But we will stand in the midst of these conflicts. We call it taking both sides; we will not promise neutrality but we will come alongside each person involved to try to support them as well as helping to find a solution to the conflict.

However, we know that if eradicating conflict is our aim then we will always fail, because there will always be conflict in our lives. But a heavenly peace, that has the potential to break in through any locked door, happens in the midst of conflict.

† Thank you, Lord, for your peace which surpasses human understanding. Today we pray for all those who are without peace, those who feel the weight of the world on their shoulders. May we all try to seek your peace today.

For further thought

As you go about your day today, consider the places and situations around you in which you would like to see Jesus' peace in action.

Wednesday 24 April
The kindness of strangers

> **Read Luke 24:13–29**
>
> *As they talked and discussed these things with each other, Jesus himself came up and walked along with them.*
>
> (verse 15)

I love travelling! However, as a single woman travelling alone in a foreign environment I often feel very vulnerable. I am often completely reliant on the kindness of strangers to help me navigate the journey.

In December 2017 I went to visit the CHIPS project in Ghana. To get to the team I had an epic journey from Accra to Nakpayili which included almost every form of transport you can imagine. But on the bus I was reminded of just how vulnerable I can be. I had already made friends with a Ghanaian woman, so when we stopped for lunch I ate a little something with her. An hour later I began to regret this decision as the bus lurched from side to side and my stomach tried (and failed!) to keep the food contained. We stopped at a river and I ran off to empty my lunch back out onto the ground; then I looked up to see that I had to try to navigate a ferry crossing. It was at this point I questioned why I had ever said yes to this trip! But then I looked behind me to find my new friend waiting for me. She smiled a compassionate smile and then proceeded to help me buy a ferry ticket, find a seat, introduce me to the other women and then reboard the correct bus on the other side. I have never been so thankful for the kindness of a stranger.

God can work in the most unlikely of places … even in the travelling companions we find. God certainly worked that way on the Emmaus road, and on many roads around the world today.

† Father, your ways are often strange and mysterious. Help us to open our eyes and see you in the most unlikely of places and people.

For further thought

As you journey through life today, find a way to demonstrate the kindness of strangers to someone. If you can't think of anything check out the ideas on the website of the Random Acts of Kindness group.

Thursday 25 April
Facing fear

Read Luke 24:30–44

They got up and returned at once to Jerusalem.

(verse 33a)

I can understand why the disciples were leaving Jerusalem. Their leader had been killed and now his grave had been desecrated; on top of all this there were some rumours beginning that there had been some kind of divine intervention. I would be terrified! What on earth would happen next?

When I volunteered as a teacher in Jamaica I met a woman called Lorna Stanley. She founded Operation Restoration Christian School in Trenchtown, and in her battle to educate the children in the area she went head to head with local gang leaders called the Dons. One story she tells is of how some of her students phoned to tell her to stay away from Trenchtown, because the Dons had put a price on her head and if she came anywhere near her life would be in danger. After praying and pondering what to do, she decided to go down and face the Dons. Apparently they sat in the room like a judging panel with her sitting opposite them. They launched all sorts of allegations against her and were ready to deal out gangland justice until she turned round and said to the leader, 'I love you.'

He broke down in tears and all these years later is still one of the strongest supporters of the school.

When the disciples had seen Jesus they were able to conquer their fears and return to Jerusalem. With God we can conquer our fears too.

† God, you hold the whole world in your hands and with you we have the ability to overcome our fears. Help us today to come face to face with our fears and take the first step to conquering them.

For further thought

What do you fear at the moment? What do you wake up worried about or what stops you from doing something? What is the first step you can take to come face to face with it?

Friday 26 April
Not afraid to fail

Read Luke 24:45–53

'You are witnesses of these things.'

(verse 48)

When Jesus chose the disciples he chose regular, ordinary people. Those regular, ordinary people changed the world. Christianity can be found in every country, and Jesus' birth is the point from which we now measure time. Some of the most inspiring points of history were in turn inspired by his words.

For 18 months I had the unique opportunity of being a Christian working in a West London synagogue. Never before had I felt such a weight of the responsibility of witnessing my faith. I do not mean that I went in every day and told my colleagues about Jesus; I have never been very good at very vocal evangelism. Instead by witness I mean that the way I live my life should be a representation of Christ. This is all well and good at the beginning of the day when you can offer to make everyone a coffee, but becomes a different kettle of fish when you have 101 things to do and none of them seem to be going well.

It was my job to start different community projects and some of these projects did not go well. And when I failed I realised that my biggest witness was in how I dealt with failure. I was vulnerable with my colleagues when I told them I had begun to have panic attacks before work. When I shared my problems with them they felt able to share theirs with me. It led to a huge conversation about mental health and we started to make some changes to our office to improve our working environment.

Jesus called regular, ordinary people to be his witnesses. You are one of them.

† Father, thank you for trusting us to be your witnesses, even in our failures. Help us to demonstrate your love to those around us today.

For further thought

When you go to work, school or the supermarket tomorrow, take a look at the people around you. Encourage someone who looks like they might need it.

Saturday 27 April
Local hero

Read John 21:15–19

Jesus said, 'Take care of my sheep.'

(verse 16b)

Angell Town Estate, Brixton, London is renowned for the violence that takes place here. The mothers on this estate have seen and experienced some of the horrors that this has brought. Many of these tremendous women are doing all they can to change it.

There is Mary who gives up almost seven days a week to open the community centre, Angell Delight, every day. She has built it from nothing and has often kept it open through her own pure determination. The young people know that they can always come to her.

There is Lorraine who, in memory of her son, has created Dwaynamics: a boxing club for young men and women. She has become their champion, pushing them to achieve their potential and being an endless supporter. The young people know that they can always come to her.

There is Kamika who runs creative projects all over Brixton. The young women on the estate describe her as their second mum, always open for a conversation and willing to help them to carry their burdens. The young people know that they can always come to her.

Mary, Lorraine and Kamika (along with many other women) are famous on our estate, but they will rarely be recognised by the rest of the world. They are inspirational in the selfless care they take of the young people in our community. They are living models of Jesus' words to 'take care of my sheep'.

I hope to live by their example each and every day.

† Lord, thank you for the incredible people who do inspirational acts that no one but you will ever know about. Help us to follow in their example.

For further thought

These incredible people in our communities need help. Can you commit to spending time each week helping them? Find out who they are in your community and go and ask how you can help.

Music in the Bible – 1 Sing a new song

Notes by **Ian Howarth**

Ian is a Methodist Minister and Chair of the Birmingham Methodist District. He has served as Precentor to the Methodist Conference, and was on the editorial committee of *Singing the Faith*, the latest Methodist hymn book. To help keep him sane in ministry, he sings in the City of Birmingham Symphony Chorus. He is married, with three adult children, the youngest of whom is autistic with severe learning difficulties. Ian has used the NRSVA for these notes.

Sunday 28 April
Clarion call

Read Joshua 6:1–20

You shall march … with seven priests bearing seven trumpets of rams' horns before the ark. On the seventh day you shall march around the city seven times, the priests blowing the trumpets.

(verses 3–4)

The sound of the shofar, the ram's horn trumpet, has great significance throughout the Hebrew Bible. It is first mentioned in Exodus 29:16 as a sign of the presence of God on Mount Sinai, and its use comes to be symbolic of God's voice and divine action.

It reminds us that from earliest times the sound of music carried with it a sense of otherness, of mystery. It can suggest a power that goes beyond human understanding. Historically, that suggestion of mystic power in music can be used for good or ill. Music was significant in generating enthusiasm and unity in many great freedom struggles, but also in Nazi rallies! It is not so much that music itself contains the meaning, but it gives the message it bears added, and potentially spiritual, significance.

Music is a great gift. It reaches parts that other things cannot reach, and opens many out to the Other, the voice of God. However, because of its power, we need to be careful.

Was it the voice of God that brought down the walls of Jericho with the trumpets, or was the use of music trying to give divine authority to essentially human actions?

† Thank you, God, for music. May our spirits resound with your Spirit, that it may help us to experience your love and discern your truth.

Monday 29 April
David, soother of the soul

> **Read 1 Samuel 16:14–23**
>
> *And whenever the evil spirit from God came upon Saul, David took the lyre and played it with his hand, and Saul would be relieved and feel better, and the evil spirit would depart from him.*
>
> (verse 23)

The capacity of music to reach the deepest emotions of many people is one of its greatest qualities. It can soothe and help people relax, it can also excite and energise. I am reminded of Nanki Poo in Gilbert and Sullivan's operetta *The Mikado*, whose trade is to sing a song to meet the mood of his customers, and who claims he has a song to touch every emotion needed:

> *My catalogue is long, through every passion ranging,*
> *And to your humours changing I tune my supple song!*

David had quite a task trying to soothe the irascible King Saul with his lyre. At first the music did meet his mood, and offered him the soothing he needed. But once Saul became jealous of David's military success in chapter 18 we hear how the playing simply enraged him more and David had to escape Saul attacking him with a spear.

The relationship between music and feelings is mysterious, complex and powerful. In recent years it has been recognised and used skilfully by music therapists. Such therapy has been found empirically to benefit various mental health conditions. Many even without therapy find music a helpful way to process our emotions, and perhaps help us move on when stuck in one emotional state, into another.

Music can be misused to manipulate feelings, and to generate an emotionalism that bypasses rational thought. But at its best it can allow us to get in touch with our deeper selves, in a unique way that can be a symbol of God's life-giving presence with us.

† Gracious God, you know my deepest needs. Open my inward ear to hear your voice of comfort and new life, in the ways that speak to me, through the gifts you have given.

For further thought

What music touches your deepest feelings? How do you relate that to your understanding of your experience of God?

A musical catalyst

Read 2 Kings 3:13–20

And then, while the musician was playing, the power of the Lord came on him.

(verse 15)

Music here acts as a catalyst for God's Spirit to come upon Elisha. It is as if it opens a door for God's spirit to flow in a way that empowers Elisha in his ministry.

Over the centuries people have discovered various media that seem to enable that flow of God's Spirit in various ways. Not just music, but the visual arts, beautiful buildings, poetry and the wonders of nature are all examples, and it is no surprise that from the earliest times places of worship have nurtured these arts to help deepen people's experience of God.

Of course, a lot of these media are culturally conditioned, and a piece of music or a painting that enables one person to experience the presence of God may be completely alien to another person. Also, some see the investment needed to create the excellence required for the arts to be a symbol of the divine, to be an indulgence and an extravagance, a diversion from the true nature of the gospel and from our commitment to those in need.

But while some, notably the Puritans, decried the arts and wanted an emphasis solely on the Word, this story reminds us that for all the tensions, God does work through them, and uses them as a vehicle for his Spirit.

In a fast-changing cultural landscape, Christians face a real challenge in using music and the other arts appropriately so that they can continue to help people experience God's Spirit inspiring and empowering them today.

† Thank God for the things that you find help open the door to God's Spirit moving in you to inspire and empower.

For further thought

Is there a danger in making something that deepens our experience of God into an end in itself and risking idolatry?

April

Music in the Bible – 1 Sing a new song

Temple offering

Read 2 Chronicles 5:2–14

And when the song was raised, with trumpets and cymbals and other musical instruments, in praise to the Lord, 'For he is good, for his steadfast love endures for ever', the house, the house of the Lord, was filled with a cloud ... for the glory of the Lord filled the house of God.

(parts of verses 13–14)

From the earliest times, and in virtually all religious traditions, music has had an important place in the worship of God.

The combination of factors that the readings through the week have pointed to, music offering a sense of 'the other', music speaking to people's deepest feelings, music as a catalyst opening the door for God's Spirit to move, all serve to make it an appropriate element of worship.

As we read of the splendour of the music in Solomon's temple, we have to remind ourselves this was a time when music was not the ubiquitous medium it has become today, through broadcasting and electronic media. This orchestra and choir depicted by the Chronicler was something special and splendid, and the musical experience it offered was unique, precious.

Music still features centrally in much Christian worship, but when high-quality music is available to listen to all day at the flick of a switch, it is quite a challenge to how we use the sometimes limited resources we have in churches to offer that experience which enables music to fulfil its potential role in enhancing the worship of God's people.

Very few can have the resources of Solomon, but this passage speaks to the importance and value of music in worship, and challenges us to commit to using our imagination and creativity with the resources we have to use music well to enhance our worship of God.

† Thank God for all who provide music in the church(es) where you worship.

For further thought

How do we ensure that the spiritual needs of both those who are musical, and those who don't relate to music, are met in our worship?

Thursday 2 May
Singing at all times

Read Acts 16:25–31

About midnight Paul and Silas were praying and singing hymns to God, and the prisoners were listening to them.

(verse 25)

Of all the musical activities that are used to enhance people's spiritual life, the most common is singing.

Singing needs no resource other than ourselves and allows a level of expression that goes beyond words. Singing for many people serves to raise spirits, to build community, to allow participation at a deep level, to express the inexpressible.

It is singing that enables Paul and Silas to express their praise in the unlikely context of their prison, and the fact that Luke mentions that the other prisoners are listening, implies it was making an impression on them.

Singing comes from something deep within us. It comes from our breath. Just as the Holy Spirit is God's breath, singing is almost as if our spirit is made audible.

C.S. Lewis in *The Magician's Nephew* takes the image of God's Spirit brooding over creation in Genesis 1 and builds on it to have Aslan sing creation into being, which is a wonderful image.

Corporate singing can still be a powerful expression of deep things, as the work of Gareth Malone on television shows us, if in a rather formulaic way, and John Bell in his book *The Singing Thing* urges Christians to be countercultural to preserve singing together in their worship.

However, I am conscious that not everyone sings. The requirement that attendance at church involves singing can be off-putting, and the implication that the only way to praise is through singing is alienating. As always the diversity of human nature and culture offers us a challenge in how we approach singing in our worship and spirituality.

† Loving God, help me to be sensitive to the needs of others. As I give thanks for what helps me to worship you, help me rejoice in the different things that help others in their worship.

For further thought

If you like to express praise through singing, ask someone who finds that difficult what media help them to praise (or vice versa).

Friday 3 May
Different styles, one God

Read Colossians 3:12–17

… with gratitude in your hearts sing psalms, hymns and spiritual songs to God.

(part of verse 16)

In our reflections this week, we have focused on the value of music, in personal spirituality and also in corporate worship.

However, we have to acknowledge that in church life the use of music in worship has often been a source of conflict. This has been seen in the removal of the church bands and their replacement with organs in parish churches in the nineteenth century, or in the so-called 'Worship Wars' over the introduction of electronic, drum-based, popular-style songs led by worship bands. Praise bands were often introduced at the expense of traditional hymns and psalms led by choirs and organs over the last 30 or 40 years.

Music is a product of culture and the sort of music a church uses will speak in seconds to visitors about which cultures will feel at home in that church. The challenge for music not to be exclusive and divisive in modern church life is a real one.

The text above was, I am sure, not written with this in mind, but its reference to psalms, hymns and spiritual songs does seem to encourage a variety of musical forms, even if we cannot be sure what those were in first-century Colossae!

How we value the variety of music available for worship today – celebrating what has value for us, but not denigrating and putting inappropriate value judgements on that which we may find difficult, but others really appreciate – is a key concern for all who care about worship in our churches today.

† Thank God for the variety of music available for worship, and the musicians committed to writing music for worship today. Pray that variety may be a source of richness, not division.

For further thought

Reflect on the way different styles of music in worship may say something different about God and about who the church is for.

Saturday 4 May
The trumpet shall sound

Read 1 Corinthians 15:51–57

For the trumpet will sound, and the dead will be raised imperishable, and we will be changed.

(verse 52b)

This passage always reminds me of the great bass aria near the end of Handel's *Messiah* where Handel sets the words to the accompaniment of a wonderful trumpet solo.

We are back with the trumpet, the instrument, whether made of ram's horn or metal, that has special significance as representing the voice of God throughout the Bible. Through the trumpet call, God is calling the dead back to life at the day of resurrection.

The fact that musical imagery is used by Paul here, to suggest God's life-giving power, speaks to the experience of many people that music itself can have a life-giving quality.

Brian McLaren in his book *We Make the Road by Walking* talks about a universal quest for 'aliveness' which he suggests is the driver behind a lot of modern interest in spirituality. He writes that the quest for aliveness explains a lot of what we do. 'It's why readers read and travellers travel. It's why lovers love and thinkers think, why dancers dance and filmgoers watch.'[9]

For me, it is why I sing, and why I listen to music. The sound of the trumpet can indeed be a symbol of God's power to bring us alive, in this life and the next.

That aliveness is not a self-indulgent feel-good factor, but a growing awareness of what lies deep at the heart of things: God's love and life, to be treasured and to be shared.

† Pray for those who feel emotionally or spiritually dead, for whom a concept of 'aliveness' may make little sense, that the life-giving trumpet of God shall sound for them.

For further thought

Think about what God's 'aliveness' means to you, and how you might nurture it in your life.

---

9   McLaren, B.D. (2014), *We Make the Road by Walking: A Year-Long Quest for Spiritual Formation, Reorientation, and Activation* (London: Hodder & Stoughton).

Music in the Bible – 2 Sing to the Lord

Notes by **Simei Monteiro**

 Brazilian poet and composer Simei is a retired missionary and previously worked as worship consultant at the World Council of Churches in Geneva, Switzerland. Her book *The Song of Life* (ASTE/IEPG, 1991) explores the relationship between hymns and theology. She and her husband live in Curitiba, Brazil. They have two daughters and three grandchildren. Simei has used the NRSVA for these notes.

Sunday 5 May
In the beginning there was music

Read Psalm 96:1–13

Let the heavens be glad, and let the earth rejoice ... Then shall all the trees of the forest sing for joy before the Lord ... He will judge the world with righteousness, and the peoples with his truth.

(verses 11–13)

The world's musical theories are rooted in many ancient cultures, including those indigenous to Latin America. For millennia, music was connected to thinking about the cosmos, psychology, spirituality and ethics. It seems there is an understanding of cosmic harmony; an original sound pervading the universe and uniting heavens and Earth.

In this psalm, there is a similar idea: a song of praise which involves the whole universe. It is an invitation to us to listen to this music which is not any one kind of music but is instead a universal praise song! Are we able to listen? What about joining in and singing praises to God with all creation, the whole cosmos? Any sound contains many modes of vibration called harmonics. In order to develop our understanding of the relationships between humanity and nature, we have to pay attention to the harmony in our lives and in our world.

We are the guardians of our sustainable world, and in this sense music expresses our connection to it. This week we will explore the connections between music, our singing, and all aspects of God's world. As Shirley Murray says in her 'Earth Prayer': 'God is our maker: do not deny God, challenge, defy God, threaten this place: life is to cherish, care, or we perish!'[10]

† Eternal Singer, open our ears and our hearts to your voice; help us to create harmony in our personal life and in our world!

---

10   Murray, S.E. (1996), 'I Am Your Mother' in *Every Day in Your Spirit* (Carol Stream, Illinois: Hope Publishing Co.).

Monday 6 May
God's breath is our song

Read Psalm 150

Praise the Lord! Praise God in his sanctuary; praise him in his mighty firmament! ... Praise him with tambourine and dance; ... with clanging cymbals; ... praise him with loud clashing cymbals! Let everything that breathes praise the Lord! Praise the Lord!

(parts of verses 1–6)

Reading this psalm, we are invited to listen to a true symphony. And more than just listening: we are called to be part of an ethereal concert. Even if you are not a musician it is possible to understand the clear instructions! The theme is 'praise God's deeds and his surpassing greatness'.

Where is this concert performed? It can happen in a sanctuary or in the cosmos. The entire universe can become a sacred place; all available instruments are in place; all kind of sounds are acceptable, including many different tonal colours, percussion and our voices.

Yes, our breath can make music. The breath of life, the original breath of God in us can make joyful music! The best instrument is our voice and in order to play it, we will need our breath!

The music in us is God's singing. The Guarani people, an indigenous community in the interior of South America, have a myth of creation which recalls an original song called the song of completeness. It was sung in the beginning of creation and it continues resounding in the universe. According to the myth, if we forget the beautiful sounds and words we will lose our human identity. We are born in song, and we are called to sing that song to maintain our identity.

God sings inside us with the breath of life, the Holy Spirit, which is able to make us sing a song of wholeness, a song of completeness!

† Dear God, let me feel your breath in me, on me and around me, so I can sing your eternal song and feel completely still and blessed in my entire life.

For further thought

Sitting down quietly, with your eyes closed, can you feel your breath and your pulse, your inner rhythm? Can you offer it as a praise song to God?

The song of the sea

Read Exodus 15:1–12

At the blast of your nostrils the waters piled up, the floods stood up in a heap; the deeps congealed in the heart of the sea ... You blew with your wind, the sea covered them; they sank like lead in the mighty waters.

(verses 8, 10)

We realise we are facing times of hatred and war. We cannot trust in our future nor be complacent about what kind of world our children will live in. But, should the worst happen, when events will come close to destroying us, where can we go for healing our anger, our wounds or resentments? Is an idea like forgiveness or letting go possible in our world?

While reading these verses, I asked myself: is this a song of victorious vengeance over enemies or a memorial song to celebrate the mighty deeds of God in favour of his people? That is, I wonder if this song sings out the possibility that endless disgrace can be cast by God into the depths of the sea. Is it possible to find a parallel between the heart of the sea, in these verses, and God's depths of mercy? Can the infinite curse of endless hatred, be annihilated, annulled, by justice and grace?

The depths of mercy are the place of forgiveness and forgetfulness, as the prophet said: 'He will again have compassion upon us; he will tread our iniquities under foot. You will cast all our sins into the depths of the sea' (Micah 7:19).

If we want to restore balance to life on Earth, accept it as our common house and live in peace with our neighbours, we will need to find the right way. So let us ask for forgiveness and forgetfulness from the one who is able to cast our sins into the depths of the sea and welcome us in the depths of his love.

† Merciful and graceful God, clean my heart and mind from all I don't need to carry; and free our world from prejudice and hate.

For further thought

What are some practical ways your community can overcome hate and resentment?

Wednesday 8 May
Hannah's song

Read 1 Samuel 2:1–10

Talk no more so very proudly, let not arrogance come from your mouth; for the Lord is a God of knowledge, and by him actions are weighed. The bows of the mighty are broken, but the feeble gird on strength.

(verses 3–4)

As human beings, we want to be able to find immediate solutions when we are concerned about the reality around us. Soon we realise that it is not easy to find the right solution. Finding such solutions is up to God and we understand we are under God's wisdom and authority; for the Lord is a God of knowledge, and by him, actions are weighed.

In Portuguese, the meaning of the word *pesar* is close to the English verb 'to ponder'. It can have several meanings: it can be to weigh, to feel a deep sorrow or be overloaded. It can also mean to be able to evaluate, to judge someone or something.

The symbol of justice is a scale and its weight (*peso*) helps us to get the right balance, the just weight. The problem is that it is not easy to identify what we put on each platform of this scale.

Like many other countries, Brazil is facing difficult times: political crisis, corruption, low salaries, unemployment, rising prices, lack of health care. As a nation, historically we descend from oppressors and yet at the same time we find ourselves under the oppression of the very society we have created. Like Hannah, we feel the need to cry out to God.

Despite current circumstances, we believe God will give us the wisdom and strength to cope with this situation. In the midst of our troubles and indignation we can also see God acting, giving strength and courage to us. Can Hannah show us how our song can be angry and urgent, but also hopeful and constructive?

† God of Hope, guard my heart against arrogance and help me to act only for the good of my country. Let me listen to your voice and enjoy the blessings of your care.

For further thought

In many countries of the world, including among the poorest in Brazil, protest music has galvanised communities and brought strength to people who have very little.

Thursday 9 May
The wells of salvation

> **Read Isaiah 12:1–6**
>
> *With joy you will draw water from the wells of salvation. And you will say on that day: Give thanks to the Lord, call on his name; make known his deeds among the nations; proclaim that his name is exalted … let this be known in all the earth.*
>
> (verses 3–4, 5b)

Brazil has the second-largest aquifer system in the world and it is an important source of fresh water. It is named after the Guarani people: Aquífero Guarani. It is said that this vast underground reservoir could supply fresh drinking water to the world for 200 years. But if the water is hidden in the depths of the earth it is necessary to draw the water and that is the question and the problem. Who will do it? The authorities say they do not have enough money and technology to explore it. So, possibly this precious treasure will be put on auction. Some big companies in the world, such as Coca-Cola and Nestlé, dream of exploring it and reaping the financial benefit. However, in the Northeast Region of Brazil, people are dying for lack of water, helpless and ignored.

It would be easier if we could sing like Israel sang in the desert: 'Spring up, O well! – Sing to it!' (Numbers 21:17). It must have seemed like a miracle to see waters springing up in the desert!

People in these regions need fresh water for themselves but they are also thirsting for the everlasting water. They believe in God and long for fresh and precious water for their lives.

The wells of salvation come from God who provides redemption for all human beings. It is there for us to accept joyfully: the Living Water, Jesus!

† Let us pray for countries and peoples facing lack of water; let us pray for those thirsting for justice; may the river of healing waters flow in our lives and in our world.

For further thought

Wells were often sites of conflict between people in the Bible, as in our time. What can you do to cut down on your use of water at home and in your church community?

Friday 10 May
A hymn to Jesus

Read Colossians 1:15–20

For in him all the fullness of God was pleased to dwell, and through him God was pleased to reconcile to himself all things, whether on earth or in heaven, by making peace through the blood of his cross.

(verses 19–20)

The reading today says more clearly than anywhere else in the Bible that things which have been disconnected and alienated from each other are recovered and reconciled in Christ. This is for everything and for everyone! I recall the Guarani myth that says that in the beginning was 'the completeness' – a stage where all things and beings were part of a Whole Being. Maybe this is another way to understand the fullness of God.

Studying composition I learned that the best quality of a masterpiece is unity. It does not matter how diverse the musical elements are or how many sound colours we want to combine; the principle of unity seeks vibrant harmonies.

Sometimes the right instrument is needed to achieve this unity: a kind of reconciliation of sounds and rhythms. That is what gives us the artistic fruition and for the artist the joy of accomplishment.

There will be always room in God's fullness. This is the joy of reconciliation: 'God's pleasure' to provide the reconciliation of Earth and heaven. Even when things on Earth do not seem reconciled, God's love in Jesus Christ will continuously work in us and through us to build peace and reconciliation.

Like my indigenous ancestors I am longing for a real fullness of life in the midst of my human life; a time when human beings and creation are held together in the breath of God. I believe God is calling us to be agents of reconciliation for such a time as this. A time when Jesus Christ will be all in all!

† Spacious God, help us to find a place in your roomy heart and extend our arms to all creation. May the fullness of your love dwell in our lives and in our world.

For further thought

God is calling us to be agents of reconciliation in our families, communities and world. Can we hear the call?

Saturday 11 May
The guardian of our souls

Read 1 Peter 2:21–25

… so that, free from sins, we might live for righteousness; by his wounds you have been healed. For you were going astray like sheep, but now you have returned to the shepherd and guardian of your souls.

(verses 24b–25)

In many languages, a large number of words connects ideas like healing, salvation and safety. In Portuguese, we have *salvar* (to save), *sanar* (to heal), *saúde* (health), *sã, são* (be sane), *estar a salvo* (be safe).

Looking at this text from 1 Peter, some of the verses speak clearly about healing and safety. Of course, God is the Shepherd, who guards, preserves, watches over, keeps and protects our souls and lives. But it is the expression 'guardian of your souls' that strikes me the most. Do we really need a guardian for our souls? Are we not self-sufficient?

As a child, I remember my parents rehearsing the great Christian hymn 'Te Deum Laudamus' in the small church choir. It was in Belém, close to the Amazon River estuary. It seemed so difficult to sing, but I was fascinated by the harmony of voices in a block of sounds.

Later, as a young student in Rio de Janeiro, I heard the 'Te Deum' sung as a celebration on the anniversary of the Military Revolution. I was so confused and disturbed that for a time I kept this hymn out of my memory and musical experience. Then I remembered the last phrase and prayer: 'O Lord, in thee, have I trusted: let me never be confounded.' I sang it and suddenly felt completely reconciled with my memories!

God is the guardian, the preserver, of our souls. God will never let us be confounded. God is the guardian of the treaty made between us and Christ. God will keep us safe, saved, sane. The insanity will not touch our lives.

† Guardian of my soul, I belong to you and you watch over me. If I go astray, please bring me to the safety of your shelter. Heal me with your love and care!

For further thought

Which expression from today's reading brought the most comfort to you?

Readings in Daniel –
1 Dramatic stories

Notes by **Noel Irwin**

In 2000 Belfast boy Noel moved to Sheffield, working as a community outreach worker for the Church of England, Superintendent of the Methodist Mission and Director of the Urban Theology Unit in Sheffield. He is now Tutor in Public Theology at Northern College, Manchester, and trains Church Related Community Work Ministers for the United Reformed Church. In his spare time he enjoys running in the hills and martial arts. Noel has used the NRSVA for these notes.

Sunday 12 May
Exiled youths

Read Daniel 1:1–20

But Daniel resolved that he would not defile himself with the royal rations of food and wine; so he asked the palace master to allow him not to defile himself.

(verse 8)

Daniel is a tale for our times. It is a story of exile, telling of the choices facing new arrivals to a country: assimilation or separation? New names or old? New food or traditional? The story has been played out countless times down through the centuries. The choice between these two options (sometimes one of them is forced on the new arrivals by the hosts) can have huge repercussions. It is generally accepted that the Jews of Denmark largely survived the Holocaust because for the Danish population there was no 'us' and 'them' in relation to the Jews, there was only 'us'.

So, do Daniel and his companions 'assimilate' or 'separate'? Well, to be honest, it is a bit of both. They accept the Babylonian education (indoctrination?) and the changing of their names, but then draw a line in the sand when it comes to the food of the conquerors (verse 8). Why food? Is it perhaps something to do with us being what we eat? Or is it actually nothing to do with the food and more to do with wanting to show they are not entirely under the control of the king and their ultimate allegiance is to their God?

† Reflect honestly as to where your ultimate allegiance lies. What is your line in the sand?

May

Readings in Daniel – 1 Dramatic stories

The golden image

> **Read Daniel 3:1–18**
>
> *If our God whom we serve is able to deliver us from the furnace of blazing fire and out of your hand, O king, let him deliver us.*
>
> (verse 17)

In chapter 3 Daniel is absent, and the focus shifts on to Shadrach, Meshach and Abednego. Sometimes it feels in the book of Daniel as if the kings are comedy villains, prepared to slaughter people on a whim to make themselves feel powerful. Here Nebuchadnezzar builds a statue for the people to worship. We do not know what the statue was an image of; a god or the king himself. We do know that worship is central in this chapter and the purpose of it is to boost the morale and identity of the empire, of which religion was an important part.

It seems Shadrach, Meshach and Abednego were punished for not worshipping the statue. I wonder: did they have the option of keeping a low profile and not attracting any attention from the state, or did they actively go looking for martyrdom? Much of the news at the moment is about the failings and foibles of those in power, so those Christians in positions of secular authority certainly need our support and prayers.

The contention around this passage has focused on the translation of verse 17. The NRSVA translation expresses doubt whether God can, or will, deliver them. Other translations remove that doubt. For me, while the theology of the NRSVA may be difficult, it expresses best the Aramaic text (remember, from 2:4 to the end of chapter 7 the language switches from Hebrew to Aramaic). This sense of doubt in our reading provides a relevance for Christians who may be facing persecution but finding no 'miraculous' deliverance though an assurance of the presence of God in their difficulties.

† Pray for Christians persecuted around the world.

For further thought

Find out more about people persecuted for their beliefs and take some action (an email or a letter) to help them.

Tuesday 14 May
Delivery from the furnace

> **Read Daniel 3:19–30**
>
> *They disobeyed the king's command and yielded up their bodies rather than serve and worship any god except their own God.*
>
> (verse 28b)

In Roman Catholic Bibles (based here on the Greek text of the Septuagint) an extra 66 verses are slotted in between verses 23 and 24 of Protestant Bibles. Part of this extra text appears in various prayer books as a hymn entitled 'a Song of Creation' or 'Benedicite'.

However, much of the Christian focus on this passage has been on the mysterious fourth figure, who appears in verses 24–25. The build-up to this has been the mention of how the three men are bound; then three become four with them unbound and walking around unharmed. We are told the fourth figure '"has the appearance of a god"'. The biblical text does not tell us who this person is. In verse 28 Nebuchadnezzar speculates that the figure is an angel. I see a parallel in chapter 6 when Daniel is thrown into the den of lions; the interpretation of Daniel himself is: 'My God sent his angel and shut the lions' mouths' (verse 22). Saying this however, it is hardly surprising that much Christian interpretation of this story has identified the figure with Christ.

While you will read these notes in May, I am actually writing these notes just before Christmas. So, as I read this passage from Daniel I became very conscious of Matthew 1:23 where the baby Jesus is identified as Emmanuel, God is with us. This has been the experience and testimony of countless Christians throughout history that God in Jesus Christ has been present to them in a very deep and special way in times of suffering and difficulty.

† Loving God, we pray for those known to us who are suffering, in whatever way, today. We pray Emmanuel God with us for your presence and peace to be real and known to them. Amen.

For further thought

In the Old Testament, salvation is predominantly a this-worldly event. What stories of deliverance and rescue have you heard recently?

Nebuchadnezzar's dream

Read Daniel 4:1–18

I saw a dream that frightened me; my fantasies in bed and the visions of my head terrified me.

(verse 5)

Today our passage begins with a little bit of a puzzle. The end of chapter 3 in Aramaic is the beginning of chapter 4 in the English translations. Which view you take on this depends on whether Nebuchadnezzar's praise of God is best seen as the conclusion of the story of the furnace, or should it be the introduction to his second dream?

The key theme in this passage is the sovereignty of God. One of the reasons a number of people think the praise of Nebuchadnezzar belongs at the beginning of chapter 4 is how it fits in so well with this theme. You have the most powerful figure of his time, a non-Jew, acknowledging the sovereignty of the God of Daniel, Shadrach, Meshach and Abednego. Like the earlier dream of Nebuchadnezzar I am sure this dream seems rather odd to us. While later in the chapter we receive the interpretation of Daniel, the second half of verse 17 makes it clear the dream is about the sovereignty of God.

For those faithful Jews reading the account of Daniel we should not underestimate how difficult it may have been for them to accept stories like this, where they are being told that God is really in control, when the reality is that their nation and their lives are under the authority of foreign powers. The book of Daniel is really interesting because of this question of how the people of God should respond to ungodly regimes. Never mind the question as to why God allows such regimes – Daniel provides us with pictures of both compliance and resistance.

† Our sovereign God, show us when we should be compliant with the powers that be and when we should resist them. Amen.

For further thought

What are some examples of faithful people who have opposed political powers? Do you think faithful people can ever avoid confrontation with powers big or small?

Thursday 16 May
Nebuchadnezzar eats grass

Read Daniel 4:19–37

Now I, Nebuchadnezzar, praise and extol and honour the King of heaven, for all his works are truth, and his ways are justice; and he is able to bring low those who walk in pride.

(verse 37)

It is no surprise that verse 19 stresses how frightened Daniel is. I mean, the job God has given him to do is simply to say something really difficult to the ruler of the most powerful empire in the world at incredible risk to his own life. What can possibly go wrong? Here, Daniel operates as one of God's prophets and yet manages to do it in a way which has both clarity and sensitivity. To be able to hold both of those things together is quite an achievement.

Often we perhaps either shy away when we need to say a difficult thing – this could be to a colleague, friend, family member or someone from your church – or we give the right message but in a way which alienates the recipient from actually listening to us. There are many examples of that among the prophets of the Hebrew scriptures.

This is the last appearance of Nebuchadnezzar in the book of Daniel. Are verses 34–37 an account of the conversion of the king to Judaism? That does seem unlikely; perhaps he came to a position where he worshipped God among other gods. But in his final words in Daniel we see someone who has become humble, with a recognition that his own power and glory are only for a time, while the power and glory of God are everlasting. I cannot help thinking if only some of the prominent political figures of our world could have a similar experience to Nebuchadnezzar, in terms of recognising their own finitude and creatureliness, our world would be a better and safer place.

† Lord, when we know the right thing to do and say, may we have the courage and indeed the sensitivity of a Daniel to speak and act clearly.

For further thought

How should the church, locally, nationally and internationally, speak truth to power?

Friday 17 May
Ghostly writing

> **Read Daniel 5:1–9, 17–30**
>
> *'You have praised the gods of silver and gold, of bronze, iron, wood, and stone, which do not see or hear or know; but the God in whose power is your very breath, and to whom belong all your ways, you have not honoured.'*
>
> (verse 23b)

Chapter 5 starts with a bit of a bump! Without so much as a goodbye Nebuchadnezzar is gone and Belshazzar arrives without any introduction or indication of how much time has passed. Anyhow, we have arrived at a very posh event. The focus of the text is not so much the 'poshness' but on the use, or rather misuse, of the vessels from the temple in Jerusalem which Nebuchadnezzar had taken.

In the book of Daniel so far, and indeed in the rest of the book, visions and dreams are the way God has communicated. In contrast the incident (verses 5–9) of a visible hand writing on the wall is very different. Daniel though is called to do what Daniel does – and what a contrast between the prophet in the last chapter who speaks out diplomatically, and the one here who proclaims to a foreign king words the great Hebrew prophets could have spoken to kings of Judah and Israel. In Ireland we would say he does not miss him and hit the wall!

One of the legacies of this passage is the phrase which has come into the English language, though very few people nowadays would have any concept it comes from the book of Daniel, 'the writing is on the wall'. In thinking about the book of Daniel I have over the last while heard people ask 'What is the writing on the wall?' in relation to Brexit or Trump. It seems even in our days we need a Daniel to interpret and show the justice of God where it is sorely needed.

† Loving God, show us how you act in the world. Amen.

For further thought

I was taught that prophecy in the Bible was 'forth – telling' not 'fore – telling'. What does 'forth – telling' mean in your context?

Saturday 18 May
Daniel in the lions' den

Read Daniel 6:1–24

So Daniel was taken up out of the den, and no kind of harm was found on him, because he had trusted in his God.

(verse 23b)

Daniel is now on to his third king and it is all going very well as he gets promoted to third in the kingdom. Then it all goes pear-shaped when he experiences professional jealousy and scheming. He is forced to decide where his ultimate loyalty lies: is it with his career or his faith? Is it with his king or his God?

When I was in Sunday school there was a picture on the wall of Daniel in the lions' den. We also used to sing a chorus where the refrain was 'Dare to be a Daniel'. It is such a well-known story and the focus is on the faithfulness of Daniel because of which God saves him from becoming the main course for the lions. But somehow the politics was all left out of the story. We have seen elsewhere in the book how the options of compliance and resistance to the state have both been taken.

In the New Testament Jesus is presented with a similar choice between God and Caesar where he gives both a clever and an ambivalent answer. In Romans 13 Paul seems to suggest compliance. Revelation 13 sees the Roman state as being demonic and to be resisted at all costs. Despite the political sanitisation of the story of Daniel, the God or Caesar choice, whether with or without lions, confronts us still and is one we cannot avoid. Ultimately Daniel's answer was the same as that of Peter and the apostles in Acts 5:29: 'We must obey God rather than any human authority.' What is your answer?

† Reflect on how important prayer is to you. Is it important enough for you to risk your life for it?

For further thought

Darius says, 'Tremble and fear before the God of Daniel' (verse 26). There is not much trembling and fearing before God nowadays – do you think that is good or bad?

Readings in Daniel – 2 Dramatic visions

Notes by **Mark Woods**

Mark is a Baptist Minister and writer. After pastoring two churches, he joined the *Baptist Times* and then the *Methodist Recorder*. He now serves as editor of online journal *Christian Today* (christiantoday.com). Author of *Does the Bible Really Say That?* (Lion Hudson), he runs unenthusiastically to keep fit and reads a lot. Mark has used the NIVUK for these notes.

Sunday 19 May
God's power in a wicked world

Read Daniel 7:1–18

'As I looked, thrones were set in place, and the Ancient of Days took his seat. His clothing was as white as snow; the hair of his head was white like wool. His throne was flaming with fire, and its wheels were all ablaze.'

(verse 9)

Parts of the book of Daniel – like this one – belong to a kind of writing called 'apocalyptic', meaning 'hidden'. Revelation in the New Testament is the same. It uses symbolic language to refer to real situations and future events. It's highly coloured and dramatic, and it's designed to horrify and terrify. Those who first read it or heard it would have understood more clearly than we do the references to the kingdoms of the time – the Babylonians, the Persians and the Greeks.

But the fact that all this happened a long time ago doesn't mean it's ancient history. It is a present reality. There are great and wicked powers at work in the world. We live in a dangerous time. Daniel – like Revelation – is not just about the world as it was, it's about the world as it is – and the world has beasts with teeth and claws.

However, once we have been terrified by this vision, there's another. God is enthroned in power and glory. His authority extends over the beasts. And he gives it to 'one like a son of man', who receives an 'everlasting kingdom'. It is right to read this as a reference to Christ, but in context the 'son of man' refers to God's whole people of Israel. God fulfils his purposes through them – and through him.

† God, the world can be a frightening place, and I do not always feel safe. Help me to trust in your faithful loving-kindness.

Monday 20 May
Trials will have an end

Read Daniel 8:1–14

'How long will it take for the vision to be fulfilled – the vision concerning the daily sacrifice, the rebellion that causes desolation, the surrender of the sanctuary and the trampling underfoot of the Lord's people?'

(verse 13)

This vision is a way of giving a history lesson – but the lesson isn't just about the past. The ram is the powerful Persian Empire; the goat is the Macedonian or Greek Empire under Alexander the Great, who overthrew it. When he died (the broken horn) his empire divided into four (the four horns) under his generals. One of them, Antiochus Epiphanes, became very strong. He was a brutal ruler who tried to impose Greek culture on Judea and profaned the temple by sacrificing a pig on the altar – the 'rebellion that causes desolation' (verse 13). His actions sparked a successful revolt, but not until the people had suffered greatly and seen their precious faith trampled underfoot.

Daniel asks how long the suffering will last. The number is perhaps not very important, though lots of people have tried to work out what it means and apply it to modern politics. The point is that the suffering will end. When God's people are enduring terrible oppression and see everything they have treasured destroyed, it's tempting to believe that nothing will ever get better. But Daniel says, 'Have faith.'

If we are living in peace and safety, we might still apply these words to our own lives; we might very well go through times when we are bruised and battered by what life throws at us. But these words are profoundly relevant in places where the forces of hell have been unleashed against the Church – in Iraq or Syria, for instance. The powers of evil are limited. The sanctuary will be restored.

† God, when the past weighs heavy on me and the present seems unbearably hard, help me to trust in your glorious future and not to doubt your purposes for me.

For further thought
Ultimately, Christians don't just believe in healing, but in resurrection. Even when everything is gone, God can bring new life.

The pressure to conform

Read Daniel 8:15–27

'He will cause deceit to prosper, and he will consider himself superior. When they feel secure, he will destroy many and take his stand against the Prince of princes. Yet he will be destroyed, but not by human power.'

(verse 25)

Gabriel's explanation of the dream provides the key for Daniel's readers to understand what's happening in terms of their own times. But those times are a long way from ours. What does Gabriel say to us?

One answer is to say that these apocalyptic books have a double significance. They are about real historical events in the past, but they are about things that happen all the time, too. Nations do behave like beasts, and so do individuals. There is something terribly familiar about the 'fierce-looking king' of verses 23–25. He is Antiochus, who tried to wipe out Jews and Judaism. But he is any number of others, too. We might think of Hitler, or Stalin, or Pol Pot – bloodthirsty tyrants who caused the deaths of millions and developed perverted personality cults that gave them extraordinary influence over their people. Similar sorts of rule can still be found in parts of the world today.

But that's rather easy to say if you are living in a Western democracy, as I do. It means the problem is always somewhere else. The fierce king will be a 'master of intrigue' (verse 23) and will 'cause deceit to prosper' (verse 25). We need to look to our own nations and cultures, too. For us, the king might not even have a face. He might be nationalism, or greed for consumer goods, or the pressure to conform to a godless society. Antiochus' great crime was that he wanted Jews to be like everyone else. Many people today want the same thing from Christians.

† God, help me to remember who I am by your grace – called to be a citizen of a different kingdom, even when it's hard. And bless those who are persecuted for righteousness' sake.

For further thought

Can we discern the enemies we face in today's world? How can we resist the pressure to conform and be like everyone else?

Wednesday 22 May
A humble prayer for mercy

Read Daniel 9:1–19

'We do not make requests of you because we are righteous, but because of your great mercy. Lord, listen! Lord, forgive! Lord, hear and act! For your sake, my God, do not delay, because your city and your people bear your Name.'

(verses 18b–19)

Daniel's response to the humiliation of his country is to pray – and his prayer is a wonderful example of what a mature, thoughtful prayer of faith can be. He is clear-eyed about the faults of his people and his own faults. And we recognise this in our own time, too: when nations forget God, bad things happen.

Most of Daniel's prayer is an acknowledgement of shortcomings. We are not always so disciplined in our own prayers; a hasty confession, and then it's on to more pleasant themes. Daniel is remorseless in analysing what has gone wrong.

He sees the destruction of Judea as a consequence of the people's sin. Chapters like this have led people to think that when something goes wrong in their own lives, God is punishing them. That's a spiritually damaging interpretation that doesn't find much support in the Bible; the fact that God may have done it to Israel doesn't mean he's doing it to us.

Daniel's prayer, moreover, doesn't end with God's judgement. He reminds God (as if God needs reminding!) of his mercies in the past, when he brought the people out of Egypt. He asks for restoration and forgiveness. He puts God first, asking him to bring glory to himself in restoring the nation ('your city and your people bear your Name'). And he pleads not on the grounds that they deserve it, but just because God is merciful.

Daniel prays a priestly prayer for the nation. But he offers us a way of praying for ourselves, too.

† God, I know I deserve nothing from you, but you are loving and merciful. So I ask forgiveness for my sins, and I pray that I may bring glory to you by how I live.

For further thought

What lessons can I learn from the world around me today? How can I see God at work in things that happen?

May

Readings in Daniel – 2 Dramatic visions

A word of heavenly encouragement

Read Daniel 10:1–21

Again the one who looked like a man touched me and gave me strength. 'Do not be afraid, you who are highly esteemed,' he said. 'Peace! Be strong now; be strong.' When he spoke to me, I was strengthened and said, 'Speak, my lord, since you have given me strength.'

(verses 18–19)

Daniel is not exactly despairing – he is, after all, a man of faith. But he is deeply troubled at the state of his people. At this moment he sees a vision that will give him a completely different perspective on what is happening. Rather than the messy business of politics and the clashes of human empires, he sees a spiritual reality behind it all. The man he sees by the banks of the Tigris is described as a being of overwhelming splendour, of more-than-human majesty. No wonder Daniel's face turned pale and he had 'no strength left' (verse 7).

The key to this passage is understanding that it opens a window onto a different reality. The 'one who looked like a man' (verses 16, 18) speaks of spiritual warfare. The people of God are engaged in a greater struggle than they know. There are battles in the heavenly realms that are only glimpsed by those on Earth.

At one level this comes across almost as science fiction: the idea that there are ripples of cause and effect spreading out across the dimensions is one that's often been explored by fantasy writers. But if we're too literalistic about this we won't understand the truth behind what we read. In our lives today we can feel oppressed by powers greater than ourselves. We can have a sense of real evil at work in the world. Well, says Daniel, that may be: but look who we have fighting for us! He might face a temporary setback, but he is far too powerful to suffer defeat. So don't worry.

† God, help me to remember the spiritual realities behind the everyday world, and not to be afraid of the strength of the enemy; your angels are fighting for me.

For further thought

What difference does it make to how we live in the world if we are open to spiritual realities as well as material ones?

Friday 24 May
Swimming against the tide

Read Daniel 11:21–35

'Those who are wise will instruct many, though for a time they will fall by the sword or be burned or captured or plundered. When they fall, they will receive a little help, and many who are not sincere will join them.'

(verses 33–34)

In this passage we are back to Antiochus Epiphanes again, who sacrificed a pig – an unclean animal – on the altar in the temple in Jerusalem, defiling it in a horrific act of blasphemy. But the chapter is a wretched account of battles, plots and skirmishes, in which the kings of the North and South – the Ptolemies and the Seleucids, Alexander's successors – play their power games. There is no peace and no justice, and it culminates in Antiochus' 'Abomination of Desolation'. As well as his heartbreaking act of defilement, he killed many Jews in Jerusalem and sparked a bloody and ultimately successful rebellion against his rule.

Not everyone resisted the evil, though. Many went with the tide, some of the 'wise' among them. It was better to conform, they thought; better to keep their heads down. And if the scholars and pastors, the wise and respected leaders, were going astray, what chance was there for ordinary folk? In this light, one line in verse 32 stands out: 'the people who know their God will firmly resist him' (that is, the Enemy).

In other words, it isn't enough to take our cue from other people. We have to decide for ourselves to follow Christ and do what's right. The history of our own times is too much like Daniel's vision for comfort: endless wars and political intrigues that lead nowhere, and relentless pressure on God's people to conform and keep quiet. All the more reason then to be clear about what we believe, and who we follow.

† God, help me to stand up for what's right, even if it means standing on my own. Help me tell the difference between what's true and good, and what's deceptive and wrong.

For further thought

Sometimes it's easy to see an evil that has to be resisted; sometimes it isn't. How can we learn to be discerning?

May

Readings in Daniel – 2 Dramatic visions

145

The promise of resurrection

> **Read Daniel 12**
>
> *'Multitudes who sleep in the dust of the earth will awake: some to everlasting life, others to shame and everlasting contempt. Those who are wise will shine like the brightness of the heavens, and those who lead many to righteousness, like the stars for ever and ever.'*
>
> (verses 2–3)

The book of Daniel portrays a mighty struggle between good and evil. In the end, God will judge between the righteous and the unrighteous.

This is the first time in the Old Testament we read plainly about a resurrection and a final settlement of accounts. Something like it is necessary if we are to believe in a good God, because so many people die without ever receiving justice.

It's fascinating to see who is singled out for praise – those who are wise, and who 'lead many to righteousness'. In other words, wisdom is practical – it isn't just head knowledge, it leads to real goodness. And it is shared with others – wise people serve as examples to follow. It's worth asking ourselves whom around us we can influence for good, and how.

While this last chapter is full of joyful hope, it is clear-eyed about what God's people must go through first. It speaks of terrible distress. The wicked won't repent, but will still be wicked. The power of God's people will be 'finally broken' (verse 7).

At one level, this is about the dark days of Antiochus. But Jews have taken strength from them throughout their long history of oppression: God has not deserted them. And Christians today who face unimaginable trials, whether because they are actively persecuted or just because they are alive and human, and bad things do happen, can take comfort from the last message to Daniel: 'You will rest, and then at the end of the days you will rise to receive your allotted inheritance' (verse 13).

† God, thank you that when everything seems hopeless, your mercy endures forever. In the darkness of defeat, help me to trust in your glorious promise of resurrection.

For further thought

Who am I influencing for good? How am I learning wisdom, and how am I sharing it?

Struggles and surprises – 1 Struggles

Notes by **Stephen Willey**

 Stephen is a Methodist Minister who was involved in mission to the economic world. This included offering industrial chaplaincies and establishing a regional anti-trafficking network. With four churches in Birmingham, England, three in areas of multiple deprivation, Stephen is committed to seeing people's potential fulfilled within and beyond the church, especially among those who are young, vulnerable or living in challenging circumstances. Stephen has used the NRSVA for these notes.

Sunday 26 May
Jacob the wrestler

Read Genesis 32:22–32

Jacob said, 'I will not let you go, unless you bless me.' So he said to him, 'What is your name?' And he said, 'Jacob.' Then the man said, 'You shall no longer be called Jacob, but Israel, for you have striven with God and with humans, and have prevailed.'

(verses 26b–28)

I wasn't sure I'd keep the job I'd just been appointed to. In just a few weeks the company management had changed entirely and the chief executive didn't seem to think my face fitted. In an interview he asked, very pleasantly, if I'd bought my house yet. 'The church has sorted it out,' I said. His answer: 'Oh, okay then. Well, come back in two weeks and explain why we should keep you.' Sleepless nights followed as I struggled with what I should say and how I should respond. My struggles paid off on that occasion.

The day before Jacob was planning to meet his estranged brother again, he had a sleepless night. What sort of reception would he get? Feeling anxious, he spent the night wrestling and realised he was struggling with God. Jacob, who stole his father's blessing and was hoping for his brother's blessing, sees an opportunity to claim God's blessing as well. Jacob becomes wounded in the struggle but he receives God's blessing. Jacob, audacious and determined, leaves the encounter wounded and blessed! Perhaps as we reflect on struggles this week, Jacob can be our guide – one who saw that God's blessing comes *through* struggle, not by avoiding it.

† In my restless or sleepless nights, in my struggles with you, O God, dare I, like Jacob, demand a blessing?

Monday 27 May
Call me Mara

Read Ruth 1:1–21

'Call me no longer Naomi, call me Mara, for the Almighty has dealt bitterly with me. I went away full, but the Lord has brought me back empty; why call me Naomi when the Lord has dealt harshly with me, and the Almighty has brought calamity upon me?'

(verses 20–21)

In recent years I have been struck by the plight of many asylum seekers and refugees. Recently a local church provided fish and chips for refugee families. Fish and chips is a very English meal but it turned out that it was not the best food to share with the families we welcomed. After eating, no ketchup remained but quite a lot of chips were left. The families we served were thankful, but chips didn't really suit them. Coming from another reality and culture, having suffered risk, vulnerability and isolation, they were beginning to settle and embrace a new life, but they weren't ready for chips! Next time the church will try a different food. Welcoming others sometimes requires adaptation.

How could Naomi not adapt, see what Ruth had done for her and be joyful? Naomi wasn't returning empty at all, she was accompanied by King David's great-grandmother! Naomi's harsh words directed at God completely ignored Ruth's presence and potential. Maybe Naomi couldn't see through her grief that, although she had been through a terrible time, so had Ruth, her companion, now accompanying her to a strange land. Ruth, having lost her husband, chooses to go forward with her grumpy, bitter mother-in-law, however costly, risky, isolating and strange that may be. Despite Naomi's initial failure to recognise her value, Ruth brings new hope to challenging times, not just for Naomi, but to Bethlehem and all God's children. With the support of Boaz, in the arms of Naomi, Ruth's child begins a lineage which embraces the hope of a Messiah.

† God of mercy envelop, in your love, those who are lonely or grieving. Teach me the art of being welcoming to those in need without imposing my personal expectations upon them.

For further thought

How generous can my charity be? Can I accept lack of enthusiasm from someone who is grieving or sorrowful and still give my love?

Tuesday 28 May
Abigail's struggles

Read 1 Samuel 25:4–13, 23–31

[Abigail] fell at his feet and said, 'Upon me alone, my lord, be the guilt; please … hear the words of your servant. My lord, do not take seriously this ill-natured fellow Nabal; for as his name is, so is he; Nabal is his name, and folly is with him.'

(verses 24–25a)

Being a cyclist on British roads, I have come across some pretty ill-natured fellows. Occasionally a curse pierces the air as I'm cycling along. A van might come close as a passenger yells in my ear. Someone once spat at me in a park. When I'm cycling ill-naturedness can come close and I try (not always successfully) to respond with generosity and humour, aware that 'road rage' can spiral out of control.

Abigail demonstrates how, in spite of the difficulties of being married to an ill-natured husband, it is possible to alleviate the consequences of his arrogance. This man Nabal (meaning 'Fool') puts Abigail, along with her family and whole household, at risk. Abigail acts decisively without consulting her husband. Rather than wait to see what might happen as a result of Nabal's insulting behaviour, she rides out to David and skilfully turns back the potential violence of 400 men with swords coming to kill all the men in her household. David tells her that she is the reason he hasn't got blood on his hands.

Abigail's response shows that while small-minded ill-natured acts can precipitate terrible violence, violence can also be diverted. Even if things become very serious when those in power (like Nabal) are unable to be generous or (like David) increase the stakes by being intent on violent retribution, humility, generosity and humour can transform a situation. Abigail turns David around and prevents his anger boiling over into a massacre. The story of her wise intervention will be retold for generations to come.

† Help me to find a humble wisdom, generosity and humour when dealing with those who are ill-natured around me.

For further thought

How might I use wisdom, generosity and humour to turn round a situation at work or elsewhere where ill-naturedness is creating a hard-hearted response?

Wednesday 29 May
Elijah's broken night

Read 1 Kings 19:1–11

[Elijah said,] 'It is enough; now, O Lord, take away my life …' Then he lay down under the broom tree and fell asleep. The angel of the Lord came a second time, touched him, and said, 'Get up and eat, otherwise the journey will be too much for you.'

(verses 4b–5a, 7)

Worn out, fearful and grieving, Elijah says, 'It is enough; now … take my life.' But God has no intention of taking Elijah's life; rather, God wakes him, gives him nourishment and says he has a journey to go on. Things look hopeless and Elijah cannot see a future, but God still desires a unique and fulfilling life for him.

When dry-mouthed, we feel we cannot eat as fear or grief overwhelms us, sometimes someone comes to us and offers a drink or something to eat. The Salvation Army have a reputation in Britain for doing just that. They find a place for someone freed from human trafficking by a police raid, or they set up near to the site of a disaster in which people have been traumatised, shocked and grief-stricken. A cup of tea and gentle heart cannot change the terrible facts of a situation but they give a person a brief respite from the enormity of what they have experienced.

A difficult political situation with all sorts of threats and difficulties faces Elijah. His is the only voice speaking on God's behalf. He is threatened on all sides, terrified, alone and exhausted, and then an angel, God's messenger, comes: 'Get up and eat, otherwise the journey will be too much for you.'

When things seem totally pointless or hopeless, taking a drink or a bite to eat can be a powerful expression of faith. Jesus, on the night he was betrayed, took bread, and when he had given thanks he broke it and he gave it to his disciples.

† Slowly pray the Lord's Prayer. Note the demand for daily bread in it and consider what God would have you do when you have been nourished by it.

For further thought

What overwhelming challenges have I been able to overcome? Has my struggle helped others? Could my struggle help others in the future?

Thursday 30 May (Ascension Day)
Job loses all

Read Job 1:6–22

Then Job arose, tore his robe, shaved his head, and fell on the ground and worshipped. He said, 'Naked I came from my mother's womb, and naked shall I return there; the Lord gave, and the Lord has taken away; blessed be the name of the Lord.'

(verses 20–21)

Sometimes shock leaves a person only able to do what they have always done. Perhaps this is why Job worships God and blesses God's name at such a terrible time. When the news is full of fear and dread it seems that Job goes into a kind of automatic response as familiar words of worship appear on his lips.

I have seen shock and grief take people in different directions, but I am often surprised when someone, on receiving bad news about a loved one, is still able to participate in worship. I think of a father whose young daughter is going blind. He is distraught but, nevertheless, remains involved in worship. Or the widow who, after losing her husband of 50 years, comes the following Sunday and helps out a struggling mother.

Later in Job's story there comes a time when God's response, though far from straightforward, is full of wonders. Then, Job will discover that in struggling and questioning he gets to know God better. But at this point, when Job has just heard devastating news, he shaves his head and offers a prayer to God as is his practice, for he is a pious man.

Ascension Day reminds us that Christ left his disciples despite the fact that times of struggle and challenge were ahead. The disciples cannot just gaze at the sky where Jesus departed, they must discover what it means to be resilient in a hostile world. They do so through a pattern of daily prayer, fellowship and the breaking of bread. This, with the Holy Spirit, nourishes their hope.

† Look up at the sky today as often as you are able and remember Jesus' ascension. Then bring to mind someone you know who is struggling from grief, loss or sorrow.

For further thought

Have I ever surprised myself with my reaction to bad news? Is there some way I can support others through tragedy or loss?

Friday 31 May
Weeping prophet

Read Jeremiah 9:1–6

*O that my head were a spring of water, and my eyes a fountain of tears,
so that I might weep day and night for the slain of my poor people! O
that I had … a traveller's lodging-place, that I might leave my people
and go away from them!*

(verses 1–2a)

When a child falls over and is hurt, his or her face crumples, lungs
open and out comes a cry of the pain and desolation. Then, often
reaching through tears, the child tries to make contact with the
one who will provide comfort and take them away from this
overwhelming sorrow or pain. Jeremiah's tears and his longing to
get 'away from it all' may be familiar to both parents and children.

The idea that Jeremiah could escape from a painful situation
full of grief, and from the people who surround him with bad
behaviour, oppression and lies may be appealing, but it isn't
realistic. Feeling completely betrayed, Jeremiah laments, but where
else can he go through his tears except back to God? Jeremiah's
struggles and lamentations keep his prophetic voice true and help
him to continue saying what needs to be said. His message at this
point is not an easy one. The One he is reaching out to, on the
nation's behalf, to comfort and restore them, cannot work with a
people who are false and have no love for God.

Jeremiah's tears well up out of his inner conflict as he feels the
pain and desolation caused by his kinsfolk, but he remains a true
prophet, as he continues to reach through the tears to grasp the
One who alone can comfort the people.

† Pray for the courage to reach for God in the times when the tears flow.

For further thought

How do you usually reach out to God? What sort of prophet might
God be calling you to be?

Saturday 1 June
Jesus' sleepless night

Read Matthew 26:36–46

And going a little farther, [Jesus] threw himself on the ground and prayed, 'My Father, if it is possible, let this cup pass from me; yet not what I want but what you want.' Then he came to the disciples and found them sleeping.

(verses 39–40a)

The person I was visiting was in the kitchen making me a cup of tea. It was a lull in a very busy week. My head started to feel heavy, my eyelids seemed to have a will of their own, the heaviness of sleep was upon me and I drifted. Sleep completely overwhelmed me until cups rattling on saucers shocked me into wakefulness! I don't think my host noticed, but when the disciples fell asleep Jesus noticed, and he was disappointed. Those lionhearted disciples had abandoned him.

Peter, willing to do anything for Jesus, even to die for him, was unable to keep his eyes open on this night of betrayal. Alone and desperate, a terrible struggle is taking place in Jesus' heart. Perhaps he is beginning to sense the abandonment which will reach its height upon the cross. No comfort comes from those who have been closest to him and are still just a stone's throw away. The disciples sleep on, and Jesus strives to find a way forward with God. 'Not what I want but what you want,' he cries as in humility he consents to the Father's will for the sake of those he loves. Awake in the shadows, Jesus accepts a journey which will take his disciples beyond death. Having broken and shared bread, he alone remains awake. On a sleepless night, amid overwhelming shadows, not yet pierced by the light of resurrection, Jesus' struggle becomes the source of our hope.

† Risen Christ, you prayed that you might do the Father's will even though you were vulnerable and alone. Accompany us on our journey and in our struggles strengthen us to do your will.

For further thought

The mystic Julian of Norwich (1342–c. 1416) asked to see Jesus' sufferings on the cross. How is it possible to pray alongside Christ in his suffering?

Struggles and surprises – 2 Surprises

Notes by **Raj Bharat Patta**

 Raj is an ordained minister in the Andhra Evangelical Lutheran Church in India, and recently completed his PhD at the University of Manchester. He now works with the Stockport Methodist Circuit. As a creative Bible study facilitator, Raj engages with communities to bring transformation. He is married to Shiny and they have two sons, Jubi and Jai ho. He blogs at thepattas. blogspot.co.uk. Raj has used the NRSVA for these notes.

Sunday 2 June
Ascension: a bodily Jesus ascends into heaven

Read Acts 1:1–11

When he had said this, as they were watching, he was lifted up, and a cloud took him out of their sight.

(verse 9)

The early Church and the early Jewish communities were familiar with stories of ascensions into heaven from the lives of Enoch and Elijah, who were taken up into heaven. However, in defiance of the Roman Empire's injustice, God raised Jesus from death, proclaiming hope for all who undergo such unjust trials and executions. Post-resurrection, Jesus appeared to his disciples in his body and ate with them while bodily present, and then ascended into heaven bodily. The material broken-crucified-risen body now ascends into heaven, for the broken body becomes the site of a transfigured body, seated at the right hand of the Father of the Holy Trinity.

The logic of empire, which is demonstrated by violence, seeks to destroy bodies by killing, to scatter bodies through terror, to crucify bodies unjustly, to 'disappear' bodies through torture, and to disintegrate all life. In contrast to this, the love of Trinity surprises as they receive and embrace bodies into their fold, and the ascension of a bodily Jesus is a foretaste to such a reception of material bodies. Those who are embraced by the love of Trinity are called to receive the broken-hearted and partake in the healing of their broken bodies.

Like those early followers of Jesus, where can we be surprised by God in our Bible reading this week?

† Gracious God, surprise us today and every day this week by your powers of life, that we might live for your glory. Amen.

Monday 3 June
Courageous discipleship

Read Genesis 38:12–30

As she was being brought out, she sent word to her father-in-law, 'It was the owner of these who made me pregnant.' And she said, 'Take note, please, whose these are, the signet and the cord and the staff.' Then Judah acknowledged them and said, 'She is more in the right than I, since I did not give her to my son Shelah.'

(verses 25–26a)

When the sexual abuses of a famous Hollywood producer were exposed, the '#MeToo' campaign gathered speed around the world. Many women spoke out courageously against the abuses they had faced in their lives. In today's text, Tamar the ancestor of Jesus spoke out courageously to expose her father-in-law who made her pregnant. It took Judah by surprise, for he had to acknowledge that she was more in the right.

How is this surprising story the word of God? Perhaps by recording such a story in scripture, it exposes how in the Hebrew society then, and even in today's society, domestic abuse and sexual violence continue to happen. Such stories call the readers to expose perpetrators of abuse, as part of the Christian commitment to justice, and to partake in contesting and overthrowing the domination of patriarchy and all such powers. Perhaps also this text is an invitation to take courage like Tamar, to speak openly about the abuse that she had to go through. I believe Jesus inherited this courage from her, for Christian discipleship today is all about being a courageous disciple of Jesus Christ, at a time when injustice and discrimination take centre stage.

Finally, this text invites us to locate God in the voice and action of Tamar, because Judah asked that she be burned for her act. God's voice is a voice of justice, for God chooses to be found among those vulnerable voiceless communities who are abused, discriminated against and crushed by violence. A surprising God, indeed.

† God who in Jesus came from the ancestry of Tamar, grant us her courage to be bold in exposing abuse and injustice happening in our communities. Amen.

For further thought
Who are the people of courage around you, speaking out against injustice in your community?

Tuesday 4 June
The donkey speaks

Read Numbers 22:21–35

*Then the Lord opened the mouth of the donkey, and it said to Balaam,
'What have I done to you, that you have struck me these three times?'*

(verse 28)

We have seen films where animals talk to each other in human language, like *Finding Dory*, *Fantastic Mr. Fox* etc., and for kids of this generation, who have grown up watching these films, animals speaking in human wods is not a surprise. In the times of Ancient Israel, God surprises God's people with things they have not imagined. In this story, God opened the mouth of the faithful friend of the prophet Balaam, a donkey, who speaks back to Balaam when he turned away from what is pleasing to God. Funnily enough, in this passage, the angel of God is seen by a donkey and not by the prophet. The vision of God is given to a pack animal and concealed from a human being. When Balaam strikes his faithful friend, who had carried him faithfully, the donkey expresses his anger and exposes Balaam's impatience and cruelty towards him. At the end, Balaam repents that he had sinned.

Can we be surprised by a God who speaks to us not just through humans, but through his creation, to expose our disobedience to God? The presence of God is seen first by the rest of creation and only last by humanity. God's presence is spread across the creation equally, not just among the righteous and unrighteous, but also the human and non-human. Be prepared for a surprise today, that God is speaking to you through the unspeakable, and through the unimagined.

† God of all creation, help us to recognise your voice among who we think are incapable of carrying God's voice. Amen.

For further thought
What part of God's creation might be speaking to you today?

Wednesday 5 June
Peter's surprise vision

Read Acts 10:1–15

But Peter said, 'By no means, Lord; for I have never eaten anything that is profane or unclean.' The voice said to him again, a second time, 'What God has made clean, you must not call profane.'

(verses 14–15)

A public notice was posted in the office canteen of a leading Indian daily newspaper, *The Hindu*. From now on, employees were not allowed to eat non-vegetarian food on its premises, the notice explained, 'as it causes discomfort to the majority of employees who are vegetarian'. The notice was a small indication that notions of purity and pollution have been operating forces for caste practices. Vegetarianism, which is an upper-caste norm, is treated as pure, and based on its normativity the rest are considered polluted, profane and discriminatory.

The text today challenges such notions of purity and profanity, for Peter wanted to uphold his purity of not eating what is shown to him. God surprises Peter by challenging him to overcome such differentiations and to affirm all creation equally, which is the norm of the divine God. This text therefore calls us to contest dominant norms that exist in our societies, for God surprises communities by turning up in sites of so-called 'profanity'.

Let us not judge people based on their food habits, practices and histories, for what God has made no one should call profane. God also surprises by speaking the unconventional, for Peter did not anticipate that God would call him to eat what is present in front of him. Peter wanted to uphold his racially dominant identity by not eating unclean food, but God challenges Peter to identify with other people whose taste buds are not similar to his.

Our world is still divided by food today. The message of the gospel is that food builds communities, for Jesus the bread of life is inviting us all to join together, giving up our prejudices.

† Gracious God, prepare us to be surprised by your unconventional visions and voices. Amen.

For further thought

In what ways does food divide your community? In what ways does it bring it together?

Surprise hidden treasure

Read Matthew 13:44–45

The kingdom of heaven is like treasure hidden in a field, which someone found and hid; then in his joy he goes and sells all that he has and buys that field.

(verse 44)

In his famous book *The Alchemist,* Paulo Coelho tells a story of a shepherd boy Santiago, who follows his dreams of finding a treasure. On finding it he was surprised to realise that he was not only seeking the treasure of his destiny but was living out his destiny in trying to find it.

The gospel text for today is from Jesus' parables about the kingdom of God, which is a surprise. When someone finds a treasure in a field, why does he go and sell all that he has and buy the entire field? The mystery of the kingdom of God is not that it is about a precious treasure, but rather about finding the hidden treasure and then buying the entire field, which has that precious treasure in it. God in Jesus surprises us by saying that the kingdom of God is not an exclusive club of those few 'chosen' 'treasured' ones. Rather it is a field for all, for the redeemed field contains the treasure; the treasure does not contain the field. God in Jesus surprises us to say that the kingdom of God is already present in the field, and it is for us to seek and find it, and make it open and public for all people of God, not limiting it to denominations or territories or religions. The kingdom of God is that reality for which, when we seek and find it, we are called to sell all our possessions, for all that matters is to own the Kingdom of God alone. The spirituality of the kingdom of God is based on selling up and being open to all.

† Gracious God, help us to celebrate that your reign on Earth is an all-inclusive, welcome place for all creatures of God. Amen.

For further thought

What in your life might the God of surprises be asking you to sell in order to gain the kingdom?

Friday 7 June
Surprise tax!

Read Matthew 17:24–27

Jesus said to him, 'Then the children are free. However, so that we do not give offence to them, go to the lake and cast a hook; take the first fish that comes up; and when you open its mouth, you will find a coin; take that and give it to them for you and me.'

(verses 26b–27)

In the Matthew passage today, Jesus is asked about paying the temple tax in his fishing village. Peter replied 'Yes', and Jesus explains to him that children are exempted from paying temple taxes, for it is God's house. To understand this story, we need to recognise that in Jesus' time, there were two kinds of taxes: one levied by the Roman emperor for the running of their colony, and the other by Jewish leaders for the running of the temple. And it was the Pharisees who upheld the norm of paying taxes to the temple. There were others who did not feel obliged to pay the temple tax. Either in protest against the empire or for their own economic or religious reasons they did not pay.

The temple authorities wanted to know if Jesus was willing to pay these temple taxes and they ask Peter. Peter replies that Jesus will pay, for which Jesus had to engage in conversation with him, explaining that all children of God are exempted from paying these taxes collected in the name of God in the temple. In other words, by his reply, Jesus was explaining to him that he is the Son of God, the child of God, and for all children of God like his disciples it wasn't obligatory to pay these taxes. In his own way, Jesus was exposing the economic poverty in his times; with such meagre wages it was not possible for his sisters and brothers to pay, unless they found coins in the mouths of fish.

† Dear God of justice, thank you for assuring us that we are your children and co-heirs with Jesus Christ, for you have saved us only by your grace and not by our merit. Amen.

For further thought

What creative ways might Jesus find to address controversial political issues of our day?

Saturday 8 June
Coming of the Holy Spirit

> **Read Acts 2:1–13**
>
> *Divided tongues, as of fire, appeared among them, and a tongue rested on each of them. All of them were filled with the Holy Spirit and began to speak in other languages, as the Spirit gave them ability.*
>
> (verses 3–4)

The story of Pentecost happened at a time when there were fear, war and confusion among the disciples of Jesus Christ. Just after the resurrected Christ ascended into heaven, the Holy Spirit poured down on creation and the disciples of Jesus Christ were sent out. Interestingly, the God of Pentecost surprised everyone gathered there by not choosing to speak in any of the dominant languages of the day, either the language of the empire or the language of the temple. At Pentecost God spoke the language of the people in the communities. This is a call and a challenge to the Church today not to succumb to speaking the language of the powerful elite in the Church or the state but rather to speak and understand the language of those on the margins, the migrants. Unfortunately, we as a Church have typically chosen the language of the dominant and have not always considered the languages of the marginal people. Mind you, God doesn't choose one so-called 'official' tongue, for the God of Pentecost invites us to celebrate our diversities and our multicultural identities and strive to participate in the widening and deepening of God's reign here on Earth. As a Church, do we have a language? What language do we speak and hear? Is our language heard by the common people of our times?

Pentecost is a celebration of multilingualism and multiculturalism. With the recognition and acknowledgement of a multi-ethnic community with many languages, the early Church envisaged a heterogeneous community and celebrated it in their life and practice.

† God of Pentecost, pour on us your Spirit and help us to celebrate the gift of diversity you have given us. Amen.

For further thought

What other cultures around you may surprise you sometime soon?

Fruits of the Spirit

Notes by the **Revd Dr Jennifer H. Smith**

Jennifer is a Methodist Minister serving in London as the Superintendent of Wesley's Chapel and Leysian Mission, the church built for John Wesley and opened in 1778. She is committed to pastoral ministry, and teaches and visits widely. Jennifer is a US citizen, and has lived in the United Kingdom since 1993; she is married to an Anglican priest. Jennifer has used the NRSVA for these notes.

Sunday 9 June (Pentecost)
Love

Read Galatians 5:22–26

... the fruit of the Spirit is love, joy, peace, patience, kindness, generosity, faithfulness, gentleness, and self-control. There is no law against such things.

(verses 22–23)

Paul speaks of this list as one whole, one fruit together. And of course, fruit is designed both to feed folk who are hungry and to sow seed for the future. Fruit catches the eye – we climb fences to pick it ripe, and pay premium prices to get it even when wrapped in plastic. It is as if Paul is saying, '... rest in the grace of God, this is what your food will be and with this food you will feed others around you'.

Today is Pentecost, the day we celebrate the coming of the Spirit among the early disciples, a 'rush of violent wind' as they worshipped. That day brought harmony out of chaos, understanding from bewilderment. This fruit is still ours for the eating, and it is still as sweet.

Too often, this marvellous group of interrelated attributes gets treated like a 'to do' list by well-intentioned Christians, as if we could mark ourselves out of ten for each quality. Not so! It is neither a set of goals (however juicily laudable), nor a moral code. Here is the result of resting in God's grace, not a list of work to do to get it. Fruit, not works.

† You who feed and care, ripen our lives and sweeten our way. Amen.

Monday 10 June
Joy

Read Romans 15:13

May the God of hope fill you with all joy and peace in believing, so that you may abound in hope by the power of the Holy Spirit.

(verse 13)

Pause and think: with what do you associate joy? When do you remember having it? Myself, I associate joy with the freedom of walking out of an exam room, or discovering that someone unexpectedly loves me, or that something I had thought was closed is still a possibility. Even in the midst of doing something complicated or demanding like preaching or filling in a long form, joy is about a care-less security and sense of being in the right place, in God's time, and being entirely in the flow of the moment. Sometimes I notice joy only afterwards, looking back and observing myself. Paul in the letter to the Romans clearly associates joy with peace and hope: joy is not necessarily the same as pleasure or happiness.

I have a sense of joy as being hidden in plain sight, pervading the possibility of every moment if I can only get my anxiety, or pride, or complaint out of the way. I have a sense of joy as the eternal perspective that can come in the deepest grief or conflict. But here is the point: this gift is given not to those who are already wealthy in pleasure and care-less being.

Joy is offered specifically to those of us who are NOT abounding in hope, and still have hard things to do. Joy lives in the real world. It does not obscure bad feeling or avoid evil things, but persists among them.

† Give me joy in my heart, hope in my soul, love in my path this day. Amen.

For further thought

In a concordance, look up references to the command 'Rejoice'. In what situations does it occur?

Tuesday 11 June
Peace

Read John 16:33

'I have said this to you, so that in me you may have peace. In the world you face persecution. But take courage; I have conquered the world!'

(verse 33)

I love the full-page 'paradise holiday' advertisements in magazines or on the walls of busy train stations: there are white sand and shade, warmth and turquoise water. The message is, 'Come away, relax into an island idyll where you can forget to ask the hourly wages of local staff, enjoy without worrying where their children swim, and use fresh water for your Jacuzzi with abandon.'

I want these holidays, I want the 'peace' they offer. Don't we all deserve a bit of peace? Isn't that escape what we pay for? God is not against pleasure, nor relaxation. But God doesn't ask us to wait for peace until we can afford the private beach, and squint hard enough at it to make it seem our right by virtue of a handy credit card.

Today's verse gives us the last words Jesus spoke to his disciples at table at the Last Supper. Peace, this fruit of the Spirit, is not about escape from reality. Jesus is at pains to say, earlier in John 14:27, that his peace is not like that of the world: 'I do not give to you as the world gives.'

God's peace is not dependent on external things, but does transform our experience of external things. Peace is a gift from Jesus there for the asking. 'My peace I leave with you': quite literally, it is our inheritance. And in real peace, we will all get a decent wage, and share resources, and have clean water and rest.

† God of the busy unfinished tasks and unquiet spirit, give me peace today in all I do. Amen.

For further thought
What prevents you from feeling peaceful?

Wednesday 12 June
Patience

Read Romans 12:12

Rejoice in hope, be patient in suffering, persevere in prayer.

(verse 12)

Thinking about patience puts me in mind of a documentary I saw some years ago about an experiment with young children aged 3–5 years. They were placed by themselves in front of a luscious-looking marshmallow. They could either eat it at once, or wait 15 minutes and then be given two! Then they were left alone with the tape running.

As a watcher I laughed to recognise my own internal struggles in the far more honest reactions of the children: some just gobbled up the sweet, others tried to distract themselves by covering their eyes or singing, some stroked it or mimed eating it. Only 25 per cent were able to be patient and delay gratification for the whole 15 minutes. And this 'patience' correlated strongly with their success in later life.

The thing was, children who had been consistently neglected or even recently disappointed were most likely to eat the treat right away: they had little reason to trust.

The experience of having one's needs met teaches a careless lack of anxiety we would all hope for in our relationship with God. Perhaps this is why Paul links it with prayer: here is how we build our relationship and increase our trust in God's compassion for us.

Patience is much easier when we know from experience that goodness awaits us. I am sure those who truly 'live in the Spirit' will find patience an utterly predictable fruit of their relationship with God. And for those of us who find patience a more elusive gift, remember that God's patience with us is as infinite as grace.

† Give me patience, Good Lord. And help me to build patience in others. Amen.

For further thought

Pray the Lord's Prayer slowly and deliberately. Pause over the phrase, 'Give us this day our daily bread.' What do you actually hope for when you make this prayer?

Thursday 13 June
Faithfulness

Read Hebrews 11:1

Now faith is the assurance of things hoped for, the conviction of things not seen.

(verse 1)

To be assured of what I hope for, to be convicted that the good things I do not see right now will come to pass? Does this describe me? Does it describe you?

I would say I have faith, even that I am faithful, but some things I have gotten so used to as to accept as inevitable. I find it hard to hope, or have conviction that they will be different. I observe that children do starve in wartime. I see that folk who miss education in youth have a much harder life and fewer opportunities. I note that people who do not conform to culturally 'normal' standards of ability, appearance and behaviour are far more likely to get abuse in public places. Unlike me, God never gets 'used to' these seemingly inevitable truths. They are always shocking to God. And we love God for it! It is not for nothing that God's 'great faithfulness' is celebrated by the refrain of one of our most widely known and loved hymns.

If I think about it, I do have assurance in hope for a God who is faithful to the coming kingdom, not the world as it is. I am convicted that God's faithfulness awaits our movement for justice, for sharing, for peacemaking. Faithfulness to this God demands that I continue to treat the world as unfinished, that I not accept nor make peace with the world as it is. Faithfulness demands that I remain shocked by unequal situations, that I hope and am convicted they will not be so, despite their seeming inevitability.

It is God's great faithfulness to the world that keeps God at work in us, ever hoping for more abundant sharing, ever convicted that we will see the way to just living.

† Faithful God, give me endurance in times of disquiet, patience in times of change. Amen.

For further thought

'Our culture celebrates heroic, sacrificial faithfulness, even as we find it foolhardy.' Do you agree?

Friday 14 June
Gentleness

Read Colossians 3:12–13

As God's chosen ones, holy and beloved, clothe yourselves with compassion, kindness, humility, meekness, and patience.

(verse 12)

There is a sense, in considering gentleness, of power restrained. There is a sense of being alongside instead of striving or straining. I am remembering a man who was on the list to sleep in our church 'night shelter' one night several years ago. He arrived late, ranting and shouting, drunk, his face covered in blood. Attempts to restrain or reason with him made him more belligerent, and he was to be thrown out into the night.

Then there came a quieter minister of great experience. He was carrying a bowl of warm water and a soft cloth. 'See how soft this cloth is, see how lovely and warm the water is,' he said to me, not looking at the man next to me. 'I am just going to sit here, and see if anyone is cold and tired, and needs his face washing, with this warm water, this soft cloth.' He sat down.

The man and I both watched him, unspeaking. He sat a full ten seconds, and then the man sat next to him. We gently washed the man's face with the soft cloth and warm water, talking gently to each other about what we were doing, what we would do next, so he could see and know without having to give way or ask. Often in situations there is a right thing to do and a wrong thing to do, and then there is a question which cuts across both: how can I be a blessing? Gentleness is neither passive, nor a lack of strength. And it is a graceful gift, used well.

† Holy God, deal with me gently today, in my body, mind and spirit. Amen.

For further thought

Looking in a mirror, gently wash your own face, slowly with a soft sponge or cloth. Treat your face with gentle love. Remind yourself of God's care.

Saturday 15 June
Self-control

Read 2 Peter 1:5–7

For this very reason, you must make every effort to support your faith with goodness, and goodness with knowledge, and knowledge with self-control, and self-control with endurance, and endurance with godliness, and godliness with mutual affection, and mutual affection with love.

(verses 5–7)

If I'm honest, reading these verses just makes me exhausted. The 'reason' spoken of is to avoid the horrors of the corrupt world of lust, but the layers of scaffolding necessary make it a daunting prospect!

Self-control implies self-knowledge and self-awareness. It implies the existence of a critical gap of milliseconds between something happening, and my response to it. It assumes that in those milliseconds I can and will reflect and consider what I want to do, versus what I first rush into or react with. And then it implies that whatever happens during that millisecond will lead me to a better response than I might have first led with. It can be learned, and surely as the scripture suggests, it is easier with practice and in community with others.

But there are many stages there, in that process within that millisecond. And I am aware that I'm sometimes as likely to reflect my way out of a more contentious response I might have made, towards one that serves an end other than righteousness. Some things, like an experience of God's love, I hope will evoke our immediate, strong and clear response, uncensored by restraint.

Perhaps here is a clue to recovering a proper understanding of self-control: it might sometimes mean restraint, sometimes mean letting loose the depths of our spirit. It always means confidence in God's love for us and image in our deepest being. And I know I value it most in others when I find it least in myself, this fruit of the Spirit.

† Guide my senses, guard my thoughts, prevent my hands from harm. Amen.

For further thought

Are you aware of having been taught 'self-control'? By whom, and how? What is the difference between self-control and social appropriateness?

June

Fruits of the Spirit

Surprising women in the Bible – 1 Visionaries and prophets

Notes by **Lynne Frith**

Lynne loves playing with words – whether writing poems or prayers, playing Scrabble or messaging friends – and has a secret longing to write on walls with a spray can. The rest of the time she is a Methodist Presbyter in Auckland, Aotearoa (New Zealand), where she is privileged to serve with an inclusive, welcoming congregation. Lynne has used the NRSVA for these notes.

Sunday 16 June
Call the Midwife

Read Exodus 1:8–22

But the midwives feared God; they did not do as the king of Egypt commanded them ...

(verse 17)

I am an avid watcher of the British TV series *Call the Midwife*. As a former nurse, I can relate easily to the situations faced by the midwives: their joy at each new life brought into the world, their deep sorrow when a baby does not live, their determination to work for the health and well-being of the whole community.

Midwives know what is going on in the community. They see families at their most vulnerable and most hopeful moments. For Shiprah, Puah and their colleagues, being asked to kill babies must have been intolerable. Their inventiveness and faithfulness to their calling had a profound effect, not only on their community, but also on their own lives. Were these two the only ones who resisted, or are they representative of a wider group of midwives, all of whom collectively defied Pharaoh's orders? Whether alone or representative, the political action of these two women challenged the oppressive power of a new and unsympathetic king of Egypt.

This week, we read stories of political acts by women. Most are motivated by concern for the wider community. They are ancient stories that resonate with the stories of women's lives in the twenty-first century, in any part of the world.

† Give thanks to God for women of courage and faithfulness.

Monday 17 June
A first among women

Read Exodus 15:1–3, 19–21

Then the prophet Miriam … took a tambourine in her hand; and all the women went out after her …

(verse 20)

This year marks 60 years since Dame Revd Dr Phyllis Guthardt was ordained by the Conference of the Methodist Church in New Zealand, the first woman to be ordained in any denomination in Aotearoa New Zealand. The significance of this went largely unnoticed at the time. Dame Phyllis herself has reflected that she was responding to the call of God, and did not see herself as a 'first'. Subsequently, in 1985, Dr Guthardt was the first woman to become President of the Conference. In *A Kind of Opening*, a publication of the Wesley Historical Society to mark the 50th anniversary of Phyllis' ordination, a number of women reflect on the influence she was in their lives and ministries. Today, however, less than one third of the deacons and presbyters in the Church are women, and only eight women have ever been elected President of the Conference.

Verse 20 in today's text is the first time in the narrative that the sister of Moses and Aaron is named. Note that Miriam is described as Aaron's sister, without reference to Moses. Not only is she a prophet, but she is also a musician, and a leader among the women. The nameless sister who showed her initiative to keep the infant Moses safe is the first female prophet to appear in the Hebrew scriptures.

There is nothing in the narrative to indicate what qualities led to Miriam being identified as a prophet. Was her leadership exercised only among the women of the community? Was it only to fulfil ritual functions? Is the figure of Miriam representative of the wisdom and experience of women in general?

In many communities today, women's leadership continues to be behind the scenes, unacknowledged and unnamed.

† Pray for the work of leadership training for girls and young women in church and community.

For further thought

How is women's leadership reflected and named in your church? In your community?

Tuesday 18 June
Daughters have rights

Read Numbers 27:1–11

The daughters of Zelophehad are right in what they are saying; you shall indeed let them possess an inheritance …

(verse 7)

Mahlah, Noah, Hoglah, Milcah and Tirzah are the daughters of Zelophehad, and his only children. When their father died in the wilderness, the daughters challenged the laws of inheritance. Moses supported their cause, God looked favourably on their claim and a precedent was set for the Israelites.

Here we have an uncommon example in the scriptures of gender equality, recognising that the male line is not the only way of preserving inheritance.

It takes courage to challenge custom and tradition in order to bring about social change for justice and equality. Moreover, there may be other more pressing needs, like access to clean water, food security, healthcare and education, that take priority in a community's political agenda.

The World Young Women's Christian Association (the World YWCA) is one global organisation that is focused on empowering girls and young women with the provision of advocacy, leadership training and safe spaces.

In many countries, trade unions advocate for pay equity, to ensure that women and men get equal pay for equal work.

In addition to lobbying groups, there are individuals like Malala Yousafzai, a Pakistani activist for female education and the youngest winner of the Nobel Peace Prize. Through their courage and challenges to power and tradition, they give voice to the voiceless.

We too are called to stand with those who are crying out for justice, fairness and equality.

† Pray for gender equality in all aspects of human relationship and community.

For further thought

Encourage your faith community to become a member of an organisation that promotes gender equality.

Wednesday 19 June
All in good faith

Read Joshua 2:1–24

'... since I have dealt kindly with you, swear to me by the Lord that you in turn will deal kindly with my family. Give me a sign of good faith that you will spare my father and mother, my brothers and sisters, and all who belong to them, and deliver our lives from death.'

(verses 12–13)

Stories are emerging now about New Zealand women who worked in the resistance movement in Europe during the Second World War. The story of Nancy Wake, the 'White Mouse', is well-known. Others, like Pippa Doyle, who recently at the age of 96 was awarded the Legion of Honour for her work as a member of the Special Operations Executive, are only now having their courageous work acknowledged and honoured. New Zealand women such as these were 'outsiders' with experience, skills, daring and much else.

Rahab was an outsider – single, a prostitute, living in the margins of the city. She had both nothing and everything to lose. By driving a bargain with the spies she hid, she saved the life of her own family and household.

Some might call Rahab a collaborator. Others will see a story of survival, of doing what is necessary to ensure the safety of those dear to her.

It's also part of a larger story of the divinely sanctioned invasion of the city of Jericho and the lands across the Jordan. As in ancient times, so in today's world, religion or divine sanction is used to justify war, colonisation, the destruction of established peoples and communities, especially when the story is told from the perspective of the conqueror.

I find myself thinking about displaced peoples then and now, refugees fleeing from Syria and Burma, for example, or the refugees who have been held in detention for years on Manus Island. Where is God in their experience and their story?

† Pray for those who risk their personal safety in order to protect their families or to bring down unjust regimes.

For further thought

How might women's experience of war and occupation be different from men's? How might it be the same?

June

Surprising women in the Bible – 1 Visionaries and prophets

Thursday 20 June
Women in public life

Read Judges 4:1–16

At that time Deborah, a prophetess … was judging Israel.

(verse 4)

The year 2018 marks 125 years since women were able to vote in New Zealand, the first in the world who could. However, women were not allowed to stand for parliament until 1919, and it was not until 1933 that the first female Member of Parliament, Elizabeth McCombs, was elected.

In the twenty-first century, Ana L. Revenga and Ana Maria Munoz Boudet report that only around 20 women hold the office of Head of State or government around the world. Twenty-three per cent of parliamentary seats are occupied by women globally ('Women's Work', *Scientific American*, September 2017).

When New Zealand's prime minister Jacinda Ardern was elected leader of the Labour Party just seven weeks before the general election in 2017, journalists (mostly male) were more interested in whether she and her partner intended having children than they were in her political ideology or her leadership qualities. If she became prime minister, and decided to have a child, would the two roles be compatible, they asked. For example, what would happen if a prime minister took maternity leave?

In Deborah we see a confident leader, a military strategist, during a period of Israel's life in which the conquest of Canaan had failed, and 'the Israelites again did what was evil in the sight of the Lord' (verse 1). Deborah had a strategy to overthrow King Jabin of Canaan, who had oppressed the Israelites for two decades. She summoned Barak to implement her plan. He hesitated, perhaps doubting her leadership. Deborah accompanied Barak, instructing him each step of the way. Sisera's army was destroyed, and the efforts to occupy Canaan continued.

† Pray for those who hold public office, that they may act justly, with wisdom and compassion.

For further thought

What stereotypes and expectations do you hold of women in leadership or public office?

Friday 21 June
A nation saved by an outsider

> **Read Judges 4:17–22**
>
> *Now Sisera had fled away on foot to the tent of Jael wife of Heber the Kenite.*
>
> (verse 17)

The story of Israelite resistance in Canaan continues. It is a harsh story, and one that raises many questions.

With his army destroyed, Sisera fled to Jael's tent. Did he think that no one would expect to find him there? Did he think that, because her husband was an ally of King Jabin, she would hide and protect him? The peace between King Jabin of Canaan and Heber the Kenite would not protect Jael from censure if it were found that Sisera had been in her tent. Was Sisera counting on her co-operation and silence?

Jael welcomed Sisera, made him comfortable and responded to his requests. Then, when Sisera was asleep, Jael killed him, fulfilling Deborah's prophecy that Sisera would be sold into the hands of a woman.

There is a question for me about what was omitted from the story. What else was going on? Did Sisera rape Jael, or threaten her? Was there a history to the relationship that was not just about her husband's political allegiances?

Jael's co-operation with Sisera is similar to the behaviour of many women trapped in violent relationships, who acquiesce to the demands for fear of worse consequences for themselves or their family.

None of us knows how we will act in desperate or dangerous circumstances – when our family or we are threatened.

We should not leave this story without acknowledging that, as with the story of Rahab, it is through the actions of a foreign woman, an outsider, that there is a change in Israel's fortunes.

† Pray with compassion for those who are caught in desperate or dangerous situations, and act to preserve their safety.

For further thought

When have so-called outsiders been catalysts for social change, justice and peace?

Saturday 22 June
Royal succession

Read 1 Kings 1:5, 11–31

Now therefore come, let me give you advice, so that you may save your own life and the life of your son Solomon.

(verse 12)

Emperor Akihito of Japan has announced that he will abdicate from the throne in 2019. He will be succeeded by his son Crown Prince Naruhito. When King Bhumibol Adulyadej of Thailand died in 2016, having reigned for seven decades, his son Crown Prince, now King Maha Vajiralongkorn, succeeded him. From time to time there is media speculation about the intentions of Queen Elizabeth II with regard to succession to the British throne.

In each instance there are traditions and protocols that determine succession to the throne.

In today's reading, we have an account of a struggle for the throne of Israel. Adonijah, one of the sons of David, has declared himself to be king, even though David, though advanced in years, has not announced who will be his successor to the throne.

Enter the prophet Nathan, who was not invited to Adonijah's ritual sacrifices. Nathan breaks the news to Bathsheba, disclosing his plan to remedy the situation. Bathsheba acts on Nathan's advice and petitions David, reminding David that protocols have not been observed.

Bathsheba is fearful for her and her son's future should Adonijah become king. Is Nathan exploiting Bathsheba's love of her son Solomon for his own ends? Are Nathan and Bathsheba collaborating for the future of the nation? Is Bathsheba's primary concern to ensure security and safety for herself and Solomon? The outcome of her and Nathan's interventions is that David declares Solomon to be his successor.

It's not only royal families and governments that have traditions and protocols about succession. Religious communities also have traditions, church laws and protocols that determine leadership succession.

† Pray for those who are taking up new leadership roles in church, community or government in your country.

For further thought

How is continuity of leadership enabled in your church or community? Are changes needed to the protocols to ensure transparent processes?

Surprising women in the Bible – 2 Evangelists and leaders

Notes by **Clare Nonhebel**

Clare is a published fiction and non-fiction author on diverse topics such as childhood, faith, doubt, the homeless heart, the self-help industry, gardening, genius and Death Row. She lives in Dorset, UK. Find out more on her website, clarenonhebel. com. Clare has used the NIVUK for these notes.

Sunday 23 June
It's only old Anna

Read Luke 2:21, 36–38

She was very old; she had lived with her husband seven years after her marriage, and then was a widow until she was eighty-four. She never left the temple but worshipped night and day, fasting and praying.

(verses 36b–37)

In many cultures women have little status, especially if they are childless, elderly, unmarried, widowed or have no home, career or role. By these criteria, Anna the prophetess had no impact on the society of her day. If she was noticed at all she was possibly seen as some old lady hanging around the building day after day with nowhere to go.

But Anna was a powerhouse, investing her riches of time and faith in worshipping God and sharing his goodness with anyone who would listen. Her undistracted focus on God meant that when a poor, young couple walked by, obeying the Law of Moses by bringing their firstborn son to the temple to dedicate him to God, Anna saw not just a baby (my husband swears all babies look alike) but recognised the promised saviour of the world.

Unusually for someone in the Bible described as a prophet, none of Anna's words are recorded. Like all the women in this week's readings, she's low-profile – a secret weapon in God's armoury! Perhaps it's not the words that matter in a prophetic life, but a humble heart fully open to God. Thank God for prophets like Anna!

† Abba, Father, give us insight and wisdom like your servant Anna, to keep an open heart and clear focus on the realities of your kingdom.

Surprising women in the Bible – 2 Evangelists and leaders

Monday 24 June
Mary, mother of God

Read John 19:16b–18, 25b–27

When Jesus saw his mother there, and the disciple whom he loved standing near by, he said to her, 'Woman, here is your son,' and to the disciple, 'Here is your mother.'

(verses 26–27a)

To understand why Mary has been a role model for generations of Christians requires us to read between the lines. The bare facts recorded in the Gospels reveal a woman out of her depth: bewildered to be chosen as a virgin to mother the Messiah and concerned when Jesus went missing at age 12 and, later, was reported by family members as not eating or taking care of himself.

We can only imagine how alone Mary felt, standing under the cross, spattered by the blood of her tortured son, breathing with him each agonised breath. Close by were his executioners and the taunting crowd. Beside her were Mary Magdalene, whose association had tarnished her son's reputation, and John, who had run away terrified. But there she was, standing with them. How could she open her heart, bled dry, to welcome another son at that worst moment of her life?

In recent years, some murder victims' families have joined campaigns against the death penalty for their loved one's killer, whom they recognise as another family's son or daughter. Even in their darkest hour they keep their hearts open to compassion rather than clenched in revenge.

At Pentecost, Mary would be there (Acts 1:14) still standing with all those 'friends' who left her son to die alone, still praying with and for them. A prophetic figure to all who suffer, who struggle to understand God's ways and who strive to keep forgiving, Mary stands with us, for all time.

† My soul, glorify the Lord; my spirit, rejoice in God my Saviour, for he has been mindful of the humble (and often jumbled) state of his servant and stands me with blessed companions.

For further thought

How do you see Mary? Do you see any resemblance to your own faith?

Tuesday 25 June
Dinner party from hell

Read Mark 14:3–9

While Jesus was in Bethany, reclining at the table in the home of Simon the Leper, a woman came with an alabaster jar of very expensive perfume, made of pure nard. She broke the jar and poured the perfume on his head.

(verse 3)

Luke (7:36–50) gives a fuller version of this dinner party from hell but omits Jesus saying that the woman's action was prophetic – anointing his body for burial, in advance of his death. The trouble was, no one else saw it that way.

I was in a prayer group where, one evening, a woman who had been in prostitution for 20 years had a life-changing encounter with Jesus. Shortly afterwards the Holy Spirit prompted her to pray with people for healing, with beautiful outcomes – except among some long-term Christians who took exception to 'that kind of woman' laying hands on anyone.

It's interesting that in Luke's account the host, Simon, has given Jesus a terrible welcome: not even water to wash after a long, hot day. He must have been dirty, sweaty and uncomfortable. Why has Simon invited him? To make himself and his fellow Pharisees feel superior? But Simon is, or was, a leper. Shouldn't he, of all people, know how it feels to be treated as unclean?

It's the woman, with her bad reputation, her bold public show of emotion, her embarrassingly inappropriate touchy-feely action and her extravagant outpouring of priceless perfume, who has surely been moved to pity for a fellow outcast. Like all prophets, she doesn't necessarily know the significance of her action. She comes to share Jesus' humiliating situation, knowing only too well how it feels. And he shares and then banishes her shame, because whoever stands up for him on Earth, he will stand up for them. Including in heaven.

† Lord, persecution can be so subtle. Give us courage not to join in with those tiny hurtful signs: the raised eyebrow, amused half-smile or in-joke that conveys an 'us and them' message to someone.

For further thought

If God gives a double portion of honour to those who have been shamed, can we do the same?

Surprising women in the Bible – 2 Evangelists and leaders

Wednesday 26 June
They have taken my Lord away

Read John 20:1, 11–18

Jesus said, 'Do not hold on to me, for I have not yet ascended to the Father. Go instead to my brothers and tell them, "I am ascending to my Father and your Father, to my God and your God."'

(verse 17)

Every time I think I've got my theology sorted, God does something unexpected and I feel totally out of my orbit. All the things I know about him have to be viewed in a new context. It's unsettling. And inspiring.

Mary Magdalene's cry from the heart, 'They have taken my Lord away!' marks the end of her hopes – but the dawn of a new hope, not only for her but for anyone who will hear the news she is sent to tell. Not only is God still Father to the Son who died feeling forsaken by him, but still Father to the friends who ran away or denied him.

This isn't Mary's first major shift in perception. She was delivered from seven demons that overshadowed her whole life and mind, and was released by Jesus to love and be lovable again. Now she has to let go of the Jesus she loves because there is more of him than she knows. It's the beginning of a wider love story – with the Father and Holy Spirit as well as the Son, with fellow disciples and with many people who don't yet know what she knows. And, bless her, Mary runs to do what she is told. She lets go of the Jesus she knows and runs to share the good news: there's more to come! God hasn't rejected anyone and Jesus' death hasn't cancelled his promises.

Not only is there light at the end of the tunnel but there is a whole wide world waiting to know: God hasn't finished with us! Prepare to be surprised!

† Jesus, help me not to cling to what I know of you or to jealously guard my theology. Help me let go, trusting that there's more than I've ever dreamed or imagined.

For further thought

Am I ready to learn more of God? Even if it means unlearning some of my certainty?

Thursday 27 June
Grandma's prayers

Read 2 Timothy 1:3–7

I am reminded of your sincere faith, which first lived in your grandmother Lois and in your mother Eunice and, I am persuaded, now lives in you also.

(verse 5)

There's a saying that 'God has no grandchildren,' meaning that we can't coast along on other people's faith but need to form our own relationship with him. In our reading today, Paul goes on to remind Timothy to use his faith and his anointing and develop God's gift to him. But it certainly does help to have back-up from other people of faith.

Our plumber called round with his arm in a sling, having fallen three storeys through a house on a building site. The hospital doctor said he was lucky to be alive. I said, 'Someone must have been praying for you!' and he said, 'That'd be my mother-in-law – a terrible holy woman. I'll never complain about her again!'

Lois and Eunice must have been a strong influence on Timothy's growing faith and eventual ministry, for Paul to specially mention them. What a bonus for him and a privilege for them.

Whether or not we have family with a history of faith or are first-generation believers, we are part of a mega-family of faith, a whole cloud of witnesses on Earth as well as in heaven, and never need feel we're struggling on alone.

No one can do for us the part that God asks us to do, and most of our praying will have to be done on our own as we step out in faith. But if you have a Lois or Eunice to pray for you, thank God for them. And maybe you 'parent' or 'grandparent' other Christians, who are not related to you. One family. It works well.

† Father, you give us a spirit of power, love and self-discipline. Prompt us to use it to pray for believers who struggle against a spirit of timidity.

For further thought

If we take a step of faith, it may mean that others connected to us move forward too.

Surprising women in the Bible – 2 Evangelists and leaders

Come home

Read Acts 16:14–15

The Lord opened Lydia's heart to respond to Paul's message. When she and the members of her household were baptised, she invited us to her home.

(verses 14b–15a)

Visiting families in a slum in Mumbai, India, with a worker from the charity Oasis, the narrow path between the small dwellings was blocked by a tiny girl with a big voice, shouting, 'Now come to my home!' She wouldn't move till we followed her into a small, dark room with holes in the roof. And she carried on shouting until we sat down and her mother told us how fearful she was for her older daughter, who had trouble breathing. The child only settled down when we prayed for her sister. Then she let us go.

Prophets of all ages, male or female, can have very insistent voices. Lydia doesn't just invite Paul and Silas to stay in her home; she persuades them, using a bit of moral blackmail: 'If you really consider me a believer, come to my home.' Put your faith where your mouth is, in other words. It's the one-big-family theme again: childless Anna and the baby Jesus; Mary and new son John; outcast woman and unwelcomed Jesus; Lois and Eunice and Timothy.

If we say we're God's children, we shouldn't be surprised when we're recognised by our siblings, even when we haven't met them before. And what do family do, when one member has a home and others are far from home? Bring them to their own home. It speaks volumes.

The Lord really did open Lydia's heart to respond; she got the point very quickly. It takes some of us a bit longer.

† Lord, who are our brothers and sisters? When we're slow on the uptake, point out to us the ones you want us to notice. Help us to make them feel at home.

For further thought

How easy is it to get the balance between caring for our own families and caring for God's family members who need a welcome home?

Saturday 29 June
Helping the helper

Read Romans 16:1–2

I ask you to receive Phoebe … and to give her any help she may need from you, for she has been the benefactor of many people, including me.

(verse 2)

A homeless lady sat by the door of the church, exhausted and wearing broken shoes. A kindly woman coming out offered to bring her home and give her some shoes. She refused. Another woman came out, walking with a limp, and made the same offer, which she accepted. At home, Siobhan made her tea and gave her shoes, then explained she had had a stroke and her hands didn't work very well and asked if the lady might help her peel some potatoes. She became a frequent visitor to Siobhan's home.

The secular world – and sometimes, sadly, churches and charities as well – tends to divide people into helpers and those in need of help. Or into useful people and useless. Or givers and takers. But that's not real. In our reading today, Phoebe, having been a useful contributor to her own community in Cenchrea, is recommended by Paul to the church in Rome as someone who might need a bit of help herself.

As children in a low-income family, my sister and I used to beg our mother at birthday times, 'Don't give me a useful present!' It's very tempting to sum up a new person's value to a community according to how much they might have to offer. But sometimes the useless gifts are treasured most. I like to think Phoebe was welcomed into her new church in Rome, not as a useful helper in all its projects but just for being herself, and that the people who helped her felt blessed by getting to know her.

† Lord, you said it's more blessed to give than to receive. If we're generous in giving, let us be generous in letting others have the blessing of helping when we're in need.

For further thought
It feels good to be the giver but how good am I at letting others help when I'm in need?

Readings in Luke (3) – 1 Who do you say I am?

Notes by **Erice Fairbrother**

 Erice is a Solitary of the Order of the Holy Cross Associates in New Zealand. Called to this work by her community, she is the chaplain and leads the order's spiritual centre in Napier. Her work includes teaching, leading courses in formation and prayer, and offering meditation and retreats. She is a published writer, poet, pastoral supervisor and Anglican priest. Her work includes editing, fostering local writing opportunities and publishing. Erice has used the NRSVA for these notes.

Sunday 30 June
Staying in the peace

Read Luke 8:26–39

Then people came out to see what had happened, and when they came to Jesus, they found the man from whom the demons had gone sitting at the feet of Jesus, clothed and in his right mind. And they were afraid.

(verse 35)

Some years back I had a friend who taught her daughter from a young age that when life was frustrating and made her angry, she should try to 'stay in the peace'. It was a great alternative to the naughty step process of being alone and apart.

The Gospels open us to the loving presence of the one who came to bring peace, reconciliation and restoration – the presence of Christ. It is in this presence of acceptance and embrace that we are able to face our dark places, hurt places, hidden shames we carry, our hates, prejudices, old beliefs and all that binds us to past fears and behaviours. It is no easy thing to take time to let go of all that we have carried over long periods of time. For many it is a frightening process to consider.

The man we read of today experiences the presence of Christ as a process that brings peace – a presence that restores him in mind, drawing him into a close relationship with God.

To 'stay in the peace' is a choice made daily, moment by moment to stay in the company of the Christ who heals, restores and, as we will read this week, strengthens us.

† Recall a time of being with someone whose very presence has brought you peace. Have you ever been that presence for another?

Monday 1 July
Making room for healing

> **Read Luke 8:40–56**
>
> *As he went, the crowds pressed in on him. Now there was a woman who had been suffering from haemorrhages for twelve years …*
> *She came up behind him and touched the fringe of his clothes, and immediately her haemorrhage stopped. Then Jesus asked, 'Who touched me?'*
>
> (part of verses 42–45)

Societies have increasing demands placed on them to meet incredible needs; to assist the least able, empower the most impoverished, provide healthcare for the sick and pastoral support for the dying. The ability to make space for those needs to be heard, to give healthcare to those who need it, to provide resources for those who need family support is, sadly, in many places found to be less than adequate. Communities experience this at a local level, as do many church communities also facing crowds needing hope restored and a practical response.

The crowd eager to be with Jesus included many in need, yet despite this and the press of those surrounding him, Jesus makes room for them all. Though the noise is great he still has ears for the voice of need; though many touch him he can still feel the hopeful touch of the one among the many. Confronted with despair, he restores life and hope. Making room remains a challenge in a world of constant noise drowning cries for help, and of individualism that would keep us removed from feeling the touch of others reaching out.

What would our world be like if social policy was based on a priority of making room – for the homeless, the unemployed? Last year I passed two homeless men leaning on a rubbish bin. As I passed, one was saying to the other, 'Happy to share my bin with a mate.' I walked on, challenged to ask myself; how am I making room – like them, like Jesus – for my neighbour?

† Pray for community and political leaders, that they may be responsive to the needs of the suffering.

For further thought

Consider ways in which you are able to be present to the needs around you. What will enable you to be responsive to them?

Tuesday 2 July
Making room together

Read Luke 9:1–17

And taking the five loaves and the two fish, he looked up to heaven, and blessed and broke them, and gave them to the disciples to set before the crowd. And all ate and were filled.

(verses 16–17a)

Some of the most effective social justice work I've had the privilege to be part of, has been achieved through building partnerships. In one instance, a parish joined with mental health services to bring a youth suicide prevention strategy to the city. It involved building partnerships with schools to ensure all students had access to care and support. There are similar partnerings occurring to address social housing initiatives, support free-store centres, and foster understanding through interfaith opportunities. It is less about being like-minded, and more about sharing a vision of compassion, and mutual respect.

Who was on the hillside when Jesus invited everyone to join him to provide enough food? When he invited them to share their resources, were some present who weren't sure about Jesus, some more deserving than others among those that were there? Such distinctions didn't seem to concern Jesus – or the size of the crowd. While the latter worried the disciples, the need for food for all was the greater issue. Jesus modelled a human/divine partnership of compassion and respect in his invitation to mutual giving and receiving.

When we let go of feeling helpless, or of worrying about the size of the problems, we make room for that human/divine presence. It frees us to be actively alongside those who know their own needs best. Recognising them as our neighbours, we can begin to build partnerships based on compassionate respect. What might we discover of God when we include all in mutual partnering to ensure the well-being of everyone?

† Pray that we might share with Christ in making room for others meeting common needs together.

For further thought

Discuss with groups you are part of, how you attend to the balance between necessary help and sharing responsibility for change.

Wednesday 3 July
Naming what is true

> **Read Luke 9:18–36**
>
> *He asked them, 'Who do the crowds say that I am?' They answered, 'John the Baptist; but others, Elijah; and still others, that one of the ancient prophets has arisen.' He said to them, 'But who do you say that I am?' Peter answered, 'The Messiah of God.'*
>
> (verses 18b–20)

A group of friends gathered outside the High Court to support a colleague who was about to be sentenced for a serious crime. As they waited, their friend's lawyer arrived. They were unprepared, however, for the way he addressed his client: 'And how's the crim this morning?' One of those gathered there was challenged. Until that moment she thought she knew who her friend was. While the rest of the group debated whether one was a criminal or a friend first, she began to see her friend more honestly – as a criminal as well as a friend. It was an insight that demanded more from her in the years ahead, changed the support she offered, and developed a friendship based on truth and deepening understanding.

Despite how others see Jesus, Peter doesn't hesitate to name the truth. Jesus in turn responds by inviting the disciples into a deepening relationship. He outlines for them the costliness of seeing him for who he is. He doesn't protect them from the reality that they are already living in the shadow of what is ahead. Although the resurrection is yet to come, God responds to Peter by taking him, with James and John, into the transfiguring presence of Christ. In that moment the truth Peter had named became a reality.

The one, who was the way they followed, was now the truth they would come to know. It is the same truth we have come to know. Can we like Peter speak it courageously into a world disfigured by fake news and alternative facts?

† Pray for the courage of Peter to name the truth we see when we encounter fake or false representations of what is happening in our own context.

For further thought
It can be hard to identify and name the true needs facing our communities. Find others who share your feelings and support one another.

Thursday 4 July
True greatness benefits all

Read Luke 9:37–50

'Whoever welcomes this child in my name welcomes me, and whoever welcomes me welcomes the one who sent me; for the least among all of you is the greatest.'

(verse 48)

In the sixth century St Benedict taught his community concerning humility: 'Do not wish to be holy before you really are.' In the Tao we find similar teaching: 'The best people are like water; they benefit all things and do not compete with them. They settle in low places.'

A lowly child healed by Jesus evoked acknowledgement of God's greatness – greatness all the more powerful because it took nothing away from those to whom it was given. Immediately Jesus realises his disciples are being seduced by the wonder of the healing itself and, despite his warning, they soon begin competing for the right to be the greatest. Their idea of greatness meant power that could be grasped whereas God's greatness means a power found in vulnerability. Society treats vulnerability as weakness and the cost of seeing weakness instead of need is revealed in the difficulty society has working with issues such as child abuse, end-of-life care and refugee resettlement. Thankfully there are many who, in spite of prevailing attitudes, do respond with compassion. They may not be of our faith community, or hold the same views, but when the needs of the least are met, God's greatness continues to be revealed.

In a world yearning for peace, these teachings from the gospel and ancient traditions may very well be the key that will unlock and restore hope. Our part is to be like water that settles among the lowly, to find our service in benefiting all things, trusting it is the greatest thing we can do.

† Pray today that God renew our passion for humble service in Christ's name.

For further thought

For the rest of this week, commit to noticing where God's greatness is quietly at work in your life and delight in it.

Friday 5 July
Leavings and beginnings

> **Read Luke 9:51–62**
>
> *When the days drew near for him to be taken up, he set his face to go to Jerusalem.*
>
> (verse 51)

In the 1840s my paternal forebears set their face to the south, sailing to New Zealand, never to return. They were among the pioneers who arrived and travelled by foot over high ranges on paths still not fully cut through the hills – men and women for whom the work of carving out a new life from scratch was hard and demanding. Felling bush, and building homes and businesses was a commitment though made in faith. It was costly and difficult in an alien environment of icy southerlies and scorching summer heat. Nearly a hundred years later my mother sailed from London as a child, not realising she too would never return.

In the poem 'Settlement', New Zealand poet Kerry Hines (Auckland University Press, 2014) explores the impact on settlers leaving everything they knew. Her words 'he left forever/ when he left'[11] catch the sense of finality and the grief many experienced. She could have been writing of my forebears who did indeed leave forever when they left. Many still do, not by choice but because of conflict and oppression, knowing there will be no returning.

When Jesus set his face to Jerusalem he knew there was no going back 'when he left'. Many have followed his example: missionaries, social reformers, pioneers, protestors for justice and peace. In the current refugee crisis, we are called to set our face towards them, making room in our communities and hearts and supporting agencies that minister to them.

† Pray for agencies and community leaders as they work to make room for those who have had to leave everything and begin again.

For further thought

Is there anything that keeps you from setting your face towards God's call on your life?

---

11 Hines, K. (2014), *'Settlement'*, Young Country (Auckland: Auckland University Press).

Saturday 6 July
Journeys are best taken with others

Read Luke 10:1–16

The Lord appointed seventy others and sent them on ahead of him in pairs ... He said to them, '... Go on your way. See, I am sending you out like lambs into the midst of wolves.'

(parts of verses 1–3)

To be sent on a journey is to accept that there will be tough moments. In 1990 I set out backpacking from the southern to the most northern parts of Indonesia. Over six enriching weeks I encountered many challenges, some of them daunting. At those times, travelling with a friend made it possible to keep going and between us we were able to offer mutual encouragement and support.

There are many kinds of journeys, not all of which take us far from home. In New Zealand, one of the journeys we are on as a nation is that of addressing our high rates of violence affecting women and children. The most effective work is occurring where people are coming together; setting aside differences to share experiences, to listen to stories and create stronger relationships – locally, regionally and nationally. Our national rates of youth suicide are among the worst in the world yet for years it was an issue that was deliberately kept from public scrutiny. Currently this attitude is being challenged. Families and friends most affected by suicide are making it clear that they cannot continue to carry the weight of it on their own, in isolation. Through community groups connecting with each other, open support and honest discussions are beginning.

There are many roads travelled all over the world by women and men working together to make a difference. Today's reading reminds us that the 70 were not asked to go it alone. Neither are we. God asks us to work together as we journey with the good news that God is near.

† Give thanks that we are not called to work alone as we seek to share the good news.

For further thought

Look for opportunities where you can offer company to someone who may need a companion on their journey.

Readings in Luke (3) –
2 Pray like this

Notes by **Bola Iduoze**

Bola is a qualified accountant with over 20 years' experience in the marketplace. She has a passion for coaching and mentoring and jointly manages a mentoring platform with her husband Eddie (mentoringplatform.com). Bola assists her husband in pastoring at Gateway Chapel, in Kent, UK, and is a published writer and speaker. Bola and Eddie have two children. Bola has used the NIVUK for these notes.

Sunday 7 July
Eyes that see, ears that hear

> **Read Luke 10:17–24**
>
> *Then he turned to his disciples and said privately, 'Blessed are the eyes that see what you see. For I tell you that many prophets and kings wanted to see what you see but did not see it, and to hear what you hear but did not hear it.'*
>
> (verses 23–24)

The disciples of Jesus, having spent so much time with him, went as he told them and came back excited about their result. Jesus was full of joy and praised God. He then commented on the disciples' privilege, not just at what they've experienced, but at what they've seen and heard with him.

It is so easy to be moved more with the spectacular without giving as much attention to our experience of the things that really matter to God. A short while ago, I decided to look out for the things God is doing around me that would not have caught my attention otherwise. I decided to keep a journal. By the end of that week, I had noted so many surprising things that astonished me. Our eyes see many things and our ears hear, but our heart never records them, unless we take the effort. We are too engrossed looking for the spectacular so that we miss what God is doing in and around us.

You and I are very privileged. God is doing astonishing things all around us. Will your heart record them as you read Luke this week?

† Lord, open my eyes and my ears to see and hear what you will have me hear and see today.

189

Monday 8 July
Who is our neighbour?

Read Luke 10:25–37

The expert in the law replied, 'The one who had mercy on him.' Jesus told him, 'Go and do likewise.'

(verse 37)

In my teen years growing up in Idiban, Nigeria, my neighbour was a single mum of three. One day she lost her son in an unexpected university accident. Some of the university representatives had to come and break the news to her.

During this tragic time, as is typical in Nigeria, people visited this family to offer condolences. What, however, left a major impact on me was a group of people from a certain church group who never knew my neighbour, but learned of her experience. They came daily to assist my neighbour in practical ways. They took care of the other children and they sorted out dinner. They visited my neighbour until she was strong enough to start doing things by herself. Even though these people never knew my neighbour, they showed so much care that everyone else around wanted to know more about them, their church and their God. The good deeds of these people drew many to Christ.

A neighbour is not just someone close to you, but the one that cares enough to show mercy in all circumstances. In our scripture today, Jesus' parable of the Good Samaritan states our need to go out of our way to be a blessing and help to the people around us, even if we have nothing to gain by such actions.

Our love for God is reflected in our actions towards others. Today I pray that you will receive the grace to show mercy to everyone around you just as Jesus commanded us to do (verse 37).

† Lord, grant me the grace to see and show mercy to all those around me who need help. Use me to share your mercy in the world. Amen.

For further thought

Who around you needs unexpected help today?

Only one thing is needed

> **Read Luke 10:38–42**
>
> *'Martha, Martha,' the Lord answered, 'you are worried and upset about many things, but few things are needed – or indeed only one. Mary has chosen what is better, and it will not be taken away from her.'*
>
> (verses 41–42)

In my teen years, my family lived in a housing estate called Owode in Ibadan. Our estate has a local Baptist church where we had large church celebrations from time to time. At these services, our preacher took time to explain the reason for the season and the significance of each of those days to us. On more than one occasion, however, my family as well as many others arrived so late that we missed the bulk of the sermon!

We were late to church because we were busy preparing for the festive periods. Our business meant that we missed the most important part of the festival: the lesson and purpose of the day. Our time spent cooking, getting our clothes together and preparing to host visitors from church became a major distraction.

When I read this scripture, I notice that Martha was so concerned about being a great host that she never got to sit at Jesus' feet. She wanted to impress so much that she received nothing impressed upon her heart from the special guest in her home. She overlooked the significance of Jesus' teachings and even found herself irritated with the person who sat down to learn.

Jesus told Martha to focus on the important things. Many things will pull on our time, but it is our responsibility to protect our time and choose what is the most important. Never get too busy to sit down and learn from God daily – it will smooth out the rough patches in your day and in your life!

† Father, I pray that you will help me set aside all distractions and sit at your feet to learn from you daily. In Jesus' name, Amen.

For further thought

Your best investment in your day will be doing the needful thing first. Sit at Jesus' feet; then every other thing can follow.

Wednesday 10 July
Pray like this

Read Luke 11:1–13

'If you then, though you are evil, know how to give good gifts to your children, how much more will your Father in heaven give the Holy Spirit to those who ask him!'

(verse 13)

The disciples of Jesus came to him. They had noticed something that John's disciples had which seemed missing in their camp. Jesus did not rebuke them for wanting to emulate the spiritual things they had observed. Instead, he gave them what they wanted, and more. As they requested, he gave them a prayer model; he taught them how to pray, and he dug deeper to give them further pointers. He assured them they could be confident God will hear them; God is a helper who listens to prayers.

Having a helper makes all the difference in life. Knowing there's a resource available to assist us in praying and even in articulating our needs should give us that assurance when prayers go unanswered.

My earthly father is a very loving man. When we were young and had requests, he listened. Equally I had some friends whose mothers stepped in as helpers.

When we submit ourselves to the Holy Spirit, he will help us in prayers as well as show us the will of God. The Holy Spirit teaches us how to pray and prays in us, but also provides us with the assurance of God's presence. As the scripture today says, your Father is keen to give you good gifts: so do pray!

† Lord, thank you that you answer our prayers when we come to you. Create in me a fresh passion to pray and follow your leading all my days. In Jesus' name, Amen.

For further thought

When and where do you find it easiest to pray? Where could you find five minutes in your day in which to bring your concerns to God?

The kingdom of God is here

Read Luke 11:14–28

'But if I drive out demons by the finger of God, then the kingdom of God has come upon you.'

(verse 20)

I have witnessed change of regime and government a few times while growing up in Nigeria. While explaining this story from Luke to my children, I have also had to describe regime change, as they haven't experienced anything like it in their lifetimes.

Whenever the military government takes over power from politicians, it brings nervousness to the nation. Although they project confidence and stability, they are only in charge of things until another regime takes over. If a politician is elected as the new ruling power, again, they set up their own rules and the military men return to their barracks. Despite their ammunition, power and visual demonstrations of being in power, they vacate the government and disappear. This has been the situation in my home country for over 30 years now.

God's rule is different. In today's reading, Jesus shared with his audience how the presence and power of God can overshadow and overtake that of the enemy in someone's life. Yet when Jesus comes as ruler, he does not disappear after a few years. Jesus remains and rules with justice and peace. Even if we can't see his rule now, we can be confident it is coming – and is now present in ways we can't see clearly.

Jesus is all-powerful and his kingdom can surely be established in our lives, overpowering all the challenges and strongholds of the past if we let him in. How can we let God's rule be manifest in our lives today?

† Lord, let your kingdom be established in my life, defeating every form of oppression and any limitations set by me. In Jesus' name, Amen.

For further thought

What are the hidden signs of God's rule around you today?

Light in the darkness

Read Luke 11:29–36

'Your eye is the lamp of your body. When your eyes are healthy, your whole body also is full of light. But when they are unhealthy, your body also is full of darkness.'

(verse 34)

Growing up in a community where electricity supply is irregular has made this scripture significant to me. My childhood years coincided with a period when the electricity board of my nation had to ration electricity supplies. We were all forced to get alternative sources of light into our accommodation to avoid accidents.

We used gas lamps around the house when the power was shut off. Sometimes the lanterns we had at home might need trimming and cleaning; without this care, the lamp wouldn't create as much light as it could otherwise do. Sometimes, we had to make do with only a little light in one corner, plunging the rest of the house into darkness.

In today's scripture, Jesus was teaching his disciples about the value of the eyes as the lamp or light of the body and the need to ensure we keep this lamp bright and healthy, healthy enough to ensure our whole body is full of light. Like my family's lamps growing up, our eyes need care to ensure we can see truly. We are to ensure we are lighting the world around us as fully as we can.

We are charged in this scripture to ensure the light in us does not fail. This suggests that we have control over the light in us. To keep our eyes and lamp sharp is our daily responsibility. Unless we clean our lanterns, our vision and brightness will be limited.

God seeks to illumine our world; will we be the ones to keep our eyes and lamps healthy and shining brightly?

† Father, help me to be conscious of the fact that my eyes are the lamp of my body and give me grace to see that the light within me is shining brightly. In Jesus' name, Amen.

For further thought

What can you do today to see truly and well, the way God sees the world?

Saturday 13 July
The six woes

Read Luke 11:37–54

'Woe to you experts in the law, because you have taken away the key to knowledge. You yourselves have not entered, and you have hindered those who were entering.'

(verse 52)

While Jesus was teaching his disciples, a group of scholars approached him. Jesus started sharing with them the dangers of what they had practised to date. They were sorting out the outward matters, but were not mindful of the internal things that really do matter to God.

Many of us today still find ourselves more mindful of the things that are seen, noticed and expected by religious leaders. We work hard to please other people rather than God.

Answering his challengers, Jesus also indicated his unhappiness about the fact that these so-called experts have taken away the key of knowledge from the people. Jesus made clear that he wants us all to have access to that knowledge and to readjust our lives based on the truth that is revealed to us as we walk into the newness of life in him.

What does this mean for us today? We can enter into God's provision and plans for our lives if we take the knowledge that is now available to us in the word of God with the help of the Holy Spirit as our best teacher. The Spirit will inspire our own study and help us to live the truth – for the betterment of the whole world.

† Father, thank you that you have given us the key of knowledge, which no one can take away from us. Help us to rely on the Holy Spirit every day. Amen.

For further thought

What kind of learning and study takes place in your church community? How can you join in, or what changes can you suggest?

Readings in Luke (3) –
3 The narrow door

Notes by **Shirlyn Toppin**

Shirlyn is a presbyter in the Methodist Church in Ealing, London. She believes passionately in the preaching of the word of God, without compromise or fear, and exercising a pastoral ministry of grace. She enjoys various forms of leisure and relaxation and her favourite pastime is shopping, especially for shoes. Shirlyn has used the NRSVA for these notes.

Sunday 14 July
Be on your guard

Read Luke 12:1–12

'I tell you, my friends, do not fear those who kill the body, and after that can do nothing more. But I will warn you whom to fear: fear him who, after he has killed, has authority to cast into hell.'

(verses 4–5)

Fear is one of the most powerful of human emotions! It can be a crippling factor for many people – whether it's the anxiety of losing keys or the impending loss of life. Death is the pathway for all of God's created beings, but our natural human inclination is to stay alive. The fear of death may stir us into action, cause us to take everyday precautions like visiting the doctor or even cancel trips and worry about leaving the house.

However, Jesus' words to his disciples that they must be on guard against those who would kill them were not about physical death, but about spiritual death: eternal separation from God. Jesus wants us to be aware of the greater threat to our lives, and that threat is the devil, who masquerades himself as light. Scripture tells us that he is a murderer, stalker and the most vicious enemy of the church.

If you knew that a murderer was roaming freely in your neighbourhood, would you not take necessary precautions to protect yourself? In like manner Jesus' warning cannot go unheeded: 'fear him', 'be on your guard'!

† Father, grant me discernment to see the attacks of the enemy and let me put on the armour of God. Amen.

Monday 15 July
Think less of self

> ### Read Luke 12:13–26
> *He said to his disciples, 'Therefore I tell you, do not worry about your life, what you will eat, or about your body, what you will wear.'*
>
> (verse 22)

To say that you should not worry about what you eat or wear in this fashion- and body-conscious society might be too hard to accept. The influence of magazines, television and social media networks can easily make one believe that security is found in material possessions. Perhaps accumulating material possessions is simply a matter for individual choice?

Jesus' words in today's reading are clear. The teaching of Jesus warns against taking false refuge in that which is temporary like wealth and beauty. These things last only for a moment and in a twinkle of an eye could be gone. Natural disasters are reminders of this reality, as many are left with nothing, devastated by the loss of years of hard work. In such cases, while thankful for their lives, they are still wrestling with the loss of things they valued as important to their being, which may or may not be of monetary worth.

Jesus' words about worrying could be summed up by the phrase, 'Store your treasures in heaven.' Sometimes our preoccupation with self and what we have or do not have can be detrimental to our relationship with God. When we worry, we can be implicitly saying that God cannot meet our needs. Yet at no time has worrying about a situation changed it. Jesus cautions us about expending useless energy worrying!

† Remind us to decrease so you can increase in us, Father. Help us to be aware of the danger of trusting in possessions. Amen.

For further thought
What possessions might you be holding onto for security?

Tuesday 16 July
Be generous, be ready

Read Luke 12:27–40

'Blessed are those slaves whom the master finds alert when he comes: truly I tell you, he will fasten his belt and have them sit down to eat, and he will come and serve them.'

(verse 37)

Generosity means hospitality! To receive an unexpected visitor in your home shows an attitude of welcoming. Generosity is extending grace! The ability to be ready to entertain when the situation is inappropriate is commendable. This viewpoint is also endorsed by Jesus' story of the master who comes unexpectedly and finds his servant receptive of his visit. The servants are not only blessed for their patient endurance, they are also rewarded by the master who proceeds to serve them a meal, a fitting testimony of his affection for them in their devotion to him.

Wisely or foolishly, once I allowed a stranger to stay in the manse for three days, a Christian minister who found himself stranded in London from the Seychelles. My generosity and preparedness to entertain 'angels unawares' could have been costly, but no harm came to me. On reflection, did I only entertain him because he was a minister? Or was Jesus' teaching that we must help the 'least of his brothers' the compelling factor for my generosity? I would like to think it was a combination of both.

Jesus' challenging words are about living our lives in the present in a way that is oriented to the future. When Jesus returns, will he find believers watching, waiting and ready for his return? Will we be ready to welcome Jesus, even if he comes as a stranger in need?

† Lord, help me to be alert to your coming and enable me to be practical in my stewardship and discipleship. Amen.

For further thought

When have you entertained an angel unawares?

Wednesday 17 July
Be wise, be vigilant

Readings in Luke (3) – 3 The narrow door

July

Read Luke 12:41–59

'Truly I tell you, he will put that one in charge of all his possessions.'

(verse 44)

In yesterday's reading we see Jesus commending the servants for their alertness to the master's return. Today he sets a challenge: how should they behave as they wait for the arrival of the master who may be delayed?

Jesus poses two different scenarios of stewardship. In one, the master finds the slave at work when he arrives, and puts him in charge of all his possessions. By contrast, the servant used his master's late arrival to dominate and belittle the other slaves while living sumptuously himself at the expense of his master. He was not rewarded favourably, because he wasn't ready at the coming of his master.

In this parable, Jesus is referring to the attitudes in our hearts, not just the way we behave. I recall how my pattern of driving changed one Sunday morning on my way to church, noticing a police vehicle behind me. Immediately, I decelerated to the speed limit, hoping they would go in another direction. Needless to say, I was not fortunate, as both of us were heading into the same area. Do I believe in breaking the law? No, but most importantly I should behave wisely at all times, not knowing when I may have to give an account for my driving.

Jesus' word of warning to be ready is a constant challenge on how we exercise our discipleship. How do we fulfil his task, while preparing for his return?

† Lord of grace and mercy, let your spirit of wisdom be exercised always in me as I prepare for your coming to reign in glory. Amen.

For further thought

Are you ready to receive the Lord with joy? What can you change in your life to be ready?

Thursday 18 July
Precious lives

Read Luke 13:1–17

'No, I tell you; but unless you repent, you will all perish just as they did.'

(verse 5)

The demands that Luke placed on a believer's life to be ready for the coming of Jesus in chapter 12 seem to have tapered off. In today's reading, the focus is on another demand: to recognise one's guilt and seek repentance. The examples Luke posed are a reminder that radical change is needed in order that one should not perish.

So often we believe that good things should happen to good people and bad things to those who are considered bad. Jesus, however, dispels this notion. He reminds his audience that the sudden death of the Galileans or the 18 in Siloam was not because they were more guilty than the survivors. The loss of precious lives is a reminder that we all will die, and in this perspective repentance is of utmost priority. It is often said that married couples should not go to bed angry in the event that one of them dies and the opportunity to say sorry is lost. As Ephesians 4:26 puts it: 'Do not let the sun go down on your anger.' Jesus' chilling words 'unless you repent, you will all perish as they did' (verse 3) point not to guilt, but to the suddenness of death and the urgent task of repentance, or changing one's mindset. However, all is not lost. The parable of the barren fig tree is symbolic of a space or opportunity left for repentance. It shows how the gardener sees the preciousness of the fig tree and willingly offered to tend it, so it could flourish and not die. The message of repentance still echoes today. Are we listening?

† Lord, may I take every chance to repent and change my ways, that the sun might not go down on my anger. Amen.

For further thoughts

What damaged or broken relationships in your life need attention?

A narrow door

Read Luke 13:18–35

'Strive to enter through the narrow door; for many, I tell you, will try to enter and will not be able.'

(verse 24)

Another summons to wake up to the gift of salvation comes in the warning of the narrow door. Salvation is free, yet Jesus says to strive to obtain it, which connotes the need to purposively struggle. Salvation might be free, but one has to desire it because it is not forced upon anyone. Freedom of choice plays an integral part in the choosing or refusing of it. Therefore, those who desire eternal life are invited to strive to find the way, which is through a narrow door.

The narrow door suggests that entering it is demanding, not easy. People might think that living a good life is enough, being a good person is enough, but salvation is a free gift and is not conditioned by one's behaviour or character. So often this principle is subtly branded in the church that being good is the key to eternal life, with no transformative process, clearly contradicting Jesus' message.

I have been asked on many occasions that if someone is sincere and good, but not a Christian, will God not welcome them into heaven? But is sincerity enough without seeking the truth? Proverbs 16:25 warns us: 'Sometimes there is a way that seems to be right, but in the end it is the way to death.' We are warned to be less accommodating of any kind of cheap grace and instead, to strive and struggle in order to enter the door that leads to eternal life.

† Heavenly Father, give me courage to strive and grace to persevere that I may enter the narrow door to eternal life. Amen.

For further thought

What in your life won't get past the narrow door? How about in your church's life?

Saturday 20 July
Traditions challenged

Read Luke 14:1–14

And Jesus asked the lawyers and Pharisees, 'Is it lawful to cure people on the sabbath, or not?'

(verse 3)

Today's reading draws us to see how in challenging traditional beliefs, one man received freedom in the form of healing. The dos and don'ts of the Sabbath laws, though restrictive for many in their application, gave the Jewish authorities prestige and clout. But they were also instrumental in rendering these authorities speechless before Jesus. Why should such a question be asked of them by one who is of the Jewish faith? Should he not know better than to challenge them? Jesus' argument builds on the logic of the laws themselves. Surely if it is legitimate to help a beast of burden on the Sabbath, it should also be applicable to human beings.

Often in ministry we encounter traditions that started as an act of kindness. At one church in which I ministered I learned it was the tradition that the stewards came forward to receive the offering but did not bless it. I later found out that in order to assist an aged and frail preacher who took the service in the pulpit, a member of the congregation decided to receive the offering, which the preacher blessed from the pulpit. And as such, a tradition was born in which the offering was received by the steward and blessed by the preacher. A tradition no one challenged, until I asked about it.

Challenging traditions does not mean undermining them. Jesus himself maintained traditional respect of the temple by purging it of practices that were not becoming to it. However, for Luke the emphasis of the thought-provoking query of Jesus moves one to see the liberation from that which hinders wholeness of being.

† Gracious Father, may my actions speak of your love and grace. Stop me from merely maintaining traditions that impede restoration and renewal. Amen.

For further thought

Can you call to mind practices in your church/Christian discipline that have become traditional burdens?

Where did I hear that before? – 1 Famous sayings from the Old Testament

Notes by **Deseta Davis**

Deseta is currently an assistant pastor of a Pentecostal Church. Her main vocation is as a prison chaplain helping to bring hope to those who are incarcerated. Having obtained an MA in theological studies, she previously worked as a tutor in Black Theology bringing the study of theology to a range of people who had not considered such study. Deseta is married to Charles, they have two grown-up children and a granddaughter. Deseta has used the NIVUK for these notes.

Sunday 21 July
By the skin of my teeth

Read Job 19:20

I am nothing but skin and bones; I have escaped only by the skin of my teeth.

(verse 20)

This week we will be concentrating on common sayings from the Old Testament. As common as these sayings are, many people may not realise their origins – and these sayings may not be common to all countries and may have different meanings in different contexts.

Today's saying is attributed to Job who went through a very difficult period in his life, losing everything he owned including his children. He had an awful skin disease and believed he had escaped by the skin of his teeth, that is, perhaps, just by the thin porcelain covering of his teeth. Today, the phrase means narrowly or barely escaping from disaster.

Once I watched a programme on TV regarding a missionary who went abroad where he was kidnapped. He watched as one of his colleagues was murdered in front of him and he was expecting to be next. After ten gruelling days, one of the kidnappers took pity on him and helped him escape into the night. He felt he had escaped by the skin of his teeth.

In today's world, many people are escaping atrocities with barely the clothes on their backs. Many are fleeing wars, tortures, famine and degradation. Many die on the way but others know that they have escaped by the skin of their teeth.

† Pray today for missionaries and others fleeing wars and torture. Ask God to be with them in their plight.

Monday 22 July
At my wits' end

> **Read Psalm 107:27**
>
> *They reeled and staggered like drunkards; they were at their wits' end.*
>
> (verse 27)

This is another phrase used quite significantly in British circles; it is defined in the Cambridge Dictionary as being so worried, confused or annoyed that you do not know what to do next.

The psalm reviews Israel's history and tells of Israel turning time and again to their own devices and getting in over their heads. Not knowing how to deal with their situation, all they could do was call on God. Yet, no matter how many times they were in this desperate state, God had mercy and helped them in their time of need.

Sometimes we become so overwhelmed by our situations that we are at a loss as to what to do. When we are at our wits' end, that's where faith takes hold. When we don't know what to do, we can rely on God.

As Israel did, sometimes we put ourselves in situations that we cannot get out of, we lose total control, but that is sometimes where we can find God. The psalmist in Psalm 139 said 'if I make my bed in the depths, you are there' (verse 8). When I consider this, I am humbled to think that even if I am the cause for the hell I am in, at my very wits' end – God says, 'I am there.'

Faith helps us to hold on when we are at the end of our tether and do not know what to do. It helps us to trust in God who is willing to help us through the most difficult circumstances.

† Pray for those who are going through difficulties and at their wits' end, that their faith may be strengthened rather than weakened.

For further thought

When were you last at your wits' end? Where did you find the strength to carry on?

Tuesday 23 July
Pride goes before a fall

Read Proverbs 16:18–19

Pride goes before destruction, a haughty spirit before a fall. Better to be lowly in spirit along with the oppressed than to share plunder with the proud.

(verses 18–19)

Pride is generally seen as very negative. However, it is more helpful, and more biblical, to distinguish between good and bad pride. Good pride is a kind of dignity one feels for services well rendered, whereas bad pride is about self-worship, power and taking glory for oneself alone.

Pride is something that each human being has the capacity to engage in whether good or bad. Bad pride has brought down many kingdoms, toppled empires, caused wars, destroyed marriages, ruined friendships, led many to prison and is something that no one is immune from.

Daniel 4 tells the story of King Nebuchadnezzar. His heart was lifted up in pride after viewing his kingdom and praising himself. He then becomes as an animal, perhaps suffering from mental illness, eating the grass of the field and living among the animals. All this happened after being warned by Daniel the year before about his pride. When he comes back to his senses he humbles himself and honours God for his grace.

Governments today throughout the world are still vying for the place of honour; they try to become the superpower, to take pride in what they have done and leave their name in history. In doing so, many are arguing and warring against one another, bringing countries closer to conflict and destruction. Pride tends to be centre stage in a lot of these disputes!

† Loving God, I pray for the governments throughout the world. Help them to lead with humility and to work in collaboration with other governments for peace and unity.

For further thought

Where have you experienced good pride recently? Where have you known bad pride?

Wednesday 24 July
Nothing new under the sun

Read Ecclesiastes 1:9–11

*What has been will be again, what has been done will be done again;
there is nothing new under the sun. Is there anything of which one can
say, 'Look! This is something new'? It was here already, long ago.*

(verses 9–10)

I feel I am getting old when I see the same styles coming back around that I wore as a teenager. I hear my mother in myself when talking to my children and granddaughter. I say the same things she said that *I* did not like at the time, and I know my children do not like them now, but I say them anyway! No doubt my daughter says the same things to my granddaughter.

However, I do sometimes wonder about this phrase. With the advent of technology, new things seem to come out year in and year out, and if you do not get the latest gadget you seem to be left out. Advertisers push their newest device, telling you that you cannot live without it. At a push we could say that technology has been with us throughout history, from the skills given to our forefathers who were carpenters and masons such as the tabernacle artisan Bezalel, who was skilled in wood, gold and silver, to the apostle Paul who made tents.

However, the cyclical nature of life does remain the same and could be seen as emptiness and futility if we are only living for the 'rat race'. Each generation seems to be facing the same problems of life as the last generation. Nothing seems really new, no real refreshing or renewal. In fact it could be said that life is getting worse. As depressing as this may sound, the biggest problem would be if one generation does not learn from the previous generation's mistakes.

† Pray for the young people of today, that they do not make the same mistakes as the last generation.

For further thought

Young people are very technologically savvy. Could you use technology to share the wisdom you have gained to help them navigate life?

Thursday 25 July
Eat, drink and be merry

Read Ecclesiastes 8:14–15

So I commend the enjoyment of life, because there is nothing better for a person under the sun than to eat and drink and be glad. Then joy will accompany them in their toil all the days of the life God has given them under the sun.

(verse 15)

Today's phrase has all the hallmarks of enjoyment and living for pleasure. Isaiah 22:13 takes it a step further: 'Let us eat and drink for tomorrow we die.' Life does need to have some pleasure, especially after working hard, but today we live in a selfish world. We seek enjoyment and self-gratification, sometimes becoming very selfish in the process. We live to eat rather than eat to live and forget about the needs of others. We become lovers of pleasure seeking to feed our need in any way possible – not thinking about anyone else's need or how our pleasure-seeking would affect them in any way.

The gap between the rich and poor is becoming greater within countries and between countries. Recent statistics suggest a world we do not see: three billion people in the world struggle to survive on less than US$2 (£1.20) a day to eat and feed their families. It is estimated that one third of the world is well fed, one third is underfed and one third is starving. To satisfy the world's sanitation and food requirements would cost only US$13 billion (£8 billion) per year – which is what the people of the United States and the European Union spend on perfume (or pet food) each year.

Yet if we take this phrase literally – we should eat, drink and be merry, for tomorrow we die. It reminds us that while we are eating, drinking and making merry, there are many people *already dying* from poverty and hunger.

† Compassionate God, may we remember those living in poverty in our world. Help us to participate in what you are already doing to help and support them.

For further thought

What is being done for the poor in the village, town or urban neighbourhood where you live?

Friday 26 July
Seeing eye to eye

Read Isaiah 52:7–10

Listen! Your watchmen lift up their voices; together they shout for joy. When the Lord returns to Zion, they will see it with their own eyes.

(verse 8)

The New Living Translation and NRSVA translate the second part of this verse, 'for in plain sight they see the return of the Lord'; the KJV has, 'they shall see eye to eye'. The phrase is about seeing distinctly and clearly; another interpretation which is more common today is being united, looking steadily at the same thing.

The eye is said to be the window to the soul. Through the eyes you can see what is going on deep down within. That said, I had a close friend who was completely blind and he was an excellent judge of character. It is said that when sight is impaired, other senses become heightened to help 'see' without the use of eyes. My friend and I worked very well together and saw 'eye to eye' on many things. I believe he could see deep into the soul, even if not physically.

In British society today, the phrase 'seeing eye to eye' is mainly defined as 'agreeing with each other'. It could be seen as unity and collaboration, which is a major part of the Christian message. It takes effort and agreement to work together in unity. I work with a number of prison chaplains in a multifaith team. It takes a unique perspective to work in such a team and respect goes a long way. We work well together and know that our heart and duty are towards the men that we work with. We do not always see things the same way, nor always agree, but we see clearly that our work is in collaboration for the good of the men.

† Loving God, help us to see clearly that we are your people and can work together for the good of others.

For further thought

Does Christian ecumenism – working and worshipping with Christians from other churches – require 'seeing eye to eye' on all things?

Saturday 27 July
A leopard can't change its spots

Read Jeremiah 13:23

Can an Ethiopian change his skin or a leopard its spots? Neither can you do good who are accustomed to doing evil.

(verse 23)

I hear this phrase used time and again regarding prisoners and ex-prisoners. They bear the scars of their crime for life. People do not let them forget and expect them to commit other crimes as 'a leopard can't change its spots'.

Many prisoners seem to prove the point, returning to prison time and again, sometimes released on Friday and back in by Monday through the revolving door – they just can't change their spots!

Yet then there are the others, the ones who slowly change in front of you, little by little. We may not see this as often as we would like, and it may be a very slow process, but we all can talk about the one or two that have changed. And then there is the one who makes a dramatic change and becomes a great pillar in society.

Throughout the Bible we see many who were changed or transformed. I consider the little-known story of Ahab, a very wicked king who with his wife Jezebel killed and destroyed many people, yet he turned around in repentance and even God commended him to the prophet Elijah (1 Kings 21:25–29). Ahab made a dramatic change.

People can and do change, and many times all they need is help and support from society. A leopard changing its spots does not apply to human beings, but only to leopards. Because people have proved time and again that they can change.

† Pray for the prisoners and ask God to help them to change for the better.

For further thought

Who in your life do you need to allow the chance to change? What can our society do to help those incarcerated to better their lives?

Where did I hear that before? – 2 Famous sayings from the New Testament

Notes by **Lesley George Anderson**

Lesley is pastor of Thomas Memorial Wesleyan Methodist Church in Harlem, New York City, USA. He is a Methodist Minister in the Caribbean and the Americas, and former President of the United Theological College of the West Indies in Jamaica. He is the author of *Baptism, Superstitions and the Supernatural* (Faith Works, 2010) and many articles. He is married to Verna and they have one son, Lesley III, a daughter-in-law, Kayla, and two grandchildren, Quentin and Brayden. Lesley has used the NRSVA for these notes.

Sunday 28 July
Eye for an eye

Read Matthew 5:38–40

'You have heard that it was said, "An eye for an eye and a tooth for a tooth."'

(verse 38)

As a youth I was fascinated with famous sayings from the New Testament and during this week we will examine some of them. We begin with the old 'law of retaliation' (Exodus 21:23–25), known also in Latin as '*lex talionis*'. The applicable principle of the law was judicial. It was the prerogative of the court of the day to ensure a punishment equal to the crime committed.

Some of us, if not all of us, have been hurt by an enemy, a friend, a relative or other persons. Some have intentionally tarnished our names, wilfully destroyed our reputation and spread false information about us. How do we cope with such hurt and pain? Often, our first desire is to retaliate, to seek revenge or to get even.

In response, Jesus comes, not to abolish the law or the prophets (Matthew 5:17), but to make a paradigm shift that will provide us with a new, better and higher standard of justice – to 'love [our] enemies and pray for those who persecute' us (Matthew 5:44).

† O God, when our lives become entangled with hate and vengeance, lead us to the living Christ, who suffered death by crucifixion and still forgives.

Fresh From the Word 2020

It may seem early, but *Fresh From the Word 2020* is now available to order.

Order now:

- direct from IBRA
- from your local IBRA rep
- in all good Christian bookshops
- from Amazon and other online retailers

To order direct from IBRA

- website: shop.christianeducation.org.uk
- email: ibra.sales@christianeducation.org.uk
- call: 0121 458 3313
- post: using the order form at the back of this book

£9.99 plus postage and packaging.

Fresh From the Word is available for Kindle, and in ePub and PDF format from online retailers such as Amazon.

Become an IBRA rep

Do you order multiple copies of *Fresh From the Word* for yourself and your friends or people in your congregation or Bible study group?

When you order three or more copies direct from IBRA you will receive a 10% discount on your order of *Fresh From the Word*. You will also receive a free promotional pack each year to help you share IBRA more easily with family, friends and others at your church.

Would you consider leaving a legacy to IBRA?

What's valuable about a gift in your will to IBRA's International Fund is that every penny goes directly towards enabling hundreds of thousands of people around the world to access the living Word of God.

IBRA has a rich history going back over 135 years. It was the

vision of Charles Waters to enable people in Britain and overseas to benefit from the Word of God through the experiences and insights of biblical scholars and teachers across the world. The vision was to build up people's lives in their homes and situations wherever they were. His legacy lives on today in you, as a reader, and the IBRA team.

Our work at IBRA is financed by the sales of the books, but from its very start in 1882, 100% of donations to the IBRA international fund go to benefit our local and international readers. To continue this important work, would you consider leaving a legacy in your will?

Find out more

Leaving a gift in your will to a Christian charity is a way of ensuring that this work continues for years to come: to help future generations and reach out to them with hope and the life-changing Word of God – people we may never meet but who are all our brothers and sisters in Christ.

Through such a gift you will help continue the strong and lasting legacy of IBRA for generations to come!

To find out more please contact our Finance Manager on 0121 458 3313, email ibra@christianeducation.org.uk or write to International Bible Reading Association, 5–6 Imperial Court, 12 Sovereign Road, Birmingham, B30 3FH.

• To read more about the history of IBRA go to page 28

• To find out more about the work of the IBRA International Fund go to page 369

Monday 29 July
Go the extra mile

Read Matthew 5:41–42

'And if anyone forces you to go one mile, go also the second mile.'

(verse 41)

During the time of the Roman Empire it was customary practice for Jewish civilians to be forced to carry the military equipment of a soldier for at least a mile or perform other forms of labour. This was both humiliating and embarrassing. Jesus, in alluding to this exceedingly hurtful practice, departs from inciting hate, rage, peaceful disobedience or even non-violent resistance. Rather, he encourages his followers to 'go also the second mile' (verse 41). Jesus is intentionally calling you and me to radically move away from attitudes of revenge in order to live out our personal relationships at a higher standard.

Over the years I have learned that when we have been used, abused and misused, we do not have to retaliate; we can use our afflicted situation or hurtful circumstance as an opportunity to witness for the cause of Christ, even though some persons will consider us weak for not retaliating. Are you willing for the sake of Christ to suffer insults and injury? Does Christ invite you to allow evil persons to walk all over you? How do you maintain your human dignity when others seek to take advantage of you?

Your responses will depend on how far you are prepared to go; the first mile or the second mile with Christ. There are times in life when we all have to make tough choices and difficult decisions. Some of these may involve our making great sacrifices.

In 1 Corinthians 9:19–23, Paul identified himself as a 'slave to all' to 'win more' persons for Christ. Like Paul, are you able to identify yourself in this way?

† O Lord, as we endeavour to go the extra mile in our relations with those who misuse and humiliate us, may our lives be consistently channels of love and forgiveness.

For further thought

Where can you be challenged to 'go the extra mile' today?

Tuesday 30 July
Wolves in sheep clothing

Read Matthew 7:15–19

'Beware of false prophets, who come to you in sheep's clothing but inwardly are ravenous wolves.'

(verse 15)

'Beware of false prophets' is Jesus' warning to us. Who is a false prophet? The Greek word for 'false prophets' is *'pseudoprophetes'*. Pseudo means 'false' or 'fake'; Jesus was concerned that such persons would present themselves as spokespersons for God, persons in 'sheep's clothing', but in fact were 'ravenous wolves'. Paul picks up the theme in 2 Corinthians 11:13–15 and calls them 'boasters': 'false apostles, deceitful workers', who disguise 'themselves as apostles of Christ' and 'ministers of righteousness'. Jesus warned in Matthew 24:24–25: 'For false messiahs and false prophets will appear and produce great signs and omens, to lead astray, if possible, even the elect. Take note, I have told you beforehand.' False prophets will certainly mislead the sheep and bring them to their ruin. The end result will be the destruction they will bring upon themselves (2 Peter 2:1–2).

'Street Preachers' of Harlem can still be seen and heard on 125th St, known locally as Harlem's 'Main Street' (or High Street, for the British equivalent). Some are articulate misleading prophets, mortal enemies of God's sheep, while others are proclaimers of the work of Christ on Calvary's cross and of his glory in his resurrection from the dead. This is the gospel – the Good News proclaimed that is the power of God to salvation!

The true spokesperson of God is known and recognised by 'his/her fruit of the Spirit' which is 'love, joy, peace, patience, kindness, generosity, faithfulness, gentleness, and self-control' (Galatians 5:22–23). These are the evidences to be seen in the life of the person.

† Lord, protect us from deceivers, imposters – wolves in sheep's clothing. Teach us to look to you in trust as our true shepherd who cares for the sheep.

For further thought

Read and contrast John 10:1–18 with Ezekiel 22:25–27. What similarities and differences do you notice between these passages of scripture?

Wednesday 31 July
Blind leading the blind

Read Matthew 15:10–14

'Let them alone; they are blind guides of the blind. And if one blind person guides another, both will fall into a pit.'

(verse 14)

Our text reminds us of the existential reality of 'blind leaders' being guides of the blind. The key word we must bear in mind in this meditation is 'trust'. Persons to whom we look up to as our leaders, particularly our heads of state, teachers, and in this context, bishops, ministers, priests and pastors, both males and females, must be deemed 'trustworthy' as spokespersons for God.

'Blind' leaders are a danger in every age, and in recent times have been particularly misleading, misguiding, corrupting and destroying the lives of the young and vulnerable aged who cry out for help and protection. When in the midst of these leaders we must keep our eyes and ears open (Matthew 13:16–17); and in Matthew 23 Jesus denounces the leaders of his day, calling them 'blind guides' and pointing out to them that they stressed tithing, but 'neglected the weightier matters of the law: justice and mercy and faith' (Matthew 23:23–24).

Hold on to Jesus, the good news of salvation, who has the power to give sight to the spiritually blind! In John 9:39 we are informed by Jesus that the blind see and those who see are blind. Admitting we are blind is the avenue that moves us from spiritual blindness to the road of gaining spiritual sight. Having gained spiritual sight, we are able *to see* God's continuing presence with us in all of life. We live boldly, clearly and fervently the gospel in the face of death, mounting sorrows and pain. We take Jesus seriously which results in making our lives sparkle with marked manifestations of Holy Spirit power.

† Gracious Lord, cleanse our lives of the darkness of sin and teach us to trust in you more, so that we may wisely live to experience your marvellous light.

For further thought

The 2016 film *Notes on Blindness* tells the story of British theologian John Hull's experience of losing his sight. Consider today what vision means, and what it means to see truly.

Thursday 1 August
Cast the first stone

Read John 8:1–11

When they kept on questioning him, he straightened up and said to them, 'Let anyone among you who is without sin be the first to throw a stone at her.'

(verse 7)

Jesus did not condemn the woman caught in the act of committing adultery – it was unnatural for him not to have condemned such a sin. Why did Jesus make an exception in her case? Jesus is pointing out that her accusers failed to remember that a man was also involved in the act. He, too, was guilty, but was invisible to the woman's accusers. What spiritual implications can we identify in the words of Jesus?

Jesus no doubt contrasted the woman's accusers' boastings and bursting arrogance with the woman's humility in her time of humiliation. He saw in their self-righteousness, not just a willingness to condemn the woman, but also their violent readiness to stone her to death. They felt secure that they were incapable of committing sin, and this was in fact their besetting sin.

Oftentimes we find it easier to condemn and point the finger at others. We are eager to find faults and throw stones. We never seem to notice our indulgence in wickedness nor the terrible things we often do. We may not be engaged in adulterous behaviour, but we are envious, hateful and malicious. Jesus pricked the consciences of the crowd to recognise that 'all' sin is grievous! He said: 'Who is without sin be the first to throw a stone at her' (verse 7). In the end, the crowd came to recognise their own sinfulness and Jesus liberated the woman from their condemnation and told her: 'Go your way, and from now on do not sin again' (verse 11).

† Lord, forgive our foolish, boastful ways that lead to bloated pride. Cleanse us from sin and renew within us a new heart and mind. Amen.

For further thought

Examine yourself today. Are you able to cast or throw the first stone at anyone?

Friday 2 August
Fallen from grace

Read Galatians 5:1–6

You who want to be justified by the law have cut yourselves off from Christ; you have fallen away from grace.

(verse 4)

For Paul, the way we live has to match what we believe. If we want to bear fruit in the Spirit, we have to align ourselves with that Spirit through faith. Paul highlights his point noting that circumcision does not and cannot lead to salvation, for Christ is the only way.

Paul considered himself the supreme example of God's saving grace. His story is very much like my story and possibly like yours. We were lost, but now we are found. We were blind but now we see. Paul received mercy and forgiveness because he believed the truth that the grace of God is powerful enough to redeem the worst sinner who repents. Paul knew the depth of his sins as a persecutor of followers of Christ and certainly the height of his salvation in Christ after his conversion on the road to Damascus (Acts 9:1–19).

Paul as a result dismisses the argument that circumcision is an essential path to salvation. Salvation is experienced only in the perfect and complete sacrifice of Christ upon Calvary's cross. When we put our trust in anything other than God, we 'cut' ourselves 'off from Christ' and fall 'away from grace' (verse 4). To fall from grace is to be 'cut off' – severed from Christ, to whom we once belonged, and by whom we were saved. To live under the law to gain salvation is to reject salvation by grace. The work of salvation totally belongs to God, through his perfect gift to us, Jesus Christ! In Hebrews 12:15 the writer warns us: 'See to it that no one fails to obtain the grace of God …' Our challenge is to live by grace through salvation. Let us keep our trust and faith in Christ alone for our salvation, lest we fall from grace!

† O God, enable us by faith to receive your grace and rejoice in the precious gift of your son, Jesus Christ. Amen.

For further thought

What has falling from grace taught you about God's grace?

Saturday 3 August
In the twinkling of an eye

Read 1 Corinthians 15:51–54

Listen, I will tell you a mystery! We will not all die, but we will all be changed, in a moment, in the twinkling of an eye ...

(verses 51–52a)

These verses infer and emphasise the revelation of a 'new secret', a mystery revelling in the unknown, and paradoxically, in the revealed known: 'We will not all die, but we will all be changed, in a moment, in the twinkling of an eye' (verse 52). Believers in Christ will not all die, but all will be changed 'in the twinkling of an eye'. This great experience will be sudden, in a moment, like lightning flashing in the sky.

In 1 Corinthians 15 Paul draws us into the depth of an unfathomable mystery which is partly linked to Psalm 23, wherein without our ever having to walk through the valley of the shadow of death, we are translated into the realm of heaven to be present with our Lord and Saviour Jesus Christ, the conqueror of death and giver of everlasting life. This is the mystery of 'the twinkling of an eye'.

There is such certainty about this mystery that Paul writes to the Corinthians: 'Death has been swallowed up in victory.' 'Where, O death, is your victory? Where, O death, is your sting?' (verses 54–55).

Christians all over the world share in Christ's victory over his death on Calvary's cross and his resurrection victory over the grave, through the power of the living God. Paul speaks quite profoundly of the experience of living saints being 'caught up', 'in the twinkling of an eye' with our departed Christian brothers and sisters in the arms of the Lord forever (1 Thessalonians 4:17).

† O Lord, allow nothing to separate us from your love. Keep us safe and steadfast in our life's journey until we come to rest in you.

For further thought

Read again 1 Corinthians 15:51–54. Why is such detailed information given us about the 'mystery' by Paul?

Gossip

Notes by **Lynne Frith**

For Lynne's biography, see p. 168. Lynne has used the NRSVA for these notes.

Sunday 4 August
Wild fires

Read James 3:1–12

How great a forest is set ablaze by a small fire!

(verse 5b)

During summer, most parts of New Zealand have a total fire ban imposed – no campfires, barbecues or rubbish fires are permitted. It takes only a spark, or a cigarette butt, and a breeze, and before long there is a blaze that is difficult to control.

We seldom see the scale of wild fires and devastation that are a frequent occurrence in California or Australia, but from time to time, there are scrub fires of sufficient magnitude to be a threat to houses and human life.

In the same way that a spark can rapidly become a wild and ferocious fire, consuming grasslands, forests, buildings and destroying everything in its path, so too can an unkind comment on any of the social media be magnified and spread around, with devastating effect.

This week, the readings invite us to think about how and what we communicate to and about others, whether with our tongues, our keyboards or any of the devices that are available to us.

They also remind us that the way in which we communicate, the words we use, reflects the kind of person we are. The same tongue, or language, or medium of communication may be used for good or ill.

† May the words of my mouth and the meditation of my heart cause no harm or offence.

Gossip

August

Monday 5 August
Fake news and alternative facts

Read Exodus 23:1–8

You shall not spread a false report.

(verse 1a)

As I write this, the world continues to struggle with discernment in regard to 'fake news' and 'alternative facts'. These two phenomena have gained prominence in public life, particularly in global politics.

Sometimes fake news is created with an obvious agenda. Other times, it is the result of careless reporting. In either case, the speed with which such news is liked and shared quickly fools us into thinking that there may be truthfulness in these stories.

It is not only in public life that we see false news and the presentation of alternative facts shaping public opinion.

Among teenagers, the use of social media to spread false or malicious information about an individual – about his or her behaviour, appearance and personality – can have a devastating effect on the individual under attack.

Today's reading requires us to be discerning in what we 'like' and 'share', to avoid 'join[ing] hands with the wicked to act as a malicious witness' (verse 1).

Further, we are to be impartial in pursuit of justice, not siding with the majority if doing so will pervert justice being done.

Perhaps verse 8 could be rendered, 'you shall not like and share everything that presses your emotional buttons, for such liking and sharing gives a false impression of public support, and distorts truth'.

† Pray for discernment and wisdom about the reports you read on social media.

For further action

Make a commitment for this week to refrain from sharing or commenting on what appear to be false reports.

Those who cause mischief by what they say

Read Psalm 36

O continue your steadfast love to those who know you, and your salvation to the upright of heart!

(verse 10)

I knew of a woman who wrote a vitriolic letter to her sister, outlining her sister's many faults and accusing her of deceitful behaviour. She sent copies of the letter to her other siblings. The damage it caused to both the relationship of the sisters and the wider family was immense. While with time the rift in the family has softened, it is far from healed.

With contemporary communication methods like email, such damage is so much more immediate, especially if the email is copied to a wide circle. I have seen this happen in congregations, where an individual has a concern about another and, rather than address it one to one, copies in a wide group of people. Such action often appears to be out of malice rather than any desire for resolving the issue.

At another level, hate speech in all its forms does not have the well-being of the community at heart, but foments discontent and division, with the potential to erupt into acts of violence. I find it hard to comprehend what influences have been at work to shape such hatred in a person's life.

Psalm 36 eloquently describes those who mean mischief and harm.

However, the larger part of the psalm declares that God's steadfast love and faithfulness, God's righteousness and judgement are protection and refuge from the acts of the arrogant and the wicked.

It concludes with a heartfelt plea from the writer to be strengthened rather than cowed in the face of mischief making.

† May I not keep silent, O God, in the face of hate speech of any kind.

For further action

Send a message of support to victims or recipients of hate speech or other malicious communications such as graffiti.

Gossip

August

Wednesday 7 August
What you say reveals who you are

Read Proverbs 10:10–20

The mouth of the righteous is a fountain of life, but the mouth of the wicked conceals violence.

(verse 11)

In the section of Proverbs of which this chapter is a part, much attention is given to the impact on individuals and the community of all kinds of careless and harmful speech and attitudes.

Some people only speak to be critical and judgemental. They are convinced of their own 'rightness' and are unable to consider any other point of view. I have often been in committee meetings where such a person has a profound effect on the mood and effectiveness of the meeting. It seems that people are so intimidated by the anger and violence that lie behind the spoken words that they do not challenge the speaker. By their silence, they assent; the person is never confronted with the effect they have and the level of power remains unchecked.

A researcher found that nurses in New Zealand not only have to deal with traditional forms of abuse, but now face being bullied and harassed by email, with voicemail messages and on social media (*New Zealand Herald*, 21 November 2017). Many have been the focus of attention from former students they had taught, patients or families of patients. Nurses talk of being worn down, of being stalked through social media, of being fearful of damage to their professional reputation, and of the difficulty in escaping this and similar intimidating behaviour.

The pairings in each verse of today's reading from Proverbs not only caution about what lies behind harmful words and attitudes, but also offer advice about the path to wisdom, which is marked by growth in understanding and knowledge. The disposition of the righteous is life giving. The reading does not condone abusive behaviour, but offers and commends an alternative way of being, marked by restraint and wisdom.

† Pray for victims of bullying, harassment, slander and other forms of bullying and intimidation.

For further action

Find out how to access internet safety organisations in your community.

Thursday 8 August
Zip up your lips

Read Proverbs 11:9–13

A gossip goes about telling secrets, but one who is trustworthy in spirit keeps a confidence.

(verse 13)

How often have you told someone something in confidence, only to hear it back in unexpected places? Have you sometimes inadvertently or intentionally passed on information with which you are entrusted?

In every social group, including the church, there is at least one person who always talks, the person of whom it is said that if you want something spread around, tell him or her. Sometimes, in the telling, as in the childhood whispering game, the original information is distorted in some way, however small, that then leads to misunderstanding.

How easily a careless word can cause unintended hurt to another. Those who sow seeds of mistrust, fear and suspicion can damage the stability of a community or even a nation. Whether it's the fear of Islam that is promulgated as a reaction to the extreme actions of a few, or the generalisation that lays the blame on refugees and migrants for all kinds of social and economic ills, the potential for undermining civil society is great.

The ancient wisdom collected in Proverbs has a strong sense of the contribution righteous, upright and intelligent people make to the well-being of the city. The sense that individual well-being is bound up with the welfare of the city is echoed elsewhere in the scriptures, in Jeremiah 29, for example. Whether this is about respecting the confidences entrusted to us or about refusal to participate in promulgating a climate of mistrust and suspicion, people of faith have a vital part to play in maintaining the welfare of the community.

† May I always be respectful of the confidences entrusted to me.

For further thought

What contribution might you make to the well-being of the whole community?

Be a model of good works, integrity, and sound speech

Read Titus 2:1–8

Show yourself in all respects a model of good works, and in your teaching show integrity, gravity, and sound speech that cannot be censured.

(verses 7–8a)

During 2017, sexual harassment claims concerning celebrities sparked an amazing social media response. The #MeToo campaign empowered women and some men to speak out about the sexual abuse and blackmail they had suffered, from the famous or from the everyday bullies and harassers in the workplace.

There has been a change in public consciousness. Women who speak up are being believed. Men who may themselves not have abused their power are beginning to acknowledge that by doing nothing while other men abused power, they were complicit.

Public figures can no longer assume that their power, fame and wealth will protect them from prosecution.

This is one way that social media may be used for empowering people, and for speaking out for justice.

Excluding the troublesome verses encouraging young women to be submissive to their husbands, and slaves to be submissive to their masters, the letter of Titus is a reminder that, whatever our social status or our calling, how we conduct ourselves in the everyday aspects of our lives is vital, whether in good works, speech or the click of a key.

† Pray today for those who speak out about misconduct, abuse and harassment.

For further thought

In what ways might you be a model of good works and sound speech?

Saturday 10 August
Rules for the New Life

Read Ephesians 4:17–32

Be kind to one another, tender-hearted, forgiving one another, as God in Christ has forgiven you.

(verse 32)

Most of us are familiar with codes of conduct for behaviour in particular environments. They provide a clear framework for what is expected – how we interact with colleagues, clients, people seeking our help and support. They usually include standards for things such as sexual conduct, what to do with unsolicited gifts, and may include requirements for self-care, professional supervision and accountability. The purpose is both to provide a safe environment for those whom we serve, and to ensure high professional standards.

This week's readings conclude with what the NRSVA calls 'Rules for the New Life'.

Verses 17–24 identify some of the behaviours that are inconsistent with a life in Christ. Paul reminds the Ephesian Christians that they have been taught to put away their former way of life, and to put on a new self.

And so a framework, or code of conduct, follows in verses 25–32. These 'rules' are in the context of being members of the one body. They are about building up community and individuals within it, working in order to share with the needy, having a disposition of kindness, tender-heartedness and forgiveness.

† O God, keep me living kindly and tender-heartedly in all that I do.

For further thought

What might rules for a new life look like in a world of individualism and immediate communication?

Gossip

August

Readings in Deuteronomy – 1 Do not fear

Notes by **Joshua Taylor**

Joshua is Vicar of St John's Anglican Church in Timaru, New Zealand. He and wife Jo have two daughters (Phoebe and Esther) and together they've been exploring what it means to be a family on mission. Josh recently completed his Master's thesis on consumerism and its impact on how we do church. He writes a blog (longstoryshort.nz) and spends days off being mocked by fish while holding a fishing rod. Joshua has used the NRSVA for these notes.

Sunday 11 August
Following God's lead

Read Deuteronomy 1:6–11

'See, I have set the land before you; go in and take possession of the land that I swore to your ancestors, to Abraham, to Isaac, and to Jacob, to give to them and to their descendants after them.'

(verse 8)

The people of God are packing their bags and are on the move once again. What prompts their move? The opening line gives us a clue: 'The Lord our God spoke to us at Horeb' (verse 6).

It is God's initiative and promise that take pride of place in Deuteronomy and in this week's readings.

Our world offers us so much choice. The other day I stood transfixed in the yoghurt aisle looking for a treat for my daughter's lunchbox. There must have been 30 different kinds of yoghurts to choose from: a choice that was oddly paralysing. There are of course more important decisions in life than yoghurt. The point is that the weight of the decision often rests on our own shoulders. We will ask serious questions about our vocation, our relationships and the very direction of our lives. In a world without God, each decision sits with us. What Deuteronomy invites us to do is to see life in light of God's promises. This changes the game entirely. God goes before the people and prepares the way; their response is to be obedient.

Life isn't simply about finding our purpose, but rather it is about hearing how we fit in with God's mission in the world. Deuteronomy invites us to think as a people who live in response to God's promises. To do that requires that we pause to listen for God's lead.

† Faithful God, your promises are good and true. When you call me to follow you may I respond with trust and obedience. Amen.

Monday 12 August
You'll never walk alone

Read Deuteronomy 1:12–18

'But how can I bear the heavy burden of your disputes all by myself?'
... So I took the leaders of your tribes, wise and reputable individuals,
and installed them as leaders over you, commanders of thousands,
commanders of hundreds, commanders of fifties, commanders of tens,
and officials, throughout your tribes.

(verses 12, 15)

Growing up in Sunday school many characters of the Bible were presented to me as 'heroes'. Moses, that sagely bearded prophet, was of course one of the greatest. There is something problematic in this thinking. Our contemporary celebrity culture likes to have people to idolise and put up on a pedestal; however, it seems that in God's economy leaders are not called to be heroes but rather servants.

Moses displays a great amount of vulnerability in the admission that he can't bear the heavy burden of the people's disputes all on his own.

The solution is to create a team of leaders who act as commanders, officials and judges. Each of these leaders plays a particular role in upholding the law and ensuring God's justice is done. They are to judge fairly and wisely in accordance with the view that God's leadership and guidance matter the most.

Jesus himself takes on a team of disciples who undertake his mission alongside him. They are called not to be heroes but rather to be co-workers in God's mission. When they quibble over who is the greatest they are quickly reminded that this is not the point. The hero goes out on their own for their own glory, but the team who serve with Moses are reminded that God's opinion matters more than anyone else; they are told, 'you shall not be intimidated by anyone' (verse 17).

True Christian leadership as modelled by Moses seeks not to exercise power but rather to serve God's purposes in the world. Bearing the burden alone will cause us to boast or bust, but bearing it together will bear fruit for God's kingdom and for his glory.

† Lord, help us to share the burdens of leadership and service with each other that we may bring glory to your name. Amen.

For further thought
Who are the people in your life whom you are called to serve God with? What further support do you need?

227

Tuesday 13 August
Focus in a distracting world

Read Deuteronomy 2:1–23

'Today you are going to cross the boundary of Moab at Ar. When you approach the frontier of the Ammonites, do not harass them or engage them in battle, for I will not give the land of the Ammonites to you as a possession, because I have given it to the descendants of Lot.'

(verses 18–19)

We live in an age of distraction. We have emails and social media notifications at our fingertips, full schedules and 101 good things we might like to do. It isn't often enough that I pause to pray and take time to figure out what it is that I really ought to give my time to.

In today's reading from Deuteronomy we get a picture of the Israelites wandering through the desert and being prompted by God not to start skirmishes with the locals. God asks them to bypass various tribes and peoples because he has given these peoples the land. Here we are reminded that even though the land is a part of the promise of the people, it is not the point. Israel isn't defined by inheriting land; many of the other peoples have been gifted land by God as these scriptures tell us. Israel is defined by God's covenant relationship. They are a light to the nations and God has called them to represent him in the world.

This passage invites us to think about first things first. Where we might get distracted with our own projects or agendas it invites us to be focused on who God is calling us to be and what God is calling us to do.

† Lord, I am prone to wander and lose sight of your call on my life. Help me to focus my eyes on you and share in your mission of love in the world. Amen.

For further thought

What distractions are present in your life? What stops you from hearing God's promptings and being obedient? What do you need to bypass right now to follow God?

Wednesday 14 August
God has gone before you

Read Deuteronomy 2:24–37

'Proceed on your journey and cross the Wadi Arnon. See, I have handed over to you King Sihon the Amorite of Heshbon, and his land. Begin to take possession by engaging him in battle. This day I will begin to put the dread and fear of you upon the peoples everywhere under heaven ...'

(verses 24–25a)

One question that many people stew over is 'Am I living God's will for my life?' It's a big question with no answer that can be given in a couple of hundred words. But in Deuteronomy we do get a glimpse of the dynamic of following God's lead. In the mix of God's leadership of the people and their following, we see God's plan unfold.

Sihon the Amorite king stood in the way of the Israelite people getting to the promised land, yet another obstacle in God's plan. It looks rather bleak for the Israelites, but God intervenes once again. Right from the beginning of the story of the Exodus it is God who is the main character of this story. It is God who goes before the people. God gives the land over to the people by making Sihon's heart hard so that a battle ensues. The people aren't merely puppets in God's plan, though. The Lord has handed over the king, but the people are to take possession of the land – there is the dance of God's will and plan together with the responsibility and obedience of the people.

Perhaps discerning God's will is less like waiting for a train to arrive at the station and more like being on a tandem bicycle. From my experience riding tandem requires a good level of communication. This is modelled by the relationship between Moses and God and later in the Gospels we see Jesus model it in his prayer life with the Father. May we be encouraged to seek God's will and find our part to play in God's mission in our world.

† Holy Spirit, you are at work in the places we go long before we get there. Help us to follow where you lead and share in your mission of love. Amen.

For further thought

How open are your communication lines with God? When you have had a sense of something God wants you to do, how have you responded?

Do not fear

Read Deuteronomy 3:1–11

When we headed up the road to Bashan, King Og of Bashan came out against us, he and all his people, for battle at Edrei. The Lord said to me, 'Do not fear him, for I have handed him over to you, along with his people and his land.'

(verses 1–2a)

The violence of these stories of conquest in Deuteronomy has made many modern readers squirm, and rightly so. We hear of the destruction of cities and people with horror. These kinds of passages have raised the question for the new atheists and believers alike: 'Is God a tyrant?' What is easily forgotten though is the people for whom Yahweh, the God of the Hebrews, is contending. They not long ago were slaves, oppressed peoples who were wandering the wilderness. God is delivering them and in doing so God stands against the powers of the day, the ones with war machines that struck fear into the hearts of those around them. The tyrant in the story is Og, and the other kings who proudly asserted their own violent will in the world. God in this story is the defender of the weak, giving courage and strength to his wandering, once-enslaved people.

The question of violence still lingers. In light of the history of Western Christianity it is still a stain on our conscience. Much forgiveness and reconciliation are needed in this area. Today's passage invites us to see a God who gives courage and strength to the fearful and the weak as they face the powers that dominate. Today there are many violent and oppressive powers that stand against God's will in the world. We might think of corporate greed and consumerism, leaders of nations bent on power and destruction, or much closer to home the rebellion in our own hearts. God gives his people courage to face these powers with hope that he can overcome.

† Lord, we are often afraid to face the powers that stand against you. Give us courage today that we may proclaim your love and hope in the world even when it meets opposition. Amen.

For further thought

I invite you to wrestle with this question of violence in Old Testament passages. Find a good commentary or a wise friend to converse with.

Friday 16 August
The cost of leadership

Read Deuteronomy 3:21–29

'Look well, for you shall not cross over this Jordan. But charge Joshua, and encourage and strengthen him, because it is he who shall cross over at the head of this people and who shall secure their possession of the land that you will see.'

(verses 27b–28)

The term FOMO or 'fear of missing out' is the anxiety that something great is happening and we are missing it. Reading this passage, I get the feeling that Moses was suffering what we would call serious FOMO. He has laboured and led the people through much, following God's call through the wilderness and various trials, only now at the very end of the journey to miss out on entering the promised land.

Moses is one of the most persistent petitioners of God we see in the Bible and it seems he has talked with God about this matter of entering the land more than once. God replies, 'Enough from you! Never speak to me of this matter again!' (verse 26). It seems harsh, doesn't it? Of all people wouldn't Moses deserve to enter the land? We are told that Moses will not enter the land because of God's anger with the people. Here we see Moses absorbing the punishment the people deserve for their disobedience. In fact, none of the people deserve to enter the land God is giving them, rather it is God's gracious gift to enter the land because of the promises he has made. Joshua will inherit this gift and Moses' death outside the boundary will be a reminder to the people that God's promises aren't simply dished out to the deserving. Moses rightly wants to step into the land, but the true promise of intimacy and relationship with God is already his. Looking forward in the biblical story, we may think of the cost Jesus will pay on the cross to lead us into the promised land of his kingdom.

† Jesus, you bore the punishment for our sin and disobedience on the cross. Thank you for your sacrifice for us so that we may enter the promised land of your kingdom. Amen.

For further thought

I invite you this week, like Moses, to bring before God your disappointments. The Bible gives us language for petition and lament.

Take a closer look

> ### Read Deuteronomy 4:1–19
>
> *But take care and watch yourselves closely, so as neither to forget the things that your eyes have seen nor to let them slip from your mind all the days of your life; make them known to your children and your children's children … take care and watch yourselves closely, so that you do not act corruptly by making an idol for yourselves.*
>
> (verses 9, 15–16a)

If you are a new Christian, you might be experiencing the wonder of the 'mountaintop experience'. These moments are times of clarity where God speaks clearly and we experience God's presence so closely it is tangible.

If like me you have been a Christian for some time you will know that it's quite easy to forget all that God has done for us. Deuteronomy warns the people not to forget that God delivered them from slavery miraculously and gave them a new way of life in the law. In the story of Exodus Moses had barely begun his own mountaintop encounter with God when the people decidedly forgot what God had done and created a golden calf to worship instead.

There are many idols that lure us in today's world. Some of them are obvious; the classic three are money, sex and power. Simply put, an idol can be anything we put before God. God knows that these idols will never fulfil and so the people of God are always called to remember God first. The best way to cultivate our memories is to pass on the story of God to those around us with our words and our deeds. One old Russian saint, St Tikhon of Zadonsk (1724–83), puts it this way:

'Beloved Christians, you and your children shall appear at the Judgement of Christ, and you shall give account for them to the just Judge. He will not ask you whether you have taught them to speak French, or German, or Italian, but whether you have taught them to live as Christians.'

† Lord, forgive my forgetfulness of all you have done for me. May I remember your mighty deeds and may the stories of your goodness be on my lips all the days of my life.

For further thought

Time/money/talent audit: take a moment to write a list of what you spend your time, money and talent on. Whom or what do you worship?

Readings in Deuteronomy – 2 Remembering the word

Notes by **Nathan Eddy**

Nathan is editor of *Fresh From the Word*, a parent, chicken rustler, aspiring poet, and an amateur singer and pianist. He is ordained in the United Church of Christ (USA) and has served in the United Reformed Church (UK). He recently acted in two plays, the first translations into Hebrew of *Othello* and *Romeo and Juliet*. He lives in London with his wife Clare, a vicar in the Church of England, Mahalia and Elise. Nathan has used the NRSVA for these notes.

Sunday 18 August
Hear, O Israel

Read Deuteronomy 5:1–5

Hear, O Israel, the statues and ordinances that I am addressing to you today; you shall learn them and observe them diligently.

(verse 1)

The reading today is short, only six verses, and it stops just before Deuteronomy's version of the Ten Commandments, which continue to verse 21. Have a read of these six verses. Like so many verses in Deuteronomy, at first glance they might seem like Bible 'boilerplate', like verses we've read in many places.

But have a closer look. Moses is clear that the covenant is a present reality for his audience: 'Not with our ancestors did the Lord make this covenant, but with us, who are all of us here alive today' (verse 3). But elsewhere in Deuteronomy, Moses says that God made the covenant with the first generation who came out of Egypt 40 years ago (as in 1:34–40); it was that generation's children whom Moses is addressing here, not the first generation. It appears, then, that for Deuteronomy covenant includes these future generations, indeed, all future generations of Israelites.

God is still speaking these words, and hoping his people will follow them. God is even still speaking them for you and for me, and for all who listen.

† God of the covenant, open my ears to listen and help me walk your path of life today.

Monday 19 August
With all your muchness

Read Deuteronomy 6:1–22

Hear, O Israel: The Lord is our God, the Lord alone. You shall love the Lord your God with all your heart, and with all your soul, and with all your might.

(verses 4–5)

Deuteronomy 6:4 is called the Shema after its first word, the imperative 'hear' (or 'obey'). Observant Jews traditionally recite this prayer twice a day, and Jesus affirmed it as the greatest commandment (Mark 12:29). The verse affirms that God is 'one' (NIVUK), or, translating the Hebrew word differently, 'alone' (NRSVA).

Deuteronomy is known, not always positively, for its rigorous monotheism and programme of centralisation. God is to be worshipped in one sanctuary, not many (Deuteronomy 12:2–7). But Deuteronomy is also profoundly holistic and humane. Look at the diversity of ways we are commanded to revere God: keeping the words in our heart, reciting them to our children, talking about or reciting them at home, away from home, when we go to bed and when we wake up. They are to be a physical sign on our hands and between our eyes. They are to be written on the doorposts of our homes and on our gates (verses 6–9). These ways of remembering God incorporate mental, spiritual and physical acts at home and away from home. Traditionally these verses are associated with Psalm 1:1, and the righteous person who delights in the teaching of the Lord.

Deuteronomy 6 commands far more than mere assent to a creed. It commands us to offer our whole lives to God, to practise what we preach. The word translated 'might' in verse 4 is the adverb 'greatly' or 'muchly', and in this verse one dictionary even translates it with the word 'muchness'. We are to acknowledge God as one, as our only God, with our 'muchness'. We might even say, with Psalm 35:10, 'All my bones shall say, "O Lord, who is like you?"'

† God, help me worship and follow you with all of myself today, wherever I go.

For further thought

What words would you use to describe this kind of life? Is it attractive to you?

Tuesday 20 August
Exclusive embrace

Read Deuteronomy 7:1–9

But this is how you must deal with them: break down their altars, smash their pillars, hew down their sacred poles, and burn their idols with fire. For you are a people holy to the Lord your God …

(verses 5–6a)

Yesterday we looked at the way Deuteronomy draws us in, body, mind and spirit, to a life devoted to God. Deuteronomy is attractive to me as I seek to find a faith that is also a whole way of life, not just an intellectual assent. In Deuteronomy, the word of God is in reading and doing as well as thinking; it is 'very near to you; it is in your mouth and in your heart for you to observe' (Deuteronomy 30:14). In today's reading, we see how that gift of God's word to the Israelites is sheer grace, not given on the basis of any worthiness on their part (verses 7–8).

I find this nearness of God in Deuteronomy attractive and affirming. But in today's reading we also see the very deuteronomic idea that does, or should, repel us: the so-called ban imposed by God on the other peoples that live in the land of Israel. It is a threat to Israel's faith and her very existence that the seven tribes listed in verse 1 continue to live in the land. Israel is to 'utterly destroy them' (verse 2). Historically, it is unlikely that this ban was ever enforced, but that is hardly comforting.

Yet Deuteronomy also makes clear that Israel is to care for the resident alien, the orphan and the widow (14:29). Leviticus 19:18 commands us to 'love your neighbour as yourself'. The ban is abhorrent, but the Bible itself, including Deuteronomy, shows us how to care for others and live in harmony. Belief in one God is a way to peace amid diversity; belief in one God need not lead to violence in God's name.

† God of peace, root out the seeds of violence in my community. Help us live together for your name's sake.

For further thought

How can you cherish diversity in your walk of discipleship today?

Wednesday 21 August
Not by bread alone

Read Deuteronomy 8:1–20

One does not live by bread alone, but by every word that comes from the mouth of the Lord.

(verse 3b)

I spent a summer once in the mountains of southern Colorado, USA, interviewing silver miners for the US Forest Service. I think of them when I read verse 9 in today's reading, which is one of the places in the Bible where miners are mentioned. It's a reminder that the Bible already knew fairly sophisticated cultures, and that the resources of the Earth are gifts of God, not our own property to use wastefully.

But I'm especially taken with the verse that might have caught your attention: verse 3, quoted above, which Jesus quotes in the desert temptation in Luke 4:4 and Matthew 4:4. What the NRSVA translates as 'every word' could be translated as 'all'. There seems to be a pun involved which relates the gift of manna to God's causing water to 'come out' of the rock (verse 15) and to the way God caused Israel to 'come out' of Egypt (verse 14). Perhaps the focus is not so much on the word of God, but on the way God brings life to Israel. God brings life through words and commandments as well as through bread, water, saving action and the gifts of the Earth.

Perhaps this passage is an invitation to live as if everything we have is a gift from God: the food on our tables, the minerals in our phones and computers, and the words in our Bibles. God in Deuteronomy is certainly a God of life, a God who invites us to choose life (Deuteronomy 30:19) and live it with all we've got.

† God of life, thank you for your gifts to me, which bring me life.

For further thought

Scholars have identified a 'V' shape to this passage; it moves from the desert (verses 2–5), to the Promised Land (verses 7–10, 11–14) and back to the desert (verses 14–16). What effect does this have, do you think?

Thursday 22 August
Look again

Read Deuteronomy 9:1–6

Know, then, that the Lord your God is not giving you this good land to occupy because of your righteousness; for you are a stubborn people.

(verse 6)

In 2017 the British artist Rachel Whiteread had a major show at a London museum. The show featured her trademark casts of everyday household objects. Whiteread would painstakingly create plaster moulds of tables, chairs, toilet rolls and even bookshelves. She would then fill the casts with resin, and the result would be a hauntingly beautiful shape: the space around a chair or a table. It made me think about the space we all live in every day, the space in which we move and go about our day.

Deuteronomy in fact is a Greek word that means 'second law', in part perhaps because it repeats much of the story and detail of the giving of the Torah, the Law, in Exodus. Deuteronomy, in a sense, is about a second perspective. In today's reading Moses reminds the Israelites to cultivate this second perspective on their lives. They may think that coming into the Promised Land will be their doing. They may say, one day, that God gave them the land because they deserved it (verse 5). Their forebears, verse 7 continues, tested and provoked God with their unfaithfulness, and Israel still has some things to learn, or even unlearn. They must develop another perspective on the gifts all around them. These gifts, the gift of the land itself, are God's doing, not theirs. The gifts are sheer grace.

Even if we have strength and means to acquire many possessions, this section of Deuteronomy reminds us that it is God who gives strength (8:17–18). Deuteronomy invites us to look again at all we have, to see it truly and give thanks.

† Giving God, help me see today that all I have is from you. And thank you.

For further thought

What impact do you think this second perspective might have on a modern nation's political decisions?

Love is all

> ### Read Deuteronomy 10:12–22
>
> *Yet the Lord set his heart in love on your ancestors alone and chose you, their descendants after them, out of all the peoples, as it is today.*
>
> (verse 15)

Despite being lord over all the Earth and the heavens, God chose Israel to love (verse 15). And God asks Israel to love him in return (verse 12). We know what love means. Or do we? What does Deuteronomy mean by love?

Deuteronomy is not unique here. Powerful rulers across the Ancient Near East commanded love from their empires, and professed to love them in return. Scholars typically relate the love of God in Deuteronomy to this kind of treaty or covenant agreement that was common in the ancient world.

It is certainly true that love in Deuteronomy is not gushy. Israel must love the stranger (verse 19). Israel must be practical and devoted, not just star-struck, in their love of God. But in both Jewish and Christian traditions the love of God has an emotional, even romantic dimension. Jewish tradition compares the kisses of the lovers in the Song of Songs to God's giving of the Law at Sinai. Even in Deuteronomy there is an intimacy and an emotional element, it seems to me, to God's love.

My grandparents, readers of this book, have been married more than 70 years. My grandmother told me once that the secret to a good marriage was never letting the sun go down on your anger. Deuteronomy models just this kind of healthy (even angry) communication. Israel and God may fall out and have harsh words, but they will have it out and work through it. In the final consideration, practical, devoted love is the most powerful kind of love there is.

† God, you love me extravagantly, practically and devotedly. Help me love others in this way.

For further thought

Is it possible to command love? What would Deuteronomy say?

Saturday 24 August
Words to live by

Readings in Deuteronomy – 2 Remembering the word

Read Deuteronomy 11:16–21

You shall put these words of mine in your heart and soul, and you shall bind them as a sign on your hand, and fix them as an emblem on your forehead.

(verse 18)

Chapter 11, like the Shema in chapter 6, contains some of the most pointed descriptions of Bible reading in the Bible. We saw in Monday's reading a similar passage describing where, and how, to read the Bible.

Even among churchgoing Christians, the kind of scripture familiarity described in today's reading (and Monday's) is rare. That's a shame. The presence of scripture in daily life – having it on your hand and doorposts, in your heart and soul and perhaps in your memory – is, in Deuteronomy, not just for religious professionals, but for ordinary people.

Memorising scripture is out of fashion, but in my experience it provides a gift that keeps on giving. Even committing a single verse to memory is like eating a slow-release energy bar. Days, months, years later a word will strike you in a new way. Even writing out a verse by hand, either artistically or just on a piece of paper tucked in your Bible, helps commit it to memory.

This kind of Bible reading is different from reading just for the story, or for a teaching you take away from the Bible itself. It is a deeper level in which you put the words themselves in your heart, on your hand, between your eyes. One way I do this is by reading psalms on my phone as I walk – taking care not to step out into traffic! A single verse, even a single word, can suddenly seem as deep and beautiful as an emerald.

† God, I will place your word in my heart. Help it bear fruit, for the sake of my community.

For further thought

Consider a creative way of writing out a verse, or a word, from Deuteronomy which has spoken to you.

Interconnected world – 1 From beginnings to empire

Notes by **Wendy Young**

Wendy is worship and theology partnerships co-ordinator at Christian Aid. She organises worship resources for the website and facilitates 'Just Scripture', an Intercultural Biblical Dialogue project connecting local and global groups around the Bible and their lived experience. She studied Bible and the contemporary world at St Andrews University and while from Northern Ireland lives in Glasgow and can increasingly be found on a croft on the Island of Mull. Wendy has used the NRSVA for these notes.

Sunday 25 August
Table of nations

Read Genesis 10:1–5, 21–32

To Eber were born two sons: the name of one was Peleg, for in his days the earth was divided, and his brother's name was Joktan.

(verse 25)

On a recent visit to Northern Ireland my brother sat with me and talked me through the family tree on our father's side. What was initially presented as little more than a collage of names and lines on a screen took on increasing meaning as I asked about random names and a story was triggered. And so it is with the history of humankind.

Choose any name from Noah's family tree in Genesis 10 and there is a story behind it. Not just from the meaning given to each name but from the life that lived behind it. Peleg is one such name tucked right in the middle of the Genesis 10 passage and it is the only name that is defined. His name meant 'division' since in his days 'the earth was divided'.

It is a phrase easily passed over, yet it is a line that itself causes division as to how it is understood. Demographic division in the time of the tower of Babel or geological division in the time of Pangaea and Gondwanaland? And if these names sound ancient, distant and strange to us, Peleg connects us with that timeless need to work through division towards reconciliation.

† God of all time, of all ages and generations, give us the grace, courage and wisdom to dialogue through difference, to disagree agreeably.

Monday 26 August
Babel

Read Genesis 11:1–9

'Come, let us build ourselves a city, and a tower with its top in the heavens, and let us make a name for ourselves; otherwise we shall be scattered abroad upon the face of the whole earth.'

(verse 4)

The tallest tower in the world was due to be completed in 2018 but is now scheduled for 2019 or 2020. First named Kingdom Tower it has been renamed as Jeddah Tower, after its location in Jeddah, Saudi Arabia. Initial ambitions for it to be a mile high have been scaled back to a kilometre, but it will still be the tallest tower in the world.

There is something about tower building that equates to status, wealth and prominence. This desire to 'make a name for ourselves' by building a city with a tower reaching the heavens in Genesis 11 is a desire fuelled by the fear of insignificance. The scattering intervention of the Divine prevented the colossal downfall that would inevitably have come from a community built on ego and fuelled by the fear of being forgotten.

The fear of being forgotten is a legitimate fear. It is a fear realised by the more than 40 million people scattered from their homes within their country of origin. The internally displaced, scattered within their own countries but not given support or resources in the way that those seeking refuge across borders receive. This fear is not caused by ego but the need to survive.

And in these days of scattering and displacement due to conflict, climate change and inequality we do well to note that God does not favour fortresses of homogeneity.

† God who gathers and scatters, may we realise the enrichment that comes from diversity and be unified in our appreciation of difference.

For further thought

How can you and your community welcome newcomers?

Tuesday 27 August
Priestly nation

Read Exodus 19:1–6

'Indeed, the whole earth is mine, but you shall be for me a priestly kingdom and a holy nation.'

(verses 5b–6a)

I'm more familiar with the West of Scotland landscape than I am with the sand dunes of the Sinai. But what the scene set in the early verses of Exodus 19 has in common with my wilderness experience are the moonlight, the camping and the mountains. Two years ago I spent three weeks walking from Glasgow to Ben Hope, the most northerly Munro (Munros are mountains over 3,000 ft in Scotland). I journeyed along the West Highland Way and the Cape Wrath Trail, often wild camping and occasionally enjoying the brightness of the moon when clouds didn't get in the way.

The landscape was rugged and harsh and sometimes sheltering and protective. It was always revealing, reflecting back the contours, valleys and crests of life's journey so far. To pilgrimage in the wilderness is an exposing experience.

It was after walking for three cycles of the moon, three months rather than three weeks, that the Israelites set up camp and finally got to rest in the shadow of the mountain. Three months of journeying towards their true identity. The identity of a priestly kingdom and a holy nation. An identity granted to all of us who are followers of the way (1 Peter 2:9). An identity that calls us to the task of serving our neighbour in love and proclaiming the merciful works of God.

This is the priestly work that I witness every day in my work with Christian Aid when I see the generous and tenacious work of partners and supporters who journey towards the promised land where all flourish and know fullness of life.

† Journey with us, God who is found in the wilderness places and help us to find our true identity in you.

For further thought

Reflect on the wilderness experiences of your life. What was revealed to you there?

Wednesday 28 August
Foreigners and the temple

> **Read 1 Kings 8:1, 41–43**
>
> '... when a foreigner comes and prays towards this house, then hear in heaven your dwelling-place, and do according to all that the foreigner calls to you.'
>
> (verses 42b–43a)

I have little experience of any hostility for being a foreigner. The Northern Irish are on the whole very welcome on Scottish shores. It's been disappointing then to see the sometimes negative response to those more recently arrived to the countries of the United Kingdom. Frustrating to see the hostility rather than hospitality offered to those who have travelled to work and live and build their lives in other countries.

The term 'foreigner', like 'migrant', has become a loaded and pejorative term, particularly in some parts of the media. The term 'refugee' has taken on something of a more compassionate or sympathetic tone, evoked in large part by the image of little Alan Kurdi washed up on the shores of the Mediterranean now almost three years ago. He would be six by now, if he'd survived the voyage.

The reality is that people travel to places foreign to them for many and complex reasons. There is rarely one single cause. What is refreshing and inspiring in this passage from 1 Kings is that among the incredible dedication of the temple is the anticipated welcome of foreigners. Solomon even tells the Lord to make them welcome! There is a generous welcome and hospitality anticipated in this revered and holy place.

May it be an inspiration to us all to ensure sanctuary and welcome are provided for all foreigners who arrive in our local communities and places of worship. And like Solomon to insist that those in positions of power listen to the demands and respond to the needs of those needing asylum.

† God who welcomes us, may we be a source of welcome and hospitality and provide sanctuary for all who find our communities foreign.

For further thought

Find a wide range of resources to inspire and assist on the 'Focus on Refugees' pages of Churches Together in Britain and Ireland, focusonrefugees.org.

Thursday 29 August
Vision and hope

Read Micah 4:1–5

... but they shall all sit under their own vines and under their own fig trees, and no one shall make them afraid.

(verse 4)

And no one shall make them afraid.

What an image of security, of having a place to be, to sit and to flourish. And crucially, not living with the fear of violence. What comforting words, what hopeful words, what necessary words in a time when the newspaper headlines speak daily of extreme terror threats on the doorstep of the United Kingdom. Bringing home a fear that is the daily experience of millions living in conflict areas across the world.

Violence and conflict affect almost one fifth of the world's population, or 1.5 billion people. The daily fear, uncertainty and suffering borne by people living through violent conflicts in countries such as Syria, Iraq and South Sudan are immeasurable and unimaginable. In Micah we have an image of how things can be, of swords being beaten into ploughshares and of living without fear.

This is a reality that Christian Aid works for through its work to tackle violence and build peace. In Colombia, which has the second highest number of people displaced by conflict in the world, a Christian Aid partner, the Inter-Church Commission for Justice and Peace, has played a crucial role in setting up zones to offer a safe refuge to people living in areas of conflict. Providing a place where people can sit under their own vines and fig trees, where no one shall make them afraid.

May we all work and pray for the day when all shall have a place to be, to sit in contentment and see their community flourish, without fear of violence.

† Pray for all working to support and care for those who long for home.

For further thought
What can your church do to help peace flourish in your community?

Friday 30 August
God is king

Read Psalm 46

The nations are in an uproar, the kingdoms totter; he utters his voice, the earth melts.

(verse 6)

Passages and verses often take on a new perspective in the context of local and global events. The rediscovery of Jesus being a child refugee became pertinent during the media attention given to the refugee 'crisis' unfolding in 2015. The references to Syria in many passages provide a renewed poignancy as we see how it has been affected by conflict since 2011, even if the geographical entity may differ from biblical times. And so, too, with Psalm 46, which is truly a psalm for our time.

In a world where 65 million people are in need of refuge, the understanding of God as refuge and ever-present help in times of trouble takes on a new perspective and becomes an even more comforting truth to meditate on and trust.

In a time when news headlines tell of chaos within and between nations; when peace agreements and treaties become as flimsy as the paper they're written on; and when the ideas of empire and kingdom building are tottering like the final stages of a game of Jenga®, Psalm 46 tells of another order.

In these times of geopolitical uncertainty we find in Psalm 46 the stability and grounding we need for a sense of security.

We may read these words with curious disappointment, asking in the way of the psalmist that if they can be ceased, why do wars still rage in Syria, South Sudan, the Democratic Republic of Congo and to the ends of the Earth? And in the midst of our wrestling questions may we hear the words of reassurance: 'Be still, and know that I am God!' (verse 10).

† Be still and know.

For further thought

Read a national newspaper with Psalm 46 open beside you, bringing each incident of concern to God in prayer.

Saturday 31 August
Empire, exile, resettlement

Read 2 Kings 17:5–6, 24–33

Then the king of Assyria invaded all the land and came to Samaria; for three years he besieged it ... This occurred because the people of Israel had sinned against the Lord their God, who had brought them up out of the land of Egypt from under the hand of Pharaoh king of Egypt.

(verses 5, 7)

It is the end of an era. The final king wasn't as bad as the others, we are told, but to be fair they had set the bar low. The demise and scattering of the Israelites was brought on by themselves. The Bible makes clear that they had been told time and time again to live by the way of Torah but they had broken the covenant and are now displaced into exile.

The story doesn't go with them in their scattering but remains on the land, not to be left empty of people but to be cultivated and grazed and lived on. And so people come from many places with different beliefs and religious practices. And rather than becoming a melting pot of diversity there is an expectation that they would do what the people of God failed to do, that is worship the Lord God with singular devotion on this land designated for such a purpose.

There is an incredible inclusion of those new to Samaria into the covenant community, and with inclusion no excuses are allowed for, the Lord deploys lions to ravage them into devotion. In a bid to retain order it is the king of Assyria who decides to follow more conventional means and insists that the newcomers be taught the ways of Yahweh by a priest brought back from exile.

While this method works to mixed effect this is at least a recognition by the Assyrian ruler that there is a higher and more ultimate authority to which everyone must bow the knee.

† Lord of all the Earth, may we learn how to follow you with the devotion you desire for the restoration of your will in fullness. Amen.

For further thought

In the end of eras that exist in our global experience today, take a moment to bow to the One who is eternal and constant.

Interconnected world – 2 Living with difference

Notes by **Michael Jagessar**

Michael is a storyteller and writer on theology and Caribbean Literature 'at large'. More on Michael's biography and writings can be found at caribleaper.co.uk. Michael has used the NRSVA for these notes.

Sunday 1 September
All the Earth – sing!

Read Psalm 100

Make a joyful noise to the Lord, all the earth. Worship the Lord with gladness; come into his presence with singing.

(verses 1–2)

In a world of the forced displacement of peoples, inequality, an economic system that favours the privileged few, perhaps nothing is more radical or countercultural than the ability to exude joy, praise and gratitude. The people of Haiti, as one example among many, in defying all the odds can testify to this.

Perhaps, in the psalmist people like this can find confident solidarity. With a global view, the psalmist calls every person in every time and place (all the Earth) to offer thanksgiving, singing and grateful devotion to God. Yes, the call is for the whole Earth, not just people, to make that joyful noise. Can these words push each of us, and every nation state beyond our boundaries to embrace every 'other'?

Listen well – can you hear the outbreak of jubilation in this call to praise, despite the evidence around us contrary to such a need? And, consider the significance of the verbs deployed: make, serve, come, know, enter, give thanks and bless. All add to the creating of that joy-filled sound. Imagine a whole community of people rising up in such praise; we should never underestimate the power of praise in non-violent resistance!

† Creator of goodness, fill us with the music of your grace, shape us to your open-ended will, and grant us the confidence and courage of your unbounded Spirit.

Good news for all ... stay with the message

Read Mark 13:3–13

'And the good news must first be proclaimed to all nations.'

(verse 10)

Death, disaster, worry, anxiety, fear, hatred, injustice, terror, wars and talk of wars – these are only a few of the things that cause anxiety and despair today. It is tempting to consider looking for some saviour-like figure to arise and step forward. Perhaps what may be more appropriate is a reminder of the fragile state of our world and our vocation as people of the Jesus way. As truth-bearers, we are called to share good news despite the evidence around us. *The Message* translation puts this commitment brilliantly: 'Stay with it – that's what is required. Stay with it to the end. You won't be sorry; you'll be saved.' The dream is of a world of peace, not violence.

Mark takes on the great fears of the times. He is imagining the birthing of a different world: from violence to peaceful places; from an unequal world to a just one; from a hateful world to one pulsating with love. The cycle must be broken. So: beware, watch, keep alert, stay awake, mind the prophets of doom – don't be fooled. And watch those alliances that will quickly lure us into their way to maintain the status quo. After all, to neutralise Jesus, a coalition was formed largely by groups who refused to see that those on the margins should be set free. The system needed protecting for them to enjoy their privileges. Even the good news and the messenger will be sacrificed. At least, this is what they thought!

† Come, God our great midwife, into the midst of our world's birth pangs. Help us birth a new world for the renewal of all.

For further thought

Are we as the body of Christ any different today with our various alliances? When we manipulate the gospel for our own ends, what do we turn the good news into?

Interconnected world – 2 Living with difference   September

Tuesday 3 September
Sharing all – eating with generous hearts

Read Acts 2:43–47

Day by day, as they spent much time together in the temple, they broke bread at home and ate their food with glad and generous hearts.

(verse 46)

Here is a glimpse of church alive, church as movement – a community of the Jesus way. Inspiring, is it not? Look, though, at the whole story of Acts and what do we see? Sure, there is excitement and a roller-coaster ride of a fledgling community. But do not miss the stories of embezzlement, church conflict, exclusions, leadership crises, congregational anxiety and infighting. Now look again at these early verses and consider how and why we have departed from the ideal and ethos of the Jesus way.

The above verses ought to be challenging for us today: the church communities I know aren't anything like this. We may subscribe to the picture, but to live it out will mean both a radical reorientation and having to give up too much. Would it be helpful if we read these verses as a reminder that where God is at work and where God's presence is experienced, such giving and sharing is the Jesus-way response? A community of Jesus followers cannot exist for its own sake. Care for the most vulnerable must be high on the list. Justice, worship and mutuality in giving and receiving are signs of God's Spirit within such a community of people – the Easter people.

How do I, how do we, measure up to this?

† Giving God, your grace is sufficient for us and yet we live lives that betray this. Make us and our communities a true reflection of your love shown to others.

For further thought

What signals do we convey about God by our own attitudes and acts concerning money and possessions? How can our lives better reflect what God in Christ has done for us?

Wednesday 4 September
Listen to me

Read Acts 7:1–8

*Then the high priest asked him, 'Are these things so?' And Stephen
replied: 'Brothers and fathers, listen to me ...'*

(verses 1–2a)

This dispute highlights the cultural and language battles of the
times between Hebrew Christians, Hellenist Christians and the
Jewish community. The result is a sad conclusion – a literal dead
end. Hence, Stephen the martyr.

The story highlights how when scriptures and tradition are being
critiqued it becomes difficult to listen to each other. In situations
where all parties are convinced they are correct, and appeal to the
same set of scripture, it would not be difficult to imagine how
the questioning (Stephen and the Hellenists) would have been
perceived as a betrayal by both sides. Who in such situations
has managed to grasp or to be grabbed by the heart or spirit of
scripture? Is it those who hold on to the familiar and manageable?
Is it those who give agency to justice, mercy and faith? Is it those
who sense that God's story is larger than their own small view?

If there is one thing we need to hear from the story of Stephen,
it may be the danger of rightness and self-preservation. If the way
of God is about living from the heart of the scripture, we should
be aware that the Divine is not manageable and will not be bound
by our places of worship nor by a book. Is not God larger than our
traditions and the witness to the divine word?

† God whose truth is larger than we are, enlarge our minds and hearts so that we
may catch a glimpse of truth: your truth of the way of full life for all. Amen.

For further thought

What would a church/community living from the heart of the
gospel look like? What would it give up? What must it trust?

Interconnected world – 2 Living with difference

September

Thursday 5 September
God's own people

Read 1 Peter 2:9–17

But you are a chosen race, a royal priesthood, a holy nation, God's own people, in order that you may proclaim the mighty acts of him who called you out of darkness into his marvellous light.

(verse 9)

The recipients of 1 Peter lived on the margins of society, suffering humiliation and verbal abuse. The destruction of Jerusalem in 70 AD had disoriented and drained them; they were referred to as 'transient strangers' and 'resident aliens' (verse 11). Peter's message is an invitation for them to keep coming to the living stone, Jesus, allowing themselves to be built up into a spiritual house or house of living stones. This was good news for people experiencing homelessness, dislocation, abuse and wondering where God was in all of this.

The invitation is not to be passive observers of traumatic events or powerless victims of other people's opinions. A choice is offered: there is no need to search for home. They can choose to be home and family for the dislocated. There is no need to wonder where God is in all of this. They can choose to be the place of God's presence in the world here and now. This is what makes them special as God's own people!

To be God's people in Christ? It is about becoming a spiritual house where the presence of God is known, and where all are welcomed. It is about whose ministry we are called to participate in. God's own people are called to walk the Jesus way, model the Jesus life and practise the Jesus truth. This is 'chosen-ness' – to witness to this alternative economy, this God-like way of living.

† Be always generous, live kindness well and as fully as you are able; never be hasty in judgement, put away pretence and meet the other face-to-face. We are God's own people!

For further thought

Who were God's own people whom you have encountered this week? Were you surprised? If so, why?

Beyond borders

Interconnected world – 2 Living with difference

September

Read Revelation 7:9–11

'Salvation belongs to our God who is seated on the throne, and to the Lamb!'

(verse 10)

How about a loud Amen! I can't hear it! Try again.

When faced with this arena of worshippers chanting the name of the lamb, visionary John opted not for numbers but for a description to underscore all who were there. We are all there. It is not a vision of exclusion. It is a vision of life running over with difference and grace and joy and love. All sorts of oppressive markers and walls have disappeared.

I think, though, we should shout our 'amen' for another reason: that 'salvation belongs to God'! Mercifully, it does not belong to Church or any religious institution or their leaders or any doctrinal rulings or deposit of faith. How assuring to know that salvation is God's business. We cannot offer salvation – we witness to it. We do not own salvation – it belongs to God. It is God's gift and all we can do is model a life that approaches the throne of grace with boldness so that we may receive mercy and find grace – all of which is God's gifting and doing.

From start to finish, God's purpose is to restore all people. And the vision of the vast and diverse crowd around the throne in Revelation gives us an idea of what that might look like. This makes Revelation a vision for today precisely because it is about God. Here is God bringing to an end all *our* attempts at bringing closure to God's expansive embrace of the whole of creation – a world that God loves extravagantly. Here is God calling us to participate in a vision of hope and abundance, despite all the evidence contrary to this.

Let the people sing or shout 'amen' – many times over. And please, in your own language!

† May the word of God empower our thoughts and words; the love of Jesus inhabit our hearts; and the breath of the Holy Spirit inspire our lives today and every day.

For further thought

What might Revelation's vision look like for us today? In what ways are you challenged by such a vision? How do you intend to respond?

Saturday 7 September
Come out!

Read Revelation 18:1–5, 11–24

'Come out of her, my people, so that you do not take part in her sins.'

(verse 4)

The lure and allure of wealth and privilege have a long and strong reach. Many prefer to genuflect at the altars of money, economics and profit. Wealth and the love of power rule. The question that John poses to his readers is: who is in control: God, emperor or Rome/Babylon? What will it be: our uncritical participation in an impersonal system, or a life-giving alternative?

Follow the Money, a tale of greed, corruption and death, is a Danish financial crime thriller that underscores in a simplistic way one contemporary example of the reach of the economic empire in our lives. Empires and colonising powers depend on military might to maintain its geopolitics. To fight and win battles, including the one for the mind, involves economics or money. Rome (which John in Revelation parodies as Babylon) is an economic empire and organises its life in such a way as to ensure maximum economic exploitation from the conquered provinces. No wonder Rome is 'seated upon many waters' (Revelation 17:1). 'The waters that you saw … are peoples and multitudes and nations and languages' (17:15). Rome is powerful and wealthy because Rome grabs others' wealth. Rome is an exploiter, 'the magnates of the earth' (18:23).

Hence, John's call to 'come out of her, my people' (verse 4) – to come out of the maze of economic and political exploitation. The question is: come out into what? Can we, citizens of two kingdoms, ever totally be free from the economic maze? I am not sure. What I am sure about is the need to come out and re-enter with a different tactic!

† Move us out, deliverer God, into your city of grace where love, hope and healing become the habits of our hearts and minds. In the name of the one who offers abundant life for all.

For further thought

Consider the current political, social and economic state today: what will 'come out' entail? Who will be our partners in transforming lives and the system as a whole?

Waters: from Genesis to Revelation – 1 Cosmic waters

Notes by **Ann Conway-Jones**

Ann is a biblical scholar, teacher and freelance writer. She is fascinated by the different ways Jews and Christians have read the scriptures, and passionate about making academic scholarship accessible. She holds honorary research fellowships at the University of Birmingham and The Queen's Foundation for Ecumenical Theological Education. She is an Accredited Lay Worker, occasionally preaching in her parish church. Ann has used the NRSVA for these notes.

Sunday 8 September
The waters of creation

Read Genesis 1:1–10, 20–22

God said, 'Let there be a dome in the midst of the waters, and let it separate the waters from the waters.' So God made the dome and separated the waters that were under the dome from the waters that were above the dome. And it was so.

(verses 6–7)

The Bible begins and ends with water – liquid life. We travel this week from the waters of creation in Genesis 1 to the river of the water of life in Revelation 22. In the beginning there is a turbulent mass of primordial water. God creates by dividing and separating – bringing order out of chaos. Having separated between light and darkness on day one, on day two God creates a habitable space between the waters below and the waters above. The waters above are imagined as a vast sea beyond the sun, moon and stars, held back by a solid dome. Openings in the dome provide for rain. On day three God gathers together the waters below, allowing dry land to appear. And by day five these waters are teeming with life. Our scientific understanding of the cosmos may have progressed, but this poetic evocation of rhythm and order in the natural world still speaks to us. God's creation is good. Water in its proper place is essential to life. However, as we shall discover, in biblical imagery the waters retain their primordial chaotic power, always threatening to return and engulf the created world. Forces of disorder remain an ominous presence.

† O God our Creator, send your Spirit to hover over our chaos.

Monday 9 September
The proud waves are stopped

Read Job 38:1–18

'Who shut in the sea with doors when it burst out from the womb?'

(verse 8)

God's response to Job's howls of complaint begins by evoking creation, and the dawn of time. Once again we have chaotic waters, now pictured as gushing forth from a womb. The sea becomes a newborn child, with God acting as midwife. Strips of mist are imagined as swaddling bands. And just as a wriggling infant needs to be securely held, so God keeps the boisterous sea in check. The mention of bars and doors brings to mind a cosmic playpen.

Job has been turned in on himself, imprisoned by his suffering. He has cursed the night of his conception: 'Let the stars of its dawn be dark; let it hope for light, but have none; may it not see the eyelids of the morning' (3:9). Release comes, the poetry implies, by immersing oneself in the vast panorama of God's creativity, allowing human concerns to recede into the background. Job's words are transposed, with longing for darkness replaced by affirmation of light: 'when the morning stars sang together and all the heavenly beings shouted for joy' (verse 7). Creation holds mysteries beyond our understanding, and we are not the centre of the universe. The sea may rage, but God has set shores and cliffs to rein it in. Life flourishes thanks to cosmic checks and balances. Job has been questioning God, but now the tables are turned and God questions Job. What can he know about the fashioning and operation of the cosmic elements – Earth, stars, sea, underworld, light and darkness? With a series of pounding questions, Job is invited to turn his incomprehension into wonder.

† O God our midwife, bring to birth our hopes and longings.

For further thought
Look up into the night sky tonight and marvel.

Waters: from Genesis to Revelation – 1 Cosmic waters

September

Who has the wisdom to number the clouds?

Read Job 38:19–38

'Can you lift up your voice to the clouds, so that a flood of waters may cover you? Can you send forth lightnings, so that they may go and say to you, "Here we are"? Who has put wisdom in the inward parts, or given understanding to the mind?'

(verses 34–36)

God's speech to Job moves on from cosmology to meteorology, from hedging in the sea to controlling the weather. Divine creative activity is not once and for all; God continues to sustain the world by orchestrating thunder and lightning, snow, hail and rain. There is more birth imagery: 'Has the rain a father?' (verse 28), 'From whose womb did the ice come forth?' (verse 29). These are rhetorical questions – they are not meant to be answered. But the imagery is appropriate, given the connection between water and fertility. It is only when the waterskins of the heavens (containers imagined to be above the sky dome, holding in the precious water) are tilted that rain falls through the designated channels, dust turns to clumps of mud and plants can grow.

In our scientific times, the pictures presented here may seem primitive. Our understanding of rainfall does not include heavenly jars, or storehouses of snow. No doubt there are scientists whose job is indeed to number and track cloud formations. And astronomers have established the rules governing the movements of the stars, including the Pleiades, Orion and the Bear. Yet the more we know, the more we realise how complex and fragile is the ecosystem on which we depend. Thinking that we can play God, and take charge of the natural world, we have messed with it to our peril.

† O God who numbers the clouds, grant rain to thirsty lands.

For further thought

Go out into the rain this week, and give thanks for the gift of water.

Wednesday 11 September
The floods roar

Read Psalm 93

The floods have lifted up, O Lord, the floods have lifted up their voice; the floods lift up their roaring. More majestic than the thunders of mighty waters, more majestic than the waves of the sea, majestic on high is the Lord!

(verses 3–4)

Water is essential to life. But too much water can be as disastrous as not enough. In recent years we have seen many floods across the world, devastating homes and wrecking lives. The power of a tsunami or a hurricane is awesome and destructive. So no wonder the psalmist uses the thunder of mighty floodwaters as a way to evoke all that is outside human control, all that threatens to overwhelm us. And it is God's power over these waters which establishes God's greatness and majesty.

The victory over chaos did not just happen once and for all at the beginning of time. The roaring floods remind us of the story of Noah, when each kind of created animal had to be rescued, and of the parting of the Red Sea, when the Israelites were led to safety. More widely, God's rule is continually challenged by the forces of evil. The last verse of the psalm mentions 'decrees', making a link between the created order of the natural world, and the necessary rules governing human life. We need order and stability if we are to flourish, and these are ensured by obeying God-given commands, such as loving both neighbour and alien as oneself (Leviticus 19:18, 34). The psalmist celebrates God's kingship, and affirms that the world is secure despite appearances; but also calls on us to participate in the continual battle against chaos and anarchy.

† O God our stability, keep us safe when we feel overwhelmed.

For further thought

Have you ever experienced the power of the sea?

Waters: from Genesis to Revelation – 1 Cosmic waters

September

Jesus stills the waves

When Jesus calms the sea, all the biblical imagery that we have been looking at this week comes into play. The sea represents the forces of chaos and destruction threatening to swamp the disciples. Jesus rebukes the wind just as he rebukes unclean spirits (Mark 1:25; 9:25). He tells the sea to be still, which is the same command as he gives to the unclean spirit he encounters at the beginning of his ministry in the synagogue at Capernaum (Mark 1:25) – in the original Greek the same verb is used (not always obvious in English translations). Unclean spirits, like the sea, are wild, unpredictable and outside human control. Jesus displays a divine capacity to restore stability and order.

The story ends with the disciples filled with great 'awe'. 'Fear', even 'terror', might be a better translation. The great windstorm is followed by great calm, and great turmoil in the hearts of the disciples. Just as the women flee from the empty tomb because they are afraid (Mark 16:8), so the disciples are shaken when faced with the inexplicable. We too might feel that this story faces us with the inexplicable. And what does it mean to have faith, when we live in a world in which the forces of destruction, be they natural or man-made, still so often wreak havoc?

† O God the stiller of storms, protect those undertaking perilous journeys across the sea in search of a better life.

For further thought

What threatens to swamp you at this stage in your life?

Friday 13 September
A river of fresh water

Read Ezekiel 47:1–12

'On the banks … there will grow all kinds of trees for food. Their leaves will not wither nor their fruit fail, but they will bear fresh fruit every month, because the water for them flows from the sanctuary. Their fruit will be for food, and their leaves for healing.'

(verse 12)

Ezekiel's world has fallen apart. His beloved Jerusalem has been razed to the ground, and its magnificent temple, home to the living God, is no more. He is living in exile, along with many of the elite of the Judean community, and he is convinced that they have brought the disaster upon themselves. Much of his prophecy has been indictment of the people's failure to respect God's holiness. But towards the end of the book, hope reasserts itself. The best-known expression of this hope is Ezekiel's vision of the dry bones (37:1–14). That is followed by the vision of a restored temple, described in painstaking detail. A spring wells up from within the temple which flows out into the desert, getting deeper and deeper as it goes. An abundance of water pours into the Dead Sea, so that it becomes like the Great Sea (i.e. the Mediterranean), swarming with fish. Life has come to that which was stagnant. People can now spread their fishing nets, in what had been the most inhospitable of environments. Note, however, a nice pragmatic touch: the swamps and marshes remain saline – salt too, after all, is essential to life.

On the banks of the river grow all kinds of trees, bringing to mind the garden of Eden. This is a vision of a return to paradise. A complete ecosystem flows from the temple, with religion, nature and human endeavour all intertwined. Divine grace and blessing are inexhaustible, ever gaining depth and momentum.

† O God of abundance, pour fresh life into our stagnation.

For further thought

Take a walk along a river this weekend, and observe all that is growing and living along its banks.

Waters: from Genesis to Revelation – 1 Cosmic waters

September

The river of the water of life

Read Revelation 22:1–5

Then the angel showed me the river of the water of life, bright as crystal, flowing from the throne of God and of the Lamb through the middle of the street of the city.

(verses 1–2a)

Revelation, like Ezekiel, is a book filled with terror and violence, which ends on a note of hope. Much of the imagery is inspired by Ezekiel's visions, and nowhere is this more evident than in the final two chapters. John too envisages a structure set on a high mountain – this time it is 'the holy city Jerusalem coming down out of heaven from God' (21:10). Ezekiel's river of fresh water becomes 'the river of the water of life' (verse 1). There may also be an allusion here to John 4:10–14, where Jesus promises living water, 'gushing up to eternal life'. Ezekiel's trees are replaced by just the one 'tree of life', an even more explicit reference to the garden of Eden (see Genesis 2:9). Revelation stresses the correspondence between the beginning and the end: 'I am the Alpha and the Omega,' says the one seated on the throne (1:8; 21:6; 22:13). The curse caused by eating from the tree of the knowledge of good and evil has finally been reversed, and now the fruit of the tree of life can be eaten. Water is no longer chaotic and threatening: it flows from the throne of God and of the Lamb, bright as crystal. The scene is difficult to picture: how can one tree grow on both sides of the river? But that is not the point. The point is the immediacy of the presence of God. The blessing promised in Numbers 6:25 will be fulfilled: God will make his face to shine upon us, and give us peace.

† O God our light, bring healing to the nations.

For further thought

Where could you plant a tree as a sign of hope? Or what plant can you tend as a sign of God's faithfulness?

Waters: from Genesis to Revelation – 2 Quenching thirst

Notes by **Revd Canon Dr Helen Van Koevering**

After living in Southern Africa for 28 years, Helen, raised in England, recently moved to West Virginia, USA with her husband, a bishop in the Episcopal Church. Helen previously served as a parish priest and Director of Ministry for the Anglican Diocese of Niassa in northern Mozambique during a decade of growth that doubled the church. She is now discovering new perspectives for life-giving faithfulness in the US. Helen has used the NRSVA for these notes.

Sunday 15 September
Jesus calls the thirsty

Read John 7:37–39

'Let anyone who is thirsty come to me, and let the one who believes in me drink. As the scripture has said, "Out of the believer's heart shall flow rivers of living water."'

(verses 37b–38)

It doesn't take a degree in science to know that water is essential for human life, nor a degree in theology to know that thirst is a biblical metaphor for the desire for life. In our passage today, Jesus is saying that he holds both what is essential and what is desired for overflowing life.

A tension found in moving from one place to another in today's world of increasing difference between the poorest and the wealthiest is in questioning what is 'normal' and 'enough'. Having moved recently from Mozambique to the US, I now see food left on the plate or chicken on the bone rather than a scraped-clean communal bowl of food. Instead of limiting the use of water that had been time-consuming and neck-breaking to carry from the distant well, river or lake, we leave on a tap for the water to heat and sprinklers to water a lawn. Jesus confronts us not with our own rights and privilege, but those of being counted among his beloved. We are called to live as those with enough who share the abundance of the Creator's life. For the good of the world Jesus came to save.

† Lord, our Creator and Provider, we thirst for the life you offer in right living as your beloved community. In your love and your life, may our thirst be quenched by your fullness of life. Amen.

Monday 16 September
Hagar waits for her child to die

Read Genesis 21:8–19

So Abraham ... took bread and a skin of water, and gave it to Hagar, putting it on her shoulders, along with her child, and sent her away. And she departed, and wandered about in the wilderness of Beer-sheba. When the water in the skin was gone, she cast the child under one of the bushes ... she lifted up her voice and wept ... God heard the voice of the boy ... Then God opened her eyes and she saw a well of water.

(verses 14, 15, 17, 19)

Pain is part of life. Pain seems to have a privileged place in the Bible as a place where God will happen. Think of all the stories of Israel's trials, journeys, learning, and of all Jesus' encounters with the hurt, the despised, the broken, the sick. God turns our understanding upside down and our world inside out as we hear of the transformation of hearts, thoughts and lives in the biblical narrative, and are encouraged to seek God's kingdom, God's way, through pain.

Sometimes, pain blinds us and then we need others to open our eyes to see new life. A Mozambican friend, Rosa, fell into deep grief when she lost her grown son. Her profound pain, deepened by the loss of her son's care for her future and by a physical ailment that the doctors seemed not to be able to treat, was almost unbearable. Tradition held that Rosa should wear mourning clothes for 40 days, but at 5 months, she still had not removed the black clothes. Tradition also held that pain was held in community. Her friends, moved by concern for her debilitating pain, gathered round. After prayer, they gently removed Rosa's black head-covering and her black *capulana* (the cloth skirt wrap), and replaced them with new, coloured *capulanas*. It took this circle of friends to open Rosa's eyes to new life through pain and God's healing. To be companions on the journey.

† Loving Lord, you have promised to wipe away all our tears for our pain. Remind us that we do not walk our pain alone, that we are held in our suffering by your gift of community, and enable us to know that, with you, we can learn to live the future into our present always. Amen.

For further thought

What pain does someone near you carry today? What pain do you carry?

Tuesday 17 September
Disputes over water

Read Genesis 26:17–33

He moved from there [the disputed wells of Esek and Sitnah] and dug another well, and they did not quarrel over it; so he called it Rehoboth, saying, 'Now the Lord has made room for us, and we shall be fruitful in the land.' ... Isaac set them on their way, and they departed from him in peace... [Isaac's servants dug a well] 'We have found water!' He called it Shibah; therefore the name of the city is Beer-sheba to this day.

(verses 22, 31b, 32)

Conflicts over water have impacted history since well before biblical times. Access to water has been a source of tensions between states and individuals, used as a weapon during military action, as a political goal and as a tool of violence or coercion. Water resource systems have at times been a major source of contention and dispute in the context of economic and social development. One thing is for sure: providing for water needs and demands will never be free of politics.

Increased water consumption raises the possibility of future conflict over access to water, and the Middle East lives with that possibility. Five per cent of the world's population have access to only one per cent of the world's clean water. This is not just a future threat to life: around 11 per cent of the world's population do not have improved access to water – that is, access to clean wells of water within walking distance, let alone piped private household water. Access to water impacts sanitation and health, use of time and leisure, education for girls (the traditional carriers of water for families), and the viability of commerce in agriculture, fisheries, manufacturing and tourism. And, clearly, pollution of a water source destroys life.

To see water as the gift of God for flourishing life is to reclaim our responsibility as God's images for all of God's creation; safeguarding access to water for all, and changing our risky consumption and deathly pollution of the world's water resources for the good of our global neighbours, now and in the future.

† Lord God, thank you for the beauty of creation, for the provision of our needs for life, and for the communities of which we are all part. May we learn to live responsibly, seek equitable access to the world's resources, and recognise our neighbours' needs. For your glory. Amen.

For further thought

How does knowledge that water resources carry the potential for conflict affect your prayers and your choices today?

Wednesday 18 September
Rebekah draws water

Read Genesis 24:10–27

'Drink, my lord,' she said, and quickly lowered her jar upon her hand and gave him a drink. When she had finished giving him a drink, she said, 'I will draw for your camels also, until they have finished drinking.'

(verses 18–19)

Engaging in mission, whether in a Northern urban setting or an underdeveloped rural village, brings myriad opportunities to learn. Traditional mission literature might drum up enthusiasm and excitement for attractive missionary moments, but entering another's life is deskilling and unnerving, destabilising and tiring, as well as over-stretching and repositioning of rooted opinions and perspectives. Recognising God as missionary and the mission as God's opens our eyes to God's presence and discovering humility and gentleness to join in together.

Today's mission story highlights the meaning for marriage among the people of God as covenant, grace and discipleship. Abraham's servant was to discern, within the culture, time and place where he was sent, who was to be the 'strong helpmeet' (a possible translation for Genesis 2:18) for Isaac, Abraham's son. God's choice was to be determined through cultural cues, through seeking God's leading and grace, through desiring to be a faithful servant to his master and through allowing for free choice on the part of Rebekah and her family. In these ways, Abraham's servant speaks to us today in another place about marriage. The people of God can expect God's concern and guidance over the issues of life, which includes the covenantal relationship of marriage. To covenant together as fellow believers in Christ is one of the grounds for stability in marriage and in communities as much as it is a witness to the grace and overflowing life that are God's missionary offer. Rebekah invites the servant, and even his camels, to drink of her well-drawn water. That gracious, generous hospitality is the invitation to the life of our covenant-making God.

† Lord God, we find you in new places ahead and to which you invite us. Your presence offers new insight as we commit ourselves to be your disciples and seek your grace and overflowing life to quench our thirst for what is life-giving. Bless our marriages and communities, Lord! Amen.

For further thought

How is God leading you to new insights of God's gracious, generous hospitality?

Thursday 19 September
The Nile turns to blood

Read Exodus 7:14–24

Moses and Aaron did just as the Lord commanded. In the sight of Pharaoh and of his officials he lifted up the staff and struck the water in the river, and all the water in the river was turned into blood, and the fish in the river died. The river stank so that the Egyptians could not drink its water, and there was blood throughout the whole land of Egypt.

(verses 20–21)

The ten plagues before the exodus of God's freed people started with the River Nile turning into blood. Hardly any country has been so dependent on its waterways as ancient Egypt. This transportation led to widespread shipbuilding, the development of ports, sea commerce for Egypt's produce and the annual flooding of the Nile provided new deposits of fertile soil along with much needed water in the surrounding fields. If not for this flooding, Egypt would be as barren as the deserts on either side of it.

But with this first plague, the Nile, the lifeblood of Egypt, became blood and death. What had been a blessing became a curse. Red silting of the Nile is apparently common, but never to the extent that it would seriously alter the life of the Egyptians. This river of blood now forced the Egyptians to dig along the Nile for drinking water filtered through the sandy soil near the river bank. The Nile was filled with blood for seven days, the number of completion in the Bible, and a sign of complete victory over the gods of Egypt who sustained the Nile.

On a visit to the northern communities of Lake Malawi, the lake had turned red by the gold-mining techniques along one of the tributaries. Finding clean water involved sailing into the more dangerous centre of the lake. The coal mining in West Virginia led to polluted water of the many rivers, and widespread lack of clean drinking water. What false gods have been worshipped in our time in these places?

† God, we see the power of your love around us, yet we choose to follow other ways. May we be liberated by your life-giving love to be who you called us to be with all our hearts, souls and strength. Amen.

For further thought

Consider supporting or starting a river- or stream-cleaning community, and become an advocate for clean waterways with local government and organisations.

265

Moses strikes the rock

Read Exodus 17:1–7

'I will be standing there in front of you on the rock at Horeb. Strike the rock, and water will come out of it, so that the people may drink.' Moses did so, in the sight of the elders of Israel. He called the place Massah and Meribah, because the Israelites quarrelled and tested the Lord, saying, 'Is the Lord among us or not?'

(verses 6–7)

Again, the necessity for water is providing a lesson in discipleship. Water is a gift of our Creator God, whose life and love are found in the least expected and most surprising places. Though we know that quarrelling over water is inherent with our need and desire, in our reading today we see that need and desire met differently. This time, water is found not in a well or clear water source, but from within a rock. God's gift of water, a symbol of God's presence for security, peace, blessing and flourishing, is found in an unexpected place. Like the Israelites, we can still be surprised and blessed by God's gift as provision and symbol, remembrance and promise.

Have you ever watched a child delighted to discover a water fountain in a concreted play area? Have you ever seen the delight of children able to fetch their family's daily water from a new well with a handpump that makes the chore more fun and easier? Have you ever climbed a steep hill and felt that dry-throated thirst being satisfied by a friend's offer of a bottle of water? Have you ever seen the first rain's effect on a dry land, smelled the clean earth and seen the green shoots of new life so quickly respond to the rain?

Let's live that delight in our lives, be the delight that our neighbours might need today, delight ourselves in our saving God.

† Lord of the water, may we find our delight in you today. May we find you in new and unexpected places, take time to enjoy those moments, and seek to delight our neighbours in some way in this new day. Amen.

For further thought

Make a list of delightful moments you remember. In what ways could you be a delight to someone today?

Water of eternal life

Read John 4:7–15

The woman said to him, 'Sir, you have no bucket, and the well is deep. Where do you get that living water?' Jesus said to her, 'Everyone who drinks of this water will be thirsty again, but those who drink of the water that I will give them will never be thirsty. The water that I will give will become in them a spring of water gushing up to eternal life.'

(verses 11–14)

Today, we come to another well and another conversation with another woman. This time, it isn't the servant of Abraham and Rebekah, but it is Jesus, the Master Discipler, and an unnamed woman, marginalised by both her heritage and life circumstances, alone at the well at midday, a stranger to the community of the daughters of the town. Yet, just as in the story of Rebekah at the well, we learn of covenant, grace and discipleship again. With Rebekah, the encounter at the well led to marriage; with the Samaritan woman, the encounter with Jesus at the well led to a new understanding of God as Spirit, discipleship as worship, and life as eternal.

The water that Jesus offered the Samaritan woman had another source. The depth of Jesus' understanding of the woman's pain, the breadth of her need and desire for a new way, and the height of God's love for both a whole people and a whole person are heard in this conversation and in the woman's response. She left what she was doing, went back to where she was known, and shared the invitation to come to know the Christ. There is a well in Samaria today, marked out as the well of this conversation by the church built above it. Pilgrims can descend the steps and taste the water. Yet the water spoken of in this encounter was for all those that God seeks eternally and in all places. It is the life of the Spirit of Jesus offered for the life of the world.

† With joy, we celebrate your love and life offered as the water of life eternal. With thanks, we worship you with our whole lives. Liberate us to invite others to join with us in the life you offer to the world. Amen.

For further thought

Pray for someone you might invite for a chat and cup of tea this week. Invite them again, or to another occasion, or to go to church. Accept invitations that might come your way too!

Waters: from Genesis to Revelation – 2 Quenching thirst

September

Waters: from Genesis to Revelation – 3 Waters of new life

Notes by **Pete Wheeler**

Pete leads St Peter's Church, Aylesbury, UK and is a curate licensed to the Aylesbury Deanery. After 20 years of composing, producing and licensing music for film and TV he trained at St Mellitus Theological College, London. He is married to Ali, a graphic designer, and they have two teenagers. Pete runs leadership courses for young adults. As well as music, his downtime involves not enough golf and lapsang souchong. Pete has used the NIVUK for these notes.

Sunday 22 September
Born of water and the Spirit

Read John 3:1–15

Jesus answered, 'Very truly I tell you, no one can enter the kingdom of God unless they are born of water and the Spirit. Flesh gives birth to flesh, but the Spirit gives birth to spirit.'

(verses 5–6)

In the big search for life on other planets, scientists focus their exploration on searching for the presence of a certain hydrogen and oxygen compound – H_2O. They say that the presence of water is the first indicator that the building blocks for life might exist.

Whatever we might think of that possibility, it is no coincidence that water plays a huge role throughout the Bible, literally and symbolically. John's Gospel constantly uses water symbolically to reveal who Jesus is. However, the relationship between water and God's Spirit is established at the very beginning of creation, where darkness covers the 'deep' and the Spirit hovers over the waters (Genesis 1:2).

So, as Nicodemus searches for answers by the secrecy that darkness affords him, Jesus willingly takes him back to the very beginning, acknowledging his need to be reborn of both water – believing and accepting that Jesus is the Christ, his Saviour – and the Spirit – now submitting to the will of God's Holy Spirit, to be his comfort and guide.

For humanity, water is life. It even makes up 60 per cent of our bodies. So, this week, let's explore how the flow of water and the flow of the Spirit are inextricably linked to our human condition.

† Lord Jesus, as I come in faith to you once more, fill me with your Spirit, that rivers of living water might flow from within me, and out into the world around me.

Drawn from the water

Read Exodus 2:1–10

But when she could hide him no longer, she got a papyrus basket for him and coated it with tar and pitch. Then she placed the child in it and put it among the reeds along the bank of the Nile. His sister stood at a distance to see what would happen to him.

(verses 3–4)

A Chinese friend made the agonising decision that the right place for her baby girl was not with her in the UK, but with her grandparents in China – at least until she could get a job and get a steadier, surer footing in her own life. Without any judgement, it was a tremendously hard thing for me to help her through.

The next Mothering Sunday, as I preached on the story of how Moses' mother entrusted her baby into God's care, I noticed my friend sitting in the congregation, tears streaming. At that moment, she was reliving every moment of her story as it mirrored that of Moses' own mum.

Later I reassured her that Moses means 'drawn from the water'. The water in the river safely carries Moses to a life in which God has a story waiting for him. From the waters are drawn new opportunities and new beginnings. This is water that carries new life. From this water God will even choose to draw his salvation plan for Israel.

'Not mine, but your will be done.' Are there things that you need to lower into the water, entrusting them to God, and letting the fresh waters of renewal carry them away to a place where God can bring about *his* will? God's Holy Spirit can bring new life, even through the pain of letting something go.

It is quick-thinking Miriam who ensures that Moses is reunited with his mother. The last time I saw my friend, she was a happy mum once more; reunited, and busy raising her beautiful daughter.

† Gentle Spirit, there are things I know that I need to let go of. Let your waters of new life gently carry them away, and return to me a steadfast trust in your goodness.

For further thought

How will you be a Miriam today, through quick-thinking acts of kindness and courage, bringing comfort out of confusion?

Waters: from Genesis to Revelation – 3 Waters of new life

September

Tuesday 24 September
Crossing the deep

Read Exodus 14:10–31

Moses answered the people, 'Do not be afraid. Stand firm and you will see the deliverance the Lord will bring you today. The Egyptians you see today you will never see again. The Lord will fight for you; you need only to be still.'

(verses 13–14)

Certain death lies behind. Certain death lies ahead. As the Israelite people hurriedly pour onto the beach, filling the shores of the Red Sea, they turn to Moses and start to complain. Had Yahweh deserted them, leaving them to die by sword or by water? They would have rather died of exhaustion as slaves.

Moses, however, tells them something crazy. He says that the Lord is fighting their battle for them, and to simply be still (verse 14)! It must have been an astonishing thing to hear, as they waited to look death square in the face. Throughout Moses' life, Yahweh's control of water has been a recurring theme. At the Red Sea though, Yahweh's power doesn't just control the sea waters …

In the ancient traditions of Israel's neighbours, each type of water was controlled by a separate deity. But Yahweh is the God of *all* creation, and because of this, it is only Yahweh that is able to save them. Now, Yahweh's power holds back a much deeper deep – the 'ancient deeps' – the deep waters of chaos and death, flowing downwards. These are the same chaotic waters Yahweh had ordered at the beginning of time (Genesis 1:2).

If you have ever been rescued by a lifeguard you will know that the worst thing you can do is to struggle and splash around. As the lifeguard reaches you, you must be still and let them swim for you, taking control.

There is really nothing we can do to save ourselves. God has done it all. He has crossed over. He is fighting our battles. He has made a way through the deep waters of chaos. We respond to his love, mercy and grace.

† God of grace, we worship you now as Yahweh – the God who saves. You bring us into new life with you, redeeming us from the deep, through the sacrifice of your Son. We lift you up.

For further thought

Be still. Be still. Be still. Be still. Be still. Be still. Be still. Be still. Be still. Be still. Be still. Be still. Be.

Wednesday 25 September
In over your head

Read 2 Kings 5:1–14

Elisha sent a messenger to say to him, 'Go, wash yourself seven times in the Jordan, and your flesh will be restored and you will be cleansed.' But Naaman went away angry and said, 'I thought that he would surely come out to me … wave his hand over the spot and cure me of my leprosy.'

(verses 10–11)

Naaman is in over his head.

He's used to being fully in control. This is a man with vast numbers of troops, servants and slaves at his disposal. He is a soldier, a conqueror and a hero for killing the previous king of Israel. He relies on no one. He has the world at his feet.

Yet, now at this moment, he suddenly finds himself in over his head. Out of control. Beholden to the leprosy he has contracted, to the advice of his servants, to the new king of Israel, and now a strange prophet from Samaria, named Elisha.

Naturally, Naaman wants to be healed on his own terms. But he must fully trust God not only to shed his infected skin, but to cleanse him of all that has gone before. It's time to relinquish control and start again.

Still annoyed and frustrated, Naaman reluctantly dips himself into the murky waters of the Jordan. The waters rise over his shoulders and, dipping below the water seven times, for a moment Naaman is completely submersed. His future is out of his control – he is truly in over his head.

When I baptise adults I always ask them if they would like a 'full immersion' baptism. Why? Because there is nothing like that split-second feeling of being fully in over your head; momentarily held in trust, completely out of your control; fully covered by the waters of new life.

In that moment you know you are all-in. Wholly invested. This is it … rising from the water, you find that God is – eternally – faithful. New life has begun.

† Jesus, let your healing waters wash away my own desire for control – for it is strong within me. Come and have your way. Your will be done.

For further thought

'Shedding your skin' might be interpreted in many ways. Is this a prophetic word for you today? Are you being called to 'shed your skin', letting new life come and the old be cast away?

Thursday 26 September
Water to go

Read Mark 1:1–13

'I baptise you with water, but he will baptise you with the Holy Spirit.' At that time Jesus came from Nazareth in Galilee and was baptised by John in the Jordan. Just as Jesus was coming up out of the water, he saw heaven being torn open and the Spirit descending on him like a dove.

(verses 8–10)

This morning, while on retreat in Arizona, and before writing today's notes, I decided to meet with God up a mountain. However, after an hour of tough uphill walking and praying I reached into my bag and realised I had forgotten to fill my water bottle. My time of walking and prayer quickly became a time of fasting. Plain old water, I discovered first-hand, is the stuff of life, without which we are both thirsty and unclean.

In Exodus, the Israelites begin to live a new life in the truth that Yahweh (unlike other regional gods) is not restricted to a mountain or to any one place. Instead, he travels with them. Before entering the tent of meeting, Aaron and the other priests are washed clean with water (Exodus 29:4).

Why then is Jesus baptised? Isn't he already clean? Part of the answer must be that, as the waters of new life wash over him, Jesus models this same truth to all – that even his own ministry must be fully reliant on, empowered by, and filled with the Holy Spirit. This is the God who goes with us. No part of life is off-limits.

This water is dynamic, running, free-moving, hard to contain and, if you let it, it will soak into every nook and cranny. Likewise, in baptism the waters of new life not only bring us to repentance, but to a fully charged, life-giving, free-flowing, dynamic relationship with God, regardless of any possible circumstance in which we find ourselves.

I didn't only meet with God on that mountain – I walked every step up and down it with him.

† Come Holy Spirit and fill me, enable me, guide me and comfort me, that I might love others as you have loved them, and seek your will with a ready and right heart.

For further thought

Did you know that all the water in existence today is the same water that existed on the Earth millions of years ago? Same water, same God, same Jesus, same Spirit!

Friday 27 September
Blood and water

Read John 19:28–37

… one of the soldiers pierced Jesus' side with a spear, bringing a sudden flow of blood and water. The man who saw it has given testimony, and his testimony is true. He knows that he tells the truth, and he testifies so that you also may believe.

(verses 34–35)

For Greeks, blood was associated with divinity, as water was with humanity. Some even believed a mixture of the two flowed through the veins of gods – a substance known as *ichor*.

Perhaps this is why John, intent on revealing Jesus as the Christ in his eyewitness account, draws attention to this moment where blood and water pour from Jesus' wound, going to lengths to make sure his readers take note (verse 35).

Where John (the Baptist) baptises with waters of new life, Jesus uses water to cleanse the disciples' feet. So perhaps it is unsurprising that we should see not only blood, but also water mixed together, flowing from the GodMan's side, conveying the new life and purification his death brings. In death, Jesus' body brings forth the blood of the Eucharist and the water of baptism. John makes many links between blood, water, purification and revelation. He even relocates the death of Jesus on the day *before* the Passover – the day when the lambs would be slaughtered. Jesus is the Passover lamb, whose blood takes away the sin of the world.

So it is, that as I pour the wine to share communion, I always add a little water. This is humanity and divinity. God doesn't shout from afar. He doesn't just come near. He goes much further. He is the *kenotic* God, emptying himself out into the world, giving everything.

At the point of his death, the living water flows out like a river from his body into the world, and into those who believe – it's a reminder of Ezekiel's prophecy (Ezekiel 47:1–12).

Hello Holy Spirit!

† All-giving God, I thank you that, through your Son on the cross, you chose to pour yourself out into the world. Let your living water flow through me.

For further thought

Read Ezekiel's prophetic vision (Ezekiel 47:1–12). What is your vision for how this 'living water' might flow out into your community? Spend time in prayer, articulating and envisioning where and how you want to see transformation.

Saturday 28 September
Three witnesses

Read 1 John 5:1–12

'This is the one who came by water and blood – Jesus Christ. He did not come by water only, but by water and blood. And it is the Spirit who testifies, because the Spirit is the truth. For there are three that testify: the Spirit, the water and the blood; and the three are in agreement.'

(verses 6–8)

Despite his witness account to Jesus' humanity and divinity, in John's lifetime some teachers began to claim that Jesus didn't really die, suggesting instead that Jesus was probably more divine than he was human. This *gnostic* teaching also claimed therefore that what we did with our own bodies wasn't that important either. John wasn't a fan! This was not his Gospel testimony of who Jesus is!

Later, in the fourth century, at a Council in Nicaea in 325 AD, a bishop named Athanasius spoke vociferously against gnostics, explaining that Jesus was of the *same* substance as the Father – fully human, yet fully God.

What difference does this make? If Jesus was not fully human, he would not have been exactly as we are. And how then could his conquering of death save us if he wasn't really one of us in the first place?

As we have seen, John likes to use water symbolically to identify *who* Jesus is, rather than *what* it does by way of cleansing and purification. Whereas we come into the world and enter the kingdom by the water of baptism, and live in it through the outpouring of His Spirit (John 3:5), Jesus' incarnation is by these *three*: water, blood *and* Spirit – fully human, fully divine, fully empowered by the Holy Spirit. The three testify!

The waters of new life lead us not only to repentance, but to new life in the Spirit (Psalm 46:3–4)!

† God of the three, Father, Son and Holy Spirit, may my life be testimony to who you are, and what you have done because of your great love. Lead me now into the flowing streams of new life.

For further thought

If we are to truly live a full life, how and in what ways do you think our bodies can reflect this – even in their brokenness and frailty?

Waters: from Genesis to Revelation – 3 Waters of new life

September

274

Readings in Luke (4) –
An open invitation

Notes by **Dafne Plou**

Dafne is a journalist and social communicator. Her work involves travelling to other Latin American countries to lead seminars and speak at conferences. She's a member of the Methodist Church in Argentina. In her local church, in Buenos Aires' suburbs, she works in the area of community building and fellowship in liturgy. She is a women's rights activist and participates in the women's movement in her country. Dafne has used the NRSVA for these notes.

Sunday 29 September
An open invitation

Read Luke 14:15–24

'Blessed is anyone who will eat bread in the kingdom of God!'

(verse 15b)

A few days after the economic crisis started, city dwellers were surprised by 'this people' invading streets in protest, sometimes silent, sometimes noisy. Who were they? Untidy, looking like they haven't had a shower for days, muddy shoes, darker skin. Has anyone invited them to the city? Are they truly Argentinian? In the meantime, we had been busy trying to invest our savings in 'safe' places or in keeping our properties and goods out of the economic devastation, or in simply putting our own personal interests in first place, thinking selfishly that the crisis would never touch us.

Our banquet hadn't been theirs. 'This people' had been off our map for ages, we had never considered them, we had never realised they had a face, a voice, needs that were never satisfied. Who would take care? Who would take responsibility? Couldn't we just organise another soup kitchen? Were we ready to include them in solidarity, in care, with justice?

The master said, 'Compel people to come in, so that my house may be filled.' Let's fill the house then! How? By recognising that we have run after false gods and that we need to accept Jesus' invitation to his open table where 'this people' have already been included.

† Let us in, Jesus, forgive our selfishness and lack of love for our neighbours. Fill us with your Spirit and renew our faith and commitment. Amen.

Counting the cost

> **Read Luke 14:25–35**
>
> *'Salt is good; but if salt has lost its taste, how can its saltiness be restored?'*
>
> (verse 34)

Visiting the Lincoln Memorial, in Washington DC, was a deep and moving experience. I felt I was inside a kind of temple, together with dozens of people from all around the world paying silent and reverential honour to a committed leader who was true to his beliefs and ideals till the end. When coming out, I stood in awe at the top of the stairs looking towards the National Mall remembering Martin Luther King's words.

And suddenly I heard this little boy asking:

'Mummy, is this where Martin Luther King spoke?'

'Yes, and he said, "I have a dream that this nation will come together as brothers and sisters."'

'And Obama is our president now!' replied the boy proudly.

What if committed people let their saltiness wash away? Would anyone be able to replace them and restore the flavour, the strength, the vision? Who would follow a tasteless cause?

Violence stopped both Lincoln and King from seeing their dreams come true. But their salt penetrated deeply and profoundly into people's minds and souls. It permeated society, shaking the very roots of inequality and racial injustice. Their commitment did not wash away, but many were inspired to pursue these dreams with more courage and boldness so that all could enjoy a new society built on freedom and democracy. Let anyone with ears to hear listen!

† Dear Jesus, keep our minds open, our ears ready to listen and our hands and feet good for action! Amen.

For further thought

Where can you add a pinch of salt to your words and actions today?

Tuesday 1 October
Lost and found

Read Luke 15:1–10

'"Rejoice with me, for I have found my sheep that was lost."'

(verse 6)

'Hey, pastor, the chapel is full; more than 100 youngsters came to the festival tonight! Why should we leave and try to find those three or four that always go astray?' they asked, quite irritated. But they knew their pastor wouldn't stay behind and that he would lead the way.

They remembered him preaching: 'We're not here to stand behind the pulpit and shout loud, "Let the sinners come to us! Let them show their repentance and kneel before our altar!" We've got to go out, reach them, talk to them!' They knew where to look first, at the bar area, under the bridge, or across the railways, in that shanty warehouse. They'll surely find them once again.

Would bringing them to the church festival do them any good? Perhaps staying away from drinks and marijuana for one night would help. If Jesus was present at any stage in that invitation, he did it in the friendly gestures of welcome, the kind glances, the community of young ones who shared the same dreams, the same concerns, the same problems but were ready to follow other ways out, to search for different answers, to find courage to overcome adversity and embrace new hopes.

The festival went well. There were good music groups with uplifting lyrics, and a lively gathering at the church garden till late. As the last participants were leaving, a boy from the group the minister had looked for approached him. 'Pastor, we hated you when we saw you coming for us this evening. But this was cool. We'll come again.'

† Dear Jesus, your call is not an easy one to follow. Keep our trust in you firm and let us share your love and acceptance at all times. Amen.

For further thought

Are you ready to listen to people whose experiences are different from ours? Where can you have lively conversations, in trust and freedom?

Readings in Luke (4) – An open invitation

October

The father's embrace

Read Luke 15:11–31

'His father saw him and was filled with compassion.'

(part of verse 20)

It seems the relations between parents and children were not easy at Jesus' time either. We can imagine the situation: the arguing, the slamming of doors, the empty seat at the table, the cross looks, the hard words. Also the dreams about a different world outside home's walls, the adventure, the fun, the new challenges and risks. The young man just wanted his money to break ground, take his own decisions, find his own way in life. He didn't consider other people's feelings or if he had any family duties. It was time to leave!

Bonds with the father seemed to have broken, but something about him remained alive deep inside his son: his generosity and his respect for other people's dignity and rights. His father would never let his workers go hungry. This memory encouraged the son to go back. The son wasn't thinking that his father was to forgive him for what he had done. He was only hoping that this generosity he remembered so well at a time of need, would move his father to count him in. But it was love and grace that he found when his father embraced him. No reproval, but joy and celebration.

In this parable Jesus tells us not only about God's forgiveness but also about his grace and redeeming actions. God doesn't ignore our own stories and he looks for us in spite of them, to transform us and make our lives meaningful.

† In your loving embrace, we find ways to turn our crying into singing, in hope and grace. Amen.

For further thought

Think of different ways in which you could see God's grace in action in your personal life, in your church, in your community. Share the experiences with others and pray.

Thursday 3 October
Whom do you serve?

Read Luke 16:1–18

'You cannot serve God and wealth.'

(verse 13b)

Unfortunately, in many countries, people suffer their authorities' greed and ambition once they become powerful. The consequences of corruption are well-known not only because a few get rich at the expense of everybody else, but also because public investments that should contribute to better health, education, housing and transportation for all, end up in hidden pockets to be spent selfishly disregarding the common good. Injustice is like a rot which sets into all of society.

Jesus is very severe here. His strict considerations determine that there's no choice, but one way to follow. And this is hard to contend in a society in which consumerism and the accumulation of unnecessary goods are the rule in order to gain prestige and social esteem. Even doing little tricks now and then, like the servant in the parable, being 'astute' when negotiating and accumulating money and wealth, are taken for a trivial matter. Are we willing to follow Jesus' hard demand when economic success is the main target in our societies?

Following God's way means recognising that he can liberate us from all ties and ambitions. Serving him leads us to build inclusive environments where everyone is valued in his and her dignity no matter their social status. God sets us free to look beyond any demands for success, to contemplate his creation, and understand that he wants us to work for a just distribution of all its richness and resources, away from exploitation and destruction.

† Dear God, help us to avoid the temptation of serving gods other than you and lead us to achieve justice and respect for all.

For further thought

What would it mean for your church to live like a lily in the field? What would it mean for you?

Friday 4 October
Who do you listen to?

Read Luke 16:19–31

'"They have Moses and the prophets; they should listen to them."'

(verse 29)

In the 1990s there was a president in Argentina who, in answer to demonstrations against his government's unjust economic policies, said very lightly, 'Well, the poor will be always with us.' He was quoting Jesus' words in the Gospel (Mark 14:7) and it was truly outrageous. We know very well that Jesus was not justifying the existence of poverty, but reminding us of our own injustices and lack of mercy towards the poor in our societies.

'For the love of money is a root of all kinds of evil,' Paul reminds us in 1 Timothy 6:10. A life centred in consumerism, money and selfish pleasure can only lead to evil, not only individual but also social, because a society that organises its life around money, disregarding the integrity of nature and human dignity and rights, will lead only to destruction. Greed and disdain for our neighbours' needs not only ruin our own personal values and spirituality but also destroy other people's lives and creation itself.

The rich man asks for mercy, for some relief to his situation, for help so that his brothers wouldn't have to face his fate. But the answer is harsh and clear: you should have listened and acted accordingly, and your brothers should have as well.

There are values, teachings, beliefs, laws that we refuse to acknowledge because our selfish interests come first. Jesus invites us to love him in those who are oppressed, those who suffer the consequences of an unjust order, those whom we don't want to see because we have become obsessed with self-indulgence. We should know enough. We have heard and seen enough. Let's listen and be ready to care and serve others in the love of Jesus.

† Help us, Jesus, to work for a just world where no one is denied dignity or rights and solidarity and where respect surpasses selfishness and ambition.

For further thought

Create a collage with your church group to show the many ways solidarity is present in our society and our world today.

Readings in Luke (4) – An open invitation

October

Saturday 5 October
A faith expressed

Read Luke 17:1–19

'Jesus, Master, have mercy on us!'

(verse 13b)

Why is it so difficult to say 'thank you'? We live in a society that makes us believe that everything we are and everything we have is just a product of our own efforts. The 'self-made man' or the 'safe-made woman' discourse has penetrated deep into our minds and souls and has shaped the way we see life, measure results and appreciate achievements. Each step we climb is a result of our own strength, our own capacity, our own merit. We don't seem to trust in anyone else. There's no one to thank, just us.

The lepers knew very well who had healed them but they were not eager to trust him, nor show faith in him. There were other more important things to do before saying 'thanks' and dedicating time to praise God. Surely they wanted to tell their families and friends that they were healed and could go back home and celebrate. Perhaps they wanted to clean their bodies and get new clothes. Or eat a proper meal with their dear ones after living a long time as outcasts. The prophet could wait; they will see him some other day. How many times have we done the same? How many times have we prioritised our own interests over thanksgiving?

Was Jesus disappointed when he saw that only one of those healed was praising God and coming back to say thanks? And a foreigner, indeed! Jesus didn't allow this situation to get him down. His grace was overwhelming and in his love he recognised the healed man's faith that would sustain him in starting a new life.

† On our knees, dear Jesus, we humbly recognise your everlasting grace that keeps us in your arms in spite of our selfishness and ingratitude. Amen.

For further thought

Think of 'success stories' in your personal life, family life or in your community. Did you acknowledge the Holy Spirit's guidance and support and thank God? Light a candle in remembrance and thanksgiving.

Readings in Luke (4) – An open invitation

October

Readings in Luke (4) –
2 The kingdom within

Notes by **Tim Yau**

Tim is a Pioneer Missioner working for the Anglican Diocese of Norwich. His role is to establish a worshipping community in Round House Park, a new housing development in Cringleford, and also be a Mission Enabler encouraging missional practice across the region; not trying to get people to go to church, but trying to get the Church to go to the people. To his children's delight, he is a *Star Wars* geek and still dreams of becoming a superhero. Tim has used the NIVUK for these notes.

Sunday 6 October
Person preservation

Read Luke 17:20–37

'Whoever tries to keep their life will lose it, and whoever loses their life will preserve it.'

(verse 33)

What is life? It is more than simple biology. We are encircled by a multitude of organisms, some of which we value, others we misunderstand and much we're merely indifferent to. However, when it comes to our lives we are immersed in cultures and customs that shape and inform us as to what it means to have a meaningful life.

I live in an affluent new housing development on the outskirts of the city of Norwich. On my street, I can see signs and symbols of wealth and aspiration representing financially comfortable and upwardly mobile twenty-first-century Western consumerism. The message that sings out from every shiny new belonging is: to live is to have.

Conversely, for the religiously pious Pharisees who questioned Jesus in today's reading, to live was to obey God's law. Seemingly, for the people Jesus mentioned in Noah's and Lot's time, to live was to revel in life.

What does life look like where you are? Whether it's discerning God's coming kingdom like the Pharisees or living in the moment under the shadow of judgement like the ancients, Jesus asks us to let go of our position and possessions because real life is found in him.

† Jesus came that we may have life to the full (John 10:10). Lord, help us to let go of ourselves and hold onto you. Amen.

Monday 7 October
Pride and position

Read Luke 18:1–14

'For all those who exalt themselves will be humbled, and those who humble themselves will be exalted.'

(verse 14b)

Norwich Anglican cathedral is over 900 years old and dates back to the Norman conquest of England. Set behind the high altar elevated by 12 steps is the 'cathedra', the bishop's ceremonial seat of power. The building's design and flow symbolically exalted the temporal and spiritual authority of the Norman bishop over the clergy, worshippers and region. In the mediaeval age, people knew their place, from prince to peasant, society was shaped around social class, and moving up the hierarchical strata was almost impossible. Today the seat is seldom sat upon and is sectioned off by velvet ropes, like a historic museum piece.

In the West, we now like to think we live in a meritocracy, where we are judged not by class or social standing, but by our ability: the best-skilled person is exalted. In applying for jobs we are encouraged to 'sell ourselves' and promote our worthiness over others. However, in our celebrity-obsessed culture, sometimes it feels like we live in a celebritocracy, where the most self-proclaiming media-savvy famous person is exalted, despite their lack of capabilities.

In today's reading, Jesus' parable has a religiously strict Pharisee exalting himself over all others because of his devotional rigour. However, it is neither ability, fame nor religiosity that Jesus exalts, but the honest, self-aware, repentant confession of a Roman-collaborating tax collector. Realising that we are sinners and recognising that we are broken, lost and needing help allows God to exalt us, lift us up from our humble demeanour and place us in an exalted position divinely forgiven, restored and reconciled to him.

† The psalmist prays: 'My sacrifice, O God, is a broken spirit; a broken and contrite heart you, God, will not despise' (Psalm 51:17). Lord, forgive our foolish pride and accept our humble hearts. Amen.

For further thought

Ask God to show you the areas of your life where pride may have grown. How will you break it and turn away from it?

Tuesday 8 October
Possibility people

Read Luke 18:15–30

Jesus replied, 'What is impossible with man is possible with God.'

(verse 27)

At 11 years old, I had an epiphany: I wanted to be a writer. It was the 1970s and I attended the local comprehensive school, a place where uniforms had been abandoned, and with them any sense of order or identity. I lived in a grim northern industrial town, where it felt like there was nothing to be proud of, and no way out. Then one day a children's author visited my class, he read us some of his work and set us an alliteration challenge. Surprisingly, he read out my attempt and praised my creativity. That was the only time I ever remember feeling truly inspired during my formative years in education. I recall running home and telling my mother that I wanted to be a writer, but she frowned, telling me I should look at the other options. It wasn't that she was being mean, it was just that people like us from where we were didn't do that sort of thing, it was impossible.

In today's reading, we meet carers bringing their children to Jesus to secure an earthly blessing, and a wealthy ruler trying to secure his eternal blessing. The first group were initially chastised by the disciples but went away with Jesus' affirmation that God's kingdom belonged to them. The ruler, however, being firstly affirmed in his religious practice retreats from Jesus feeling dejected and apart from God's kingdom.

God doesn't work to worldly standards; he chooses the simple, trusting and innocent over the seemingly successful and self-assured. God sees the possible in what the world says is impossible, even in me.

† Lord, you see our hearts and know what we are uniquely made for, help us to see a way through human limitation and cultural conditioning to be the person you made us to be. Amen.

For further thought

Where in your life have you been told 'it is impossible'? What hopes and dreams might God want to reignite in you today?

Prayerful persistence

Read Luke 18:31–43

'What do you want me to do for you?'

(verse 41a)

Buzz after buzz after buzz! That was the resounding memory of my hospital ward shifts when I trained to be a nurse in my early twenties. Being the most junior member of the staff team meant I clocked up the most miles rushing up and down the corridors attending to the flashing buzzers of patients calling for attention. The phrase, 'What do you want me to do for you?' was often on my lips. Most of the time the answers and actions were obvious, and patients were generally grateful for the help and care. However, because of language differences, speech difficulties, mental confusion or disturbed emotional states, sometimes it wasn't clear what was wanted. The consequence of the insistent buzzing from a patient was sometimes met by staff and fellow patients with indifference, if not hostility. I'm ashamed to say that sometimes the call button was removed from the most persistent offenders.

Today's reading has a blind beggar calling out to Jesus for mercy. The beggar was impoverished by his disability but also marginalised by it because the common understanding then was that physical abnormality was due to the curse of sin in your family history. Therefore, people kept their distance from the beggar, but his persistent cries invoked the crowd's intolerance and they reprimanded him to be quiet. How wrong they were! Jesus heard the beggar and saw his obvious predicament; however, he treated him as a person, not a problem and did not presume to respond to his request without dignifying him by asking, 'What do you want me to do for you?'

† Jesus, Son of David, have mercy on us. Forgive our impatience and intolerance and help us to hear and discern the true cries for help that are drowned out by our society's indifference. Amen.

For further thought

The beggar's persistence was driven by his faith that Jesus had the power to help him. What do you have faith in Jesus for today?

Readings in Luke (4) – 2 The kingdom within

October

Thursday 10 October
Personal penitence

Read Luke 19:1–10

'For the Son of Man came to seek and to save the lost.'

(verse 10)

From being distracted as a child and wandering away from my parents in a department store to foolhardy hiking in a winter blizzard, I've been lost many times in my life. I've been lost in my own stupidity, too arrogant to seek help, too confused from misreading maps and recently too reliant on fallible technology. However, in that lostness, I've always had the compulsion to find my way home to the love, comfort and care of friends and family.

Yet, there was a time when I wanted to disappear, to walk away from the huge hurt that had become synonymous with my broken home. My plan was to buy a one-way ticket to the USA and simply wander off. Looking back I had an overly romanticised view of losing myself, but the thought of being a distant nobody was more comforting than being a shambolic somebody. For a myriad of reasons people want to get lost, they'll do it through addictions, fantasies and lies, they might create new personas for themselves to fit in with the culture they adopt, but it's all a facade because somewhere hidden deep inside them there's a longing for home. Not a place of bricks and mortar, but someplace where they're loved and accepted for who they really are.

Zacchaeus was lost; he'd walked away from his culture and embraced a lifestyle which set him on a downward spiral away from his true self. Jesus saw through his despair and disdain and brought light and love to Zacchaeus' life, his hard-hearted walls came down and transformation bloomed in him.

† Lord God, you see through the flimsy image we hide ourselves behind, turn our hearts of stone back to beating hearts of flesh. Let your love find us and bring us home to you. Amen.

For further thought

What ways are you hiding your true self? What would home look like for you? Are you willing to let Jesus into your life?

Friday 11 October
Price and prize

Read Luke 19:11–27

'He replied, "I tell you that to everyone who has, more will be given, but as for the one who has nothing, even what they have will be taken away."'

(verse 26)

At a youth camp, we were all handed £10. It was a free gift; however, we were also challenged to have faith and ask God what we should do with it; how might it multiply for God's kingdom? Some immediately handed it back uninspired, or cynically asked, 'What's the catch?' Others put it in their wallets and simply forgot about it. Nevertheless, many of us prayed and imagined creative ways to grow it. I teamed up with a friend and we found that between us we had hair clippers and scissors, so we bought as much cheap hair gel as we could and advertised ourselves as 'Audrey & Alan's Psycho-Barbers: guaranteed unqualified and inexperienced'. We hoped that, if some brave and foolish souls paid our 50 pence price to look stupid in front of their peers, we might make our money back. Amazingly though, the more extreme and wild styles we created, the more the queues grew. By the end of the week, we had over £100 and over 200 teens that would have some serious explaining to do to their parents when they got home.

Today's parable seems harsh to modern sensibilities but fits the cultural setting of that day. The stakes were high, ten minas was about three months' pay, and the unsolicited command of the strict and seemingly hated king to 'put the money to work' must have caused panic. Thankfully, this story is not about God's character but warns against fruitless faith. Jesus came to Jerusalem as judge looking for evidence of a fruitful people but sadly found opposition, excuses and fear.

† Lord Jesus, forgive our fearful responses, false excuses and fruitlessness. Let our faith be in that you chose us and appointed us so that we might go and bear fruit that will last (John 15:16).

For further thought

God chooses us and gives us gifts, what is preventing your gifts from growing? How might your image of God be stunting your spiritual growth?

Passion prelude

Read Luke 19:28–48

'Blessed is the king who comes in the name of the Lord!' 'Peace in heaven and glory in the highest!'

(verse 38)

The flags had been liberally handed out, we were given strict instructions on where to stand and how to act, and we were told explicitly not to engage our special visitor in conversation unless initiated by him. He arrived with a ripple of applause, greeted by the Ridley Hall College Principal and staff. That was the cue for the rest of us to 'act normal'; however, the loitering in anticipation of the visitation had bred an air of stifled giddiness, and when it came to addressing the dignitary we forgot our instructions.

'Charlie!' I bellowed in the excitement of the moment. The future King of Great Britain stopped, turned, smiled and called back to me. His entourage looked on dismayed and my peers looked a little red-faced at my royal faux pas. In my enthusiasm, I'd broken the rules of princely etiquette, but the Prince of Wales didn't seem the slightest bit bothered by it.

Compare this with today's reading of Jesus' arrival at Jerusalem; no polite welcome party or well-orchestrated decorum, just a rowdy rabble of Galilean peasant pilgrims, Jesus' disciples and followers, proclaiming him as king with actions laden with meaning: laying down their cloaks like they did announcing Jehu as the new king of Israel (2 Kings 9:13); reimagining of the king triumphantly returning to Jerusalem from battle on a colt (Zechariah 9:9); and the declaring of the blessed king (Psalm 118:26). This raucous procession punctuated by accusations, tears, prophecy, action and judgement brought Jesus to the heart of the Jewish nation with God's unprecedented plan to bring divine peace and glory.

† Lord Jesus, you are a king like no other, you walk with the humble, stand with the accused, weep over us all and turn the tables of injustice. May we do as you do. Amen.

For further thought

Jesus' words and actions often brought him into conflict with the authorities. Who do you stand with in life? What do you stand up for?

Building and rebuilding – 1 Sacred space

Notes by **Jane Gonzalez**

Jane is a Roman Catholic laywoman and just completed the fourth year of a Professional Doctorate in Pastoral Theology. She has a keen interest in studying scripture, is a visiting preacher at a local Anglican church and occasionally pops up on local radio reviewing the Sunday papers. Other interests include singing and gardening. Now retired, she hopes to visit all the English cathedrals and walk the Camino de Santiago. Jane has used the NRSVA for these notes.

Sunday 13 October
Abide with me

Read Psalm 104:1–9

You set the earth on its foundations, so that it shall never be shaken.

(verse 5)

As I finish the reflections for this week, I am in Rome – the city that is often called 'eternal'. We will walk mainly to sites that are important in Christian history, but our pilgrimage will also take us past the partial or ruined reminders of those who preceded Christian Rome. Rome is layer upon layer of buildings, reminding us of the transience of human life and of the fragility of all our constructs. Nothing we make is eternal or unchanging. The news at present highlights this awareness: earthquakes, hurricanes across our world, with lives lost, homes flattened, livelihoods lost. There lies before the survivors the monumental task of rebuilding, repairing or relocating.

This week's readings are all taken from the Hebrew Bible. Salvation history recounts the evolution of a nomadic people into a nation of settled urban dwellers: from tent to permanent housing; from tabernacle to temple. It recounts the building up and development of a nation. Underpinning it all, and foundational in times of destruction, exile and return, all reflected in our passages this week, is the certainty of the steadfast and indestructible love of God for his people and his creation, whatever, good or bad, befalls.

† Creator God, you are the centre of my life. Keep my faith strong and my hope alive, especially in times of uncertainty and loss.

The glory of the house is hospitality

Read Exodus 25:1–9

And have them make me a sanctuary, so that I may dwell among them.

(verse 8)

Our niece has just bought her first flat. After years of sharing with friends or living in bedsit-land, she has taken the plunge and committed herself to a mortgage. For her, this is more than a step on the first rung of the property ladder. It is the start of the fulfilment of a dream (that many people share) – a home of her own. She is looking forward to creating a space in which to welcome family and friends. She has plans for the future. She does not aspire (yet) to some of the lofty projects or 'grand designs' that many of us like to watch on home makeover television programmes. But she has ideas about the decor, the kind of furniture she would like, the improvements in layout that might one day come about. It seems innate in human beings to be ever bent on improving the places where we live.

A home, however, is more than a house to be decorated or fixed up. It is much more than an investment for the future or the type of show house where image seems to matter more than comfort. A home is our place of sanctuary and a centre of hospitality. Hospitality makes our homes as much 'sacred spaces' as the conventional church or worship place and sites where people of all faiths and none may encounter, through our welcome and sharing, the generous and loving God who dwells with us. This was the 'grand design' of Jesus in his ministry of table fellowship and one which he desires us to emulate.

† Father, give me a generous heart that welcomes the stranger and exile. Help me to work for their welfare and well-being rather than my own.

For further thought

Are our churches and meeting places real centres of welcome? Is maintenance more important than mission?

Tuesday 15 October
Home is where the heart is

Read 2 Samuel 7:1–17

I have not lived in a house since the day I brought up the people of Israel from Egypt to this day, but I have been moving about in a tent and a tabernacle.

(verse 6)

One of the ambitions for our retirement is to visit all the cathedrals in England and Wales. Whether ancient or modern, each has its own character and ambience. I have to confess to a distaste for ornate baroque architecture, but whatever the style or period, there is no doubt that these sacred spaces testify to the profound faith of those who planned and built them, and their desire to glorify and honour the Creator. Many now attract those more interested in history or architecture than worship, but they still remain centres dedicated to prayer, service and the care of the community.

In my home town, one of the most prophetic and appropriate uses of our sacred spaces recently has been as night shelters for the homeless. Churches across the town responded to the need for safe and warm accommodation and food for the homeless during the winter months, with parish rooms and church halls being used and volunteers from all denominations as volunteers.

There is an anonymous saying that, 'we shape our dwellings and then our dwellings shape us'. Does God reject a permanent dwelling, a temple, because he wishes to remain unconfined? The problem with some of our sacred spaces is that we can delude ourselves that that is the only place where God is to be found. Often we have defined ourselves and separated ourselves from each other because of the way we perceive and use particular spaces. Does confining God in a church cramp his style and limit his generosity? Are our sacred spaces really used to do his work?

† Father, shape me, mould me in your image, that I may reach out in love to those who do not know you.

For further thought

How does homelessness affect your local community? Consider how you can help, as an individual or a parish community.

Building and rebuilding – 1 Sacred space

October

Built by wisdom

Researching your family tree has become more and more popular over the last few years. It is something that I have undertaken, with my sister, in a fairly low-key way, and the internet makes the research much easier today. In an age of great mobility and a world where many travel away (through choice or necessity) to live and work, perhaps we need the security of knowing who we are and where we came from, even if there are skeletons in the closet! On such foundations we can build for the future. While I may not be able to give my family a rather grandiose title like 'House of David' or 'House of Tudor', for example, I belong to a house. The structure, however ramshackle, of the lives of my ancestors is still a building, a scaffolding and foundation for my life and, I hope, for those who follow me. Other pillars in my life have been wise and loving friends who have propped me up through hard times.

It is the same for us in the Church. As it says in Paul's letter to the Ephesians (2:19–21), we are 'built upon the foundation of the apostles and prophets, with Christ Jesus himself as the cornerstone. In him the whole structure is joined together and grows into a holy temple.' The Christian heroes and heroines of the past, the saints, form pillars that support us. Their witness and perseverance strengthen us, striving in the present to cement the foundations for the future.

† Father, I thank you for the blessing of family and friends. May I, in my turn, be a pillar of strength to those who need nurture and support.

For further thought

Think about those who have supported you in your faith. Who in your family has supported your faith the most?

Thursday 17 October
A light for the Gentiles …

Read Psalm 79

O God, the nations have come into your inheritance;
they have defiled your holy temple;
they have laid Jerusalem in ruins.

(verse 1)

A 2016 UK survey indicates that people who subscribe to no religion, known as 'nones', now outnumber those who do. All around are dire predictions of the 'death' of religion and the decline of religious practice. Rather than worshipping in church, people are flocking to art galleries and museums to seek and, it seems, to find transcendence and spiritual fulfilment. Art galleries are becoming the 'new cathedrals' according to media reports. Many talk about not being religious, preferring to be spiritual.

It can be easy to become disheartened, and sometimes to feel threatened, by the statistics and our multicultural society. Yet the statistics highlight the truism that there is a great deal of spiritual hunger around. People recognise that there is something within them that seeks a deeper reality – what we call God. How can we, as churches, respond if our neighbours are seeking this fulfilment not in church but elsewhere? Many approaches have been or could be tried – outreach centres, pub churches, Christian coffee bars; non-threatening spaces where spiritual hungers can be satisfied.

In the end, I think, as with most areas of human life, it boils down to the personal touch. As Christians, we are temples of the Holy Spirit. In us, rather than in the physical spaces of worship, in our love and acceptance of others, our compassion and charity, could not the doubtful and the 'nones' start to find the God they subconsciously seek?

† Father, may I be a beacon of light and life, to guide those who seek you in ways that will find you.

For further thought

Consider whether you could keep your church open during the week so that a sacred space is available for people to 'pop in'. How welcoming is your space?

Hope springs eternal

Read Lamentations 2:1–10

The elders of daughter Zion sit on the ground in silence; they have thrown dust on their heads and put on sackcloth; the young girls of Jerusalem have bowed their heads to the ground.

(verse 10)

I write this at the end of a summer where there has been much in the way of sorrow and grieving for many at home and abroad. At the beginning of the summer, a devastating fire swept through a tower block in London and resulted in many deaths. The flats in the tower were completely destroyed and hundreds of people were left homeless and reliant on the goodwill of their neighbours for basic necessities. In the Caribbean and Central America, thousands lost their lives and homes through the relentless battering of consecutive hurricanes and earthquakes. Truly it has been a time of lamentation and mourning. We might want to echo the words of the writer of Lamentations who sees God at work not in building up, but in ruin and destruction.

It is hard at such times to find words of consolation and hope. Where is the meaning? Sometimes, although we must say something, our words can seem facile or trite. Often the best (the only?) response is to put words into action, hope into action and to sow the seeds of future good. I live in a 'New Town' – one built after the Second World War as a response to the destruction in London. The New Towns were designed as places of hope – humane spaces replacing slums and substandard accommodation. There was to be a new start and a chance for people to put down new roots: each estate had green spaces, a church, a pub and a community centre. Space for the rebuilding of lives and communities and where mourning was turned into dancing (Psalm 30:11). Where are those sacred spaces necessary today?

† Father, I know that your ways are not my ways. Help me to keep from despair when I see great sorrow; I place all my trust in you.

For further thought

Look for some uplifting news that shows communities and individuals doing good. Spend a day reflecting on this and not on the bad news.

Saturday 19 October
East, west, home's best ...

Read Zechariah 8:1–17

Thus says the Lord of hosts: I will save my people from the east country and from the west country; and I will bring them to live in Jerusalem. They shall be my people and I will be their God, in faithfulness and in righteousness.

(verses 7–8)

At present, the plight of the displaced and dispossessed is never far away from our television screens and newspapers. Natural disasters, war and terrorism all contribute to forced migration of thousands of people. Many countries have been generous in their response and welcome for people seeking a place of respite. Church communities have been at the forefront in this effort, often in spite of vocal opposition from those who fear the influx of refugees. When a local community has problems of finding accommodation, there is concern about whether 'outsiders' should be given priority in housing and welfare. What is sometimes forgotten is that many refugees do not want to be here permanently – they want to live at home, in their own beloved lands.

In the midst of the gloom and doom of much of the news this summer there have been glimmers of hope. Iraqi Christians are returning to their homes – to cities in ruins, desecrated churches, and the task of reconstruction of buildings and community. It is remarkable that they are doing so in a spirit of reconciliation – speaking about forgiveness rather than revenge, and rejoicing in their return to the places where they have their roots.

What great faith these ancient Christian communities have shown us! It is humbling to reflect on the faith and trust they have shown, in flight and in return, that they are and always will be God's people and that he is always with them to bring them home.

† Father, increase my faith; strengthen my trust. When dark times come, keep me aware of your loving presence.

For further thought
Give thanks today, and pray for the uprooted communities of the world that have to rebuild their lives.

Building and rebuilding – 1 Sacred space

October

Building and rebuilding – 2 Buildings of flesh and stone

Notes by **Paul Nicholson SJ**

Paul is a Roman Catholic priest belonging to the Society of Jesus. He works in London as Socius (assistant) to the Jesuit Provincial. He edits *The Way*, a journal of Christian spirituality, and is author of *An Advent Pilgrimage* (2013) and *Pathways to God* (2017). Since being ordained in 1988 he has worked principally in ministries of spirituality and of social justice, and was novice-master between 2008 and 2014. Paul has used the NRSVA for these notes.

Sunday 20 October
Building up, not tearing down

Read Jeremiah 24:1–7

Thus says the Lord, the God of Israel: Like these good figs, so I will regard as good the exiles from Judah … I will set my eyes upon them for good, and I will bring them back to this land. I will build them up, and not tear them down.

(verses 5–6)

As a child, building blocks were among my favourite toys. With them, I built houses, towers and palaces, limited only by my imagination – and the number of blocks I had! Now, decades later, on a day off or on holiday, I love to visit unfamiliar towns and cities, with their squares and shopping arcades, castles and churches; their almost infinite variation on a few simple patterns.

The art and craft of building is important in the scriptures. Sometimes literally – the temple in Jerusalem is built and rebuilt as centuries pass – but often as an image of God at work, patiently constructing a people of his own, and calling men and women to join him in this. Despite repeated setbacks, God's building is assured, and continues to this day.

The buildings we live among have the capacity to crush our spirits, or to help raise our minds and hearts to God. In this regard, a light-filled, airy museum atrium can be as uplifting as a cool cathedral cloister. So, too, I can build up those closest to me, or tear them down by a word or a silence. The readings this week challenge us to build on foundations that God has laid.

† Help me, Lord, to recognise you today at work in my life, building up not only me but all those around me.

Monday 21 October
The cost of building well

Read Habakkuk 2:6–14

'Alas for you who build a town by bloodshed, and found a city on iniquity!' ... But the earth will be filled with the knowledge of the glory of the Lord, as the waters cover the sea.

(verses 12, 14)

In the centre of Bristol, in south-west England, there is a large neo-Gothic tower, part of the university. A prominent landmark for the whole city, it is called the Wills Memorial Building. This, though, has led to controversy in recent years, since it is claimed that the man the building commemorates, the Victorian philanthropist Henry Overton Wills III, made his money from the slave trade. His family owned tobacco plantations in America and, in the mid-nineteenth century, these were farmed by slaves. As a result some have argued that in justice the building ought to be renamed.

The prophet Habakkuk has harsh words for those who build on the oppression of others. He imagines the buildings themselves protesting against this. Yet his message is ultimately one of hope. In time, God will intervene, and then, we are to suppose, wrongs will be righted and the oppressed liberated.

Human actions and motivations are rarely simple. They are often mixtures of good and bad, of generosity and selfishness. The generosity Henry Wills showed to a developing university has to be set alongside his apparent blindness to the suffering from which he profited. The lifestyle enjoyed by many of you who read these words (as by their writer!) would not be possible without the hard, unremitting labour of others. There is no simple way to escape from the social and political systems that I find myself a part of, yet I must work to build a better world even while I acknowledge the necessary compromises that I have to make.

† Lord, help me to be generous with the gifts that you have given me, and to acknowledge those whose hard work brings me those gifts.

For further thought

What does 'the knowledge of the glory of the Lord' spoken of here mean to you, in the context of your everyday life?

Tuesday 22 October
Dreams of a better tomorrow

Read Nehemiah 1:1–11

'They are your servants and your people, whom you redeemed by your great power and your strong hand. O Lord, let your ear be attentive to the prayer of your servant, and to the prayer of your servants who delight in revering your name. Give success to your servant today.'

(verses 10–11)

Nehemiah, living comfortably in exile, receives news of the pitiable state of Jerusalem, ravaged by war and destroyed by fire. In prayer, he recalls God's promises, and this will lead him to take a leading role in the restoration of the city.

Towards the end of the Second World War the historic centre of the German city of Dresden was utterly destroyed in a firestorm caused by Allied bombing. Within months, the war had ended, and the survivors began the decades-long task of rebuilding their city. One key building, the Frauenkirche, was left for many years as a ruin in memory of the destruction. With much of the city restored to its eighteenth-century splendour, only in 2005 was the Frauenkirche finally rebuilt, using the original plans. Now it serves as a memorial not just to the destruction of 1945, but to the later reunification of Germany and the dreams of a more peaceful Europe that have to some extent been realised since those days.

Prayer has the ability to plant dreams of a better future deep in our hearts, and then to provide us with the strength that we need to do the hard work necessary to bring those dreams into reality. This kind of prayer can be at its most powerful when everything seems hopeless, when all that is good and beautiful in a situation seems to have been destroyed. It is then that the Spirit of God seeks out receptive individuals who will respond to the Spirit's promptings by laying the foundation for a better tomorrow. Might you be one such individual today?

† Spirit of God, as I pray plant dreams of a better tomorrow deep in my heart, and give me the strength that I need to help realise those dreams in the world around me.

For further thought

Is there a building near you that speaks to you of dreams and of hope?

Wednesday 23 October
A place dedicated to God

Read Nehemiah 12:27–30

Now at the dedication of the wall of Jerusalem they sought out the Levites in all their places, to bring them to Jerusalem to celebrate the dedication with rejoicing, with thanksgivings and with singing, with cymbals, harps, and lyres.

(verse 27)

St Paul's church in Jarrow in north-east England has a stone with a Latin inscription. Translated, this reads: 'The dedication of the church of St Paul on the 9th of the Kalends of May, in the 15th year of King Ecgfrith, and in the 4th year of Ceolfrith, Abbot and, with God's help, founder of this church.' It commemorates the dedication of the building, still used for Christian worship, on 23 April 685, ensuring that the day itself is recalled even now, over 1,300 years later.

The dedication of any building to God's service gives cause for celebration. How much more when it's an entire city! Jerusalem was rebuilt not simply as capital of a restored nation, but more than that, as the city of God, with the temple, God's house, at its centre. So the whole people celebrated its dedication with great rejoicing.

If we believe that God can be found anywhere, at any time, does it make sense to speak of particular places as 'dedicated to God'? Not, surely, if this implies that other places are 'God-less', for God will not be contained in this way. But dedicated places serve as reminders precisely that God is everywhere. Until recently, the Jarrow church was surrounded by heavy industry. Even then its blackened stones recalled other values, preserving a space of quiet stillness amid the noise of production.

This prayer time may be for you a dedicated space, not implying that God is absent from the rest of your day, but serving as a reminder to rejoice in God's constant presence in your life.

† God of the universe, present at all times and in all places, help me to be aware of your presence at this moment in this place, as I dedicate my day to your service.

For further thought

Where do you usually find it easiest to pray? What makes that a good place for you?

Building the temple of God

> **Read 1 Corinthians 3:10–17**
>
> *Like a skilled master builder I laid a foundation, and someone else is building on it. Each builder must choose with care how to build on it. For no one can lay any foundation other than the one that has been laid; that foundation is Jesus Christ.*
>
> (verses 10–11)

On a recent holiday, I visited two Italian cities, each having a cathedral with a noteworthy detached bell tower. The campanile in Florence, completed in 1359, stands straight and true; that of Pisa, finished around the same time, is famous as the 'Leaning Tower'. Both are fine ornate buildings, having stood for centuries. Pisa, though, clearly lacks the firm foundations underpinning Florence.

In writing to the Corinthians, Paul is concerned both with his own work of foundation-laying, and with the labour of others in building on this. Without the firm foundation, what follows will inevitably be flawed. Yet he is confident in his own work, having preached Christ truly and fervently. He must leave it to others to carry things forward.

Nobody lays the foundations of their own faith single-handedly. We each build on the work of the apostles, of the evangelists and of generations who have carried the Christian message forward from that time. We are each, though, charged with contributing to the building project, adding our own small element to the Christian edifice.

We can be sure of the firm foundation that we have inherited. The challenge then, as Paul reminds those who hear him, is to make sure that we contribute the best that we can: not the straw or wood, but the gold and silver of our lives. It is often the generous labour of unnamed masses through the centuries that has made the great cathedrals the precious places that they are. What will your own contribution be to the Christianity that gets passed on to the next generation?

† May I bring to you, Lord, the best I have to offer, so that together we can build a church worthy of your name.

For further thought

Who do you consider has had the biggest share in laying the foundations of your own faith in Christ?

Friday 25 October
Gifts for others

Read 1 Corinthians 14:1–5

Pursue love and strive for the spiritual gifts, and especially that you may prophesy … Those who prophesy speak to other people for their upbuilding and encouragement and consolation. Those who speak in a tongue build up themselves, but those who prophesy build up the church.

(verses 1, 3, 4)

The nineteenth century was, in Britain, the era of great civic building projects. Museums and galleries, town halls and concert halls, parks and railway termini – all were built to be open to everybody. The whole population of a city shared in the benefits of these schemes, and rich and poor alike mixed under their roofs. This stands in sharp contrast to the 'gated communities', preserves of the wealthy, that often seem to most attract architects and builders today.

Paul here is not opposed to speaking in tongues, but sees it principally as a private gift. It can help the individual to grow in faith, but does little directly to contribute to the common good. Prophesying, by contrast – attempting to offer an authoritative interpretation of God's view of a situation – has the capability of building up the entire body of believers. It is a gift for all, and so to be preferred to those that are more limited.

Most of us have a range of gifts and talents. Some more obviously benefit ourselves, others more clearly can be used to serve others. Many can be used in either way or both, and I can choose how I am going to apply them. Ignatius of Loyola, the founder of the religious order to which I belong, counselled his followers to seek the magis, that path that would use my gifts in ways that would be of most use to others. Knowing what that path might be, in any given situation, requires as much imagination as the great city planners needed.

† Lord, let me see clearly the gifts you have given me, and show me how I can best use them for the good of all.

For further thought
Which buildings near you have the effect of bringing very different people together? Which act to exclude and keep out those thought to be undesirable?

Saturday 26 October
Letting your potential be realised

Read 1 Peter 2:1–5

Come to him, a living stone, though rejected by mortals yet chosen and precious in God's sight, and like living stones, let yourselves be built into a spiritual house, to be a holy priesthood, to offer spiritual sacrifices acceptable to God through Jesus Christ.

(verses 4–5)

Michelangelo's *David*, which stands in the Accademia gallery in Florence, is probably the single most famous statue in the world. It attracts hundreds of thousands of visitors each year, and is endlessly reproduced in copies large and small. Yet the block of marble from which it was carved languished in an open yard for 25 years, rejected by one sculptor after another because of imperfections in the stone. It took the genius of Michelangelo to recognise and realise its potential.

The image found in Psalm 118:22 of the stone, initially spurned by the builders, which became the key to the whole building, was one that a number of New Testament authors applied to Christ. Here the author of 1 Peter invites us to align ourselves with this living stone. It wouldn't be surprising if, in hearing this invitation, you made the same response as the sculptors who preceded Michelangelo. It's easy to be very aware of our imperfections, and so to consider it too risky to put our gifts and talents to the test. Better to stay quietly unused in the yard than to shatter under the pressure of public exposure.

God, though, sees the potential within you, and wants nothing better than to bring that potential to life. The good news is that this is something he will do himself, if you will only allow him to. You have simply to come to him, and he will do the rest, just as he did for the shepherd boy who became among the greatest of the kings of Israel.

† Lord, when you look at me, you see not just what I am but all that I can become. Let me not stand in the way of you realising your dream in me.

For further thought

Can you see gifts as yet unused in those people who are closest to you? Can you help them to release some of those gifts?

Readings from Romans (1–8) –
1 Not ashamed of the gospel

Notes by **Revd Canon Dr Helen Van Koevering**

For Helen's biography, see p. 261. Helen has used the NRSVA for these notes.

Sunday 27 October
Unashamed power

Read Romans 1:1–17

I am not ashamed of the gospel; it is the power of God for salvation to everyone who has faith, to the Jew first and also to the Greek.

(verse 16)

How should the salvation God has revealed in Jesus Christ influence the way we live and understand our relationship with God? This question is threaded through Paul's letter to the Romans written around 55 AD. Paul knew from his own experience that the gospel was the 'power of God for salvation' and he wanted to share that knowledge with others.

Does this phrase the 'power of God' trigger memories of dominating authority, abusive relationships, broken trust of those with power over us? Does it speak of privilege and oppression? Paul had grown up and lived out the meaning of that kind of power, but he had then experienced the transforming power of Jesus, God's Son, as a saving for life, a redemption by grace and a resurrection from death. New Testament stories remind us of how God inhabits God's power: as the power that protects and nurtures like the mother hen; as the friendship that empowered those who lowered their paralysed friend through the roof for Jesus to heal; as the joy and forgiveness seen in the waiting father running to welcome his returning prodigal son. This is the power of God for transformation.

† God, may your power transform our lives and bring healing, reconciliation and joy. Amen.

Monday 28 October
Visibly known

Read Romans 1:18–32

For though they knew God, they did not honour him as God or give thanks to him, but they became futile in their thinking, and their senseless minds were darkened ... they exchanged the truth about God for a lie and worshipped and served the creature rather than the Creator, who is blessed for ever! Amen.

(verses 21, 25)

Chimamanda Ngozi Adichie, the Nigerian author, once spoke of what she called the 'danger of the single story'. She had grown up reading the children's stories in imported books, where children were white, ate apples and played in the snow, whereas she was black, ate mangoes and played in dust and sand. Several years later, as a renowned author, she recognised that critics of her novels seemed surprised to read her stories of middle-class Nigerian culture. These were not the stories they expected because, as Chimamanda realised, they were used to the 'single story' of poor rural Africans.

What is the single story on which our Church has focused, rather than the complicated human story? The foregrounding of certain issues covers or distracts from others, and the truth that our human hearts, made for goodness, truth and beauty, hold godlessness and wickedness too. We say one thing and mean another. We speak of love, yet hate our neighbours. We are surprised by laughter and joy where we expected none. Seeing the visible, outer life, we forget the need for peace and our own reconciliation to outsiders and enemies. We grieve the Spirit's presence in others' and our own lives, forgetting that we are in this world together.

† Lord, open the eyes of our hearts to truly know you within others and ourselves. May we be gentle, humble and surprised by you today, and praise you for your love and life given for us. Amen.

For further thought

What single story might you be holding? Plan to listen and learn something new from a neighbour or colleague today.

God's riches

> **Read Romans 2:1–16**
>
> *'We know that God's judgement on those who do such things is in accordance with truth.' Do you imagine, whoever you are, that when you judge those who do such things and yet do them yourself, you will escape the judgement of God? Or do you despise the riches of his kindness and forbearance and patience? Do you not realize that God's kindness is meant to lead you to repentance?*
>
> (verses 2–4)

Who doesn't know that when you point a finger at someone else, three point back at yourself, and the thumb points upward to God? With this simple gesture, the thumb reminds us of the truth of God's loving faithfulness.

Life in community, whether the smallest community of marriage or a global community of like-minded individuals and groups, provides a framework for character formation. For people of Christian faith, the Bible, our liturgy and service play a large part in forming community and character not by prescribing activities but rather by orienting around values, principles and virtues that reflect God's self-disclosure in Christ. This becomes most clear when we experience church in other cultures. The dancing towards the altar and repeatedly hearing the words, 'Go out to love and serve the Lord', is a movement that has influenced the growth of the church in mission of northern Mozambique. The rhythm of the church seasons has provided an alternative interpretation and wealth of meaning to each passing year as much as for those struggling with pain as for the comfortable affluent. And throughout history, art and music have helped form communities of faith by drawing on the Christ-like character of neighbourliness, self-sacrifice, cross-bearing, forgiveness, and the compassion that leads to repentance and openness to the riches of God's goodness, truth and beauty for the world.

† Lord, thank you for the reminder not to judge others, to repent and be formed by your loving kindness, tolerance and patience in our communities. May we know the power of the Holy Spirit with us today. Amen.

For further thought

Kindness, tolerance and patience are included in our reading as 'riches' of God and character ethics to orient our lives. Where might you show more kindness, tolerance or patience?

Readings from Romans (1–8) – 1 Not ashamed of the gospel

October

Wednesday 30 October
Jesus' redemption

Read Romans 3:21–31

But now, irrespective of law, the righteousness of God has been disclosed, and is attested by the law and the prophets, the righteousness of God through faith in Jesus Christ for all who believe. For there is no distinction.

(verses 21–22)

Northern Mozambique has historically, through war and poverty, been remote and isolated. The reality of three decades of conflict and violence that ended in 1992, and ongoing trauma that threatened peace and risked development has brought out the meaning of chronic poverty. Relative poverty compares one with another, absolute poverty is often described as living on less than a US dollar a day. Chronic poverty can only be temporarily helped by a targeted project, because the poor state of health and education means ongoing development can't be sustained. One health issue among and behind much chronic poverty is HIV/AIDS.

In the place of stigma and fear, churches urged involvement in teaching and support for the affected and the infected. They encouraged drama, music, Bible study and practical support and carried the message on their T-shirts: 'There is no difference.' God only is righteous, and God's presence embodied within communities focused on Jesus Christ's work of redemption. The day before Maria died, her eyes had lit up at the taste of the bread and wine; when Gloria breathed her last, she was holding hands with her friends, women of the church; Alberto smiled from his hospital bed on hearing the Lord's Prayer in those last hours of his life. All redeemed by faith in Jesus Christ.

† Lord, we remember with joy those who have shown us the depth of the way of transformative faith. We thank you that your righteousness, and not our own, is seen through faith in your Son. Amen.

For further thought
Who has modelled the Christian redemptive life to you?

Thursday 31 October
Grace and hope

Read Romans 4:13–25

For this reason it depends on faith, in order that the promise may rest on grace and be guaranteed to all Abraham's descendants ... Hoping against hope, he believed that he would become 'the father of many nations'.

(verses 16, 18)

Grace – God's Riches At Christ's Expense. Those are the words in a discipleship course rolled out into many dioceses of southern Africa. Grace goes hand in hand with bringing hope, and for the poor finding hope in the church. Grace and hope: two riches of God that are promised by faith in Jesus.

Bringing new life to the poor, whether material, physical, mental or spiritual new life, is a sign of God's grace in this world. In Kentucky, USA, in 2017, the Presiding Bishop of the Episcopal Church (USA), Michael Curry, spoke with 1,300 young people. He encouraged them to dream big and that to change the world, they must follow Jesus. In discipleship, there is the power to renew life, create alternative community, even affect the fabric of a nation. Baptism gives us the Holy Spirit and brings us into the neighbourhood of all the baptised, so that wherever barriers are broken, communities are formed, creation is stewarded and cared for, relationships are healed, brokenness is recognised, unity is established, education is life-widening, disease is cured, addiction is broken, cities are renewed, races are reconciled, people are blessed – hope is established and God's grace is seen at work.

† God, may the riches of your grace and the love that brings hope be with us today. May we bring that grace and hope to others, and be the change we want to see in the world. Amen.

For further thought

How is your church community living out grace and hope in your community?

Friday 1 November (All Saints' Day)
Reconciliation

Read Romans 5:1–11

... we have peace with God through our Lord Jesus Christ, through whom we have obtained access to this grace in which we stand; and we boast in our hope of sharing the glory of God ... through our Lord Jesus Christ, through whom we have now received reconciliation.

(verses 1–2, 11)

In relationship with God, we enter into a whole new world of blessing and peace on which to draw, even in the midst of what holds greatest fear in our lives: grace-filled blessing for the future as well as a hope that remains even within the trials and tribulations of life. It appears that reconciliation with God, initiated by God's love towards us, is for us to hold with sacred delight. Sacred because only God can invite us to this reconciliation; delight because it's the too-good-to-be-true that is coming true. It's a sacred delight that a child knows on the shoulders of a parent on the way home, anticipating the welcoming embrace and the place already set at the table.

It is this reconciliation that is lived out in repeated remembering of the death of a loved one in Mozambican tradition. The entire extended family gather for three days at the death, and the first memorial is held at 40 days. Christians and Muslims have overlaid this 40-day tradition with prayers and ritual, including a meal for those who gather. In the Anglican Church, the service encourages a reflection on the loss and example of the loved family member, and gifts of food are brought to church to then be blessed and taken out to those struggling in the community. The service is a connection and reconciliation with those generations who have passed on and those who remain. Fear and mourning becomes a remembrance of life-death: an illustration of ultimate reconciliation with and by the Author of our lives.

† Father, while we were yet sinners, your Son died for us to know the fullness of life that is blessing and reconciliation with you. This is beyond our imagining, and we praise you. Amen.

For further thought

Take time to list all those saints you have known who have now passed on. What did you learn about God from them?

Saturday 2 November
Overflowing gift

> **Romans 5:12–21**
>
> *Where sin increased, grace abounded all the more, so that, just as sin exercised dominion in death, so grace might also exercise dominion through justification leading to eternal life through Jesus Christ our Lord.*
>
> (verses 20b–21)

It is the grace of God that affirms the goodness of human life, that takes precisely the situation where there seems no hope in human terms, and brings new life exactly there. The incarnation of Jesus affirmed the wildest dreams of God for us, sharing death with us, and then taking that fully human, deeply and richly human being Jesus to God's-self. This true image of Jesus, the One we are called to follow, should become the centre of the true picture of Life and Love that we allow to form us.

Nyama knew that truth. He was the dearly loved lay reader (catechist) of his rural Mozambican congregation. He had turned to Christ as his example for life and love when he was 60 years old, after a lifetime of deep pain. Nyama's name means 'meat', and his life had been one sad war story after another. He had lived rough for years to protect his crops from passing soldiers, and he had spent several months with the secret police being interrogated and abused for non-existent activities with those seeking Independence. It was a conversation with a faithful Anglican that began to change his life, and his baptism and confirmation where he began to know the grace of God for eternal life. It transformed him for service and pastoral care of numerous others. His is a story of grace abounding all the more where sin had increased.

† God of grace and life, with you is eternal life. We thank you for life through Jesus Christ which he shared with us, the death and the resurrection for the life of the world. May we continue to grow in the knowledge and love that the Spirit of Jesus reveals to us. Amen.

For further thought

Share with one other person today the comfort that the knowledge of eternal life brings.

Readings from Romans (1–8) – 2 Newness of life

Notes by **Catrin Harland-Davies**

Catrin is a Methodist Minister, working as chaplain at the University of Sheffield, where she is often to be found in coffee shops on campus, putting the world to rights with students. She has a PhD in biblical studies, looking at how the New Testament Church understood itself, and is fascinated by how the Church sees itself today. She is passionate about helping the Church to interpret its calling for a new age, and individuals to fulfil their potential as disciples. Catrin has used the NRSVA for these notes.

Sunday 3 November
Dead to sin, alive to God

Read Romans 6:1–14

We know that our old self was crucified with him so that the body of sin might be destroyed, and we might no longer be enslaved to sin. For whoever has died is freed from sin. But if we have died with Christ, we believe that we will also live with him.

(verses 6–8)

Recently, Facebook suggested an article which it thought might interest me. It does that a lot, and is often wrong. But this time, it caught my weak, self-doubting side.

'Train your brain to crave good habits!' it proclaimed. Well, who wouldn't want that? So I read on. Apparently, with a bit of effort, I could learn to leap out of bed in the morning as soon as the alarm rang, because I would be addicted to the resulting sense of self-satisfaction. Unfortunately, smugness never did, for me, replace the more immediate reward of a few extra warm and cosy minutes' sleep.

Paul, here and throughout the next couple of chapters, describes just this conflict between good habits and bad, between the reward of present pleasure and that of life with God. Only, in this case, there's a lot more at stake than a more enthusiastic start to the day. He urges us to reject behaviour which damages ourselves, others or our relationship with God. This is not just making small improvements to our lives, for the sake of brighter mornings, but leaving godlessness so radically behind that we might be said to be dead to it, and fully alive in God.

† Free us, God, from all that diminishes us, so that we may be free to live for you, and you alone.

Monday 4 November
Freedom from sin, slave of righteousness

Read Romans 6:15–23

But thanks be to God that you, having once been slaves of sin, have become obedient from the heart to the form of teaching to which you were entrusted, and that you, having been set free from sin, have become slaves of righteousness.

(verses 17–18)

Three days ago was All Saints' Day. I, like many of my fellow Christians, find myself reflecting on those who might be seen as 'saints' or 'holy' (the Greek word literally means 'holy ones').

Most of us know someone who seems so infused with the love of God that they truly deserve the title 'saint'. These Christians leave us in no doubt about who it is that they serve. Godliness shines in their words, their deeds – even, it would seem, their thoughts. Paul uses the analogy of slavery, using a very human image 'because of your natural limitations' (verse 19) to describe this phenomenon. If we are fully committed to God, it is as though we were slaves of God, completely obedient to God's will, and dedicating ourselves to God's service.

But I am not like those really saintly people. Like many – perhaps most – Christians, I am a work in progress and don't always live out that complete commitment. In fact, sometimes, I act as though I were a slave to forces other than God – to sin, selfishness, money, comfort, convenience.

The good news is that the New Testament does not reserve 'holy one' for the super-Christian. It refers to anyone who is part of this new covenant relationship with God. We are holy, not because we are perfect, or even close to perfect, but because the Holy God has chosen us. We may often get things wrong, and we may forget where we owe our loyalty, but we are still ultimately holy, sanctified, offered freedom from sin, and invited to be committed to God.

† Thank you that, by grace, you have chosen me and made me holy. Help me not to be complacent, but to aspire to be worthy of the holiness to which you call me.

For further thought

What does it look like, to be a 'slave to righteousness'? Is this the same as 'holiness'? Do you know anyone who fits either description?

Cutting through the red tape

Read Romans 7:1–12

What then should we say? That the law is sin? By no means! Yet, if it had not been for the law, I would not have known sin. I would not have known what it is to covet if the law had not said, 'You shall not covet.'

(verse 7)

The uniform regulations for my daughter's school used to include the simple instruction: 'black trousers'. But at some point this was qualified ('not jeans or sports wear') and questions of definition arose. Eventually, almost every pair of trousers in the schoolwear shop fell foul of the rules somehow – no button, wrong fabric, no zip. The detail which had built up around the basic 'black trousers' rule had become increasingly complicated and arbitrary.

Communities tend to generate rules, and then more rules to clarify the rules. Sometimes, these start to feel onerous, and can get in the way of the actual purpose. The school was just trying to ensure that its pupils looked fairly smart, but had unintentionally caused huge anxiety for many pupils (and parents!) over whether a new pair of trousers would be acceptable. No wonder people start to favour deregulation, or even anarchy!

The problem with deregulation, though, is human nature. Questions or disagreements arise, and someone has to resolve them, usually by setting out some broad principles. These, in turn, lead to disputes, and the need for clarity and detail.

The law was needed, Paul says, to define and clarify sin – to guide us in godly living. But what if we are, in Paul's words, 'slaves … in the new life of the Spirit' (verse 6)? We'd probably still need to agree which side of the road to drive on, but perhaps the principles of our life together could be shaped by just two basic rules: love God, and love your neighbour. If we truly understand these, we have all the regulation we need.

† Pray for those responsible for forming and enforcing laws and regulations, and for those who feel burdened by arbitrary rules. Pray also for the victims of unjust laws.

For further thought

Is the law a good thing, or a bad thing? If you had to identify just one overarching rule for community, what would it be?

Wednesday 6 November
When the spirit is willing, but the flesh weak

Read Romans 7:13–25

For I do not do the good I want, but the evil I do not want is what I do. Now if I do what I do not want, it is no longer I that do it, but sin that dwells within me.

(verses 19–20)

After challenging us to live as those who are committed to God, Paul now acknowledges that it's not always as easy as we might hope. Temptation, with human weakness, does tend to get in the way.

I've already confessed that I find it hard to get up in the morning. And, of course, I have lots of habits and weaknesses which are not ideal – sitting on the sofa and eating chocolate, when I've planned to go for a run, for example. But something remarkable happens when I do make myself run. I come back feeling happier, more positive, more productive and generally better about myself and life. Sometimes, making the effort truly bears fruit!

But I also have much more serious weaknesses. I find it hard to tolerate those whose personality differs from mine. I can't back down in an argument (even when I suspect I may be wrong). And I lose my temper far too easily, especially with those who are closest to me. These are things which harm far more than my evening's productivity or my temporary state of mind. They hurt others, damage my relationships, and make me feel deeply and genuinely unhappy with who I am.

I don't know what Paul's weaknesses and failings were, but he clearly had some. He longed to be a better follower of Christ, and to live according to God's will. But he was human. He was committed to God, but too often embodied a commitment to sin. But how much better he doubtless felt about himself and life, when his godly side won the day!

† Forgiving God, I want to be a faithful disciple, but the distractions of life often get in the way. I struggle with the inconvenience of service, and sacrificial love. Thank you for your patient grace.

For further thought

What are the weaknesses with which you struggle? Can you commit to working on just one, but being gentle with yourself if you slip up?

Adopted into the family of God

Read Romans 8:1–17

For you did not receive a spirit of slavery to fall back into fear, but you have received a spirit of adoption. When we cry, 'Abba! Father!' it is that very Spirit bearing witness with our spirit that we are children of God.

(verses 15–16)

The first baptism service I led was of a toddler who had just been adopted. He was fostered from birth and when, by his second birthday, no adoptive parents had been found, his foster carers themselves applied. His godparents were his much older adoptive sisters. The whole extended family came to the baptism, to celebrate his place in their family, as well as in God's.

This was a particularly special baptism. This child could call his parents 'Mummy' and 'Daddy', because they had consciously and deliberately chosen him to be their child. He was meant to live with them for just a few weeks, but in the end they loved him too much to let him go. In his baptism, we celebrated the One who chooses us, and loves us too much to let us go – who invites us to call him 'Abba! Father!', calls us his children and makes us fully part of his family.

Being part of a family also means we begin to live by its patterns and values. We grow more like our Father, just as we are influenced by our human parents. That child I baptised will now be nearly a grown man. I'm no longer in the area, and don't know what his relationship with his parents is like, but I'm confident that they will still love him; that relationship will have shaped him. Neither do I know what his relationship is like with his heavenly Father, but I know that God still loves him, and I pray that he is shaped by that relationship, too.

† Pray for all who are newly baptised or preparing for baptism. Pray, too, for those who are adopted, who have adopted or who are hoping to adopt, or who give children love and a home.

For further thought

In this passage, Paul contrasts 'Spirit' with 'flesh' several times. Do you find this a helpful distinction?

Friday 8 November
When prayer simply won't come ...

Read Romans 8:18–30

Likewise the Spirit helps us in our weakness; for we do not know how to pray as we ought, but that very Spirit intercedes with sighs too deep for words. And God, who searches the heart, knows what is the mind of the Spirit.

(verses 26–27a)

'Please remember me in your prayers.' That's what Mohammad, my Muslim colleague, says to me as I go to Christian Prayers in the University's Multifaith Chaplaincy. 'Only if you'll do the same for me,' I typically reply.

Very often in my job, I'm asked to pray for others. I pray about exam stress, grief, illness, homesickness, relationships, fears. Sometimes, after I've led worship, someone will ask me to sit and pray with and for them. This is a huge privilege, and I'm glad to do it.

But often, I too need someone to pray for me. And occasionally, I reach a point where the doubt, despair and darkness are too strong, and I cannot pray. That's when I really value being part of a Christian community, where others will pray when I find it too hard.

But what happens when a whole community is in shock, and cannot find words to pray after a local tragedy? Or when we look at the world and see wars, famine and injustice, it can become almost impossible to make sense of it, and our words feel inadequate. This is not a new problem. Paul recognised it, too, but he knew, as we know, that even when our prayers falter and there are no words, the Spirit is at hand to intercede on our behalf. And the Spirit is never short of words, but prays 'with sighs too deep for words' (verse 26). We can offer our words or our silence, and the Spirit knows what is in our inmost heart, and sighs for us.

† Pray for those who, because of despair or doubt, can't pray for themselves. And give thanks for those who, in your darker times, have sustained you through their own faithful prayer and faith.

For further thought

If the whole creation is groaning, perhaps it is our responsibility, as the priesthood of believers, to pray for creation. Where would you start?

Readings from Romans (1–8) – 2 Newness of life

November

Saturday 9 November
On being 'only human'

Read Romans 8:31–39

For I am convinced that neither death, nor life, nor angels, nor rulers, nor things present, nor things to come, nor powers, nor height, nor depth, nor anything else in all creation, will be able to separate us from the love of God in Christ Jesus our Lord.

(verses 38–39)

'I'm only human!' How often do we hear these words? They remind us of our limitations: 'Don't try to take on too much – you're only human.' They pardon a person's wrongdoing: 'He made a mistake, but he's only human.' They explain our imperfections: 'I can't get it right all the time; I'm only human!'

And it's true. Through this week's readings, we've remembered time and again that we're only human, and that it's inherent in human nature to give in to temptation and to have our weaknesses. But we've also remembered that we're better than that – that we aspire to, and are often capable of, a higher standard, because we belong to Christ.

Christ was, of course, unique. Fully human, sharing our human nature, he knew limitations, weakness, temptation. But fully divine, he was also able to overcome that fundamental tension and live a life genuinely and completely committed to God. He was human, yes, but he was not 'only human'. And because he united human and divine nature, he was uniquely able to bring humanity and divinity together, so that we fully belong to God.

That doesn't mean, of course, that we're no longer human, or that we don't have to wrestle with human nature and flaws. But it does mean that we're also not 'only human', because we have God on our side, and we live for God, and in God's strength. We may mess up, we may get things wrong, we may sin and fail; but still we belong to God. And nothing can get in the way of that.

† Loving God, thank you that in all things you are with us. Thank you that, in Christ, you have drawn us to yourself and give us the strength to follow and serve you.

For further thought

How easy do you find it, in difficult times, truly to accept that God is for you, and nothing can separate you from his love?

Reading the Bible with the body – 1 Sensing God's goodness

Notes by **Jan Sutch Pickard**

 Jan is a writer and storyteller living on the Isle of Mull, and a former warden of the Abbey on Iona. She has served twice with the Ecumenical Accompaniment Programme in Palestine and Israel, based in small West Bank villages but with a chance to spend time in Jerusalem and reflect on its divisions today. A Methodist Local Preacher, she leads worship for the Church of Scotland on Mull. Jan has used the NRSVA for these notes.

Sunday 10 November
Sweeter than honey

Read Psalm 19

... the ordinances of the Lord are true and righteous altogether. More to be desired are they than gold, even much fine gold; sweeter also than honey, and drippings of the honeycomb ... in keeping them there is great reward.

(verses 9b–11)

Fine gold: I am writing this on a day of autumn sunshine, which brings out rich colours of dying leaves, burnishes the rocks and shines on still water. It is the more beautiful because unexpected, coming after a storm – and probably before more wild weather arrives. In the Scottish islands we call it 'a given day'.

I find myself remembering when one of our children had her first taste of honey. She was a tiny baby, crying and crying, when a family friend, who had raised a large family, took her in his arms, dipped his little finger in the honey jar, and put it to her lips. She stopped crying, with surprise. Her eyes widened, she seemed both more aware of all around her, more relaxed, and to relish tasting the honey. This may not now be recommended childcare practice, and we didn't make a habit of 'pacifying' her in this way! But it seems to me that we can still celebrate God's gifts as 'a taste of honey' not to be taken for granted: powerful truth, transforming justice, the reassurance of life in balance, love which takes us by surprise.

† Thank God for gifts that surprise and delight: days of sunshine, the grace of time when we need it, and above all, God's love.

Taste, see and remember

Reading the Bible with the body – 1 Sensing God's goodness

Read Psalm 34:1–10

I will bless the Lord at all times; his praise shall continually be in my mouth … O taste and see that the Lord is good; happy are those who take refuge in him … those who seek the Lord lack no good thing.

(verses 1, 8, 10)

When I read this psalm, I cannot help tasting honey and salt, porridge, kale, grilled mackerel, oatcakes, cheese, wild raspberries and brambles. These are the tastes of Iona and Mull – and have been for hundreds of years. They were flavours that St Columba (also known as Columcille) and his monks knew well, as did the islanders among whom they set up their community. Simple, sustaining food, 'good things': signs of the nourishment God provides, for people who work on land and sea, and also with creative hands, words and prayer, with body, mind and spirit.

Iona was a place of peace in a dangerous, conflicted world. As well as giving spiritual and practical leadership to his community there, Columba, we're told, shared in the work of copying out the scriptures, which – before printing – was the only way of passing them on. The legend goes that, just before he died, he was working on Psalm 34. At verse 10, he put down his pen.

This is a day when we remember endings. In 1918, at the 11th hour of the 11th day of the 11th month, the First World War officially ended. The guns fell silent. Some who'd tasted the chaos and cruelty of warfare came home, to lead lives changed for ever. Many more did not. Nor was it 'a war to end wars'. Millions have died since. What can we do in the face of suffering, injustice, death? Like Columba, we can keep on sharing the good news of God's down-to-earth and redeeming love.

† Thank you, God, for the taste on our tongue – food that delights and nourishes us; for companionship – sharing daily bread. May these give us energy to work for a greater sharing in your world.

For further thought

How can you make real God's down-to-earth love today, Remembrance Day?

Tuesday 12 November
The smell of sacrifice

Read Genesis 8:20–22

And when the Lord smelt the pleasing odour, the Lord said in his heart: 'I will never again curse the ground because of humankind.'

(verse 21a)

What smells affect you most, make you happy, move you or confuse you, bring back good memories or fearful experiences?

A group of women were sitting together in a room where a fire had just been lighted. Many lived in homes with different sources of heating, but then and there the homely smell brought back many memories.

Wood fires and peat reek, bonfires of burning leaves and barbecues, paraffin firelighters and church incense, the sharp gunpowder smell of fireworks, the subtle fragrance of wax candles (not necessarily scented!) and the smoke we sniff when a candle is extinguished. But they also remembered with anger or tears the acrid smell of burning rubbish – tyres or plastic, polluting the air – pyres of cattle slaughtered during a foot-and-mouth epidemic, the terrifying smell of a house or car on fire.

The Hebrew people, long ago, believed that the smoke of sacrifices, rising up to heaven, was pleasing to God. The idea of burnt offerings is probably alien to anyone reading this. Yet we readily respond to the idea of a Creator who delights in what has been created, 'seeing that it is good'. And creation, the physical world, praises God with its great diversity of tastes and smells and touch, sounds and colours – the rainbow being a memorable example. In the Genesis story of the Great Flood, imagine the tears of a maker who has destroyed what was a labour of love; smell the hope in the words, 'Never again.'

† Take something with a smell that you find soothing, enjoyable – leaves of a plant, talc, an orange, lavender, a cup of coffee, a book. Sit holding it, thanking God for the sense of smell.

For further thought

What smells are 'pleasing odours' to you? What smells in our world today might bring delight to God?

Reading the Bible with the body – 1 Sensing God's goodness

November

Wednesday 13 November
When we falter, God gives strength

Read Psalm 31:9–24

For my life is spent with sorrow, and my years with sighing; my strength fails because of my misery, and my bones waste away … Be strong, and let your heart take courage, all you who wait for the Lord.

(verses 10, 24)

How old was the psalmist? This psalm seems to be describing the pains and indignities of ageing: 'my strength fails because of my affliction, and my bones grow weak … I am the utter contempt of my neighbours' (verses 10–11). Yet we need to avoid caricatures. And sorrow and sighing are only part of the picture. Like many of the psalms, this holds together opposites: the psalmist describes strong feelings of rejection, yet says 'In you, Lord, I put my trust' and affirms God's unfailing love.

I think of people that I know, who wear their years with dignity, who cope with disability, who possess great wisdom, alongside warm humanity. Sybil, after a stroke, has to use a wheelchair. But swimming is possible – hard work, but sheer joy. So in gratitude she undertook a sponsored swim, and raised a great deal of money for people in the developing world. Her husband, Graeme, wrote with love and pride about this and added, 'We are most grateful that in our distraught world, at the heart of every human being there is a fundamental goodness which can never be extinguished, and that we have a shining example of this in Jesus … and so we have HOPE.'

Many older people know that, as well as hope, a sense of humour helps. I know well how time has marked but also enriched me, now rather weather-beaten but, with (mostly) undaunted spirit, I'm still trying to become the person God intended, encouraged by John Bunyan's words in *The Pilgrim's Progress*: 'One here will constant be, come wind come weather; there's no discouragement shall make him once relent his first avowed intent – to be a pilgrim.'

† God, you know when we falter: lift us up, give us stout hearts, renew our strength, sustain us with hope. Amen.

For further thought

What, at your time of life, do you want to celebrate? Or are you still travelling in hope? And what do you hope for?

Thursday 14 November
Feel the consequences

Read Deuteronomy 28:1–2, 15–24

Cursed shall you be when you come in, and cursed shall you be when you go out … The Lord will change the rain of your land into powder, and only dust shall come down upon you from the sky until you are destroyed.

(verses 19, 24)

This law-book lays down rules for human behaviour, and specifies rewards and punishments. There's fierce poetry in these words: 'Cursed shall you be in the city, and cursed shall you be in the field. Cursed shall be your basket and your kneading-bowl' (verses 16–17). There's relish that wrongdoers will get their comeuppance.

Other cultures have their comminations too – the Church in the Middle Ages called down God's wrath with 'bell, book and candle'. Celtic Christians, known for their blessings, also had a tradition of curses. But there is something particularly physical about these biblical verses with their description of the pestilence, its 'consumption, fever, inflammation, with fiery heat and drought, and with blight and mildew' (verse 22). This the Hebrew lawmakers see as the inevitable consequence of disobedience. They are not imposing the penalty – they see it coming directly from God: 'The Lord will send upon you disaster, panic, and frustration' (verse 20).

We may not believe that God is like an angry human ruler. But we're well aware that our actions have consequences. These can weigh on us, even make us ill, and affect others, sometimes whole communities. As I write this, many people in Britain are reflecting with shame on the 67 words of the Balfour Declaration, signed by the British Foreign Secretary in 1917. The consequences of making a promise, only half of which has been honoured, are still being felt 100 years later, in the relationship of Israel and Palestine, in a divided land, millions of refugees, wars, injustice, anger and fear. Who feels the hard consequences of our wrong choices and actions? It isn't always us.

† Merciful God, we are children of dust, but do not send more to choke and bury us; send rain to wash away our wrongdoing – for in Christ you offer us living water. Amen.

For further thought

Where now is dust threatening your life, your community or your nation?

Reading the Bible with the body – 1 Sensing God's goodness

November

Be drunk but not with wine

Read Isaiah 29:9–14

Stupefy yourselves and be in a stupor … Be drunk, but not from wine … these people draw near with their mouths and honour me with their lips … The wisdom of their wise shall perish, and the discernment of the discerning shall be hidden …

(verses 9, 13, 14)

I watch my youngest grandchild playing in the garden. She turns round and round, as fast as she can, becoming dizzy, then tries to stand still. Her head spinning, she falls on the grass, laughing delightedly.

Some folk think that getting drunk is fun, too.

But Isaiah addresses a very different issue – the numbed senses and confusion of a people who don't want to know. Hearing God's message from the prophets, they ignore it out of prejudice or fear. Those who speak truth to power are silenced. There's no chance to hear words of wisdom. The people fall into a stupor of ignorance and inaction. All they can do is go through the motions, paying lip service.

Isaiah lived in Jerusalem, the capital of Judah. God's call to him began in the year that King Uzziah – a capable and trusted ruler – died. It was a time of crisis. The prophetic ministry of Isaiah covers a period of about 40 years from 760 bc. Successive kings were weak or corrupt. Judah, like Israel to the north, was threatened by the Assyrians, powerful neighbours. The people closed their minds to the call to turn back to God, the message of the prophets.

Two-and-a-half millennia later, citizens of the present-day state of Israel fear powerful neighbour states. Their leaders have played on that fear, building barriers against the Palestinian people living in the same land. It is as though the people are asleep. Through prejudice and apathy, the message of the prophets has been forgotten: the insights of wise men about how to live in peace.

† Wake us up, God, from the deep sleep of apathy, and avoiding responsibility. Turn us round, but not to become dizzy. Clear our heads to understand your message, open our eyes to see your way. Amen.

For further thought

How would you put Isaiah's phrase 'discernment of the discerning' in your own words?

Saturday 16 November
Embody the hope

Read Isaiah 35:1–10

Strengthen the weak hands, and make firm the feeble knees. Say to those who are of a fearful heart, 'Be strong, do not fear!' ... Then the eyes of the blind shall be opened, and the ears of the deaf unstopped; then the lame shall leap like a deer, and the tongue of the speechless sing for joy ... the ransomed of the Lord shall return ...

(verses 3–4a, 5–6a, 10a)

Imagine a crowd of people, walking through a landscape devastated by war or drought. We've seen this picture many times: 100 years ago, wounded soldiers, British and German, behind the Western Front, retreating through mud. Seventy years ago Palestinians became refugees in the Nakba, the catastrophe, as they were expelled from their homes at the foundation of the modern state of Israel; at the same time, millions were displaced by Partition in India, as Pakistan came into being. We have seen people fleeing Sudan, Somalia, Myanmar in the last few years; refugees from Syria and Iraq walking in great crowds down the motorways of Europe, before the frontiers were closed. Whole families, with all they can carry, but little to call their own, walking wearily away from their homes and into an unknown future – wounded, hungry, frightened, confused.

Now imagine something that seems impossible: the people coming home. As they walk through the land, it and they are transformed. Rivers start flowing again, grass brings hillsides alive, the desert blooms. A causeway opens up and feet that stumbled on rubble now tread on solid ground. Some people stride ahead and others dance. Their ears are no longer deafened by shellfire, nor their eyes blinded by tears. They feel in every joint of their bodies, in every fibre of their being, the hope of coming home, the joy of restoration.

In Isaiah we glimpse a vision. But is this just a dream? Whether we'll ever see it happen, we need to live as though transformation is possible, through God's grace – and to embody that hope.

† Read all of Isaiah 35, reflecting on the words: 'they shall obtain joy and gladness, and sorrow and sighing shall flee away' (verse 10). Hold in prayer places and people in the world today which need to believe this.

For further thought

Is hope ever complete without hope for bodies as well as for spirits and souls?

Reading the Bible with the body – 1 Sensing God's goodness

November

323

Reading the Bible with the body – 2 Beholding the Lord

Notes by **Vron Smith**

Vron has worked as a laywoman in the Church for over 25 years, working with young people in a parish and as a chaplain in school, university and hospice settings. She currently works between a residential spirituality centre in Wales run by the Jesuits and co-ordinating wider mission work. She accompanies others on silent retreats and delivers formation in spirituality and retreats around the UK. Vron has used the NRSVA for these notes.

Sunday 17 November
Thoroughly to hold

Read Psalm 27:1–14

... to live in the house of the Lord all the days of my life, to behold the beauty of the Lord, and to inquire in his temple.

(verse 4)

Imagine a sunset and I ask you to 'look' at it. How do you do your looking? Then imagine a sunset and I ask you to 'behold' it. Would you do it in the same way? What would change? There seems to me a very different invitation being offered in 'beholding' compared to 'looking'. To behold comes from Old English, meaning 'thoroughly to hold' and it is the word 'thoroughly' that hints of a deeper action, something that moves and stirs not only our eyes but our mind, body, senses, heart, guts, even the deeps of our being. It is to be held, to be captured by. In the psalm today it is the beauty of the Lord that can capture us and so hold us that we want to stay and drink in all that attracts us. Certainly, in beholding the Lord, this beauty is not skin deep but goes beyond to the places where the Holy Spirit shifts and shapes within us. It is living, being fully alive. This week we offer our senses and imagination as ways to encounter the Lord with our whole selves, to be thoroughly beholden by God.

† At some moment today, let yourself be beholden by a person or something in creation and notice what God is inviting in you.

Monday 18 November
I see you

Read John 1:35–39

[The disciples] said to him, 'Rabbi … where are you staying?' He said to them, 'Come and see.' They came and saw where he was staying, and they remained with him that day.

(verses 38–39)

Sometimes, when travelling around the country to deliver work, I am hosted by kind people that previously I might have noticed across the room in a meeting or had a two-minute conversation with about general things. It is not until I am invited into their home that the space opens up in which I see them, really see them, and they see me, really see me, in a way that wasn't possible before. Of course, it's not that we sit and stare at each other but in the relating in that home space, we allow ourselves, more of ourselves to be known.

Jesus could have taken the disciples' question literally and shown them where his accommodation was or even just told them the place. But Jesus is interested in seeing, seeing more of them, letting them see more of him. The disciples then not only saw where he was staying but they spent that day with him. I wonder what they all did together in that time? Did they sit on the roof of the house in the shade and chat? Maybe they cooked a meal together or went out for a walk or a swim in the Jordan. We do know that seeing touched in the disciples a deeper desire, a desire to stay with Jesus that they couldn't ignore and that led to them inviting others to come and see. Just as for the disciples, Jesus invites us to see and be seen. And if you do choose to come and see, how do you spend the day with Jesus?

† Use your imagination to spend the afternoon with Jesus. What do you both do together and what is seen?

For further thought

Remember a time you stayed with a person you did not know well. How did the experience change how you saw them and yourself?

God's muscles

Read Matthew 11:28–30

'Come to me, all you that are weary and are carrying heavy burdens, and I will give you rest. Take my yoke upon you, and learn from me; for I am gentle and humble in heart, and you will find rest for your souls. For my yoke is easy, and my burden is light.'

(verses 28–30)

In my local gym there is a section where you find the ones who are building up their muscle mass through lifting weights. When using the lighter weights they get on doing their routine on their own but when they're pushing their muscles to the max and trying to push that extra ten kilos of weight or do five extra repetitions, they ask someone to 'spot' for them. The spotter stands right alongside the lifter, hands very close to or sometimes on the weights, ready to lift the weight with the tired lifter. How many of us sometimes struggle, like the weightlifters, with the deep-down weariness and exhaustion that comes with seemingly carrying the weight of the world on our own?

On retreats, people often come burdened by life's events, thinking they have to sort it themselves and then they can be with God. The line of thought often goes, 'God surely isn't interested in my mortgage debt or that I'm struggling with my spouse or I find my work sucks the life out of me. I need to sort it myself.' But when the person is encouraged to stop, to rest, to let God place hands alongside their own to do that heavy lifting for them, something shifts within. Jesus' image of being yoked, of being placed alongside another to learn how to do the work, and to do it in a way that is not exhausting but restful, is a powerfully attractive one that speaks to worn-out hearts. And for you, now?

† Let me learn today from you, Lord, how to take up your yoke and let you give me rest.

For further thought

What is weighing upon you at the moment? How might you invite God's help?

Wednesday 20 November
God's eau de parfum

Read Psalm 23

You prepare a table before me in the presence of my enemies; you anoint my head with oil; my cup overflows.

(verse 5)

Smells can bring back all kinds of memories for us. I remember holding my baby god-daughter after her bath and kissing her head and smelling that clean baby smell, or on a coast walk smelling the salty sea air. Smells tap into experience but can also alert us to danger or decay such as the smell of gas, the reek of rubbish in a landfill site.

In early Palestine, smell played an essential part in staying alive, from determining disease and death to welcoming cleanliness, a sense of security and sacrificial offerings to God. Imagine having spent a long, hard day at work outdoors under the beating sun, the dust caked on your dried-out skin, your body tired. You go to visit a friend who washes your head and then pours soothing oil over it. You feel the oil running down over your scalp and face, breathing in the smell of the spices, relaxing you.

The psalmist uses the image of a host who anoints with oil the head of the welcomed guest who is surrounded by enemies, who walks through dark valleys. The anointing brings honour and respect and care amid danger and conflict. If God is seen as the host, then we, like Christ, the anointed one, whose aroma is pleasing to God (Ephesians 5:2), are invited as guests to be made fragrant, to become the oil of gladness and thanksgiving in the world, to let others smell God's goodness through us. To be God's eau de parfum.

† Imagine God anointing you and breathing in the aroma of God's love and care for you.

For further thought

Notice today where you catch the aroma of God's goodness through others.

God's embodied blessings

Read 1 Peter 3:8–17

Now who will harm you if you are eager to do what is good? But even if you do suffer for doing what is right, you are blessed. Do not fear what they fear, and do not be intimidated, but in your hearts sanctify Christ as Lord.

(verses 13–15)

Hassan Zubier, a British paramedic on holiday in Finland in 2017, without consideration for his own safety, was stabbed while trying to save the life of a woman who was dying after being attacked. Was he harmed for doing good? Yes. Did he suffer for what was right? Yes. Was he blessed? Only he can know the answer to that. Were others blessed as a result of his actions? I know I was.

He is one example of those ordinary people who choose to do an extraordinary thing for another because it is the good thing to do, the compassionate thing, the loving thing. There are many stories, often untold, that give flesh to the deep goodness in humanity that recognises the suffering of another and cannot stand by unaffected and unmoving. They are the people who choose peace and blessing over evil. They are people who hope in goodness and sometimes suffer for it. When I see and hear of the acts of goodness of others, I cannot but feel a stirring of joy and hope and gratitude in my heart and know I am blessed through them. With eyes of faith, I see God in action through them, working for good. I see in them the hidden face of Christ, the One who continues to walk among us, who looks out from the suffering ones and the compassionate ones. I inherit a blessing.

† Lord, I ask for the grace to choose good over harm this day, to hold hope over despair, to pursue peace not enmity.

For further thought

Consider someone you know who chose to do good. Consider how it blessed you and thank God for the person.

Friday 22 November
No body, some body, Christ's body

Read Romans 12:1–2

I appeal to you therefore, brothers and sisters, by the mercies of God, to present your bodies as a living sacrifice, holy and acceptable to God, which is your spiritual worship.

(verse 1)

Bodies. We can love them. We can hate them. We can be obsessed by them. But we can't live without them. They shape us and we shape them. They test us and we test them. They treat us and we treat them. With no body we wouldn't experience life, sense it, interact with it, be connected in it. We need some kind of body to think, to feel, to imagine, to pray, to be able to encounter God in this world, to experience the kingdom come. We cannot separate ourselves out from our bodies or minds or hearts though sometimes we might try!

God is interested in every cell in our bodies, every thought in our minds and every stirring of our hearts because God loves everything that makes up our being. After all, in Jesus we have God who knows what it's like to be born, to be embodied, enfleshed. Like Jesus, the invitation is to gift ourselves back to God, for us as part of Christ's body. This whole offering of self is a living one – engaging with others, creation, the world and God. For Paul, worship of God involves our whole selves in the whole of life and its myriad of relationships, focused on God and acting in tune with God's desires for us all. So no matter the state of our bodies, no matter how broken or fit, we can still offer ourselves to God – God who sees and is pleased with Christ's body.

† God, my Creator, I offer you my body, mind, heart, all my being. Let my living of this day be as you desire for me and others.

For further thought
Pay attention today to your body. Notice the part it plays in living out your relationship with God.

Saturday 23 November
Touch of God

Read Matthew 17:1–13

When the disciples heard this, they fell to the ground and were overcome by fear. But Jesus came and touched them, saying, 'Get up and do not be afraid.' And when they looked up, they saw no one except Jesus himself alone.

(verses 6–8)

It was just a touch, a simple touch of the hand on my shoulder. I felt the fingers, their slight squeeze reassuring me, telling me that he was there, that he hadn't disappeared into the heavens and left us all trembling in the dust. Before I could even dare to look, I groped for his hand to hold. I needed to feel that hand, with its rough calluses and little scars from years of working wood. I needed to know that the man I had followed up this mountain was still the same flesh and blood man I would follow down the mountain, even though I knew something had changed forever. I needed his touch to calm the terror of the deafening words that had named him 'beloved Son' but propelled me face down to the ground. I just needed his human love, compassion, touch.

We all fear. We all face terrors of one kind or another in life that leave us paralysed in a heap, unable to make a move. Often, in those moments, we need the touch of another human being, we need to know we are not alone, that someone understands, loves, cares for us. Touch expresses when words fail us. We do the same for others. But achingly too, there are those whom God desperately wants to reach out to and comfort through hands like ours but can't. Many hands help make love work.

† Lord Jesus, I give you my hands today. May my hands be a means of your service towards others, a touching of your love.

For further thought

Remember a time when someone consoled you through a simple touch or embrace. Pray for that person.

Plan B

Notes by **Barbara Easton**

Barbara is Director of Education for the Methodist Church in Britain. She started out as a secondary school RE teacher and wound her way to Headship, taking in many challenges on the way. A Local Preacher in the Methodist tradition, she has followed interests in world religions, mysticism and worship; pursuits that have sometime detracted from her desire to finish more quilts. Barbara has used the NRSVA for these notes.

Sunday 24 November
Forbidden by the Spirit

Read Acts 16:6–15

During the night Paul had a vision: there stood a man of Macedonia pleading with him and saying, 'Come over to Macedonia and help us.'

(verse 9)

I used to enjoy a cartoon which was a parody of the famous 'footprints in the sand'. In this version, there was only one set of footprints, criss-crossing around the page. In the middle, a man was looking towards heaven protesting that, actually, he was trying hard to follow God's way!

The path that we are to pick out on our Christian pilgrimage through life is not always as clear as we might hope. Life presents us with many choices, some of them very difficult; even when we lay them before God in prayer, the answer can be difficult to discern. Sometimes, our choices are between things that seem equally virtuous – both seem to be the work of the kingdom. Sometimes we do what we think God would want, but it doesn't work out. Maybe we get stuck in what God wanted for us in the past, instead of now.

In this story, Paul and his friends have only good intentions but they don't work out – the language used is strange to us, but the concept isn't. They are not discouraged: God wants them, but elsewhere. So with us – not everything that is good is God's purpose for us, or the world, at the moment.

† Lord, your ways are mysterious but your heart full of love. Thank you for counting me among your pilgrim people. Help me to find your wisdom in the twists and turns of the journey.

Plan B

November

Monday 25 November
Abraham blunders

Read Genesis 12:10–20

Now there was a famine in the land. So Abram went down to Egypt to reside there as an alien, for the famine was severe in the land.

(verse 10)

Our news is full of people making difficult decisions in desperate circumstances: risking their own lives and those of their children in fragile refugee boats, for example. When one of these episodes ends in tragedy, people are quick to judge – and to condemn. My friend came to England as a refugee from the Middle East. Pregnant, her husband and brothers dead, she fled with her other children and gave birth in a refugee camp. After we had known each other a while she confided, with horror, the part of her story she found most difficult to share – she had accidentally lost one of her sons on the journey. Fortunately, he had been scooped up by other refugees and the family was reunited at a later camp. For those of us with safe homes and tidy lives, it is difficult to imagine being caught in difficult circumstances where events are almost totally outside our control. We have no idea how our principles would weather.

Is that what is happening here? Fleeing famine into hostile territory, do Sarai and Abram make a decision together about how they can survive? Did Sarai volunteer? Or is this another story of one person (a man) cynically exploiting another person (here, a woman), ensuring his own survival, indeed prosperity, no matter what the cost to others? It is interesting that, at the end of the story, it is not Abram's choices which attract God's punishment but Pharaoh's – God's greatest displeasure is with the tyranny which puts people in desperate situations and not, it seems, with the ways we muddle through.

† Lord, help us to discern but not to judge: to be wise and compassionate in the way we look at others and ourselves. We hold all victims, survivors and tyrannies in your light.

For further thought

Think about a hero of the faith who lived through difficult times. What is the Christian challenge in the times in which we find ourselves?

Tuesday 26 November
Jacob marries the wrong wife

Read Genesis 29:15–30

So Jacob served seven years for Rachel, and they seemed to him but a few days because of the love he had for her.

(verse 20)

Some years ago, I listened to a nun being interviewed about her enclosed community's move from their ancient House to a new convent many miles away. Surprisingly, or perhaps unsurprisingly, the one who coped least well with the upheaval and long journey by minibus was the Order's cat. The nun described how it struggled and complained until finally resigning itself and settling down with her for the rest of the journey; 'It decided it must endure,' she said. I was struck by her easy, familiar use of the word 'endure' – a word not frequent in my vocabulary. I have always been much more fired up with the zeal to change the things I'm able to change rather than asking for the peace to accept the things I can't. One of life's Marthas rather than its Marys. Sometimes, however, life throws at us situations that simply cannot be changed – maybe a period of serious illness, of loss or of personal disaster. We might fight it and rail against the unfairness of it but, in the end, as the old saying goes, 'what cannot be helped must be endured'.

Here, Jacob's endurance means putting up with Laban's cheating, manipulative behaviour. It is uncomfortable to suggest that it might ever be right to accept injustice – isn't that how evil triumphs? But sometimes, there are no simple answers. Here, Jacob must bide his time and navigate a long path through life's unsatisfactoriness. Yet, in the end, God's purposes are worked out. Jacob and his family go on to flourish; this hardship is a mere footnote to his story.

† Lord of Martha and Mary, still, small voice: you are also Lord of the Dance. I come to you. Let me find strength in your power and patience in your peace.

For further thought

Find Kate Rusby's song about Candlemas Eve or Robert Herrick's original poem – reflecting on the ups and downs of life at a time of change.

Plan B

November

333

Wednesday 27 November
A caravan of Ishmaelites

Read Genesis 37:12–28

When some Midianite traders passed by, [Joseph's brothers] drew Joseph up, lifting him out of the pit, and sold him to the Ishmaelites for twenty pieces of silver. And they took Joseph to Egypt.

(verse 28)

Most of this week's stories are difficult and this one is no exception. A group of thuggish young men, buoyed up by imagined hurts and finding strength in numbers, see a young lad approaching on his own and let loose all their wrong-headed hatred on him. Sadly, it's not an altogether unfamiliar scenario, but these are the children of Israel – they should have known better.

Thank goodness that salvation arrives unexpectedly! God's purposes are fulfilled by the intervention of a group of unprepossessing foreigners. God is at work, but unseen. So often in the Bible story we trace God's purposes being worked out unfathomably, through the unlikely, the disreputable and here, the downright disagreeable. Their motives are not always pure and they are sometimes compromised. If we are to work for God's kingdom, we may sometimes be called to partner with people who do not share our high moral ground.

But what of Reuben in this story? His is, to me, an altogether more familiar scenario – to be caught up, very unhappy, in a situation which is spiralling out of control. Maybe you have been in a situation where you don't like the way the conversation is going? Or, perhaps, where you are uncomfortable with how people are behaving but, on your own, feel powerless to challenge it? Reuben's response is flawed, but effective. He seems to hate himself for not doing better. Yet he shows that God can work through our imperfect attempts at goodness, as much as through the grand heroic gesture.

† Holy God, help me to discern your perfect way in this imperfect world. I am your imperfect servant. Use my imperfection for your glory.

For further thought

Research organisations working against people trafficking. Is there one small thing you can do today to support their campaigns?

Thursday 28 November
The Holy Family escapes

Read Matthew 2:13–23

Now after they had left, an angel of the Lord appeared to Joseph in a dream and said, 'Get up, take the child and his mother, and flee to Egypt, and remain there until I tell you; for Herod is about to search for the child, to destroy him.'

(verse 13)

As an RE teacher, I have looked at the story of Anne Frank with many generations of children. One of the things that repeatedly strikes me in their tragedy is that the Frank family ought to have been safe – they spotted the perils of Nazism at an early stage and were wise enough to leave their native Germany and make a new life for themselves in Amsterdam. They couldn't know what would happen next. They did it all right, and yet it still went wrong. I have sometimes wondered what my family would have done in their situation – would we have been alert enough to 'read the runes' of history? I suspect we would never have moved in the first place – we are not good at change.

There are times in our lives when we do it all right, but it does not stay right forever. We may have thought carefully and prayerfully about where we should be and what we should do. We might have risen to the challenge of God's call, but few of us expect to be called onward again.

So here, the Holy Family have each, already, dealt with quite a lot. That's putting it mildly! They deserve to be able to settle down in Nazareth where they can raise the Christ child in quiet obscurity. But the world does not stand still around them. As the circumstances of their times change, God calls them to something different. They have to respond again. We can imagine that the call of God is for them unsettling – but, at the same time, it is the summons of God's love and providence. The challenge is to keep being alert to the call.

† Lord, you call your people on. Grant us the courage to listen again and follow afresh.

For further thought

Research the painting *Walking on Water* by Maggi Hambling. What does it say to you about turmoil and calm?

Jesus' mind is changed

Read Mark 7:24–30

But she answered Jesus, 'Sir, even the dogs under the table eat the children's crumbs.'

(verse 28)

Jesus is taking some time out – not alone in the desert this time, but in the Gentile territories with his disciples. It's fair to assume that he is thinking through his calling: he's had a hectic early ministry but there are worrying signs developing, perhaps most of all that his cousin and 'forerunner' has just been executed. He assumes they can get some peace here – what resonance could the Jewish Messiah possibly have among these foreigners? Yet, the encounter with this determined and desperate Gentile woman challenges Jesus' expectations. It turns out that the things that are of God – faith, hope and love – have no boundaries. Who knew!

Encounters in unexpected places can challenge even the best of us to rethink our understanding of how God works. For the woman, it is just a request for one more miracle; for Jesus, the Gospels suggest it prompted a new direction in his understanding of Messiahship, working beyond accepted boundaries. The early Church discovered that there was more interest in the gospel among the 'wrong' sort of people than among their Jewish neighbours – they valued this story. Modern readers often love it for the feistiness of the woman but are troubled by Jesus' reactions which seem to reflect too readily the casual animosities in his day. But that is not how the story ends. Through conversation and encounter, Jesus is pressed to think differently – about himself, about others and about God's kingdom. Ultimately, the woman's persistence didn't just save her daughter – it saves me!

† Gracious God, I am not the finished article; nor is your Church or your world. In the warm assurance of your love, open to me the encounters which will move me on.

For further thought

Do something different today that will bring you into contact with people or ideas outside your familiar 'bubble'. Are faith, hope and love there?

Saturday 30 November
God repents

As a classroom teacher I would often spend the holidays developing stunningly good lessons for a class, with painstakingly prepared resources. Back in the realities of school life in September, things often didn't go as well as I had planned. I had forgotten what schools, and children, are actually like. It turned out that, sometimes, they were not as keen to learn as I was to teach them! Away from the situation I had imagined the ideal, but life sometimes bowls us a different reality. That can be true of the big things of our lives like work, retirement or family life, but also of those chance, everyday incidents which show us not to be quite the people we thought ourselves. We sometimes need to step back, to take a deep breath and reconnect with the person that we aspire to be, or the vision that we have of how God's world could be, before we return to the fray. Or to have a friend who does that for us.

This story reads very oddly to our modern minds – a mere mortal manages to deflect God from doing something he might regret! But, at its climax, it draws our attention to the essential truth about the nature of God, taking pause and stepping back to ground thinking in God's enduring goodness and grace. Armed with this vision, it is Moses himself who has the confidence to challenge the wrongdoing of his community – sometimes, that's a job for us too.

† O great I Am, I am still in your presence. I lay out my life in the light of your grace and goodness. Nourish your vision in me that I may see as you see.

For further thought

Moses clings to his vision of God when the people around him have lost faith. Which character in this story do you find most sympathetic?

Plan B

November

Warnings, judgement, comfort: readings in the Prophets – 1 Warnings

Notes by **Revd Dr Sham P. Thomas**

Sham is an ordained priest sconterving the Mar Thoma Syrian Church Bangalore, India. He was the James S. Stewart scholar at the University of Edinburgh and professor of communication at the United Theological College, Bangalore. He continues to lead conferences and retreats. Sham has used the NRSVA for these notes.

Sunday 1 December (Advent Sunday)
Sleeping over ... what?

Read Micah 2:1–11

Alas for those who devise wickedness and evil deeds on their beds! When the morning dawns, they perform it, because it is in their power. They covet fields, and seize them; houses, and take them away; they oppress householder and house, people and their inheritance.

(verses 1–2)

One of my childhood memories revolves around the picnics organised from our church. The night before the picnic I hardly slept, imagining the picnic spots and the fun that I was hoping for. Preparation for a picnic was filled with excitement – though the same could not be said for the school examinations!

Whether it is for a picnic or an examination, preparation demands self-recognition, self-evaluation and self-motivation. Advent is a time of preparation. We are invited to recognise where we are and where we ought to be in relation to the birth of Jesus, the Saviour of the world. This week's readings continuously remind us that in a world where God's justice and care are not tended to, the lives of the poor are becoming increasingly difficult. Unsurprisingly, our religious observances, rituals and practices are examined by God in relation to their relevance to the poor and needy. Even our imaginations, bedtime thoughts and early morning resolutions are scrutinised as the prophet Micah suggests in today's reading. Subsequently there are warnings, which are purpose-filled communication to mend our ways to be channels of God's peace and justice. Advent is the time for us to prepare the way for the Lord in the world rather than hindering the way.

† Lord, may we reflect on the thoughts that we take to bed and sleep over. May you be our dream when we slumber and our thoughts when we are awake. Amen.

Monday 2 December
Rotten rituals

Read Amos 8:1–12

Hear this, you that trample on the needy, and bring to ruin the poor of the land, saying, 'When will the new moon be over so that we may sell grain; and the sabbath, so that we may offer wheat for sale?'

(verses 4–5a)

In recent times, the term 'ritual' has been diluted to refer to any activity mechanically and routinely repeated. Ritual, however, is important and is very relevant in our everyday life. For instance, the routine ritualistic words like 'hello' and 'bye' may not be vital to begin with, but the absence of such salutations can have grave and lasting impact.

Religious rituals are means of transporting the participants to a divine realm, puncturing the everyday routine and providing an encounter with the divine and thereby creating the possibility of renewal and reformation through the ritual enactment. The participants thereby return to their daily chores as new beings. This, however, is not automatic. At times, the rituals can become ends in themselves and more problematically the ritual participation can remain without impact on the life of the participants.

The prophet Amos warns against such a happening with regard to feasts, fasts and worship. He condemned those who had hastily performed the liberative rituals only to continue with the exploitative practices in everyday life. Because they had made the rituals orchestrated, rotten and absurd, judgement and punishment would come not only on their rituals but also on the land in which they lived.

Recently my church celebrated the life of a small-time businessman. At a time when weights and measures were not calibrated, he was trading in sugar products. His Christian witness was so trusted that his buyers never questioned the weight of his products. His faith had corresponded to his dealings in the market transactions. For him, being honest was a ritual he lived out every day.

† Lord God, bestow on us the spirit of discernment to recognise the relation between faith and financial transactions. Amen.

For further thought

What would the prophet say about products made with child labour in our day?

Credibility gap

> **Read Hosea 4:1–9**
>
> *Yet let no one contend, and let none accuse, for with you is my contention, O priest. You shall stumble by day; the prophet also shall stumble with you by night, and I will destroy your mother.*
>
> (verses 4–5)

Around 75 years ago, one of the professors in a theological college in India was invigilating in an exam for the final-year ministerial students. After distributing the question paper and answer scripts he left the examination hall and returned only at the end of the stipulated three hours to collect the answer scripts. His absence created a lot of discussion and debate in the community and a few among them criticised him for dereliction of duty. To this charge, his response was simple: 'These final-year students are about to enter into pastoral ministry and we will be recommending them as trustworthy ministers for the church to be entrusted with the spiritual leadership of hundreds of people. How can we recommend them for such a great task if we cannot entrust them with an exam worth a hundred marks?'

The credibility of certain offices like pastor or prophet hinges on a benchmark of trustworthiness. Acceptance and respect are by-products of the offices that they hold even before they are known personally. However, they need to justify the given respect and bring credibility to the office through their contribution. What if, as the prophet Hosea warns, the priests and prophets themselves lead the people away from God by indulging in moral degradation and unethical corrupt practices? If they lose their testimony and integrity, generations may lose their interest in Christian life. This is applicable to all the 'children of God' as they have a responsibility of spiritual leadership at different levels, be it in their families or in their circles of influence.

† May our life bring credibility to our calling to be your ambassadors in this world, O Lord. Amen.

For further thought

How would you respond to someone who leaves the church because of mismanagement and misbehaviour of church leaders?

Wednesday 4 December
Beware – a dog that barks does not bite

Read Joel 2:1–14

Blow the trumpet in Zion; sound the alarm on my holy mountain! Let all the inhabitants of the land tremble, for the day of the Lord is coming, it is near ...

(verse 1)

In my local culture, there is a saying that barking dogs seldom bite. The corollary is, biting dogs won't bark! The logic behind this is simple. Generally, if a dog wants to bite, it cannot afford to bark and thereby make the intended victim alert or even escape. It acts in a smarter way in order that its victim is caught unaware and realisation dawns only once bitten. A barking dog, in this sense, does not want to bite and its barking is a warning and an opportunity given for avoiding the very biting.

The prophet Joel paints God's stark warnings of doom to the people of Israel as a warning and opportunity to avoid the predicted catastrophe. God, like a strict but loving parent, is asking the prophets, who were traditionally called barking dogs, to bark, bark and bark! It suggests that God is not a passive and disinterested onlooker of human affairs but intervenes when the people move away from their intended course of life.

Sounding the alarm is a divine call even though there is no guarantee that it will be appreciated or accepted. In a free and open society, many shy away from warning even a toddler. Even though there are statutory warnings, the general climate of today's world is to let each one live according to his or her will without much interference or imposition from anyone! We are not God's moral police, but it is our sacred responsibility as children of God to bark on behalf of God.

† Lord, give us the grace to accept your warnings with a repentant heart; give us the grace to issue your warnings courageously and without malice. Amen.

For further thought

Where do we draw the line between moral policing and permissiveness?

Warnings, judgement, comfort: readings in the Prophets – 1 Warnings

Pain of God

Read Isaiah 5:1–7

... judge between me and my vineyard. What more was there to do for my vineyard that I have not done in it? When I expected it to yield grapes, why did it yield wild grapes?

(verses 3b–4)

The readings of the week thus far suggest that the warnings are God's noble acts of love and mercy and are intended to ensure the good of his people. However, as suggested in today's reading, warnings stem from God's pain and frustration. Contrary to popular imagination, God need not be in supreme happiness all the time and heaven may not be a place of unbridled joy. God, as the prophet Isaiah suggests, is deeply disturbed and disappointed with the unapproved behaviour of his people.

God's disappointment is very deep because God's devotion to creation is absolute. God does not spare anything in providing all for them. Isaiah uses the metaphor of a vineyard to illustrate this luxurious care and commitment of God. With so much care and love invested, God is justified in expecting a faithful response from the recipients of his grace. However, what would it mean if the fruits turn out to be 'wild grapes' defying common sense and minimal reciprocity? What did God do to receive such rejection and ungrateful responses? How can God not be angry? How can his own creatures go on paining him day in and day out?

Even when God is humiliated and shamed, if God is giving another chance, it is only because God alone can offer it. It must be our minimum responsibility to be grateful to God for such a chance and produce fruits that would gladden God rather than sadden him.

† May we not turn out to be a disaster in your sight, O Lord! May we offer you our fruits which would justify, albeit in a minimal way, your investment of grace in us. Amen.

For further thought

What do we make of the biblical instruction not to grieve the Holy Spirit? What shall we tell those parents who are troubled because of the rebellion of their children?

Friday 6 December
Fast! Fast! Fast!

> ### Read Isaiah 58:1–14
>
> *Is not this the fast that I choose: to loose the bonds of injustice, to undo the thongs of the yoke, to let the oppressed go free, and to break every yoke? ... Then you shall call, and the Lord will answer; you shall cry for help, and he will say, Here I am.*
>
> (verses 6, 9a)

Yesterday, our focus was on God's warning against the rebellious people. In today's reading Isaiah shifts the focus to those who are very religious in fasting and praying. Isaiah, however, decries their fasting and prayer for two reasons.

First, they make a spectacle of their religious observances. What was on show was their suffering and sacrifice for God which they used in turn to bargain favours from God. Their self-obsession was such that God became one whose will they tried to twist rather than the one to whose will they submitted. Even today many people fast and pray in the hope of converting God and to have their 'needs sanctioned'! Sadhu Sundar Singh (born 1889), a North Indian missionary, once said that fasting and prayer should be like an egg placed under a hen. The longer it is kept there, the egg will be converted to a chick; the hen won't be converted!

Isaiah also criticises their failure to understand the social meaning of their fasting in relation to the poor and oppressed around them. They may have forgone a meal but failed to work for a system where people don't have to live in poverty and hunger. They observed it as a personal custom but were not committed to get over the corporate and structural sins that make the poor more helpless and hapless.

The remedy, however, is not to condemn or discard the religious practices but to reclaim them. That's why the prophet is inviting them to fast in a liberative and redemptive way. During this Advent season we are also invited to fast and pray in a way acceptable to God by committing ourselves to empathise with the suffering and oppressed world, conveying how much God cares for them.

† May our Advent preparations be pleasing before you, O Lord. May we not use worship practices for our own glory, but for yours. Amen.

For further thought

Who are the oppressed in your context, and what would freedom mean for them? How can your Advent fast help bring it about?

Renewal offer

Read Jeremiah 18:1–11

Can I not do with you, O house of Israel, just as this potter has done? says the Lord. Just like the clay in the potter's hand, so are you in my hand, O house of Israel.

(verses 5–6)

During this first week of Advent, we have been reflecting on God's warnings issued through prophets to the people of Israel at different times. These were very harsh in tone and bleak in content. These doom-sayings, however, were not meant to be the last pronouncements from God. Rather, it was the desperate and clarion call of a devoted God to prevent the pronounced disaster and to open a fresh beginning with God.

God, like the potter whom the prophet Jeremiah visited, can define the future of the people independent of their past or the present. Being the master potter, God can bring about marvellous vessels from otherwise marred clay: a master craftsman with the master stroke.

God's daily menu is simple: turn away from evil ways, and God will change the course of action from disaster to blessing. God is 'slow to anger' and is merciful. God revokes destruction and decides in favour of redemption. On the other hand, if God's people turn to evil ways, God will change the offer of blessing to disaster. Just as God is merciful and willing to bless, God cannot be taken for a ride. Jeremiah made it very clear: God changes his mind depending on the way people respond to him. Repentance opens the gateway to redemption.

Advent is a time when we can turn back from where we are to where we ought to be. Our deviant past or blemished present will not prohibit God from blessing us provided we remain waiting, like the clay, to be moulded in the hands of God.

† Thank you Lord, for you are not only forgiving but forgetting as well. May this Advent be a time of remoulding for us in line with your Son, Jesus Christ our Lord. Amen.

For further thought

What are the areas of your life that you need God to remould?

Warnings, judgement, comfort: readings in the Prophets – 2 Judgement

Notes by **Mark Woods**

For Mark's biography, see p. 140. Mark has used the NIVUK for these notes.

Sunday 8 December
Judgement is costly, like grace

> **Read Hosea 6:1–11**
>
> *'What can I do with you, Ephraim? What can I do with you, Judah? Your love is like the morning mist, like the early dew that disappears.'*
>
> (verse 4)

Judgement is an uncomfortable idea in today's world. We don't like talk of sin – it's notable how many powerful men caught out in sexual misbehaviour have opted for 'therapy' as a way of deflecting responsibility for what they've done, rather than acknowledging their shame.

The Bible is clear-eyed about right and wrong. God sets standards and we fall short. But these failures aren't just like getting a low mark in an exam; they cause deep sadness, damaged relationships and social disruption.

In Hosea, sin is deeply personal, but national and corporate as well. It's built round the story of the prophet and his unfaithful wife, who stand for God and his unfaithful people. In the usual way of things, such a story would involve terrible retribution. In Hosea, God's desire is for repentance and healing. The tone is grief, not anger. 'What shall I do with you?' asks God of people who have thrown his gifts in his face. His love never fails.

Hosea's power comes from its portrayal of how much this forgiveness costs. It is not cheap grace. There's grief at what God's people have done to him, anger and hurt. Judgement is personal, because sin is personal.

† God, help me to see the depth of my own sin, so that I can understand the depth of your mercy.

The unwelcome party guest

Read Malachi 3:1–5

But who can endure the day of his coming? Who can stand when he appears? For he will be like a refiner's fire or a launderer's soap.

(verse 2)

Advent leads up to Christmas, and Christmas is lovely. Jesus is born in a stable and laid in a manger, 'little, weak and helpless', as the carol says. We look forward to it: the gifts, the food, the glitter, the music, the family reunions.

But part of Advent is remembering that Jesus comes in judgement. The world is expecting a party. But the guest arrives as a judge. When God comes into our world it's a terrible thing. Because while Jesus is for the poor and downtrodden, those who suffer needlessly and unjustly, he is against those who make them suffer or who do nothing to help them.

And Malachi starts his list of those the Messiah will judge with those we might least expect. Before he moves on to sorcerers, adulterers, perjurers and the rest, he talks about religious people. No one can 'endure the day of his coming'. He will purify the Levites, who serve in the temple. Above all, the worship of God must be pure; nothing else works if that's wrong.

When we read in the Bible about judgement, the temptation is always to think that we're reading about someone else. It's easy to read the list of 'real' villains in verse 5 and feel rather smug that none of them are like us. But Malachi doesn't allow us that luxury. Jesus is coming to us, and we must not be complacent: we are sinners too. At Christmas we will have our party, but it's only because he is gracious, not because we deserve it.

† God, help me to hear the warnings of scripture as well as its comfort. Teach me to see myself as I really am, not just as I would like to be.

For further thought

Christmas is cosy and fun, but Christ is demanding as well as gracious. Have I grasped both of these aspects of his coming?

A small crumb of comfort

> **Read Lamentations 2:1–5**
>
> *How the Lord has covered Daughter Zion with the cloud of his anger!*
> *He has hurled down the splendour of Israel from heaven to earth; he*
> *has not remembered his footstool in the day of his anger.*
>
> (verse 1)

Lamentations is a book of grief. It laments the fall of Jerusalem to the Babylonians, the dreadful scenes of famine and violence, the collapse of the kingdom and the end of temple worship. Everything's gone.

The author speaks of this disaster in terms that are shocking to us: God has done it. The Babylonians might be his instrument, but God is responsible. He has turned on 'Daughter Zion', 'Daughter Judah'. He has behaved like an enemy (verses 4–5).

But that word 'like' represents a tiny spark of hope and faith. 'The Lord is like an enemy' – but he is not actually Judah's enemy. Even at this lowest point of their national life, God is still Israel's God. They are not finally abandoned.

We need to be careful how we handle texts that speak of judgement. If God brought disaster on Judah because of the people's sins, as the prophets said, it doesn't mean that when we go through dark times ourselves he is bringing disaster on us because of ours. At the same time, when trouble strikes us it can drive us to seek God again. Part of that is confession and repentance.

But a passage like this, which at first sight appears so bleak in its sense of abandonment, still speaks to us of grace. God is not our enemy. The ties that bind us to him are never broken. He is always, ultimately, on our side. The last word is always mercy, not judgement.

† God, when it seems that everything is against me and there's very little hope, help me to remember that I am never forsaken, and to trust in your good purposes for my life.

For further thought

How do I respond when everything falls apart? Is my reaction to blame God or to repent of my sins?

Warnings, judgement, comfort: readings in the Prophets – 2 Judgement

December

Wednesday 11 December
Another brick in the wall

Read Isaiah 59:1–8

They hatch the eggs of vipers and spin a spider's web. Whoever eats their eggs will die, and when one is broken, an adder is hatched. Their cobwebs are useless for clothing; they cannot cover themselves with what they make.

(verses 5–6a)

There is a verse in our reading today that is frightening. The people's sins, says God's prophet, have 'hidden his face from you, so that he will not hear' (verse 2).

Familiar denunciations of their behaviour follow. They are violent, deceitful and generally wicked. But the startling thing is the prophet's characterisation of how this affects their relationship with God. They are living entirely in aimless evil – they 'hatch the eggs of vipers' (instead of birds) and 'spin a spider's web' (instead of cloth); even food and clothing come second to doing wrong for the sake of it. These actions and this disposition create a barrier between God and the people. It's not that he is incapable of saving them (verse 1) but that brick by brick they have walled themselves off from him.

We should not take God for granted. Alongside the painful faithfulness he shows in Hosea, there is a sternness that comes from his intolerance of evil. That prevents us seeing him as some sort of divine safety net, there to catch us if we fall through indifference to his laws.

It's sometimes said that God always answers our prayers. Sometimes he says 'Yes', sometimes 'No', and sometimes 'Wait'.

But this passage gives us a fourth option. Sometimes he says, 'I am not listening.'

So we're faced with a God who is not nice and cuddly, infinitely approving of everything we do and are. This God is demanding. He says, 'Shape up. If you don't listen to me, I won't listen to you.'

† God, forgive me if I have taken you for granted and assumed you are indifferent to my faults. Help me to listen to you, and don't stop listening to me.

For further thought

Am I living a life that's really worth living, or am I wasting time on things that don't matter because they satisfy unworthy desires?

Thursday 12 December
We're all in it together

Read Isaiah 59:9–15a

Like the blind we grope along the wall, feeling our way like people without eyes. At midday we stumble as if it were twilight; among the strong, we are like the dead.

(verse 10)

Today's reading follows straight on from yesterday's, but there is a change. Instead of 'they', the prophet talks about 'we'. To portray the effect of turning from God, he describes the people as blind, weak and helpless. Truth, he says, has 'stumbled in the streets' (verse 14).

It's easy to blame other people for the things they do wrong. But the prophet is wiser than that. He realises that when there is a culture of godlessness, in which wrongdoing is routine, everyone risks being infected by it. At the very least, it's harder to do the right thing if you're the only one. And so he says 'we' because he's involved too.

Whether it's financial or sexual ethics, behaviour at work or in personal relationships, there's always a prevailing tone that can be healthy and righteous, or damaged and damaging. Furthermore, when the culture is dark – tearing people down rather than building them up, seeking personal advantage rather than the good of others – it can be hard to see it. It's just normal – it's what people do. And standing against that culture can leave someone exposed to the hostility of those who gain by it – 'whoever shuns evil becomes a prey' (verse 15).

So this passage tells us two things. It tells us not to be judgemental of the people among whom we live. It's 'we', not 'them'. And it warns us to be discerning. It may be dark all around, but we are children of light.

† God, forgive me if I have looked down on people because of their sins, and not recognised my own; and help me to stand up for what's right, even when it's hard.

For further thought

Do some people just find it easier to be good than others? Have I really tried to understand people before condemning their behaviour?

Friday 13 December
When leaders go bad

> **Read Isaiah 3:13–26**
>
> *The Lord enters into judgement against the elders and leaders of his people: 'It is you who have ruined my vineyard; the plunder from the poor is in your houses.'*
>
> (verse 14)

The Bible has particularly harsh things to say about powerful people who abuse their position to harm the vulnerable. There can be a sense of entitlement: I can do what I like because I have money and status. In one of his books, the late Terry Pratchett suggested that 'sin begins when you treat people as things'.[12] It's a very perceptive remark.

This passage condemns people who do this. It appears to be particularly harsh on women, but this is not the whole story. The context is male bad behaviour. The female luxuries referred to have been bought for them by men and paid for with what they have looted from the poor. Everyone is involved. Corruption starts at the top, with those who 'grind the faces of the poor' (verse 15) and use the money to satisfy their desires, but it draws in others as well, because they are vulnerable or because they give way to the same temptations.

One of the reasons wickedness in high places matters so much is because it infects whole societies. It warps human relationships. It seems to justify ways of treating people that should fill us with horror.

The prophet is speaking to 'elders and leaders'. What about the leaders of churches? In this context, it's a plea for integrity. Weak and vulnerable people are to be cared for, not oppressed. Financial and sexual temptations are to be resisted.

It's very basic stuff, but leaders need to take note. God will judge those who betray their calling.

† God, help me to act with integrity even when others don't. Help me to pattern myself on Christ, rather than on flawed human beings, however important or powerful they might be.

For further thought

Does modern celebrity culture encourage us to idolise the wrong people for the wrong reasons? What about Christian 'celebrities'?

Warnings, judgement, comfort: readings in the Prophets – 2 Judgement

December

---

12   Pratchett, T. (2006), *Wintersmith* (NY: Doubleday).

Keeping the faith and building the wall

Read Ezekiel 22:23–31

'I looked for someone among them who would build up the wall and stand before me in the gap on behalf of the land so that I would not have to destroy it, but I found no one.'

(verse 30)

Ezekiel's focus in these verses is the wrongdoing of the priests who were responsible for interpreting God's laws to the people. They twist the scriptures to suit themselves and they fail to condemn the 'conspiracy of princes' who oppress the people.

There are fierce denunciations here not just of the ill-treatment of the poor but of the failure of the priests to resist it. Bound up with this is their failure to keep the faith.

We should be careful with passages like this. They are sometimes seized on by conservatives and used as sticks to beat those whose opinions might challenge theirs. Not all disagreement is because one side is faithless; different views might be held with integrity.

The chapter ends with a poignant image. The 'wall' – the boundaries that define the community and keep them safe – has been broken down. God looks for someone – anyone – who will build it up and 'stand in the gap', but finds no one. The city is open to invaders. Its defenders are preoccupied with their selfish concerns.

This picture is a challenge to Christians to step forward. We are to be morally and spiritually alert, aware of what is going on in church and society. We can't dodge our responsibilities.

But also, see what side of the wall God is on. He is not inside, helping to defend it. He is on the outside, in the place of the attacker. He wants the city to be defended by the righteousness of the people. But it is not, and judgement is coming.

† God, help me to be faithful to your word in scripture, even when it's easier to believe something different. Help me to resist evil, even when it seems as though I'm the only one who cares.

For further thought

What does it mean to 'stand in the gap' today? What are the things that undermine the 'wall'?

Warnings, judgement, comfort: readings in the Prophets – 2 Judgement

December

Warnings, judgement, comfort: readings in the Prophets – 3 Comfort

Notes by **Catherine Williams**

For Catherine's biography, see p. 6. Catherine has used the NRSVA for these notes.

Sunday 15 December
Foundations

Read Isaiah 51:1–3

Look to the rock from which you were hewn, and to the quarry from which you were dug.

(verse 1b)

This week we continue listening to the prophets. We've heard warnings and judgement: now we turn to comforting words of promise given to God's people in order to restore hope to their devastated lives in exile. In order to look forward Isaiah urges the people first to look back – to remember their ancestors and recall God's love and faithfulness throughout their history. From barren places and people a great nation has come, and will flourish again.

Isaiah calls the people to wake up and listen. God promises to bring comfort, life and liberty. Desert places will blossom again; there will be joy and gladness; a time of singing is just around the corner. In the days leading up to Christmas we will read and hear again of the extraordinary new life that God is yearning to give his people, and of God's desire and longing to bring people back home into relationship with him.

As we hear the call of the prophets to prepare the way of the Lord, we are reminded to get ready to welcome Jesus this Christmas and to make his presence real for those who will visit our churches and homes to celebrate this great festival.

† Lord God, help me to take time with your word this week, in order to prepare fully my heart for you this Christmas.

Monday 16 December
A fleshy heart

Read Ezekiel 36:22–32

A new heart I will give you, and a new spirit I will put within you; and I will remove from your body the heart of stone and give you a heart of flesh.

(verse 26)

When life is very demanding; when someone has wronged us; when a situation continues for a long time or we can't see a way forward, we can begin to retreat into ourselves and become hardened or bitter. Our hearts become stony and it's hard for us to look outwards or be open and loving towards others. This was the situation in which the house of Israel found itself during exile in Babylon. Captivity led them to retreat from God and forget his holy name. Ezekiel gives words of promise and comfort. God will bring Israel home into their own land which will be abundantly fruitful. God promises to cleanse Israel, giving a fresh start. God promises to replace stony hearts with fleshy hearts and to place his spirit within so that Israel becomes obedient and dwells in God's love again. God promises to transform hard and inflexible human nature by restoring and renewing his people.

This close to Christmas we are reminded that God's promises come to fruition in the Christ child. Through the incarnation God becomes flesh and models for us an abundant life with a fleshy heart and a new spirit. God is working from the inside out: coming among us, as one of us, in order to live with us, in us and through us. In baptism we are outwardly cleansed with water and inwardly renewed by the Spirit. When challenges tempt us to harden our hearts let's remember that we've been given a heart of flesh and a new Spirit by our God who came to save us.

† Father, where my heart has become stony, make it fleshy again, so that I am able to love others and serve them as you did in Jesus.

For further thought

Give thanks today for your baptism.

Tuesday 17 December
Flourishing

Read Joel 2:21–29

The tree bears its fruit, the fig tree and vine give their full yield.

(verse 22b)

The prophet Joel speaks to the people of a time to come when everything will flourish. Armies of both foreign invaders and destructive insects have devastated the land and the people have experienced brokenness and loss. Joel looks to a time of plenty when neither the soil, nor the fauna and flora need fear. Fruitfulness and flourishing are promised, and the longed-for rain will be plentiful throughout the year. In Isaiah the prophet declares that when the Lord comes the desert places will blossom and burst into song. This is the reason that Jesus curses the fig-tree in Mark 11 – because it has not recognised that the Messiah is present.

But it isn't just the soil, animals and plants that will flourish. God promises to pour out his Spirit on humanity. Rather than the Spirit being given to a specific individual for a particular purpose, a time will come when everyone, young and old, male and female, powerful and powerless will receive God's Spirit. This is the prophecy that comes to fulfilment in Acts 2, when following the resurrection and ascension of Jesus, the Holy Spirit enters the disciples at Pentecost and they are empowered to take the good news to the ends of the Earth. Today we are the inheritors of Joel's vision – we too are enabled to flourish through the work of the Holy Spirit within us. Through the power of God we can live life in all its fullness, giving our 'full yield' to the glory of God, and for the good of our world.

† Lord God, thank you for your promise that all will flourish. Fill me afresh with your Holy Spirit this Christmas, so I may witness to your love given to the world in Jesus.

For further thought

Pray that all those who come to services in your church this Christmas will be enabled to flourish.

Wednesday 18 December
Sing aloud!

Read Zephaniah 3:14–20

The Lord, your God, is in your midst, a warrior who gives victory; he will rejoice over you with gladness, he will renew you in his love; he will exult over you with loud singing as on a day of festival.

(verses 17–18)

Zephaniah calls the people of Israel to rejoice – there is much to celebrate. God has not abandoned his people but is present with them. There is no longer any need to fear – all enemies will be dealt with, and God will bring victory. More importantly God will renew the love he has for his people and will sing loud and long of that love, joy and delight until all creation joins in with the love song of salvation. This rescue and restoration will include gathering the people together, bringing them home, restoring their fortunes and raising them up. The future is bright! Sing aloud!

In a week's time, at the great festival of Christmas, we will celebrate again, with joy and excitement, God coming among us: 'in our midst' in Jesus. But the preconceptions of the great 'warrior' spoken of by Zephaniah are seriously challenged. The Lord will be a helpless baby, born in a backwater, to a poor family soon to be refugees. There seems no victory in this inauspicious entrance of God into our world. But God is full of surprises and this infant will eventually claim victory over the biggest enemy of all: death. In this child the impossible will become possible and an abundance of miracles will indicate that God is indeed in our midst, rejoicing over us with gladness and renewing us in his love. This love will be worked out in astonishing self-giving and ultimate sacrifice – for all of us, for eternity. The future is bright! Sing aloud!

† Lord, thank you that the future with you is bright. Teach me to sing love songs to you and with you. Help me to keep hope alive for others.

For further thought

When singing Christmas carols this week remember Zephaniah's prophecy. Sing loudly and joyfully to our God who chooses to be with us in Jesus.

Thursday 19 December
A straight path

Read Jeremiah 31:2–14

With weeping they shall come, and with consolations I will lead them back, I will let them walk by brooks of water, in a straight path in which they shall not stumble; for I have become a father to Israel, and Ephraim is my firstborn.

(verse 9)

Throughout this week we are eavesdropping on the prophets as they speak God's words of comfort to those in exile who are far from home, downtrodden and struggling to maintain hope. Today Jeremiah paints a picture of God's salvation for the Israelites. God promises to gather them from wherever they are scattered and draw them to himself. He will wipe away their tears and lead them in safety and security to a place of fruitfulness. There will be 'brooks of water', 'grain, 'wine' and 'oil' in abundance. It will be a time of dancing, singing and merry-making. God promises that the way will be on a 'straight path' – indicating that it will be by the quickest route and one on which even the youngest, frailest and disabled will be able to travel. In an image similar to that in Hosea 11 God is described as a father who teaches his children to walk and who loves them with an everlasting love. Jesus reminds us of this relationship when he uses the intimate word 'Abba' – meaning 'Daddy' – as he addresses God.

If you are struggling with life today, you feel far from home or you are finding it difficult to hold onto hope, remember that God promises to gather you and bring you home – to a place filled with life, joy and healthy loving relationship both with God and with others. Remember too that however tough the road currently seems, God promises to lead you on straight paths so that you will eventually arrive home in good shape.

† Lord God, when the way seems tough remind me that you promise to lead me home on a straight path.

For further thought

Where is 'home' for you?

The breath of life

Read Ezekiel 37:1–14

'Thus says the Lord God to these bones … I will lay sinews on you, and will cause flesh to come upon you, and cover you with skin, and put breath in you, and you shall live; and you shall know that I am the Lord.'

(verses 5a, 6)

Today's reading comes from one of the most well-known passages in Ezekiel: the valley of dry bones. By God's Spirit Ezekiel is shown a place of desolation – characterised by a vast number of bones which are very dry. In this place of desperate aridity everything is dead and all hope is lost. It seems that Israel as a people are finished: the nation is no more and all life has ceased. But with God nothing is impossible and as Ezekiel prophesies to the bones so we witness the rebirth of a nation. Firstly the people are rebuilt from the inside out – bone, sinew, flesh and skin come together. Then God's breath – *ruach* in Hebrew – fills the people and life is restored. The breath of God is invisible but strong, like the wind. It's a powerful force for good which turns despair into rejoicing.

This passage recalls for us the creation stories in Genesis where our forebears are formed from the dust of the earth and God breathes life into them. It also points forward to the miracles that will take place when Jesus the Messiah enters into human history. Extraordinary life springs from the barren Elizabeth and the Virgin Mary as they conceive the cousins John and Jesus. The adult Jesus will raise both Lazarus and Jairus' daughter from the dead. And all these miracles are precursors, 'hints' of the greatest resurrection of all: Jesus – who conquers death and opens for everyone the promise of eternal life with God.

† Lord, thank you for Ezekiel's vision which teaches us that your Spirit can bring new life where all seems lost and hopeless. Breathe into the dry and desperate places in our world.

For further thought

Could you plant seeds or bulbs today to remind you of God's promise of new life?

Warnings, judgement, comfort: readings in the Prophets – 3 Comfort

December

Saturday 21 December
Speak tenderly

Read Isaiah 40:1–11

'In the wilderness prepare the way of the Lord, make straight in the desert a highway for our God.'

(verse 3)

As we end this week we are just a few days away from the celebration of Christmas. Today's passage returns us to Isaiah and to one of the most popular Advent readings. We are urged to prepare, to get ready for the Lord who will come from desert places to straighten out, level, correct our ways and gather us together to bring us home. God's glory will be revealed and as we witness God in our midst so we are called to lift our voices and sing of God's glory from the rooftops. We are given a picture of the Lord who is both a mighty warrior ruling his people, and a comforter who will speak tenderly: forgiving, feeding, nurturing and carrying his people.

These words from Isaiah 40:3 are used in Matthew's Gospel as John the Baptist heralds the way for Jesus – calling people to turn their lives around and get ready to meet the Messiah. It's a reminder to us to prepare our hearts to welcome again the Christ child this Christmas. What are you carrying that might stop you entering into the joy of this festival? Where are the sharp corners in your life that need to be made smooth? Who might appreciate you speaking tenderly to them so that they are released from fear or guilt, or comforted in their grief or troubles? When the glory of the Lord is revealed in the crib in a few days' time, be ready to join with the angels in singing of God's love, faithfulness and peace – with all your heart.

† Prepare my heart Lord Jesus, to receive you again into my life this Christmas.

For further thought

Spend some time straightening things out on the run-up to Christmas.

Christmas with the Gospel of Matthew – 1 What a day!

Notes by **Jarel Robinson-Brown**

Jarel was born in London and is currently a Methodist Minister in the Cardiff Circuit in South Wales. He has the privilege of working with many ages in many different churches. Passionate about issues of justice and equality, Jarel finds his rootedness in sacramental Methodism and Benedictine spirituality. He enjoys spending time at the piano, or with his Jack Russell enjoying the Welsh outdoors! Jarel has used the NRSVA for these notes.

Sunday 22 December
Family: loved no matter what

Read Matthew 1:1–17

So all the generations from Abraham to David are fourteen generations; and from David to the deportation to Babylon, fourteen generations; and from the deportation to Babylon to the Messiah, fourteen generations.

(verse 17)

Family portraits tell us quite a bit about the general composition of a family. I may be able to ascertain that there are many men in the family, a few widows and very few small children. I may also be able to join the dots between people's lives and experiences … that Great-Uncle X was married to Y. One thing I can't ascertain though, is the true character, history or identities of those in the frame. Yet, if I am to understand my place within it all, I need more than faces and names!

The long (and tedious!) genealogy that opens Matthew's Gospel serves to tell us one thing: Jesus is special, and Jesus is unique! Some things that are easy to forget about Jesus are that Jesus has a context, a history and an earthly family to which he belongs. Seeing Jesus in this wider picture helps us understand his humanity and, to the people of his day, Jesus belonging to a line of prophets, priests and kings would not be insignificant. We ought to ask ourselves, 'How do we see Jesus?' – and in light of who he is, how do we then see ourselves?

† In your mind's eye, how do you think God actually sees you? Try to remember that you are fearfully and wonderfully made by God.

The wise men cometh

Read Matthew 2:1–6

In the time of King Herod, after Jesus was born in Bethlehem of Judea, wise men from the East came to Jerusalem, asking, 'Where is the child who has been born king of the Jews? For we observed his star at its rising, and have come to pay him homage.'

(verses 1–2)

There are some things that no amount of preparation can get us ready for – and it's fair to say that very little was ready for Jesus' arrival. Only one group of people in the whole story at least give the appearance of being ready – the wise men! It's very easy to miss, but they are proactive, on the lookout, asking without any angelic host needing to visit. 'Where is the child who has been born king of the Jews?' These are people who find the birth of Jesus almost no surprise, and what's more? They have gifts!

The wise men in their readiness reveal to us something of the importance of being watchful, for if they had not been looking and listening, they'd have missed an opportunity to pay homage to the newly born Saviour. A once-in-a-lifetime gift. It's hard to imagine how useful gold, frankincense and myrrh could be to a newborn, but of course what mattered was the love with which the gifts came.

I remember receiving a gift from my cousin, who'd particularly gone out of his way to buy me exactly what I wanted. What worried me was how quickly I forgot the gift-giver, and focused just on the new, bright and shiny gift. We mustn't do that with God, we have to be thankful for his gifts but thankful also, always, for him.

† Loving God, help us give the gift of our hearts to you this Christmas.

For further thought

What gift will we bring to the Saviour, and what love will come with it?

Christmas with the Gospel of Matthew – 1 What a day! December

360

Tuesday 24 December
God's get-out clause

Read Matthew 2:7–18

Then Herod secretly called for the wise men and learned from them the exact time when the star had appeared. Then he sent them to Bethlehem, saying, 'Go and search diligently for the child; and when you have found him, bring me word so that I may also go and pay him homage.'

(verses 7–8)

Herod took his power and authority for granted, even in this very moment. He seems to think that he can outsmart God, and do away with the infant Jesus – but God had other plans, plans for life and not for death. Herod's sense of self-certainty led him to think he could guarantee exactly where Jesus would be, and that he had a right to know and to be told. In all things, God is always a few steps ahead of us, and thank God for that!

What Herod did in secret was very soon to come to light, as God sent warning to the wise men in a dream – not to guide Herod to the baby Jesus. Their obedience to the leading light of God prevented Herod from following through with his evil and hatred. Herod feared his loss of power more than anything and sadly he didn't have the wisdom to see that rather than taking away power, Jesus came to give power away himself – to give us a new power, a new way of living.

† Loving God, help us use our power wisely, for the building of your kingdom.

For further thought

The wise men were truly wise – wisdom saves us. Maybe we need to ask for that gift to help us throughout the coming week, and year.

Wednesday 25 December (Christmas Day)
What a day!

Read Matthew 1:18–25

'Look, the virgin shall conceive and bear a son, and they shall name him Emmanuel', which means, 'God is with us.'

(verse 23)

Some people, so they say, have that amazing ability to simply walk into a room and light it up! Well, Jesus lights up the world just by coming into it. In Isaiah, we hear of a people walking in darkness finally setting their sights on a marvellous light which has shone upon them. Christ, called 'Emmanuel', is of course more than just a newborn baby. In Jesus, the fullness of God was content to live and dwell among us – to live our life, bear our griefs, and even die our death that we might experience eternal life.

Christmas is indeed a special day in the life of the world, after all it is the day when we remember Christ the Son of God breaking into our world at his birth, but it isn't the end of the story – rather it is the beginning. To be a people upon whom light has shone is to be a people who see in a new way – the light, life and love that Jesus brings don't allow us to remain the same. When Jesus comes to us, he asks us to reconsider all those things we thought we knew or understood and have taken for granted – he asks us, if you like, to understand ourselves afresh as those unto whom God has come.

Today, Jesus has come into the world. Will we allow him, for the first time, or simply anew, to be born and make his dwelling in the stable of our hearts?

† Lord, Jesus Christ. As we remember your birth today, we pray that you might make your home in our hearts and dwell there forever. Amen.

For further thought

What in your community can the light of God illuminate this Christmas?

Thursday 26 December
God's deliverance promised

Read Matthew 2:19–23

There he made his home in a town called Nazareth, so that what had been spoken through the prophets might be fulfilled, 'He will be called a Nazorean.'

(verse 23)

It may be said, with some truth, that I am not always the most patient of people. Among my friends, I can often be on the receiving end of a little dig in the middle of a sentence highlighting the fact that I don't cope well in queues, with delays or with things changed last minute! I like things to move along in a sensible pattern and usually to move along quickly. Scripture, if it shows anything about God, certainly reveals to us that God doesn't work according to our human timetables, ideas or plans. God's time is truly God's time and if you want a plan unplanned inconveniently … simply involve God!

Waiting is a central theme to the scriptures and their characters. Different biblical narratives involve the theme of waiting – Abraham and Sarah, the Israelites in the desert, the people of Isaiah's time, Elizabeth, Peter and Paul … and many others. In the moments when we are waiting for God's deliverance it is important to remember those who have been in that place of waiting before us, and for us to remind ourselves of God whose promises are trustworthy. The people who were waiting for a Messiah waited for years, but in the end he did come. All around my manse I have framed photographs of those whose lives and witness have inspired me, people like Martin Luther King Jr, Pope John Paul I, James Baldwin and others – all those who in one way or another have known the pain but also the joy of waiting – and who, in the end, found God's promises to be true.

† Faithful God, you come to your people in their distress. Help us to wait patiently on you in the hardship of our lives.

For further thought
What is God waiting for in your life?

Christmas with the Gospel of Matthew – 1 What a day!

God's word fulfilled

Read Matthew 3:1–6

Now John wore clothing of camel's hair with a leather belt around his waist, and his food was locusts and wild honey.

(verse 4)

What might a modern John the Baptist look like? It's actually quite hard to imagine. John the Baptist is one of those likeable, misunderstood, yet slightly loveable characters to whom no one really knows how to respond. I sometimes feel a little like a John the Baptist-type walking around the streets of a city in my cassock. Heads turn and cries of 'Alright, Father?' fly across the street. In what we say and how we appear we can evoke curiosity, opening up opportunities for us to share the gospel. John the Baptist certainly stood out, and it seemed to help!

Again and again, throughout the Bible, God seems to choose the most unlikely characters as messengers, prophets and preachers. It begs the question, where do we expect truth, honesty, decency, integrity and prophetic vision to exist? In today's world we certainly do not tend to look for the wisdom of God to come from those who do not conform to our understanding of society's norms, and yet God is speaking clearly through a man shouting his head off on the riverbank wearing camel fur, and living on a diet of pests and honey …! John the Baptist reveals to us that God can use the most unusual of people, in the most unusual of ways to communicate the hope and truth of the gospel. If we don't want to miss God's voice, we need to look in the unusual places for God's word.

† God of the prophets, strengthen me to speak your uncomfortable truth today.

For further thought

Which voices do you think might be speaking words you need to hear?

Saturday 28 December
John the Baptist brings hope

Read Matthew 3:7–12

But when he saw many Pharisees and Sadducees coming for baptism, he said to them, 'You brood of vipers! Who warned you to flee from the wrath to come? Bear fruit worthy of repentance.'

(verses 7–8)

For many today, talk of wrath may seem outdated. While this may be true, through John Wesley's input and direction, a question the early Methodists regularly asked new members was: 'Do you desire to flee from the wrath that is to come?' This question asked first by John the Baptist, and later by John Wesley might not seem particularly hopeful at face value, but in reality it was. I have even asked the question of my congregations I preached to in Cardiff. The question can only be asked because the person asking believes that it is in fact possible to flee from the wrath that is to come, that a different life can indeed be lived, that salvation really can be the fruit of repentance. I have seen and known the lives of those who have decided to follow Jesus, and left much of their old lives behind.

John the Baptist challenges the Pharisees and Sadducees who perhaps weren't taking his message of repentance seriously enough, but too often relied either on intelligence or on lineage for salvation. For John the Baptist, hope was the result of repentance – when we repent, we put things back in the right order, when we start again we have confidence in God's grace. In that confidence we find our hope, our joy and our life … for repentance is about death to sin, and new life in God.

† Lord Jesus Christ, help us to remember that through your sacrifice on the cross we can all become new creations. Help me to start anew with you. Amen.

For further thought

What in your life needs changing (repenting for and seeking to amend) in 2020?

Christmas with the Gospel of Matthew – 2 The beloved son

Notes by **Jarel Robinson-Brown**

For Jarel's biography, see p. 359. Jarel has used the NRSVA for these notes.

Sunday 29 December
Jesus leads the way

Read Matthew 3:13–17

And when Jesus had been baptised, just as he came up from the water, suddenly the heavens were opened to him and he saw the Spirit of God descending like a dove and alighting on him.

(verse 16)

Baptisms are one of the most joyful occasions in the life of the Church. To this day, I can and will always remember the very first baptism I ever conducted – the wonder of that little baby girl totally fascinated by my glasses, the water and the people in the church! It always gives me great joy to witness a new Christian becoming a full part of the body of Christ in a community. The joy that comes from seeing someone make the next step, or being offered up to God by their parents, always speaks of God's grace alive and active in the world today. The joy that comes from obedience – knowing that to be baptised is not only to follow the way of Jesus, but to be obedient to Jesus in his command that the world be baptised.

Jesus' baptism doesn't represent everything that our own baptisms represent. Jesus had no sin to wash away, but by being baptised he ties himself into a common human experience, allies himself with this future sacrament of the Church, like the Lord's Supper which he partakes in. Jesus leads the way in a number of ways, but primarily through showing us how we ought to live both in faith and in practice – we need the waters of baptism, that we can live like Christ. We should, because Jesus has, and it is Christ's baptism which marks the beginning of his ministry and prepares him for his witness in the world.

† Gracious God, these holy days, let me hear again your claim on my life. Help me live only for you in the coming year, in the strength of your Spirit. Amen.

For further thought

How do we show obedience in our daily lives? Are there more areas in which we can be obedient to God's word?

Monday 30 December
Jesus overcomes

Read Matthew 4:1–10

… and he said to him, 'All these I will give you, if you will fall down and worship me.'

(verse 9)

Temptation is part of the Christian life. However much we might despise it. This is a fact. As we see today, Jesus himself had to face and endure the temptation of the devil. But what exactly is happening? At first glance it may seem a little like a typical temptation scenario, but there is a deeper element in this encounter. Satan is trying to give Jesus three shortcuts away from the cross:

Turn stones into bread.

Throw yourself off the temple.

Bow down and worship me.

Each option, a path of pure disobedience to God, and to God's will. Had Jesus done any of these, he never would have made it to Calvary. In short, the devil would have won, and God's plan been abandoned by Jesus. None of this was just incidental; Satan knew exactly what he was doing up there on the pinnacle of the temple, trying to catch Jesus in what should have been and could have been his weakest moment.

We need, in our moments of weakness as well as strength, a similar kind of obedience to that of Jesus. In those moments when we are tempted to not 'take up our cross and follow', we need to remember to trust God, praise God, and press on to the goal God has in mind for us. Confident always in his all-sufficient grace.

† God of the desert, help me withstand every temptation with the help of the one who was tempted but withstood evil. Amen.

For further thought

Do we call upon Jesus, or upon his words, in the moments when we face temptation? Perhaps we need to do so more often.

Tuesday 31 December
Jesus' ministry: no limits

Read Matthew 4:12–22

And he said to them, 'Follow me, and I will make you fish for people.'

(verse 19)

Standing at the altar reminds me constantly of one thing: how God can take the most simple, everyday objects of our life and turn them into his glorious, fathomless riches. Staring at the bread and wine, the work of human hands which earth has given, and seeing the way God nourishes and sustains his people through them, and through my weak service, serves as a constant reminder to me that nothing is beyond God's use … even you and I! Jesus truly has no limits.

In the calling of the disciples, Jesus seems to be revealing the fact that he isn't too concerned about the CVs the disciples might come with, he isn't interested in their qualifications for the role – more with their willingness (not their ability!) to follow. Are they able to leave themselves behind, to begin a journey upon which they find their true selves, to follow the one who calls them by name? Jesus wants willing hearts, and he is willing to take and make disciples no matter what state they come in. If we want to know how limitless Jesus' love is, we need only look at the people he called to 'follow'! I am reminded every day of the grace of God, who throughout history has called and made useful the most unlikely of people and turned them into instruments of his love.

† Lord God, as you called the disciples so you call each of us. Help us to trust you, to follow you and never to count the cost. Amen.

For further thought

Where is God calling you to deepen your walk with him in 2020?

IBRA International Fund: would you help us?

Will you work with us and help us to enable Christians from different parts of the world to grow in knowledge and appreciation of the Word of God by making a donation of £5, £10 or even £50? 100% of your donation will be used to support people overseas.

How your donations make a difference:

£5.00 prints 6 translated copies of *Fresh From the Word* in Ghana
£10.00 buys 14 translated copies for India
£25.00 sends 5 copies of *Fresh From the Word* (including postage and packaging) to Nigeria
£50.00 would fund 1,000 IBRA reading lists to be sent to a country that does not currently receive IBRA materials

Our partners are based in 11 countries, but the benefit flows over borders to at least 32 countries all over the world. Partners work tirelessly to organise the translation, printing and distribution of IBRA Bible study notes and lists into many different languages, from Ewe, Yoruba and Twi to Portuguese, Samoan and Telugu!
Did you know that we print and sell 8,000 copies of *Fresh From the Word* here in the UK, but our overseas partners produce another 42,000 copies in English and then translate the book you are reading to produce a total of 136,000 copies in 11 local languages? With the reading list also being translated and distributed, IBRA is still reaching 1,081,113 Christians around the world.

Faithfully following the same principles developed in 1882, we still guarantee that 100% of your donations to the International Fund go to support our international brothers and sisters in Christ.

If you would like to make a donation, please use the envelope inserted in this book to send a cheque to **International Bible Reading Association**, *5–6 Imperial Court, 12 Sovereign Road, Birmingham, B30 3FH* or go online to **shop.christianeducation. org.uk** and click the '**Donate**' button at the top of the page.

Global community

Our overseas distribution and international partners enable IBRA readings to be enjoyed all over the world from Spain to Samoa, New Zealand to Cameroon. Each day when you read your copy of *Fresh From the Word* you are joining a global community of over one million people who are also reading the same passages. Here is how our readings impact people across the globe:

American Samoa

The Congregational Christian Church in American Samoa say the following about IBRA daily readings:

> The IBRA materials encourage you to read the Bible every day and meditate on the Word. It empowers people to know God in their own terms. It strengthens and bonds families together in Christ Jesus. It waters the thirst of our souls with spiritual food.

Reverend Reupena Alo feels that the IBRA notes help transform people from their self-centred thinking into being mission-oriented, and has seen people going out to help others in need.

India

The Fellowship of Professional Workers in India value the global community of IBRA readers:

> The uniqueness of the Bible reading is that the entire readership is focusing on a common theme for each day which is an expression of oneness of the faithful, irrespective of countries and cultures.

Cameroon

Reverend Doctor Peter Evande of the Redemptive Baptist Church in Cameroon has distributed IBRA daily readings for ten years, and says:

> The use of writers from different cultural backgrounds makes IBRA notes richer than others. That aspect also attracts people from different backgrounds to love them. The structure and seasons of the Christian year help many people.

United Kingdom

Sue, from the UK, has read IBRA notes for 22 years:

> I have had many days where it feels as though the notes have been written just for me. I like the short reading for each day as this can easily fit into a daily routine and be kept up with. I also really like reading the views of the writers from overseas for an international view.

Where people are following IBRA daily readings

We love to hear our readers' favourite places to read and reflect on our daily readings. Get in touch and tell us where YOU'RE reading – perhaps you too have a favourite, or an unusual or exciting place to enjoy your Bible reading. Email **ibra@christianeducation.org.uk**

66 *My favourite place is my home in Nottingham, but over the past 25+ years, the IBRA daily notes have travelled with me to Nevis in the Caribbean, Australia, Malawi and India as well as many locations in the UK!* 99

66 *Luxembourg – sat with a coffee outside my caravan.* 99

66 *When I wake up – in bed with a cup of tea!* 99

66 *A small hut in Tonga – the very first thing in the morning.* 99

66 *In my sitting room by the side of my wife (so I can share).* 99

To find out more visit: **www.ibraglobal.org**

International Bible Reading Association partners and distributors

A worldwide service of Christian Education at work in five continents

HEADQUARTERS
IBRA
5–6 Imperial Court
12 Sovereign Road
Birmingham
B30 3FH
United Kingdom

www.ibraglobal.org

ibra@christianeducation.org.uk

SAMOA
Congregational Christian Church in Samoa
CCCS
PO Box 468
Tamaligi
Apia

isalevao@cccs.org.ws / lina@cccs.org.ws

Congregational Christian Church in Tokelau
c/o EFKT
Atafu
Tokelau Island

hepuutu@gmail.com

Congregational Christian Church in American
Samoa
P.O. BOX 1537
1 Kanana Fou Street
Pago Pago, AS 96799

cccasgs@efkas.org

FIJI
Methodist Bookstore
11 Stewart Street
PO Box 354
Suva

mbookstorefiji@yahoo.com

GHANA
Asempa Publishers
Christian Council of Ghana
PO Box GP 919
Accra

gm@asempapublishers.com

NIGERIA
IBRA Nigeria
David Hinderer House
Cathedral Church of St David
Kudeti
PMB 5298 Dugbe
Ibadan
Oyo State

SOUTH AFRICA
Faith for Daily Living Foundation
PO Box 3737
Durban 4000

ffdl@saol.com

IBRA South Africa
The Rectory
Christchurch
c/o Constantia Main and Parish Roads
Constantia 7806
Western Cape
South Africa

Terry@cchconst.org.za

DEMOCRATIC REPUBLIC OF THE CONGO
Baptist Community of the Congo River
8 Avenue Kalemie
Kinshasa Gombe
B.P. 205 & 397
Kinshasa 1

ecc_cbfc@yahoo.fr

CAMEROON
Redemptive Baptist Church
PO Box 65
Limbe
Fako Division
South West Region

evande777@yahoo.com

INDIA
All India Sunday School Association
NCCI Campus
Civil Lines
Nagpur
440001
Maharashtra

sundayschoolindia@yahoo.co.in

Fellowship of Professional Workers
Samanvay
Deepthi Chambers, Opp. Nin.
Tarnaka
Vijayapuri
Hyderabad 500 017
Telangana

fellowship2w@gmail.com

The Christian Literature Society
No.68, Evening Bazaar Road
Park Town
Chennai 600 003
Post Box No.501

clschennai@hotmail.com

REPUBLIC OF KIRIBATI
KPC Bookstore
PO Box 80
Bairiki, Antebuka
Tarawa
Republic of Kiribati

Fresh From the Word 2020
Order and donation form

IBRA
International Bible Reading Association

ISBN 978-0-85721-938-1	Quantity	Price	Total
AA180101 *Fresh From the Word* 2020		£9.99	
10% discount if ordering 3 or more copies			
UK P&P			
Up to 2 copies		£2.50	
3–8 copies		£5.00	
9–11 copies		£7.50	
12 or more copies		Free	
Western Europe P&P			
1–3 copies		£5.00 per copy	
If ordering 3 or more copies please contact us for revised postage			
Rest of the world P&P			
1–3 copies		£6.00 per copy	
If ordering 3 or more copies please contact us for revised postage			

Donation Yes, I would like to make a donation to IBRA's International Fund to help support our global community of readers.

£5.00 ☐   £10.00 ☐   £25.00 ☐   £50.00 ☐   Other ☐

TOTAL FOR BOOKS, P&P AND DONATION

Title: _____   First name: _____   Last name: _____

Address: _____

_____

Postcode: _____   Tel.: _____

Email: _____

Your order will be dispatched when all books are available. Payments in pounds sterling, please. We do not accept American Express or Maestro International. HOW WE USE INFORMATION ABOUT YOU AND RECIPIENTS OF YOUR INFORMATION: We will use your information in performance of your contract with us and the provision of our services to you including our legitimate interests. For further details please view our full privacy policy and your rights at www.ibraglobal.org/privacy

---

CARDHOLDER NAME: _____

CARD NUMBER: ☐☐☐☐ ☐☐☐☐ ☐☐☐☐ ☐☐☐☐

START DATE: ☐☐ ☐☐   **EXPIRY DATE:** ☐☐ ☐☐

SECURITY NUMBER (LAST THREE DIGITS ON BACK): ☐☐☐

SIGNATURE: _____

Please fill in your details on the reverse

Ebook and Kindle versions are available from Amazon and other online retailers.

Gift Aid declaration *giftaid it*

If you wish to Gift Aid your donation please tick the box below.

I am a UK taxpayer and would like IBRA to reclaim the Gift Aid on my donation, increasing my donation by 25p for every £1 I give.

☐ I want IBRA to claim tax back on this gift and any future gifts until I notify you otherwise. I am a UK taxpayer and understand that if I pay less Income Tax and/or Capital Gains Tax than the amount of Gift Aid claimed on all my donations in that tax year it is my responsibility to pay any difference.

Signature: _____   Date: _____

Thank you so much for your generous donation; it will make a real difference and change lives around the world.

Please fill in your address and payment details on the reverse of this page and send back to IBRA.

☐ **I have made a donation**

☐ **I have Gift Aided my donation**

☐ **I would like to know more about leaving a legacy to IBRA**

☐ **I would like to become an IBRA rep**

☐ **I enclose a cheque (made payable to IBRA)**

☐ **Please charge my MASTERCARD/VISA**

Card details will be destroyed after payment has been taken.

Please return this form to:
**IBRA
5–6 Imperial Court
12 Sovereign Road
Birmingham
B30 3FH**

You can also order through your local IBRA rep or from:
• website: shop.christianeducation.org.uk
• email: ibra.sales@christianeducation.org.uk
• call: 0121 458 3313

International Bible Reading Association

Registered Charity number: 1086990